Programming Sound
for DOS and Windows

Programming Sound for DOS and Windows

Nathan Gurewich
Ori Gurewich

PUBLISHING

A Division of Prentice Hall Computer Publishing
11711 North College, Carmel, Indiana 46032 USA

Trademarks

Overview

Contents

Chapter
4

The Hello.c Program   **55**

Chapter
12   **Sound C Programming for DOS`**   **465**

Acknowledgments

We would like to thank Stacy Hiquet, Acquisitions Editor at Sams Publishing, for accepting this project, and especially for the various suggestions and recommendations that she made during the development and production of the book.

We would also like to thank Judy Brunetti, the editor of this book, for her superior work in editing the manuscript, and for her many suggestions, inquiries, and discussions during the development of the manuscript.

We would also like to thank Bruce Graves, the technical editor, who actually compiled and linked all of this book's programs and verified that the programs compiled, linked, and executed properly.

About the Authors

Nathan Gurewich holds a master's degree in electrical engineering from Columbia University, New York City, New York, and a bachelor's degree in electrical engineering from Hofstra University, Long Island, New York. Since the introduction of the PC, the author has been involved in the design and implementation of commercial software packages for the PC. He is an expert in the field of PC programming, and in providing consulting services in the area of local area networks, wide area networks, and database management and design.

Ori Gurewich holds a Bachelor of Engineering degree from Stony Brook University, Stony Brook, New York. His background includes working as a senior software engineer and as a software consultant engineer for companies developing professional multimedia and Windows applications. He is an expert in the field of PC programming and network communications, and has developed various multimedia and sound algorithms for the PC.

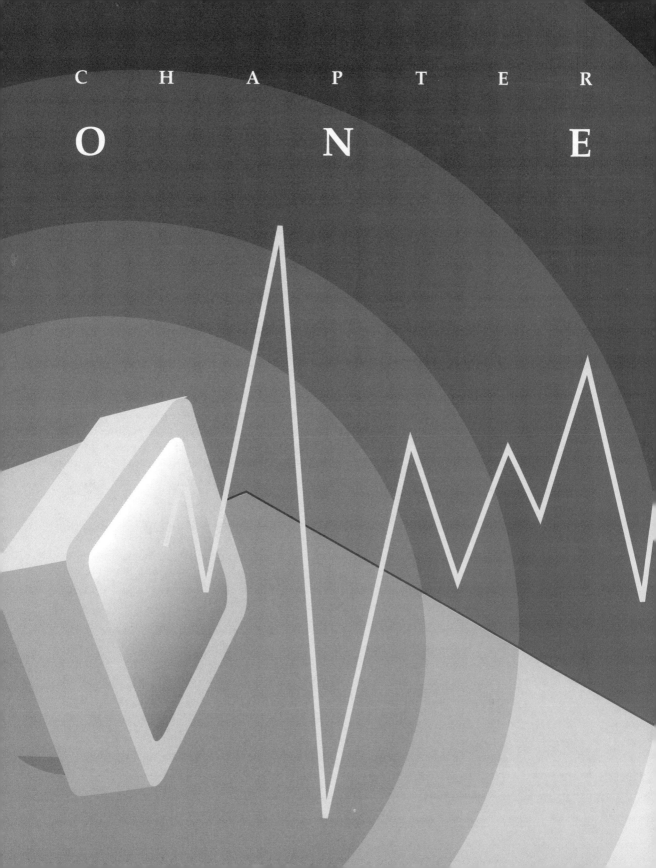

ONE

Sound Programming

Do you want your PC to speak and play music from within your C programs? If so, then this book is for you.

The Concept of the PC Speaking and Playing Music

PCs are becoming less expensive, more powerful, and more popular. They can be found in almost every business and many homes. An integral companion to the PC is the software that operates the PC. PC software has become more powerful, more competitive, and less expensive. For example, several years ago, there were only a few good word processing software packages. Today, you can find many excellent word processing packages at a fraction of the price that was offered several years ago.

Because of the PC's increased speed and power, users expect the software to perform more tasks, to be faster, and to take full advantage of the PC power. The MS Windows operating system is an example of this hardware and software evolution. This operating system works best on powerful PCs that have fast 80386/486 processors, plenty of RAM, plenty of hard drive, and a VGA or other high-resolution monitors.

Programmers are now faced with a new challenge: the challenge of writing programs that attract many PC users by fulfilling the users expectations. Several years ago, it was expected from a PC user to possess the technical ability to operate a powerful software package. It was common practice to blame the end user for not knowing how to operate the software correctly.

With the introduction of Windows, the border is now very well defined. A qualified user is one who knows how to operate the Windows operating system. The user is expected to know how to start a program by clicking the program icon, how to execute several programs, how to copy, paste, and cut text and graphic objects from one program to another, how to access the program menus, and how to perform other common Windows tasks.

As a programmer, you are faced with the challenge of writing your program so that a user who is equipped with the knowledge of performing these basic operations will be able to operate your program without any difficulties.

Programs that Appeal to the Human Senses

Besides being easy to operate, your programs should be attractive to the user and pleasant to use. To make a program attractive and pleasant to use, you should appeal to the human senses: to the visual sense and to the hearing sense.

To make a program pleasant and appealing to the visual sense of the user, the application should be displayed in a graphics mode, with colors. When applicable, the program should include animation (for example, the illusion of a moving, mechanical pushed button when the user clicks a push button in a Windows application).

To make a program pleasant and appealing to the hearing sense of the user, the application should talk and play real music.

Several years ago, almost all programs used the internal built-in speaker to produce beeps that alerted the user of certain conditions and events that occur during the program's execution. Nowadays, a well-written program should speak to the user, telling the user in human voice the reason for the audio alert rather then producing annoying beeps.

There are two ways to enable the PC to produce human voice: by using a sound card, and by using the internal built-in speaker that already exists in every PC.

The Concept of the PC Speaking With and Without Additional Hardware

The Personal Computer (PC) is a computing machine designed to accomplish almost all conceivable tasks. There is one task, however, that the PC is not designed to do: to speak in real human voice, and to play real music.

To add this capability to the PC, the sound card was invented. The sound card is a card that is plugged into one of the slots of the PC's motherboard. It includes jacks to connect an external microphone and external speakers to it. Your program may send commands to the sound card, telling it to play sound files.

The sound card is a peripheral that introduces sophistication to your programs. Sound cards need devices such as a microphone and external speakers. The reality, however, is that not all PCs have sound cards installed.

In this book you will learn how to write C programs that make the PC play sound through both a sound card as well as through the PC's internal built-in speaker.

This book teaches you how to write C programs that make the PC play sound for programs that are executed under the DOS operating systems and for programs that are executed under the Windows operating system. The speech files played by the PC are real human voice (not synthesized voice), and the music files played by the PC are real music.

You will also learn how your program can detect the presence or absence of a sound card in the PC, and how to direct the sound to either the sound card or to the internal built-in speaker. If your program discovers that the PC does not have a sound card installed, it will play through the internal built-in PC speaker. This little speaker (that already exists on all PCs) can produce real human speech and real music. This concept is illustrated in Figure 1.1.

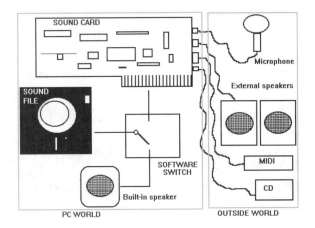

Figure 1.1. The concept of playing through the internal built-in PC speaker instead of through the sound card.

Once you learn how to incorporate sound into your programs, you'll never be able to write a program that does not include sound. As a programmer, you probably already utilize the PC speaker to produce some primitive beeps during program execution. No more! From now on, you'll replace those nasty annoying beeps with intelligent audio prompts.

Installing this Book's Disk

To write C programs that can record and play sound files, you need various software. The book's disk includes software libraries of C functions that your program can use. Thus, to use these C functions, your program has to be written in the C language, and then compiled and linked using either the Microsoft C compiler or the Borland C compiler.

The TSEngine

The libraries of the C functions included on the book's disk are *regular* C functions that can be called from your C programs for DOS, and from your C programs for Windows. They enable you to incorporate sound into your programs with great ease. This powerful collection of C functions is referred to in the book as the TSEngine.

This Book's Disk

This book's disk includes the C source code of this book's

Programs

Software utilities

Sound files

Libraries of C functions for the Microsoft C compiler for creating Windows applications

Libraries of C functions for the Borland compiler for creating Windows applications

Libraries of C functions for the Microsoft C compiler for creating DOS applications

Libraries of C functions for the Borland compiler for creating DOS applications

Other software utilities

This software is the short version of the TS Sound Plus library by TegoSoft Inc. Although it is the short version, the supplied software enables you to compile, link, and execute all the book's program examples by yourself. It also enables you to write similar programs by yourself.

Installing this Book's Disk

The software included with this book is stored in a compressed form. You cannot use the software without first installing it on your hard drive.

Follow these steps to install the files on your hard drive:

1. From a DOS prompt, set your default drive to the drive that contains the installation disk. For example, if the disk is in drive A:, type **A:** and press Enter.

2. Type **INSTALL** and press Enter.

This will create a directory named C:\SPSDK and install all the files to that directory. You will need at least 4.6M of free space on your hard drive to install the files.

NOTE   The files must be installed on your C: hard drive. This drive letter is hard-coded in some of the programs. If you wish to change this, it's an easy matter to change the drive references in the code.

Once the files are installed in your hard drive, several subdirectories are created. Make sure you read the software license agreement that resides in the subdirectory, LICENSE.

The text of this book corresponds to the content of the book's disk. However, you may find some minor differences between some sections of code that appear in the book to the code that appears on the book's disk. These differences may be due to last minute changes, and they are minor. (For example, the book's disk may include different program icons.) In any event, all the book's programs were compiled, linked, and tested. So always refer to the code in the book's disk as the most upgraded code.

As stated, you'll be able to compile and link all the book's program examples by yourself. Nevertheless, the book's disk also includes the already compiled and linked Windows programs. This enables you to immediately execute the book's programs and *hear* the programs. This way, you'll gain a better understanding of what you are expected to learn from this book. The next chapter shows you how to execute these programs.

The program examples of this book are explained in an easy-to-learn, step-by-step manner. So relax, and prepare yourself for a very pleasant journey.

TWO

Sound Programming Techniques and Sound Libraries

There are two separate sound-programming topics to learn:

1. How to make the PC play sound (either through the PC's internal built-in speaker, or through an installed sound card).

2. How to best utilize the PC's ability to speak and play music for the creation of powerful and impressive programs.

How To Make the PC Play Sound

Throughout this book, you learn about making the PC play sound by:

- Recording sound files from within your programs

- Playing sound files from within your programs

- Determining whether the PC has a sound card installed, and based on this determination

- Directing the sound to either the PC internal built-in speaker or to the sound card

All these tasks are performed under the Windows operating system as well as under DOS.

Learning to accomplish these tasks is simply a matter of learning how to use the appropriate C functions. Throughout this book you will encounter many program examples that show you step-by-step instructions on how to do it.

How To Best Utilize Sound from Within Your Programs

Once you know how to produce sound from within your programs and are able to grant the PC the power of speech, you'll have to think of how to best utilize this new dimension into your programs. This is where you will apply your technical artistic talent and ingenuity. Sound programming can be incorporated into all types of programs: serious business programs, word processors, software utilities, animation, demo programs, and so on.

When you study the program examples in this book, you will learn how the sound playing ability is used. You will be instructed to compile, link, and execute the program examples of this book. The book's disk includes all the source code of the programs.

We will now go over some of the programs found in the book. We recommend that you execute the programs before learning their codes, this way you'll *hear* and *see* what you are expected to gain and learn.

The Windows Operating System

The Windows operating system is becoming very popular. Currently, almost all PC vendors ship their PCs with a mouse device and with the Windows operating system already installed.

Creating New Icon Groups in the Program Manager

If your PC has the Windows operating system installed, you may follow the proceeding steps to create a new icon group in the Program Manager of Windows that contains the icons of the book's programs.

There are two methods for creating this icon group:

Method 1

To begin with, look at Figure 2.1 where you will see several icon groups in the Program Manager of Windows (for example, Main, Accessories, and so on). We will now add a new group of icons to the Program Manager—a group of icons that includes the programs of this book.

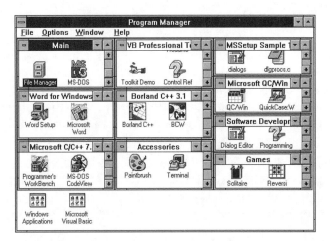

Figure 2.1. Several icon groups found in the Program Manager of Windows.

- Click the File menu of the Program Manager. The File menu appears, as shown in Figure 2.2

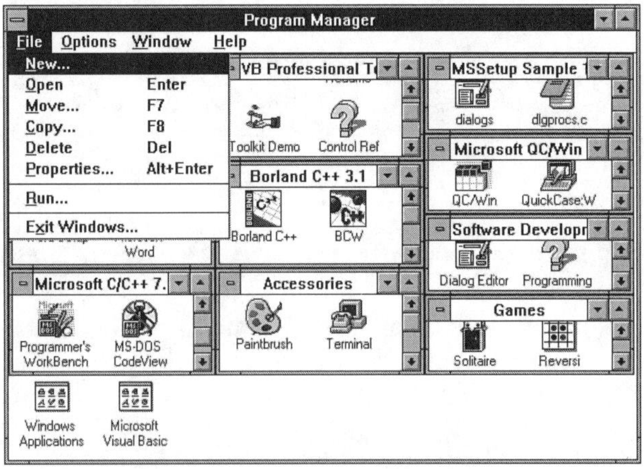

Figure 2.2. The File menu of the Program Manager.

- Select the New option from the File menu. The New Program Object dialog box appears, as shown in Figure 2.3. This dialog box lets you create either a new program group or a new program item. Because we are now trying to create a new program group, click the Program Group radio button (see Figure 2.3).

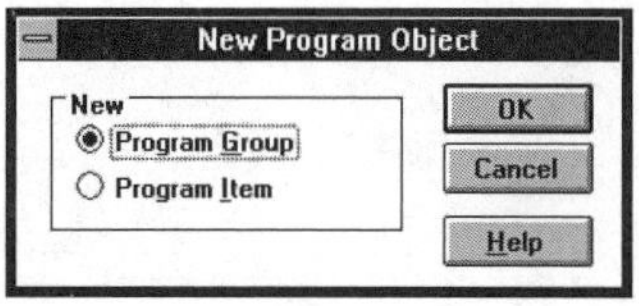

Figure 2.3. The New Program Object dialog box.

- When you select the OK push button, the Program Group Properties dialog box appears. Type `Gurewich book` in the Description field of the Program Group Properties dialog box (see Figure 2.4). (You may leave the Group File field empty.)

  When you select the OK push button, a new icon group appears, as shown in Figure 2.5. As you can see, there are no icons in this group. We will now add some icons, each representing a different program from the book.

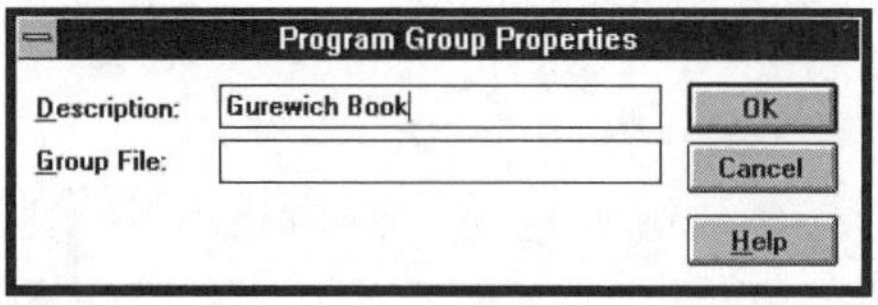

Figure 2.4. The Program Group Properties dialog box.

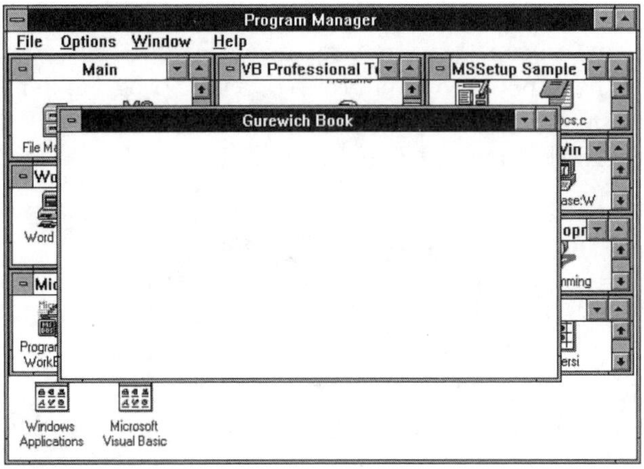

Figure 2.5. The Gurewich Book group.

We will now add icons to the Gurewich Book group.

- While the title of the Gurewich Book group is highlighted, click the File menu of the Program Manager. The File menu appears, as shown in Figure 2.2.

- Select the New option from the menu. The New Program Object dialog box appears, as shown in Figure 2.3.

  Because we are now adding a new program item (not a new program group), make sure that the Program Item radio button is pushed (not the Program Group radio button).

- Select the OK push button of the New Program Object dialog box. The Program Item Properties dialog box appears, as shown in Figure 2.6

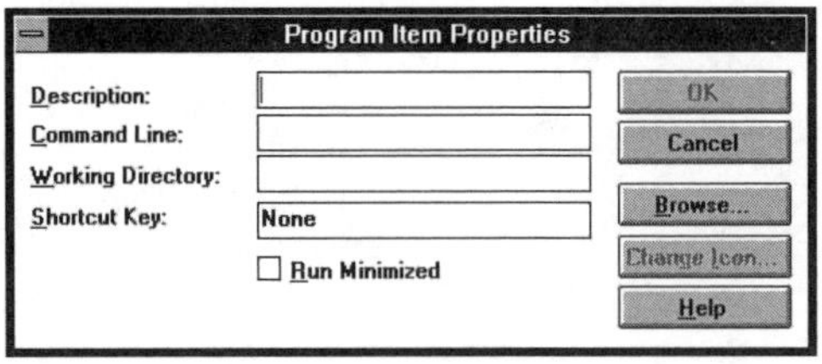

Figure 2.6. The Program Item Properties dialog box.

For our first icon, we'll add the Dog program.

- In the Description field of the Program Item Properties dialog box type **Dog**.

- Fill in the Command Line field of the Program Item Properties dialog box by typing

  c:\spSDK\Samp4Win\Dog.exe

  An alternative way to fill the Command Line field is to use Browse:

- Click the Browse push button and select c:\spSDK\Samp4Win\.

- Select the DOG.EXE file.

After you push the OK push button, the Command Line field should contain

C:\SPSDK\SAMP4WIN\DOG.EXE

You may leave the Working Directory field of the Program Item Properties dialog box empty.

When you push the OK push button of the Program Item Properties dialog box, a new icon is added to the Gurewich Book group of icons, as shown in Figure 2.7. You may now execute the Dog program by double clicking the Dog icon.

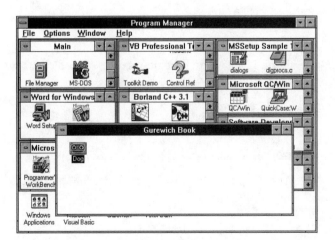

Figure 2.7. The Dog icon is added to the Gurewich Book group.

You can add more icons to the Gurewich Book group of icons by just re-peating the process. Add an icon for each of the .EXE files that reside in c:\spSDK\Samp4Win\.

Once you finish creating icons to each of the programs of c:\spSDK\Samp4Win\, the group will contain the icons shown in Figure 2.8

Figure 2.8. The Windows programs of the book.

Method 2

An alternative method for creating the new group of icons lets you create the new icon group faster:

- Log into c:\spSDK\Misc\.

- Copy the Gurewich.grp file to the Windows directory:

  ```
  Copy c:\spSDK\Misc\Gurewich.grp c:\Windows  {Enter}
  ```

- From the Program Manager, double click the File Manager icon (see Figure 2.9).

Figure 2.9. The File Manager icon.

The File Manager window appears, as shown in Figure 2.10.

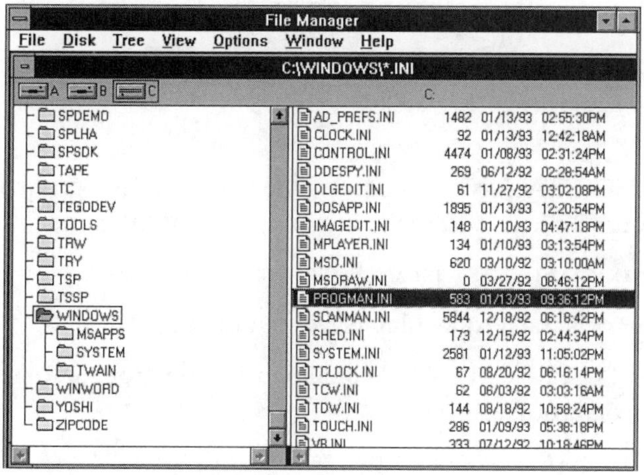

Figure 2.10. The File Manager window.

- Double click the PROGMAN.INI file. (This file resides in c:\Windows\.)

  The Notepad program appears with the PROGMAN.INI file ready to be edited (see Figure 2.11).

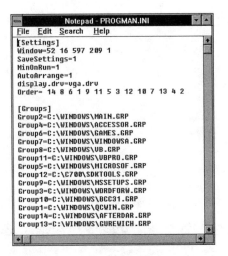

Figure 2.11. The Notepad window.

- The PROGMAN.INI file contains the list of the icon groups, as shown in Figure 2.11. To add the new icon group, add the line

```
GroupXX=C:\WINDOWS\GUREWICH.GRP
```

(Note: XX is the next available group number.)

In our PC, PROGMAN.INI contained 12 icon groups, so we added the new icon group as

```
Group13=C:\WINDOWS\GUREWICH.GRP
```

- To make the addition of the new group effective, restart Windows. (You may do so by exiting Windows, and then starting Windows again.)

Executing the Applications

As you can see, there are different forms of icons: tape-recorder cassettes, external speakers, and other customized icons (see Figure 2.8).

The programs identified by the tape-recorder icons as well as the customized icons can be executed by any PC. You don't need additional hardware or software. The sound is played through the internal built-in speaker that exists in every PC.

The programs that are identified by the external speaker icons, are programs that can be executed only if the PC has a sound card installed. The programs will be able to play through any Windows-compatible sound card.

Try to execute some of the programs. For example, to execute the Dog program, double click the Dog icon; to execute the Dance program, double click the Dance icon, and so on.

Most of the programs are self-explanatory; other programs require some explanation. For example, to execute the SayName program, double click the SayName icon. Then switch to the Program Manager and try to exit from Windows, or try to execute the Paintbrush program.

This book teaches you how to write these programs.

How This Book Is Organized

The book is composed of the following chapters:

Chapters 1 and 2: These chapters provide an overview of sound programming.

Chapters 3 through 9: This part of the book teaches how to write Windows applications that can play sound through the internal speaker of the PC without any additional hardware or software.

Chapters 10: This chapter teaches how to write stand-alone sound Windows applications. A stand-alone sound application is an .EXE file that contains the sound files, and thus requires no external sound file(s).

Chapter 11: This chapter teaches how to write Windows applications that play and record sound through a sound card. The sound card may be any Windows compatible sound card.

Chapter 12: This chapter teaches how to write DOS applications that can play sound through the PC speaker without any additional hardware or software.

Chapter 13: This chapter teaches how to write DOS applications that can record and play sound through the Sound Blaster sound card.

Appendix: The appendix teaches how to use the DLL sound library. The DLL can be utilized by C programs, by Visual Basic for Windows, and any other Windows programming languages that can utilize DLLs.

Sound Programs for DOS

The directory c:\spSDK\SampMS\ contains C programs that need to be compiled and linked with the Microsoft C compiler. The directory c:\spSDK\SampBL\ contains C programs that need to be compiled and linked with the Borland C compiler. In Chapter 12, you'll be instructed to compile and link these programs. (Due to disk-space limitation, we did not compile and link these programs.) However, to provide you with a taste of these programs, the book's disk includes two sample DOS programs that are already linked in the directory c:\spSDK\Util\. These programs can play the S sound files that reside in c:\spSDK\Sfiles.

You can execute the GR1.EXE program as follows:

- Log into c:\spSDK\Util\.

- To play the file Day.s, at the DOS prompt type

    `GR1 c:\spSDK\Sfiles\Day.s` {Enter}

Similarly, you can play the other .S files that reside in c:\spSDK\Sfiles\.

You can execute the GR2.EXE program as follows:

- Log into c:\spSDK\Util\.

- To play the file Day.s, at the DOS prompt type

    `GR2 c:\spSDK\Sfiles\Day.s` {Enter}

Similarly, you can play the other .S files that reside in c:\spSDK\Sfiles\.

The sample programs, GR1.EXE and GR2.EXE, play only S-Type sound files. Later in the book you will learn how to write programs that play other types of sound files (for example, .TS sound files, .WAV files, .VOC files, and others).

THREE

The Generic 1 Windows Program

In this chapter, we will write the Generic1.c Windows program, on which many subsequent programs are based.

Generic1.c and Generic2.c

As you know, C programs for Windows tend to be longer than C programs for DOS. However, all Windows applications look alike, and indeed, many Windows programing books teach Windows programing by first showing a simple template program, usually called *Generic.c.* All subsequent programs are built around the Generic.c program. That is, once you understand the program and all its associated files, you simply copy Generic.c and all its associated files to other files. Then you make minor changes to the new files and create a new Windows application without the need to type the lengthy parts of the program that are common to all Windows applications.

This book follows the same Generic.c technique. When you program Windows applications that contain sound, however, there are basically two methods for writing such applications. Because the two methods are different from each other, we need two "Generic" programs: Generic1 and Generic2.

We begin with the Generic1.c program, a program which you may already be familiar with. Once we cover writing Windows applications that have the Generic1.c format, we'll write programs that are based on the Generic2.c format.

The Generic2.c-based programs are by far more powerful than the Generic1.c-based programs. You will have a chance to appreciate the extreme power of Generic2.c-based programs later in the book. For now, just note that with a Generic2.c-based program you can write some fancy, advanced multitasking programs. For example, a Generic2-based program may play a sound file, and while the sound file is playing, you may switch to the Program Manager of Windows, click the MS-DOS icon (usually in the Main group of icons), and go to a DOS shell. While in a DOS shell, the PC keeps playing the sound file. You can also execute a regular DOS program, during which the sound file still plays in the background. Another option is switching to Word for Windows, Paintbrush, or any other Windows application; and while you work with the other application, the PC keeps playing the sound file in the background.

The Generic1.c Program Files

The Generic1 program includes the following files:

Generic1.c	The C source code of the program.
Generic1.h	The #include file of the program.
Generic1.rc	The resource file of the program.
Generic1.def	The module definition file of the program.
Tape.ico	The icon of the program.

To compile and link Generic1, you need a sixth file, the Generic1.mak file:

Generic1.mak	The .MAK file of the program.

These files are provided for you in c:\spSDK\Samp4Win\.

The complete listing of Generic1 is shown in Listings 3.1 through 3.5.

Listing 3.1. Generic1.h.

```
/*==================================================
FILE NAME: Generic1.h

(C) Copyright Gurewich 1992, 1993
==================================================*/
```

continues

Listing 3.1. continued

```
/*---------
 prototypes
 ---------*/
long FAR PASCAL _export WndProc       ( HWND, UINT, UINT, LONG );
BOOL FAR PASCAL _export AboutDlgProc ( HWND, UINT, UINT, LONG );

/*-------
 #define
 -------*/
#define IDM_QUIT  1  /* The Quit option in the menu */
#define IDM_ABOUT 2  /* The About option in the menu */

/*-------------
 Global variables
 -------------*/
char        gszAppName[] = "Generic1" ; /* Our application name. */
HINSTANCE  ghInst;                        /* current instance.     */
```

Listing 3.2. Generic1.c.

```
/*==============================================================
  PROGRAM: Generic1.c
  -------
  (C) Copyright 1992, 1993 Gurewich. (R) All rights reserved.

  PROGRAM DESCRIPTION:
  -------------------
  This is the Generic type 1 program.
  ==============================================================*/

/*---------
 #include
 --------*/
/*------------------------------------
 Required for all Windows applications.
 ------------------------------------*/
#include <windows.h>

/*------------------------------------------------------------------
 Required so that sp_ functions, SP_ macros, and #definitions
 from the TS sound library may be used in this applications.
 ------------------------------------------------------------------*/
#include "c:\spSDK\TegoWlib\sp4Win.h"

 /*-----------------------------------------------------
```

```
    Definitions & prototypes specific to this application.
    -------------------------------------------------------*/
    #include "c:\spSDK\Samp4WIN\Generic1.h"


    /*==================
     FUNCTION: WinMain()
     ==================*/
    int PASCAL WinMain ( HANDLE hInstance,
                         HANDLE hPrevInstance,
                         LPSTR  lpszCmdLine,
                         int    nCmdShow )
    {
    /*-------------------------
     Local and static variables.
     -------------------------*/
    HWND      hWnd;    /* Handler to the window of our application.   */
    MSG       msg;     /* Message to be processed by our application. */
    WNDCLASS  wc;      /* Window class of our application.            */

    /*----------------------------------------------
     Make the hInstance variable a global variable.
     ----------------------------------------------*/
    ghInst = hInstance;


    /*----------------------------------------------
     Update the window class structure and register
     the window class.
     ----------------------------------------------*/
    if ( !hPrevInstance )
       {
       /*-------------------------------------------
        The "if" is satisfied, this is the very 1st
        run of this application.
        -------------------------------------------*/
       wc.style         = CS_HREDRAW | CS_VREDRAW ;
       wc.lpfnWndProc   = WndProc ;
       wc.cbClsExtra    = 0 ;
       wc.cbWndExtra    = 0 ;
       wc.hInstance     = ghInst ;
       wc.hIcon         = LoadIcon   ( ghInst, "IconOfTape" ) ;
       wc.hCursor       = LoadCursor ( NULL, IDC_ARROW      ) ;
       wc.hbrBackground = GetStockObject ( WHITE_BRUSH );
       wc.lpszMenuName  = gszAppName ;
       wc.lpszClassName = gszAppName ;

       /*------------------
        Register the window.
        ------------------*/
       RegisterClass ( &wc );
```

continues

Listing 3.2. continued

```
    }/* end of if(!hPrevInstance) */

/*-----------------------------------
  Create the window of our application.
  ---------------------------------*/
hWnd = CreateWindow ( gszAppName,
                      gszAppName,
                      WS_OVERLAPPEDWINDOW,
                      CW_USEDEFAULT,
                      CW_USEDEFAULT,
                      CW_USEDEFAULT,
                      CW_USEDEFAULT,
                      NULL,
                      NULL,
                      ghInst,
                      NULL );

/*---------------------------------------------
  Show and update the window of our application.
  -------------------------------------------*/
ShowWindow   ( hWnd, nCmdShow );
UpdateWindow ( hWnd );

/*---------------
  The message loop.
  --------------*/
while ( GetMessage ( &msg, NULL, 0, 0 ) )
      {
      TranslateMessage ( &msg );
      DispatchMessage  ( &msg );
      }

return msg.wParam ;

} /* end of function. */
/*========================= end of WinMain() ====================*/

/*==================
 FUNCTION: WndProc()
 =================*/
/*-----------------------------
 DESCRIPTION: Processes messages.
 ----------------------------*/
long FAR PASCAL _export WndProc ( HWND hWnd,
                                  UINT message,
                                  UINT wParam,
                                  LONG lParam )

    {
```

```
/*-------------------------
Local and static variables.
-------------------------*/
HDC          hdc;       /* Needed for displaying text. */
PAINTSTRUCT  ps;        /* Needed for displaying text. */
RECT         rect;      /* Needed for displaying text. */


/*------------------------------
 Needed for the About dialog box.
------------------------------*/
static FARPROC lpfnAboutDlgProc ;

switch ( message )
      {
      case WM_CREATE:
            /*-------------------------------------------
            Typically, you will open a sound session here.
            -------------------------------------------*/
            /*.........................................*/
            /*........ Opening a sound session ........*/
            /*.........................................*/


            /*-----------------------------------------------------
            Obtain the lpfnAboutDlgProc of the About dialog box.
            -----------------------------------------------------*/
            lpfnAboutDlgProc =
            MakeProcInstance (( FARPROC) AboutDlgProc, ghInst);
            return 0;

      case WM_PAINT:
            hdc = BeginPaint ( hWnd, &ps );
            GetClientRect ( hWnd, &rect );
            DrawText ( hdc,
                      "Demonstration",
                      -1,
                      &rect,
                       DT_SINGLELINE ¦ DT_CENTER ¦ DT_VCENTER );
            EndPaint ( hWnd, &ps );
            return 0;

      case WM_COMMAND:
            /*-----------------
            Process menu items.
            -----------------*/
            switch (wParam)
                   {
                   case IDM_QUIT:
                         /*-------------------------
                         User clicked on Quit option.
```

continues

Listing 3.2. continued

```
                                         --------------------------*/
                                    DestroyWindow (hWnd);
                                    return 0L;

                              case IDM_ABOUT :
                                    /*--------------------------
                                    User clicked on About option.
                                    --------------------------*/
                                    DialogBox ( ghInst,
                                                "AboutBox",
                                                hWnd,
                                                lpfnAboutDlgProc );
                                    return 0;
                              }/* end of switch (wParam) */

                   case WM_DESTROY:
                         PostQuitMessage (0);
                         return 0;

                   }/* end of switch (message) */

/*----------------------
 Message was not processed.
 --------------------*/
return DefWindowProc ( hWnd, message, wParam, lParam ) ;

}/* end of WndProc() */
/*================== end of WndProc() ====================*/

/*=======================
 FUNCTION: AboutDlgProc()
 =======================*/
/*-------------------------------------
 DESCRIPTION:
 This is the About dialog box procedure.
 -------------------------------------*/
BOOL FAR PASCAL _export AboutDlgProc ( HWND hDlg,
                                       UINT message,
                                       UINT wParam,
                                       LONG lParam )
{
switch ( message )
       {
       case WM_INITDIALOG :
             return TRUE;
```

```
        case WM_COMMAND :
            switch ( wParam )
                {
                case IDOK :
                case IDCANCEL :
                    EndDialog ( hDlg, 0 );
                    return TRUE;
                }
        }

return FALSE ;

}/* End of function. */
/*=============== end of AboutDlgProc() ===============*/
```

Listing 3.3. Generic1.rc.

```
/*==================================================
 FILE NAME: Generic1.rc
 ---------

 FILE DESCRIPTION:
 ----------------
 The resource file.

 (C) Copyright Gurewich 1992, 1993

 =================================================*/

/*-------
 #include
 -------*/
#include <windows.h>
#include "Generic1.h"

/*---
 Menu
 ---*/
Generic1   MENU
BEGIN
   POPUP   "&Menu"
       BEGIN
```

continues

Listing 3.3. continued

```
            MENUITEM "&Quit",  IDM_QUIT
            MENUITEM "&About", IDM_ABOUT
        END
END

/*-----------------------------------------
 Definition of the Cassette tape icon.
 File name: Tape.ico
 Icon name: IconOfTape
-----------------------------------------*/
IconOfTape ICON Tape.ico

/*------------------
 The About dialog box.
------------------*/
AboutBox DIALOG 81, 43, 160, 100
STYLE DS_MODALFRAME ¦ WS_POPUP ¦ WS_VISIBLE ¦
                      WS_CAPTION ¦ WS_SYSMENU
CAPTION "About this program"
FONT 8, "MS Sans Serif"
BEGIN
    PUSHBUTTON      "OK", IDOK, 64, 75, 40, 14
    CTEXT           "(C) Copyright Gurewich 1992, 1993", -1,
                    13, 47, 137, 18
    ICON            "IconOfTape", -1, 14, 12, 18, 20
END
```

Listing 3.4. Generic1.def.

```
;=====================================
; module-definition file for Generic1.c
;=====================================

NAME          Generic1

DESCRIPTION   'The Generic1 program. (C) Copyright Gurewich 1992, 1993'

EXETYPE       WINDOWS

STUB          'WINSTUB.EXE'

CODE  PRELOAD MOVEABLE DISCARDABLE
```

```
DATA   PRELOAD MOVEABLE MULTIPLE

HEAPSIZE      1024
STACKSIZE     8192
```

Listing 3.5. Generic1.mak.

```
#=============
# Generic1.mak
#=============

Generic1.exe : Generic1.obj Generic1.h Generic1.def Generic1.res
    link /nod Generic1.obj, Generic1.exe, NUL, \
        slibcew.lib oldnames.lib libw.lib commdlg \
        c:\spSDK\TegoWlib\TegoWin.lib, \
        Generic1.def
    rc -t Generic1.res

Generic1.obj : Generic1.c Generic1.h
    cl -c -G2sw -Ow -W3 -Zp Generic1.c

Generic1.res : Generic1.rc Generic1.h Tape.ico
    rc -r Generic1.rc
```

Because all the subsequent Generic1-based programs are based on the preceding files, we will quickly review these files.

A Quick Review of Generic1

The Generic1.c file resides in c:\spSDK\Samp4Win\. Although Generic1.c is a simple program, you should go over its listing and gain a full understanding of its code, because all subsequent Generic1-based programs are based on it.

Later chapters discuss some advanced Windows applications that include sound, synchronization of moving text and graphic objects with the playback of sound (animations), multitasking, and other interesting topics. During the discussions and explanations of those topics, we assume that you are familiar with the Windows operating system and already know how to write simple C programs for it. Thus, we assume that you know about topics such as `WinMain()`, `WndProc()`, the resource file (.RC), the module definition file (.DEF), dialog boxes, push buttons, and other related Windows topics. Because different readers come from different backgrounds and with different levels of Windows programming experience, we go line by line over the code of the Generic1.c program and its associated files.

If you are an experienced Windows programmer, you may find the material presented in the rest of this chapter somewhat simple. If so, just browse through it rather than read it with great concentration; it presents several new topics that you'll need in subsequent chapters. We particularly suggest reading the section entitled "The TegoWin.lib Library."

If you haven't programmed for Windows lately, the material presented in the rest of this chapter will serve as a refresher course.

The *#include* Section of Generic1.c

Generic1.c includes the following three `#include` statements:

```
#include <windows.h>
#include "c:\spSDK\TegoWlib\sp4Win.h"
#include "c:\spSDK\Samp4WIN\Generic1.h"
```

The first `#include` file, windows.h, is required for all Windows applications. This file came with the MS SDK for Windows package.

The second `#include`, sp4Win.h, resides in c:\spSDK\TegoWLib\. As you read this book, you will write C programs that call C sound functions that are part of the sound library, TegoWin.lib. The prototypes of those C sound functions are declared in the `#include` file, sp4Win.h. The file sp4Win.h also includes #definitions and macros related to the sound library, TegoWin.lib.

The third `#include` file, Generic1.h, contains function prototypes and definitions that are specific to Generic1.c.

The *WinMain()* Function of Generic1.c

The Generic1.c program then proceeds with a standard WinMain() function and its standard four parameters:

```
int PASCAL WinMain ( HANDLE hInstance,
                     HANDLE hPrevInstance,
                     LPSTR  lpszCmdLine,
                     int    nCmdShow )
{
........................
... body of WinMain() ...
........................
}
```

Every Windows application must have a WinMain() function, as every DOS C program must have a main() function.

The Local Variables of *WinMain()*

WinMain() has three local variables:

```
HWND      hWnd;
MSG       msg;
WNDCLASS  wc;
```

Those variables are used in the body of WinMain() to perform various standard initializations.

Globalizing the Instance of Generic1

Generic1.c then makes the hInstance variable that came from the Windows operating system as the first parameter of WinMain() a global variable, ghInst:

```
ghInst = hInstance;
```

The global variable ghInst is defined in the Generic1.h file:

```
HINSTANCE  ghInst;
```

We make this variable global to make it visible in the WndProc() function, discussed later in this chapter.

Our convention for variable naming is using *g* as the first character of the variable name. For example, ghInst is a global variable.

Updating and Registering the Window Class

If this is the first instance of the program, we then update the structure wc, as in the following:

```
if ( !hPrevInstance )
    {
    /*-------------------------------------------
    The "if" is satisfied, this is the very 1st
    run of this application.
    ------------------------------------------*/
    wc.style          = CS_HREDRAW | CS_VREDRAW ;
    wc.lpfnWndProc    = WndProc ;
    wc.cbClsExtra     = 0 ;
    wc.cbWndExtra     = 0 ;
    wc.hInstance      = ghInst ;
    wc.hIcon          = LoadIcon  ( ghInst, "IconOfTape" ) ;
    wc.hCursor        = LoadCursor ( NULL, IDC_ARROW      ) ;
    wc.hbrBackground  = GetStockObject ( WHITE_BRUSH );
    wc.lpszMenuName   = gszAppName ;
    wc.lpszClassName  = gszAppName ;

    /*-----------------
    Register the window.
    -----------------*/
    RegisterClass ( &wc );

    }/* end of if(!hPrevInstance) */
```

Note that the global variable gszAppName is used to fill the last two elements of the wc structure: lpszMenuName and lpszClassName. This string variable gszAppName was initialized in Generic1.h:

```
char gszAppName[] = "Generic1" ;
```

We use the name of the program, Generic1, for the menu name and the class name (the last two elements of the wc structure).

Create, Update, and Show the Program Window

We then create, update, and show the program window with the
CreateWindow(), ShowWindow(), and UpdateWindow() functions:

```
hWnd = CreateWindow ( gszAppName,
                      gszAppName,
                      WS_OVERLAPPEDWINDOW,
                      CW_USEDEFAULT,
                      CW_USEDEFAULT,
                      CW_USEDEFAULT,
                      CW_USEDEFAULT,
                      NULL,
                      NULL,
                      ghInst,
                      NULL );

ShowWindow   ( hWnd, nCmdShow );
UpdateWindow ( hWnd );
```

Note that we again use the global variable gszAppName as the first two parameters of CreateWindow(). This way, when you write other Generic1-based
programs, the only place that will require a change is a single statement in the
Generic1.h file where gszAppName is defined.

The Message Loop of Generic1.c

The message loop of Generic1.c is the standard while() loop:

```
while ( GetMessage ( &msg, NULL, 0, 0 ) )
    {
    TranslateMessage ( &msg );
    DispatchMessage ( &msg );
    }
```

The Windows operating system generates messages based on events that
occur. For example, if the user selects an item from the menu, the Windows
operating system generates a message that indicates the user selected the menu
item, and then it stores the message in a message buffer. The message loop in
WinMain() extracts the message using the GetMessage() function. If there is no
message for our program, the Windows operating system executes the
WinMain() of other programs. The Windows operating system returns control
to our program when there is a message for our program.

If an event took place that caused the Windows operating system to generate and store a message for our program (for example, the user chose an item from the program menu), the `GetMessage()` in `WinMain()` extracts this message, and the body of the `while()` loop is executed: the message is translated with the `TranslateMessage()` function, and then dispatched back to the Windows operating system using the `DispatchMessage()` function. Upon receiving the dispatched message, the Windows operating system executes the function mentioned as the `lpfnWndProc` element of the `wc` structure. Because we updated this element as

```
wc.lpfnWndProc    = WndProc ;
```

`WndProc()` will be executed.

The *WndProc()* Function

The Windows operating system executes the `WndProc()` function, as in the following:

```
long FAR PASCAL _export WndProc ( HWND hWnd,
                                   UINT message,
                                   UINT wParam,
                                   LONG lParam )
{
.............................
... The body of WndProc() ...
.............................
}
```

The prototype of `WndProc()` is declared in Generic1.h as:

```
long FAR PASCAL _export WndProc ( HWND, UINT, UINT, LONG );
```

The Message Switch of *WndProc()*

The parameters of `WndProc()` are the description of the message. `WndProc()` analyzes the message, and based on its content executes code that corresponds to the particular message.

This is accomplished by using the `switch()`, as in the following:

```
switch ( message )
      {
      case WM_CREATE:  .......
                       .......
                       .......
                       return 0;
      case WM_PAINT:   .......
                       .......
                       .......
                       return 0;
      case WM_COMMAND:
          switch (wParam)
                 {
                 case IDM_QUIT:  .......
                                 .......
                                 .......
                                 return 0;
                 case IDM_ABOUT: .......
                                 .......
                                 .......
                                 return 0;
                 }
      case WM_DESTROY: .......
                       .......
                       .......
                       return 0;
      }
return DefWindowProc ( hWnd, message, wParam, lParam ) ;
```

Each case is terminated with return 0, indicating to the Windows operating system that the message was processed. If a message is not processed, WndProc() uses the DefWindowProc() function.

Processing the *WM_CREATE* Message

The Windows operating system sends a WM_CREATE message to our program upon creating the program window.

The WndProc() function processes the WM_CREATE message as follows:

```
case WM_CREATE:
    /*-------------------------------------------
    Typically, you will open a sound session here.
    ---------------------------------------------*/
    /*.............................................*/
    /*........ Opening a sound session .........*/
    /*.............................................*/
```

```
/*--------------------------------------------------
Obtain the lpfnAboutDlgProc of the About dialog box.
------------------------------------------------*/
lpfnAboutDlgProc =
MakeProcInstance (( FARPROC) AboutDlgProc, ghInst);
return 0;
```

The first section of the WM_CREATE case opens a sound session. The code for opening a sound session is discussed in the next chapter.

The second section of the WM_CREATE case has to do with the program's About dialog box. We update the variable lpfnAboutDlgProc using the MakeProcInstance() function. The variable lpfnAboutDlgProc is used later to create and display the About dialog box with the DialogBox() function under the IDM_ABOUT case. Note that the first parameter of MakeProcInstance() is AboutDlgProc, which means we are naming the dialog box procedure AboutDlgProc().

The prototype of the AboutDlgProc() function is declared in Generic1.h as:

```
BOOL FAR PASCAL _export AboutDlgProc ( HWND, UINT, UINT, LONG );
```

which is a standard call-back function prototype.

Processing the *WM_PAINT* Message

The WndProc() processes the WM_PAINT message, as in the following:

```
case WM_PAINT:
     hdc = BeginPaint ( hWnd, &ps );
     GetClientRect ( hWnd, &rect );
     DrawText ( hdc,
                "Demonstration",
                -1,
                &rect,
                DT_SINGLELINE ¦ DT_CENTER ¦ DT_VCENTER );
     EndPaint ( hWnd, &ps );
     return 0;
```

The WM_PAINT case extracts the device context hdc using the BeginPaint() function, gets the client area using the GetClientRect() function, and then displays the phrase Demonstration at the center of the window.

The Windows operating system sends a WM_PAINT message to WndProc() whenever there is a need to repaint our program window.

The code under the WM_PAINT case simply displays the message Demonstration at the center of the Generic1 window.

Processing the *WM_COMMAND* Message

WndProc() processes WM_COMMAND messages—messages that are generated because the user chose an option from the program's menu.

Whenever the user selects a menu option, the Windows operating system sends the WM_COMMAND message to WndProc(). We open a new switch under the WM_COMMAND case. This switch further investigates which menu option the user selected.

```
case WM_COMMAND:
    switch (wParam)
            {
            case IDM_QUIT:
                DestroyWindow (hWnd);
                return 0L;

            case IDM_ABOUT :
                DialogBox ( hInstance,
                            "AboutBox",
                            hWnd,
                            lpfnAboutDlgProc );
                return 0;
            }
```

As shown in Figure 3.1, the Generic1.c program menu contains two options: Quit and About. Subsequent programs have more menu options, and their switch(wParam) extends to include more cases.

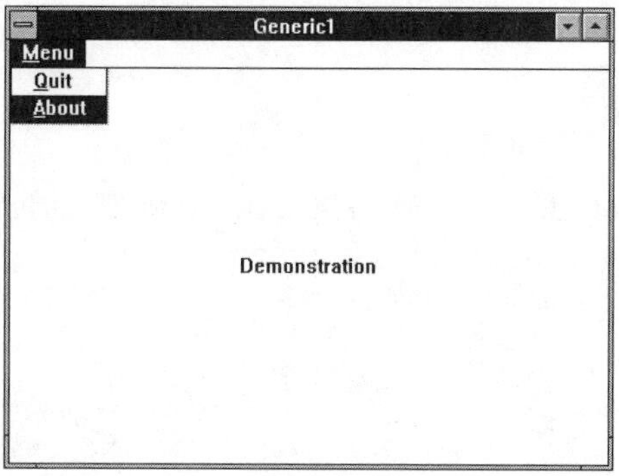

Figure 3.1. The Generic1.c program menu.

The fact that the user selected the Quit option is sensed by WndProc() by catching the WM_COMMAND message with wParam equal to IDM_QUIT. The IDM_QUIT is #defined as 1 in Generic1.h. Under the IDM_QUIT case we execute the DestroyWindow() function, which causes the Windows operating system to generate the WM_DESTROY message as the next message. We terminate the case by returning 0, indicating to the Windows operating system that the message was processed by WndProc().

If the user chooses the About option, the Windows operating system executes WndProc() with message equal to WM_COMMAND and wParam equal to IDM_ABOUT. IDM_ABOUT is #defined in Generic1.h as 2. The IDM_ABOUT case will be executed, and the AboutBox dialog box displays. The layout of the AboutBox dialog box is defined in the Generic1.rc file. Note that the fourth parameter of DialogBox() was previously updated under the WM_CREATE case.

The dialog box procedure of the About dialog box is the AboutDlgProc() function:

```
BOOL FAR PASCAL _export AboutDlgProc ( HWND hDlg,
                                       UINT message,
                                       UINT wParam,
                                       LONG lParam )
{
switch ( message )
        {
        case WM_INITDIALOG :
                return TRUE;

        case WM_COMMAND :
                switch ( wParam )
                        {
                        case IDOK :
                        case IDCANCEL :
                            EndDialog ( hDlg, 0 );
                            return TRUE;
                        }
        }
return FALSE ;
)
```

The prototype of AboutDlgProc() is declared in Generic1.h, and the body of the AboutDlgProc() function is a standard dialog box procedure with the WM_INITDIALOG case and WM_COMMAND case.

The WM_INITDIALOG message is received when the dialog box is first created. The WM_COMMAND message is received when the user selects an option from the dialog box menu.

Processing the *WM_DESTROY* Message

WM_DESTROY is the last message that WndProc() processes:

```
case WM_DESTROY:
    PostQuitMessage (0);
    return 0;
```

The Windows operating system sends this message to WndProc() whenever a request to terminate the program is generated. Such a request is generated when

1. The user clicks the Close option from the system menu of our program window. This causes the Windows operating system to send a WM_DESTROY message to WndProc().

or,

2. The user selects the Quit option from our program menu. This causes the Windows operating system to send to WndProc a WM_COMMAND message with wParam equal to IDM_QUIT. The IDM_QUIT case is then processed, executing the DestroyWindow() function, which causes the Windows operating system to send a WM_DESTROY message to WndProc().

Under the WM_DESTROY case, we execute the PostQuitMessage() function which causes the generation of a null message. The GetMessage() function receives the null message that was generated due to the execution of PostQuitMessage(). The body of the message loop in WinMain() is not executed, and the program terminates.

The Resource File, Generic1.rc

The resource file of Generic1.c is Generic1.rc.

This file contains two #include statements:

```
#include <windows.h>
#include "Generic1.h"
```

These #include files are necessary because the following lines of the .RC file use #definitions that are #defined in them.

The next section in the .RC file is the menu outline definition. The Generic1 menu contains two options: Quit and About. This is accomplished as in the following:

```
Generic1  MENU
    BEGIN
      POPUP   "&Menu"
      BEGIN
          MENUITEM "&Quit",   IDM_QUIT
          MENUITEM "&About",  IDM_ABOUT
      END
    END
```

The menu is called Generic1 (as was committed in WinMain() when the element wc.lpszMenuName was updated with gszAppName).

Next in the .RC file is the IconOfTape icon definition:

```
IconOfTape ICON Tape.ico
```

which defines the IconOfTape icon made from the Tape.ico file. You will find Tape.ico in c:\spSDK\Ssmp4Win\. Tape.ico was generated using the Dialog Image Editor program that comes with the Microsoft SDK for Windows. This icon is used in two occasions:

1. As a small picture in the About dialog box (see Figure 3.2). This is specified in Generic1.rc in the line of the section that defines the About dialog box:

   ```
   ICON "IconOfTape", -1, 14, 12, 18, 20
   ```

2. As the icon of our program when the user minimizes our program window. This was defined in WinMain() when we updated the element wc.hIcon with the following statement:

   ```
   wc.hIcon  = LoadIcon ( ghInst, "IconOfTape" ) ;
   ```

The IconOfTape icon is shown in Figure 3.3.

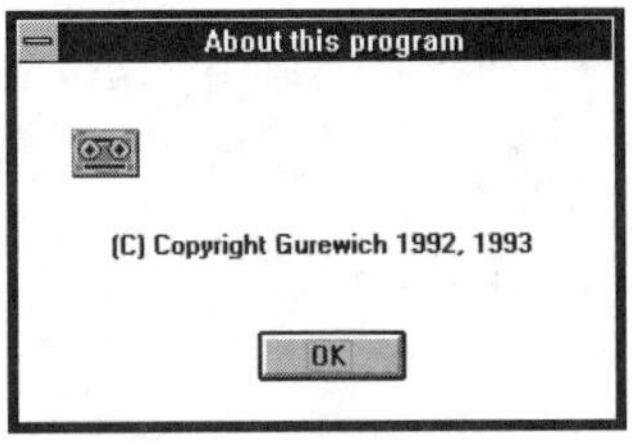

Figure 3.2. The About dialog box.

Figure 3.3. The `IconOfTape` icon.

The next section in the .RC file defines the About dialog box outline:

```
AboutBox DIALOG 81, 43, 160, 100
STYLE DS_MODALFRAME ¦ WS_POPUP ¦ WS_VISIBLE ¦
                    WS_CAPTION ¦ WS_SYSMENU
CAPTION "About this program"
FONT 8, "MS Sans Serif"
BEGIN
  PUSHBUTTON      "OK", IDOK, 64, 75, 40, 14
  CTEXT           "(C) Copyright Gurewich 1992, 1993", -1,
                  13, 47, 137, 18
  ICON            "IconOfTape", -1, 14, 12, 18, 20
    END
```

The Module Definition File, Generic1.def

All Windows applications require a module definition file. The module definition file of Generic1 is Generic1.def, and it resides in c:\spSDK\Samp4Win\.

This file is needed for the compiling/linking process of all Windows applications.

The Make File, Generic1.mak, for the Microsoft Compiler

The make file of Generic1.c is called Generic1.mak, and it resides in c:\spSDK\SampMS\. This make file is used for compiling and linking the Generic1 program with the Microsoft compiler.

Generic1.mak consists of three sections. The Generic1.mak file will be executed by a program called NMAKE.EXE which came with your Microsoft Compiler/Linker package. The NMAKE program executes the Generic1.mak file from bottom to top—that is, the NMAKE will first execute the third section, then the middle section, and finally the first section.

The last section in the Generic1.rc file is:

```
Generic1.res : Generic1.rc Generic1.h Tape.ico
    rc -r Generic1.rc
```

The first line of the preceding section instructs the NMAKE.EXE program to execute the second line of this section whenever the time and date of the file Generic1.res is older than the time and date of Generic1.rc, Generic1.h, or Tape.ico.

Thus, modifying either Generic1.rc, Generic1.h, or Tape.ico causes the execution of the line

```
rc -r Generic1.rc
```

This line is an instruction to compile the Generic1.rc file—that is, to create Generic1.res from the Generic1.rc file.

The -r switch tells the rc program to compile but not to link—that is, not to add Generic1.res to the Generic1.exe file which we did not generate yet.

The middle section of Generic1.mak is:

```
Generic1.obj : Generic1.c Generic1.h
    cl -c -G2sw -Ow -W3 -Zp -Tp Generic1.c
```

The first line of this section is an instruction to the NMAKE program, telling it that the second line of this section should be executed whenever the time and date of the Generic.obj file are older than the time and date of the Generic1.c file, or the Generic1.h file. Thus, a modification to either the Generic1.c or the Generic1.h file, will cause the second line of this section to be executed.

The second line of this section is:

```
cl -c -G2sw -Ow -W3 -Zp Generic1.c
```

cl is the program that compiles Generic1.c to create Generic1.obj.

The switches between the cl and the Generic1.c are explained next.

The -c Switch

The -c switch tells the cl program to compile (make a Generic1.obj file from the Generic1.c file) but not to link yet (not to create the file Generic1.exe yet).

The -G2sw Switch

The cl accepts the -G2 switch, the -Gs switch, and the -Gw switch. As a short-cut, you can supply the three switches in a single word, as -G2sw.

The -G2 switch tells the cl compiler to generate code that is compatible with 80286 and better PCs—that is, 80386 and 80486.

The -Gs switch disables the stack overflow checking.

We specified 8KBytes for the stack in Generic1.def, so we should be OK.

The -Gw switch tells the cl program to add a small program at the beginning and at the end of each function defined as FAR. This is needed during execution for moving code and data segment in memory.

The -Ow Switch

The -Ow switch tells the compiler not to perform certain types of optimizations. By using this switch, we are ensuring that the code generated is the code that we intended to write. (Sometimes, due to optimization, you get an optimized code, but the resultant code is not exactly what you wanted it to be.)

The -W3 Switch

The -W3 switch stands for "Warning level number 3." When you compile, the cl program prompts you for certain compiling warnings that are predefined in the compiler program to be of that level. You should not ignore these warnings because they might indicate the presence of bugs during the execution of the program.

The -Zp Switch

You don't have much of a choice regarding this switch; it is simply required. It has to do with the way windows.h defines certain structures. Some of these structures are saved on byte boundaries. The -Zp switch tells the compiler to pack the structures—that is, to save the structures on byte boundaries.

The Linking Section of Generic1.mak

Here is the first section in Generic1.mak:

```
Generic1.exe : Generic1.obj Generic1.h Generic1.def Generic1.res
    link /nod Generic1.obj, Generic1.exe, NUL, \
        slibcew.lib oldnames.lib libw.lib commdlg \
        c:\spSDK\TegoWlib\TegoWin.lib, \
        Generic1.def
    rc -t Generic1.res
```

The first line is an instruction to the NMAKE program to generate Generic1.exe whenever its date and time are older than any of the files following the colon (:). Thus, a modification to Generic1.obj, Generic1.h, Generic1.def, or Generic1.res causes the generation of a new Generic1.exe. The generation of Generic1.exe is specified by the next lines in the first section of Generic1.mak.

The remaining lines of the first section of Generic1.mak are:

```
link /nod Generic1.obj, Generic1.exe, NUL, \
    slibcew.lib oldnames.lib libw.lib commdlg \
    c:\spSDK\TegoWlib\TegoWin.lib, \
    Generic1.def
rc -t Generic1.res
```

The backslash "\" at the end of the lines is an indication that the line continues on the next line.

The first word, link, is the name of the program that causes the linking. The /nod switch that follows link is an instruction to the link program to not perform a default library search, but instead to use the libraries mentioned on the link command line.

Following /nod is Generic1.obj, the file to be linked.

The next field is the name of the Generic1.exe file, which is the name of the resultant file.

The next field is the name of the .MAP file to be created. We don't need a .MAP file, so we supply the keyword NUL.

The next field is a list of libraries that the link should use. These libraries are:

1. slibcew.lib

2. oldnames.lib

3. libw.lib

4. commdlg.lib

5. c:\spSDK\TegoWLib\TegoWin.lib

Note that the libraries are listed between two commas: the comma after NUL and the comma after c:\spSDK\TegoWLib\TegoWin.

The slibcew.lib is the small model Windows library.

The oldnames.lib is a library that enables you to use nontraditional C function names that are not ANSI C library functions.

The libw.lib is a library from the Windows SDK. It is needed so that your program can use functions from the Windows DLL libraries.

The commdlg.lib is the common dialog box library.

The TegoWin.lib is a library that resides in c:\spSDK\TegoWLib. By including this library, your program may call C sound functions that reside in this library. This is only a short version of the TegoWin.lib library, but it contains enough to link all the program examples presented in this book.

The next file name that appears is Generic1.def, telling the linker to link in accordance with the Generic1.def file.

The last statement in the link process is:

```
rc -t Generic1.res
```

which tells the linker to include the Generic1.res file in the linking process. (Generic1.res was previously generated from the Generic1.rc file in the third section of Generic1.mak.)

The TegoWin.lib Library

To compile and link the Windows C programs of this book, you need a C sound library. The TegoWin.lib file resides in c:\spSDK\TegoWLib\. This library file is the limited edition (short version) of the TegoSoft sound library for the Microsoft C compiler and SDK for Windows. Although it is the short version of this library (courtesy of TegoSoft Inc.), it contains all the necessary software to enable you to compile and link all the book's examples with the Microsoft C compiler and SDK for Windows.

Again, note that this library must be used during the link process, and indeed it is mentioned among the list of libraries to be linked in the first section of the .MAK file.

The NMAKE Program

The NMAKE program that came with your Microsoft package acts upon the Generic1.mak file. First, it executes the last section of instructions in Generic1.mak, generating Generic1.res. Then NMAKE executes the middle section, generating the Generic1.obj file. And, finally, the NMAKE program executes the first section of Generic1.mak, generating the Generic1.exe file.

Compiling and Linking with the Microsoft C Compiler

To compile and link the Generic1 program with the Microsoft C compiler:

- Make sure your PC is in a DOS-protected mode.
- Log into c:\spSDK\Samp4Win\.
- At the DOS prompt type

    `NMAKE Generic1.mak` {Enter}

The Microsoft C compiler requires that your PC be in a protected mode during the compiling and linking process. There are two methods to put your PC in a protected mode:

1. Start Windows, and then select the MS-DOS icon from the Main group of icons. This takes you to the DOS shell. While in the DOS shell, your PC is in a protected mode, so you may compile and link with the Microsoft C compiler.

2. Use any memory manager software package that can put your PC in a protected mode such as the Qualitias 386MAX or BlueMAX version 6.x.

Compiling and Linking with the Programmer Working Bench of Microsoft

If you prefer to utilize the Programmer Work Bench (PWB) that came with the Microsoft compiler, add c:\spSDK\Tego4Win\TegoWin.lib to the library list.

The Make File, Generic1.mak, for the Borland Compiler

The book's programs may be compiled and linked with both the Microsoft C compiler and the Borland C compiler. The Borland version uses .BMK extensions (for example, Generic1.bmk).

The make file Generic1.mak (for the Microsoft C compiler) is similar to the make file Generic1.bmk (for the Borland C compiler). The differences between these two files are essentially syntax differences. For example, the compile command in the file Generic1.mak is cl, while the compile command in the file Generic1.bmk is bcc.

To compile and link the Generic1 program with the Borland compiler:

- Log into c:\spSDK\Samp4Win\.

- At the DOS prompt type

  `MAKE -f Generic1.bmk` {Enter}

Note that the Borland compiler uses the MAKE.EXE program (not the NMAKE.EXE program). Also note that the Borland compiler requires you to type the -f switch.

You may use the -B switch to compile and link all the files regardless of the times and dates of the files by executing the MAKE.EXE program as follows:

```
MAKE -f Generic1.bmk -B {Enter}
```

Note that the Borland C compiler program may be used in both modes: regular DOS session, and DOS protected session.

Executing the Generic1.exe Program

You can execute the Generic1.exe program using any of the following four methods.

Executing Generic1 From Within Windows

- Select the File menu.
- Select Run from the File menu.
- Type the name of the program to be executed:

  c:\spSDK\Samp4Win\Generic1.exe

  Or use the Browse button to select Generic1.exe from c:\spSDK\Samp4Win\.

Making an Icon for the Program

Although Generic1 is a simple program, other programs that you'll write will be more complex. As such, you'll write the code in several logical steps: you'll write some code, compile and link it, and execute it. Then, if you are satisfied with the results, you'll write more code, compile and link it, and execute it. In such cases, it is best to create an icon for the program so that you don't have to waste time going through the File->Run->Browse process. Instead, you simply click the icon of the program to execute it.

Executing Generic1 From the DOS Command Line

To execute Generic1 from the DOS command line, make sure that you completely exit Windows—that is, make sure you are not in a DOS shell.

- Log into c:\spSDK\Samp4Win.

- At the DOS prompt type

    WIN Generic1   {Enter}

Writing Generic1.c-Based Programs

As previously discussed, you can write Windows applications that include sound using the Generic1 files as templates. You can also write more advanced Windows applications based on the Generic2.c program later in this book.

Make sure that you understand the Generic1.c program and its associated files (that is, Generic1.rc, Generic1.h, Generic1.def, and Generic1.mak), that you know how to compile and link them either with the Generic1.mak file or with the Programmer Work Bench (PWB), and that you know how to execute the resultant Generic1.exe program.

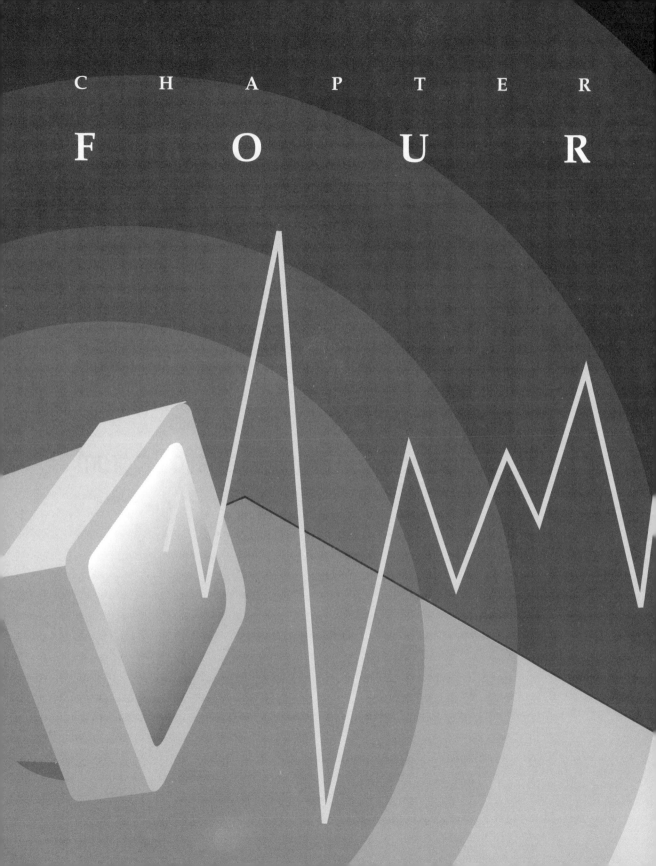

The Hello.c Program

Most programming books start teaching a programming concept by introducing as their first program a program that displays the phrase Hello. We follow this tradition, except that our first program literally says *Hello*.

In this chapter, we will write our first Windows program that includes sound, a simple Windows application called *Hello.c*. This program is a Generic1-based program.

We recommend that you compile, link, and execute the program before studying its code. This way you'll gain a better understanding of what the program can do.

Compiling and Linking the Hello Program with the Microsoft Compiler

To compile and link the Hello program with the Microsoft compiler:

- Make sure your PC is in a DOS-protected mode.

- Log into c:\spSDK\Samp4Win\.

- At the DOS prompt type

    NMAKE Hello.mak   {Enter}

Compiling and Linking the Hello Program with the Borland Compiler

To compile and link the Hello program with the Borland compiler:

- Log into c:\spSDK\Samp4Win\.

- At the DOS prompt type

  `MAKE -f Hello.bmk` {Enter}

Executing the Hello Program

To execute the Hello program:

- Select Run from the File menu of the Program Manager of Windows.

- Use Browse to select the file

  `c:\spSDK\Samp4Win\Hello.exe`

The Hello program menu contains three options: Play, Quit, and About. The Hello.c main window is shown in Figure 4.1, and its About dialog box is shown in Figure 4.2.

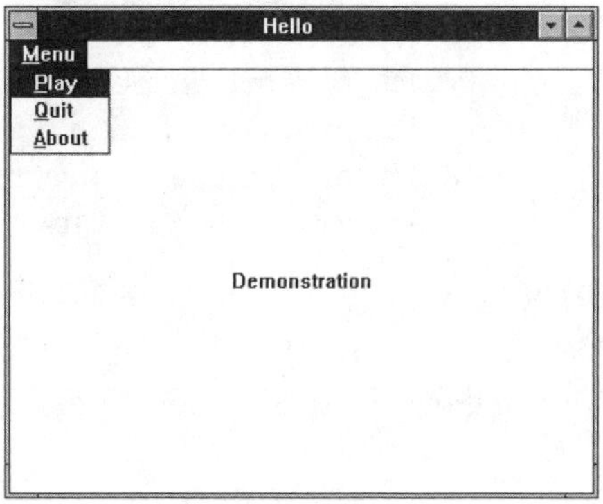

Figure 4.1. The Hello.c main window.

Figure 4.2. The About dialog box of the Hello program.

Here is how the Hello.c program works:

- When the user selects Play from the menu, the program plays the phrase *Hello, have a nice day. Good-Bye.*

- When the user selects About from the menu, the program says *Hello* and displays the About dialog box.

- When the user selects Quit from the menu, the program says *Good-Bye* and terminates.

The Files of the Hello Program

The complete Hello program consists of the following files:

Hello.c	The C code of the program.
Hello.h	The .h file of the program.
Hello.rc	The resource file of the program.
Hello.def	The module definition file of the program.
Hello.mak	The make file of the program.
Tape.ico	The icon of the program.

These files are provided for you on the book's diskette, and reside in c:\spSDK\Samp4Win\.

The complete listing of the Hello files is shown in Listings 4.1 through 4.5.

Listing 4.1. Hello.h.

```
/*===================================================
 FILE NAME: Hello.h

 (C) Copyright Gurewich 1992, 1993
 ===================================================*/

/*---------
 prototypes
 ---------*/
long FAR PASCAL _export WndProc       ( HWND, UINT, UINT, LONG );
BOOL FAR PASCAL _export AboutDlgProc ( HWND, UINT, UINT, LONG );

/*------
 #define
 ------*/
#define IDM_QUIT  1  /* The Quit  option in the menu */
#define IDM_ABOUT 2  /* The About option in the menu */
#define IDM_PLAY  3  /* The Play  option in the menu */

/*---------------
 Global variables
 ---------------*/
char       gszAppName[] = "Hello" ; /* Our application name. */
HINSTANCE  ghInst;                  /* current instance.     */
```

Listing 4.2. Hello.c.

```
/*===========================================================
 PROGRAM: Hello.c
 -------
 (C) Copyright 1992, 1993 Gurewich. (R) All rights reserved.

 PROGRAM DESCRIPTION:
 -------------------
 This program has a Play menu in it.

 ===========================================================*/

/*-------
 #include
 -------*/
/*-----------------------------------------------
 windows.h required for all Windows applications.
```

continues

Listing 4.2. continued

```
--------------------------------------------*/
#include <windows.h>

/*----------------------------------------------------
  sp4Win.h required so that sp_ functions, SP_ macros,
  and #definitions from the TS C sound library may be used
  in this application.
  --------------------------------------------------*/
#include "c:\spSDK\TegoWlib\sp4Win.h"

/*----------------------------------------------------
  Definitions & prototypes specific to this application.
  --------------------------------------------------*/
#include "c:\spSDK\Samp4WIN\Hello.h"

/*==================
  FUNCTION: WinMain()
  ==================*/
int PASCAL WinMain ( HANDLE hInstance,
                     HANDLE hPrevInstance,
                     LPSTR  lpszCmdLine,
                     int    nCmdShow )
{
/*------------------------
  Local and static variables.
  ----------------------*/
HWND     hWnd; /* Handler to the window of our application.   */
MSG      msg;  /* Message to be processed by our application. */
WNDCLASS wc;   /* Window class of our application.            */

/*----------------------------------------------
  Make the hInstance variable a global variable.
  --------------------------------------------*/
ghInst = hInstance;

/*----------------------------------------------
  Update the window class structure and register
  the window class.
  --------------------------------------------*/
if ( !hPrevInstance )
    {
    /*----------------------------------------
    The "if" is satisfied, this is the very 1st
    run of this application.
    --------------------------------------*/
    wc.style        = CS_HREDRAW | CS_VREDRAW ;
    wc.lpfnWndProc  = WndProc ;
    wc.cbClsExtra   = 0 ;
```

```
   wc.cbWndExtra     = 0 ;
   wc.hInstance      = ghInst ;
   wc.hIcon          = LoadIcon   ( ghInst, "IconOfTape" ) ;
   wc.hCursor        = LoadCursor ( NULL, IDC_ARROW      ) ;
   wc.hbrBackground = GetStockObject ( WHITE_BRUSH );
   wc.lpszMenuName  = gszAppName ;
   wc.lpszClassName = gszAppName ;

   /*-----------------
   Register the window.
   ----------------*/
   RegisterClass ( &wc );

   }/* end of if ( !hPrevInstance ) */

 /*--------------------------------------
  Create the window of our application.
  ----------------------------------*/
hWnd = CreateWindow ( gszAppName,
                      gszAppName,
                      WS_OVERLAPPEDWINDOW,
                      CW_USEDEFAULT,
                      CW_USEDEFAULT,
                      CW_USEDEFAULT,
                      CW_USEDEFAULT,
                      NULL,
                      NULL,
                      ghInst,
                      NULL );

/*---------------------------------------------
 Show and update the window of our ts
 application.
 -------------------------------------------*/
ShowWindow   ( hWnd, nCmdShow );
UpdateWindow ( hWnd );

/*----------------
 The message loop.
 ---------------*/
while ( GetMessage ( &msg, NULL, 0, 0 ) )
      {
      TranslateMessage ( &msg );
      DispatchMessage ( &msg );
      }

return msg.wParam ;

} /* end of function. */
/*======================= end of WinMain() ===================*/
```

continues

Listing 4.2. continued

```
/*==================
 FUNCTION: WndProc()
 ==================*/
/*----------------------------
 DESCRIPTION: Processes messages.
 ----------------------------*/
long FAR PASCAL _export WndProc ( HWND hWnd,
                                  UINT message,
                                  UINT wParam,
                                  LONG lParam )
{
/*------------------------
 Local and static variables.
 ------------------------*/
HDC            hdc;    /* Needed for displaying text. */
PAINTSTRUCT    ps;     /* Needed for displaying text. */
RECT           rect;   /* Needed for displaying text. */

static FARPROC lpfnAboutDlgProc ; /* For the dialog box. */

switch ( message )
        {
        case WM_CREATE:
                /*------------------
                Open a sound session.
                --------------------*/
                sp_OpenSession ( "c:\\spSDK\\TSfiles\\Hello.ts",
                             SP_NON_STAND_ALONE,
                             0L, /* Not applicable. */
                             SP_TS_TYPE);

                /*-----------------------------------------------------
                Obtain the lpfnAboutDlgProc of the About dialog box.
                -----------------------------------------------------*/
                lpfnAboutDlgProc =
                MakeProcInstance (( FARPROC) AboutDlgProc, ghInst );
                return 0;

        case WM_PAINT:
                hdc = BeginPaint ( hWnd, &ps );
                GetClientRect ( hWnd, &rect );
                DrawText ( hdc,
                        "Demonstration",
                        -1,
                        &rect,
                        DT_SINGLELINE ¦ DT_CENTER ¦ DT_VCENTER );
                EndPaint ( hWnd, &ps );
                return 0;
```

```
case WM_COMMAND:      /* Process menu items. */
     switch (wParam)
              {
         case IDM_PLAY:
              /*-----------------------------------------
               Play the sound file.
               Range to play: very beginning to end.
               Phrase: "Hello, have a nice day. Good-Bye"
               --------------------------------------*/
               sp_PlayF ( SP_START_OF_FILE, SP_END_OF_FILE );
               return 0L;

         case IDM_QUIT:
              /*-----------------------------------------
               User selected the Quit option from the menu.
               -------------------------------------------*/
               DestroyWindow (hWnd);
               return 0L;

         case IDM_ABOUT :
              /*------------------------------------------------
               User selected the About option from the menu.
               -------------------------------------------*/
              /*------------------------------------------------
               Play a section of the sound file.
               Range to play: 0 to 10,000
               Phrase: "Hello"
               -------------------------------------------*/
               sp_PlayF ( SP_START_OF_FILE, 10000L );

               DialogBox ( ghInst,
                           "AboutBox",
                           hWnd,
                           lpfnAboutDlgProc );
               return 0;
          }/* end of switch(wParam) */

case WM_DESTROY:
     /*-------------------------------
      Play a section of the sound file.
      Range to play: 30,000 to 40,000
      phrase: "Good-Bye"
      -------------------------------*/
     sp_PlayF ( 30000L, 40000L );
```

continues

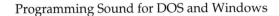

Listing 4.2. continued

```
                PostQuitMessage (0);
                return 0;
        }/* end of switch(message) */

/*----------------------
 Message was not processed.
 ----------------------*/
return DefWindowProc ( hWnd, message, wParam, lParam ) ;


}
/*================= end of WndProc() ====================*/

/*=======================
 FUNCTION: AboutDlgProc()
 =======================*/
/*------------------------------------------
DESCRIPTION:
This is the About dialog box procedure.
------------------------------------*/
BOOL FAR PASCAL _export AboutDlgProc ( HWND hDlg,
                                       UINT message,
                                       UINT wParam,
                                       LONG lParam )

{
switch ( message )
        {
        case WM_INITDIALOG :
                return TRUE;

        case WM_COMMAND :
                switch ( wParam )
                        {
                        case IDOK :
                        case IDCANCEL :
                            EndDialog ( hDlg, 0 );
                            return TRUE;
                        }
        }
return FALSE ;
}/* End of function. */
/*=============== end of AboutDlgProc() =============*/
```

Listing 4.3. Hello.rc.

```
/*======================================================
 FILE NAME: Hello.rc
 - - - - - - - - -

 FILE DESCRIPTION:
 - - - - - - - - - - - - - - -
 The resource file.

 (C) Copyright Gurewich 1992, 1993

 ===================================================*/

/*------
 #include
 ------*/
#include <windows.h>
#include "Hello.h"

/*--
 Menu
 --*/
Hello   MENU
BEGIN
    POPUP   "&Menu"
        BEGIN
            MENUITEM "&Play",   IDM_PLAY
            MENUITEM "&Quit",   IDM_QUIT
            MENUITEM "&About",  IDM_ABOUT
        END
END

/*-----------------------------------------
 Definition of the Cassette tape icon.
 Filename: Tape.ico
 Icon name: IconOfTape
 ----------------------------------------*/
IconOfTape ICON Tape.ico

/*--------------
 The dialog box.
 --------------*/
AboutBox DIALOG 81, 43, 160, 100
STYLE DS_MODALFRAME ¦ WS_POPUP ¦ WS_VISIBLE ¦
                     WS_CAPTION ¦ WS_SYSMENU
CAPTION "About this program"
```

continues

Listing 4.3. continued

```
FONT 8, "MS Sans Serif"
BEGIN
    PUSHBUTTON      "OK", IDOK, 64, 75, 40, 14
    CTEXT           "(C) Copyright Gurewich 1992, 1993", -1,
                    13, 47, 137, 18
    ICON            "IconOfTape", -1, 14, 12, 18, 20

    CTEXT           "The Hello program", -1, 46, 13, 79, 12
    ICON            "IconOfTape", -1, 132, 63, 18, 20
    CONTROL         "", -1, "Static", SS_BLACKFRAME, 43, 9, 87, 18

END
```

Listing 4.4. Hello.def.

```
;=======================================
; module-definition file for Hello.c
;=======================================

NAME          Hello

DESCRIPTION   'The Hello program. (C) Copyright Gurewich 1992, 1993'

EXETYPE       WINDOWS

STUB          'WINSTUB.EXE'

CODE   PRELOAD MOVEABLE DISCARDABLE

DATA   PRELOAD MOVEABLE MULTIPLE

HEAPSIZE      1024
STACKSIZE     8192
```

Listing 4.5. Hello.mak.

```
#=============
# Hello.mak
#=============

Hello.exe : Hello.obj Hello.h Hello.def Hello.res
    link /nod Hello.obj, Hello.exe, NUL, \
        slibcew.lib oldnames.lib libw.lib commdlg \
        c:\spSDK\TegoWlib\TegoWin.lib, \
        Hello.def
    rc -t Hello.res

Hello.obj : Hello.c Hello.h
    cl -c -G2sw -Ow -W3 -Zp Hello.c

Hello.res : Hello.rc Hello.h Tape.ico
    rc -r Hello.rc
```

The Make File, Hello.mak

The Hello.mak file was created by copying the Generic1.mak file into Hello.mak, and then replacing each occurrence of `Generic1` with the string `Hello`.

The Resource File, Hello.rc

The Hello.rc file is identical to the Generic1.rc file, except that we replaced each occurrence of Generic1 with the string `Hello`, and added the Play option to the menu. We also modified the About dialog box by adding a second `IconOfTape` icon, and the text `The Hello program` is enclosed inside a square frame (see Figure 4.2).

The Module Definition File, Hello.def

The Hello.def file is identical to the Generic1.def file, only that we replaced each occurrence of *Generic1* with the string `Hello`.

The #*include* File, Hello.h

The Hello.h file is identical to the Generic1.h file, except that we replaced each occurrence of Generic1 with the string `Hello`, and we added a new #define statement:

```
#define IDM_PLAY  3
```

This statement accounts for the new Play option in the Hello.c menu.

The Hello.c File

Hello.c was created from Generic1.c by replacing each occurrence of `Generic1` with `Hello` and adding several statements. We'll now go over those added statements.

The *sp_OpenSession()* Function

The `WM_CREATE` case of Hello.c calls the `sp_OpenSession()` function:

```
sp_OpenSession ( "c:\\spSDK\\TSfiles\\Hello.ts",
                 SP_NON_STAND_ALONE,
                 0L, /* Not applicable. */
                 SP_TS_TYPE);
```

That is, upon creating the program window, we also create a sound session by using the `sp_OpenSession()` function. The prototype of `sp_OpenSession()` is included in the sp4Win.h file that you #included at the beginning of the program.

The `sp_OpenSession()` function loads the TSEngine for Windows, and tells it how to open the sound session. The `sp_OpenSession()` function does not have to be under the `WM_CREATE` case; it could reside anywhere in the program. In fact, some programmers prefer to issue `sp_OpenSession()` in the `WinMain()` function. The `sp_OpenSession()` statement should be executed only once during the life of the program, but no harm is done if it is executed more than once. The reason for executing the `sp_OpenSession()` only once is that the execution of this function may take time, so executing this function more than once just creates unnecessary delays.

The sp_OpenSession() function is a TSEngine function. You can easily recognize that fact, because the function starts with the characters sp_. All the TSEngine functions start with the characters sp_.

> **NOTE**   All the TSEngine functions start with the characters sp_. For example, sp_OpenSession().

We will soon examine the parameters and the returned value of the sp_OpenSession() function.

DLL Functions Versus the Static *sp_* Functions

Note that sp_OpenSession() is not a Windows DLL function, but a regular C function for Windows. This function resides in TegoWin.lib, which resides in c:\spSDK\Tego4Win\.

As you may already know from your Windows programming experience, a static library is linked to the program during link time. It also becomes an integral part of the program—that is, the portion of the library called by your program becomes an integral part of Hello.exe.

A DLL library is a dynamic library, containing functions your program may call. Unlike the static library, however, the DLL library does not become an integral part of the .exe file. Instead, the DLL library resides on the hard drive. If during your program's execution there is a call to a function that resides in the DLL library, the corresponding code of the called function in the DLL is loaded into memory and executed.

(See the Appendix to see how to use the sp_ sound DLL functions.)

You may wonder whether you should use static C sound functions or DLL sound functions. The answer is that in some programs it is better to use the static sound libraries, while in other programs it is better to use the DLL sound functions. Suppose, for example, that you are distributing a demo disk that contains sound. You instruct the user to insert the disk into the drive and then type **Win demo** at the DOS prompt. When implementing the demo with the static sound functions, your demo consists of a single file, and there is no need to distribute the DLL sound library with the demo. This way you don't have to concern yourself with a more complex Install program that copies the DLL into the user machine, and you don't have to worry that the user will separate the demo program from the DLL file(s) that it needs.

On the other hand, if your program is more complex and consists of several programs that each make a call to a sound function, then you should use a DLL library. By using a DLL library you save disk space, because the sound functions are not integral parts of each program, but reside as a single file on the hard drive. This single DLL file is shared by all the programs that need it.

Use of Other *sp_* Functions

Once your program issues the sp_OpenSession() statement, the TSEngine is loaded, and it is ready to play sound files and perform other chores and tasks. The other chores and tasks that the TSEngine may perform are accomplished by issuing other sp_ functions. The sp_OpenSession(), however, must be the first sp_ function that your program issues. This, of course, makes sense, because the sp_OpenSession() is the function that loads and activates the TSEngine for Windows.

NOTE   The sp_OpenSession() must be executed before any other sp_ function.

The sp_OpenSession() may reside anywhere within the code of the program.

A good place to issue the sp_OpenSession is under the WM_CREATE case in WndProc().

A good place to issue the sp_OpenSession() is a place in the program where the sp_OpenSession() is executed only once during the life of the program.

The Parameters of the *sp_OpenSession* Function

In the Hello.c program, the sp_OpenSession() function took four parameters:

```
sp_OpenSession ( "c:\\spSDK\\TSfiles\\Hello.ts",
                 SP_NON_STAND_ALONE,
                 0L,        /* Not applicable. */
                 SP_TS_TYPE);
```

The Hello.ts Sound File

The first parameter is the name of the sound file, Hello.ts. This first parameter tells the TSEngine to open a sound session with Hello.ts, which resides in c:\spSDK\TSfiles\. When you specify the path of the sound file, use double backslashes (\\), because the C language uses a single backslash (\) as a control character. If the current directory happens to be the directory in which the sound file resides, then there is no need to specify the path of the sound file.

The Stand-Alone Parameter

The second parameter of the sp_OpenSession() function is an integer called the stand-alone parameter. To understand the concept of the stand-alone parameter, assume that Hello.c was compiled and linked, and you are ready to distribute it. If you create Hello.exe as a non-stand-alone program, then the distribution disk must contain two files: Hello.exe and Hello.ts.

This presents a certain limitation, because not only do you have to distribute two files, you also have to make sure that your installation program installs Hello.ts into the directory specified by the first parameter of the sp_OpenSession() function.

To overcome this problem, you can link the sound file to the program itself, thus creating a stand-alone program. The resultant file, Hello.exe, will contain the code together with the sound file. Your distribution disk will contain a single file, the Hello.exe file. The second parameter of sp_OpenSession() specifies whether you want your program to be a stand-alone program or a non-stand-alone program.

Specifying SP_NON_STAND_ALONE as the second parameter means that the program is a non-stand-alone program, and specifying SP_STAND_ALONE as the second parameter means that the program is a stand-alone program. As you can see, Hello.c specified SP_NON_STAND_ALONE as the second parameter, and therefore the Hello.exe will be a non-stand-alone program.

It is customary to start developing Windows applications by specifying a non-stand-alone program. Once you complete the non-stand-alone program, you may convert it to a stand-alone program by simply changing the parameters of the sp_OpenSession() function. The conversion of a non-stand-alone program to a stand-alone program involves a single change in the parameters of the sp_OpenSession() function.

Later in the book you will learn how to link the sound file to the .exe part of your program, so that you will be able to generate stand-alone programs.

The Third Parameter of the *sp_OpenSession()* Function

The third parameter of sp_OpenSession() is a long integer. The value of this parameter should always be OL.

The File-Type Parameter

The fourth parameter of sp_OpenSession() is an integer that specifies the type of the sound file. For S-type sound files, the fourth parameter should be SP_S_TYPE, and for TS-type sound files, the value should be SP_TS_TYPE. Because the file we play is a TS-type sound file, we supply the value of SP_TS_TYPE.

NOTE   The four parameters of sp_OpenSession():

First parameter: A null-terminated string. This string specifies the path and name of the sound file. Remember to include double backslashes (\\) in the path, as required by the C language. If the sound file resides in the current directory, then you don't have to specify the path.

Second parameter: An integer. This integer specifies whether the program will be a stand-alone or a non-stand-alone program.

SP_NON_STAND_ALONE = non-stand-alone program.
SP_STAND_ALONE = stand-alone program.

Third parameter: The value of this parameter should always be OL.

Fourth parameter: An integer. This integer specifies the type of the sound file.

SP_S_TYPE = .S-type sound file.

SP_TS_TYPE = .TS-type sound file.

SP_WAV_TYPE = .WAV-type sound file.

SP_VOC_TYPE = .VOC-type sound file.

SP_SND_TYPE = .SND-type sound file.

The *sp_PlayF()* Function

To play a sound file or a section of a sound file, your program must issue the sp_PlayF() function.

The *F* in sp_PlayF() stands for *Forward*—that is, playing in the forward direction. The sp_PlayF() function takes two parameters, as you can see from its prototype. The prototype of sp_PlayF() is declared in the sp4Win.h file, which resides in c:\spSDK\TegoWLib\.

The first parameter of sp_PlayF() is a long integer that specifies the starting point of the section to be played. The second parameter is a long integer that specifies the last byte to be played. For example, if you wish to play the section from byte coordinate 1,500 to byte coordinate 7,500, your program will issue the following statement:

```
sp_PlayF ( 1500L, 7500L );
```

NOTE The two parameters of the sp_PlayF() function:

> *First parameter:* Long integer. Specifies the first byte coordinate of the section to be played.
>
> *Second parameter:* Long integer. Specifies the last byte coordinate of the section to be played.

The `sp_OpenSession()` function must be executed prior to executing the `sp_PlayF()` function.

You don't have to worry about any memory or allocation issues. If the particular section is not already loaded into memory, the TSEngine is responsible for loading it.

The *SP_START_OF_FILE* and *SP_END_OF_FILE* Identifiers

When the user selects the Play option from the menu, the Windows operating system will execute the `WndProc()` function with the parameter message equal to `WM_COMMAND`, and `wParam` equal to `IDM_PLAY`. Thus, the case `IDM_PLAY` will be executed:

```
case IDM_PLAY:
    sp_PlayF ( SP_START_OF_FILE, SP_END_OF_FILE );
    return 0L;
```

The `sp_PlayF()` function contains two parameters: `SP_START_OF_FILE` and `SP_END_OF_FILE`. Those parameters are #identified in the sp4Win.h file that resides in c:\spSDK\TegoWLib\. You can easily recognize that those are Sound-library-related #definitions, because their names begin with the `SP_` characters. All sound-related macros and #definitions start with the characters `SP_`. For example:

```
SP_START_OF_FILE
SP_END_OF_FILE
SP_S_TYPE
SP_NON_STAND_ALONE
```

The `SP_START_OF_FILE` tells the TSEngine to start playing from the first byte of the sound file.

Thus, the following two statements are identical, both telling the TSEngine to play the file from the first byte to byte 8,000:

```
sp_PlayF ( 0L, 8000L );
sp_PlayF ( SP_START_OF_FILE, 8000L );
```

The SP_END_OF_FILE tells the TSEngine to play the sound file up to the last byte of the file. Thus, if the sound file happens to be 10,000,000 bytes long, the following two statements are identical, both telling the TSEngine to play a section from byte location 9,000 to the end of the sound file:

```
sp_PlayF ( 9000L, 10000000L );
sp_PlayF ( 9000L, SP_END_OF_FILE );
```

The advantage of using the SP_END_OF_FILE identifier is that your program does not have to determine the size of the sound file. By supplying SP_END_OF_FILE, your program lets the TSEngine determine the size of the sound file.

> **NOTE** SP_START_OF_FILE: The SP_START_OF_FILE #identifier may be supplied as the first parameter to the sp_PlayF() function. It tells the TSEngine to play from the first byte of the sound file.
>
> SP_END_OF_FILE: The SP_END_OF_FILE #identifier may be supplied as the second parameter to the sp_PlayF() function. It tells the TSEngine to play up to the last byte of the sound file.

Because we tell the TSEngine to play the entire sound file, the phrase *Hello. Have a nice day! Good-Bye* will be played whenever the user selects the Play option from the menu.

Other *sp_PlayF()* Statements in Hello.c

The sp_PlayF() function is also used under the IDM_ABOUT case. When the user selects the About option from the menu, the Windows operating system executes the WndProc() function with message equal to WM_COMMAND, and wParam equal to IDM_ABOUT. The IDM_ABOUT case first plays the section from the beginning of the file up to byte location 10,000 of the file, and then displays the About dialog box:

```
case IDM_ABOUT :
     sp_PlayF ( SP_START_OF_FILE, 10000L );
     DialogBox ( ghInst,
                 "AboutBox",
                 hWnd,
                 lpfnAboutDlgProc );
     return 0;
```

Once the 0 to 10,000 section is played, the program proceeds and displays the About dialog box by using the DialgBox() function.

Of course, you may wonder how we knew that the Hello section resides between byte coordinate 0 and byte coordinate 10,000. We certainly didn't find out by trial-and-error, because that would've taken forever. We used the TS Sound Editor, an easy way to find the coordinates of a particular sound section within a sound file.

The TS Sound Editor Program

The TegoSoft (TS) Sound Editor program is a program that lets you load a sound file into the screen, and then lets you highlight (with mouse or keyboard) any section of the sound file. You can play the highlighted section, delete it, move it, copy it, insert sound sections to other portions of the sound file, or do to it whatever you wish. (The book's diskette does not include the TegoSoft Sound Editor program.)

In fact, the TS Sound Editor is like a regular word processor with all the features of a word processor. There are, of course, some differences between the TS Sound Editor and a word processor. Typically, in a word processor you highlight a text section and make it bold, italic, a different font size, and so on. In the TS Sound Editor, you also highlight a sound section; but instead of making it italic, bold, or a different font size, you perform sound manipulations on the highlighted section. Some of these sound manipulations include increasing or decreasing the volume of the section, adding Echo to the section, filtering noise from the section, changing the sound section to create sound distortion (for special effects), changing the characteristics of the sound section to sound like a different person, as well as other sound features.

With the TS Sound Editor, we examined the Hello.ts file and noticed that it is built as follows:

From Byte Location	To Byte Location	Sound Content in the Specified Section
0	10,000	*Hello*
10,000	20,000	*Have a nice day*
30,000	40,000	*Good-Bye*

If, of course, you have the TS Sound Editor, you will be able to determine the byte coordinates of the sound file by yourself.

A pictorial representation of the Good-Bye section is shown in Figure 4.3. The TS Sound Editor displays the sound file on-screen in a similar manner. It also lets you insert text labels to identify the beginning and end of the sound sections.

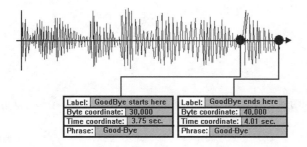

Figure 4.3. A pictorial representation of the Good-Bye section.

The preceding construction of the Hello.ts file explains the reason for supplying 0 to 10,000 as the section to be played when the user selects the About option from the menu. We want the program to say *Hello* whenever the user selects the About option.

Saying Good-Bye Upon Quitting the Program

Similarly, we want the program to say *Good-Bye* to the user whenever the user quits the program. The user may quit the program by either selecting the Close option from the system menu (the standard menu that is accessed by clicking the minus sign in the upper-left corner of our program window), or by selecting Quit from our program menu. If the user closes the program by selecting the Quit option, the Windows operating system will execute WndProc() with message equal to WM_COMMAND, and wParam equal to IDM_QUIT. This will cause the execution of the IDM_QUIT case which executes the DestroyWindow() function:

```
case IDM_QUIT:
    DestroyWindow (hWnd);
    return 0L;
```

The execution of DestroyWindow() causes the Windows operating system to execute WndProc() with message equal to WM_DESTROY.

Under the WM_DESTROY case we play the section that corresponds to the phrase *Hello:*

```
case WM_DESTROY:
    sp_PlayF ( 30000L, 40000L );
    PostQuitMessage (0);
    return 0;
```

Similarly, if the user closed the program from the system menu, the Windows operating system executes WndProc() with message equal to WM_DESTROY, and the phrase *Hello* plays.

The sp_PlayLabelF() and sp_PlayTimeF() Functions

A cousin of the sp_PlayF() function is the sp_PlayLabelF() function. This function is by far more convenient to use than the sp_PlayF() function. While sp_PlayF() requires that you know in advance the byte coordinates of the various sections of the sound file, the sp_PlayLabelF() does not require byte coordinates. Instead, the two parameters of sp_PlayLabelF() are sound labels that you insert into the sound file with the TS Sound Editor. For the Hello.ts sound file, you will use the TS Sound Editor to insert labels at the beginning and end of each section. For example, you'll insert the label GoodBye starts here at the beginning of the Good-Bye section, and GoodBye ends here at the end of the Good-Bye section. To play the Good-Bye section, your program will issue the statement:

```
sp_PlayLabelF ( "GoodBye starts here", "GoodBye ends here" );
```

When you use labels, you also can create a library of common phrases and words. You'll have a sound file called GoodBye.ts that has labels at its beginning and end, a sound file called Press.ts that says *Press any key to continue* and has labels at its beginning and end, and other common useful sound files.

As you develop your program, you'll create a single sound file containing all the audio prompts you need. To add all those little sound files to a single sound file, use the TS Sound Editor.

The TS Sound Editor also lets you delete sound files, if you decide to delete certain sound audio sections from the single file. The advantage of using labels is that you can immediately play any section from the single sound file with the sp_PlayLabelF() function, because this function does not depend on the byte coordinates of the sections, but on its labels.

In the program examples of this book, we assume that you currently do not own the TS Sound Editor, or have the advantage of inserting sound labels into the sound files. Thus, we use the sp_PlayF() function rather than the sp_PlayLabelF() function. (The sp_PlayLabelF() function is not included in the short version of the TS sound library.)

Another close relative of the sp_PlayF() and sp_PlayLabelF() functions is the sp_PlayTimeF() function. Like its relatives, the sp_PlayTimeF() function requires two parameters, both of which are floating numbers. The first parameter is the starting point of the section to be played, expressed in seconds; and the second parameter is the ending point of the section to be played, also expressed in seconds.

For example, to play a sound section from time location 7.25 seconds to 7000.0 seconds, your program will issue the following statement:

```
sp_PlayTime ( 7.25, 7000.0 );
```

Because sp_PlayTimeF() is useful only if you have the TS Sound Editor, the program examples in this book only use the sp_PlayF() function for playing. The sp_PlayTimeF() function is not included in the short version of the TS sound library.

This concludes the discussion of the Hello.c program. You may have noticed that we did not say anything yet about the returned value of sp_OpenSession() and the returned value of sp_PlayF(). The returned values from these functions are very important, and are discussed in the next chapter.

Hint

As you may recall from Chapter 2, the NMAKE program compiles and links in accordance with the contents of the .MAK file. The NMAKE program compiles and links only those files that were changed since the last compile or link. The decision to compile or link is based on the time and date of the *dependency files* (files that are listed after the colon (:) character in each section of the .MAK file). When doing Windows programming, the files are usually generated by copying previous existing files (such as the Generic1 files). Sometimes, as a result of copying and recopying files, the NMAKE utility gets confused, because when you copy files, the time and date of the original files remain the same.

If at any point during development you want to force the NMAKE program to compile and link all the files of the project regardless of the time and date of the files, you can execute the NMAKE program with the /A switch. Likewise, when using the Borland compiler, use the -B switch to compile and link all the files that appear in the .MAK file, regardless of the time and date of the files.

For the Microsoft compiler:

```
NMAKE Hello.mak /A  {Enter}
```

For the Borland compiler:

```
MAKE -f Hello.mak -B {Enter}
```

This way you are guaranteed that NMAKE will compile and link all over again.

The Sections Program

As an exercise, you may now write a new program called Sections.c. This program plays various sound sections from the Hello.ts sound file.

The Sections program has the following specifications:

- The program name is Sections.c.
- The program is a Generic1-based program.
- The program contains two menus: File and Sections.

- The options in the File menu are:

```
Menu heading: File
Items in the File menu:
```

Menu Options	Action
Play	Plays the Hello.ts file
About	Says *Hello*, and displays the About dialog box
Quit	Says *Good-Bye*, and quits the program

- The options in the Sections menu are:

```
Menu heading: Sections
Items in the Sections menu:
```

Menu Options	Action
Hello	Says *Hello*
Have	Says *Have*
A	Says *A*
Nice	Says *Nice*
Day	Says *Day*
Good-Bye	Says *Good-Bye*

For example, when the user clicks the Nice option from the Sections menu, the program says *Nice;* when the user clicks the Day option from the Sections menu, the program says *Day*, and so on.

The File menu is displayed in Figure 4.4, and the Sections menu is displayed in Figure 4.5. The About dialog box of the program is shown in Figure 4.6. This dialog box is similar to the About dialog box of Hello.c, except that we spread more IconOfTape icons in this dialog box (for cosmetic reasons).

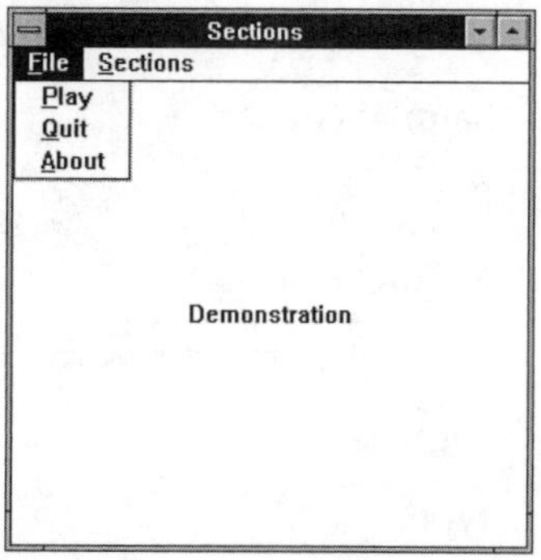

Figure 4.4. The File menu of Sections.c.

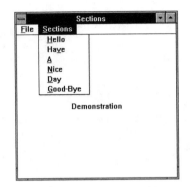

Figure 4.5. The Sections menu of Sections.c.

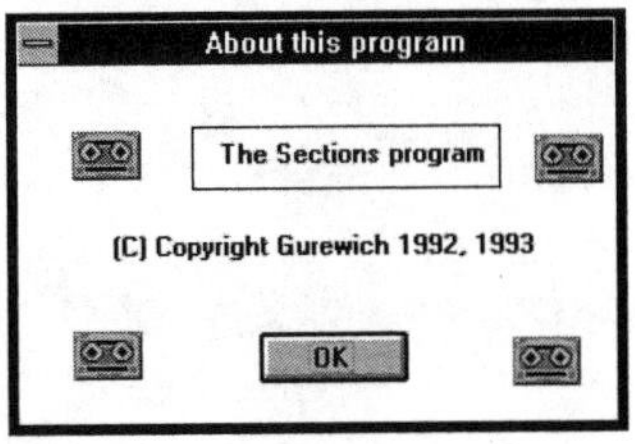

Figure 4.6. The About dialog box of Sections.c.

Compiling and Linking the Sections Program

To compile and link the Sections program with the Microsoft compiler:

- Make sure your PC is in a DOS-protected mode.

- Log into c:\spSDK\Samp4Win\.

- At the DOS prompt type

   NMAKE Sections.mak   {Enter}

To compile and link the Sections program with the Borland compiler:

- Log into c:\spSDK\Samp4Win\.

- At the DOS prompt type

   MAKE -f Sections.bmk   {Enter}

Executing the Sections Program

To execute the Sections program:

- Select Run from the File menu of the Program Manager of Windows.

- Use Browse to select the file

```
c:\spSDK\Samp4Win\Sections.exe
```

The Sound Sections of the Sections Program

To write the Sections program, we needed to know the byte coordinates of each section. Because we assume that you do not own the TS Sound Editor, here are the byte coordinates of the Hello.ts file:

From Byte Location	To Byte Location	Sound Content in the Specified Section
0	10,000	Hello
15,000	18,250	Have
18,250	18,500	A
19,000	23,000	Nice
23,000	30,000	Day
30,000	40,000	Good-Bye

(With the help of the TS Sound Editor it took us very little time to extract these byte coordinates.)

The Files of the Sections Program

The Sections program consists of the following files:

Sections.c	The C code of the program.
Sections.h	The .h file of the program.
Sections.rc	The resource file of the program.
Sections.def	The module definition file of the program.
Sections.mak	The make file of the program.
Tape.ico	The icon of the program.

These files are provided for you in c:\spSDK\Samp4Win\.

The Sections program is very similar to the Hello program. See Listings 4.6 through 4.10 for the complete listing of the Sections program.

Listing 4.6. Sections.h.

```
/*=====================================================
FILE NAME: Sections.h

(C) Copyright Gurewich 1992, 1993
=====================================================*/

/*---------
 prototypes
 --------*/
long FAR PASCAL _export WndProc       ( HWND, UINT, UINT, LONG );
BOOL FAR PASCAL _export AboutDlgProc ( HWND, UINT, UINT, LONG ) ;

/*------
 #define
 ------*/
#define IDM_QUIT    1  /* The Quit     option in the File    menu */
#define IDM_ABOUT   2  /* The About    opiton in the File    menu */
#define IDM_PLAY    3  /* The Play     option in the File    menu */
#define IDM_HELLO   4  /* The Hello    option in the Sections menu */
#define IDM_HAVE    5  /* The Have     option in the Sections menu */
#define IDM_A       6  /* The A        option in the Sections menu */
#define IDM_NICE    7  /* The Nice     option in the Sections menu */
#define IDM_DAY     8  /* The Day      option in the Sections menu */
#define IDM_GOODBYE 9  /* The Good-Bye option in the Sections menu */


/*--------------
 Global variables
 --------------*/
char      gszAppName[] = "Sections" ; /* Our application name. */
HINSTANCE ghInst;                     /* current instance.     */
```

Listing 4.7. Sections.c.

```
/*===============================================================
  PROGRAM: Sections.c
  -------
```

```
PROGRAM DESCRIPTION:
-------------------
This program has two menus in it.
The File menu and the Sections menu.

The File menu includes the following menu items:
    Play  .... Plays the entire sound file.
    Quit  .... Quits the application.
    About .... Displays an About dialog box.

The Sections menu includes the following menu items:
    Hello    ..... Says "Hello"
    Have     ..... Says "have"
    A        ..... Says "a"
    Nice     ..... Says "nice"
    Day      ..... Says "day"
    Good-Bye ..... Says "Good-Bye"

============================================================*/

/*--------
 #include
 --------*/
/*-----------------------------------------------
 windows.h required for all Windows applications.
 ----------------------------------------------*/
#include <windows.h>

/*----------------------------------------------------------
 sp4Win.h required so that sp_ functions, SP_ macros
 and #definitions from the C sound library may be used in
 this application.
 ---------------------------------------------------------*/
#include "c:\spSDK\TegoWlib\sp4Win.h"

/*---------------------------------------------------------
 Definitions & prototypes specific to this application.
 --------------------------------------------------------*/
#include "c:\spSDK\Samp4WIN\Sections.h"

/*==================
 FUNCTION: WinMain()
 ==================*/
int PASCAL WinMain ( HANDLE hInstance,
                     HANDLE hPrevInstance,
                     LPSTR  lpszCmdLine,
                     int    nCmdShow )
```

continues

Listing 4.7. continued

```
{
/*--------------------------
 Local and static variables.
 ------------------------*/
HWND      hWnd; /* Handler to the window of our application.   */
MSG       msg;  /* Message to be processed by our application. */
WNDCLASS  wc;   /* Window class of our application.            */


/*----------------------------------------------
 Make the hInstance variable a global variable.
 --------------------------------------------*/
ghInst = hInstance;


/*---------------------------------------------------
 Update the window class structure and register
 the window class.
 -------------------------------------------------*/
if ( !hPrevInstance )
    {
    /*----------------------------------------
     The "if" is satisfied. This is the very 1st
     run of this application.
     --------------------------------------*/
    wc.style         = CS_HREDRAW | CS_VREDRAW ;
    wc.lpfnWndProc   = WndProc ;
    wc.cbClsExtra    = 0 ;
    wc.cbWndExtra    = 0 ;
    wc.hInstance     = ghInst ;
    wc.hIcon         = LoadIcon   ( ghInst, "IconOfTape" ) ;
    wc.hCursor       = LoadCursor ( NULL, IDC_ARROW        ) ;
    wc.hbrBackground = GetStockObject ( WHITE_BRUSH );
    wc.lpszMenuName  = gszAppName ;
    wc.lpszClassName = gszAppName ;


    /*------------------
     Register the window.
     ----------------*/
    RegisterClass ( &wc );

    }/* end of if(!hPrevInstance ) */

/*------------------------------------
  Create the window of our application.
  ----------------------------------*/
hWnd = CreateWindow ( gszAppName,
                      gszAppName,
                      WS_OVERLAPPEDWINDOW,
                      CW_USEDEFAULT,
```

```
                         CW_USEDEFAULT,
                         CW_USEDEFAULT,
                         CW_USEDEFAULT,
                         NULL,
                         NULL,
                         ghInst,
                         NULL );

    /*---------------------------------------------
     Show and update the window of our application.
     -----------------------------------------*/
    ShowWindow   ( hWnd, nCmdShow );
    UpdateWindow ( hWnd );


    /*----------------
     The message loop.
     ---------------*/
    while ( GetMessage ( &msg, NULL, 0, 0 ) )
         {
         TranslateMessage ( &msg );
         DispatchMessage ( &msg );
         }

    return msg.wParam ;

} /* end of function. */
/*========================= end of WinMain() ===================*/

/*==================
 FUNCTION: WndProc()
 =================*/
/*-----------------------------
 DESCRIPTION: Processes messages.
 ----------------------------*/
long FAR PASCAL _export WndProc ( HWND hWnd,
                                  UINT message,
                                  UINT wParam,
                                  LONG lParam )
{
/*-------------------------
 Local and static variables.
 ------------------------*/
HDC          hdc;  /* Needed for displaying text. */
PAINTSTRUCT  ps;   /* Needed for displaying text. */
RECT         rect; /* Needed for displaying text. */

static FARPROC lpfnAboutDlgProc ; /* For the dialog box. */

switch ( message )
```

continues

Listing 4.7. continued

```
{
case WM_CREATE:
     /*-----------------
     Open a sound session.
     ------------------*/
     sp_OpenSession ( "c:\\spSDK\\TSfiles\\Hello.ts",
                      SP_NON_STAND_ALONE,
                      0L,  /* Not applicable. */
                      SP_TS_TYPE);


     /*--------------------------------------------------
     Obtain the lpfnAboutDlgProc of the About dialog box.
     ------------------------------------------------*/
     lpfnAboutDlgProc =
     MakeProcInstance (( FARPROC) AboutDlgProc, ghInst );
     return 0;

case WM_PAINT:
     hdc = BeginPaint ( hWnd, &ps );
     GetClientRect ( hWnd, &rect );
     DrawText ( hdc,
               "Demonstration",
               -1,
               &rect,
                DT_SINGLELINE | DT_CENTER | DT_VCENTER );
     EndPaint ( hWnd, &ps );
     return 0;

case WM_COMMAND:    /* Process menu items. */
     switch (wParam)
            {
            case IDM_PLAY:
                 /*----------------------------------------
                 Play the sound file.
                 Range to play: very beginning to end.
                 Phrase: "Hello, have a nice day. Good-Bye".
                 ----------------------------------------*/
                 sp_PlayF ( SP_START_OF_FILE, SP_END_OF_FILE );
                 return 0L;

            case IDM_QUIT: /* User clicked on Quit option. */
                 DestroyWindow (hWnd);
                 return 0L;
```

```
case IDM_ABOUT :
    /*----------------------------------------
    Play a section of the sound file.
    Range to play: 0 to 10,000.
    Phrase: "Hello".
    ----------------------------------------*/
    sp_PlayF ( SP_START_OF_FILE, 10000L );
    DialogBox ( ghInst,
                "AboutBox",
                hWnd,
                lpfnAboutDlgProc );
    return 0;

case IDM_HELLO:
    /*----------------------------------------
    Play a section of the sound file.
    Range to play: 0 to 10,000.
    Phrase: "Hello".
    ----------------------------------------*/
    sp_PlayF ( 0L, 10000L );
    return 0L;

case IDM_HAVE:
    /*----------------------------------------
    Play a section of the sound file.
    Range to play: 15,000 to 18,250.
    Phrase: "have".
    ----------------------------------------*/
    sp_PlayF ( 15000L, 18250L );
    return 0L;

case IDM_A:
    /*----------------------------------------
    Play a section of the sound file.
    Range to play: 18,250 to 18,500.
    Phrase: "a".
    ----------------------------------------*/
    sp_PlayF ( 18250L, 18500L );
    return 0L;

case IDM_NICE:
    /*----------------------------------------
    Play a section of the sound file.
    Range to play: 19,000 to 23,000.
    Phrase: "nice".
    ----------------------------------------*/
    sp_PlayF ( 19000L, 23000L );
    return 0L;
```

continues

Listing 4.7. continued

```
                        case IDM_DAY:
                             /*-------------------------------------
                             Play a section of the sound file.
                             Range to play: 23,000 to 30,000.
                             Phrase: "day".
                             -------------------------------------*/
                             sp_PlayF ( 23000L, 30000L );
                             return 0L;

                        case IDM_GOODBYE:
                             /*-------------------------------------
                             Play a section of the sound file.
                             Range to play: 30,000 to 40,000.
                             Phrase: "Good-Bye".
                             -------------------------------------*/
                             sp_PlayF ( 30000L, 40000L );
                             return 0L;

                        }/* end of switch(wParam) */

              case WM_DESTROY:
                   /*-------------------------------------
                   Play a section of the sound file.
                   Range to play: 30,000 to 40,000.
                   Phrase: "Good-Bye".
                   -------------------------------------*/
                   sp_PlayF ( 30000L, 40000L );
                   PostQuitMessage (0);
                   return 0;
              }/* end of switch(message) */

  /*-----------------------
   Message was not processed.
   -----------------------*/
  return DefWindowProc ( hWnd, message, wParam, lParam ) ;

  }
  /*================== end of WndProc() ====================*/

  /*========================
  FUNCTION: AboutDlgProc()
  ========================*/
  /*-----------------------------------------
  DESCRIPTION:
  This is the About dialog box procedure.
  -------------------------------------*/
```

```
BOOL FAR PASCAL _export AboutDlgProc ( HWND hDlg,
                                       UINT message,
                                       UINT wParam,
                                       LONG lParam )
{
switch ( message )
        {
        case WM_INITDIALOG :
              return TRUE;

        case WM_COMMAND :
              switch ( wParam )
                      {
                      case IDOK :
                      case IDCANCEL :
                           EndDialog ( hDlg, 0 );
                           return TRUE;
                      }
        }
return FALSE ;
}/* End of function. */
/*=============== end of AboutDlgProc() ==============*/
```

Listing 4.8. Sections.rc.

```
/*====================================================
 FILE NAME: Sections.rc
 ---------

 FILE DESCRIPTION:
 ----------------
 The resource file.

 (C) Copyright Gurewich 1992, 1993


 ===================================================*/

/*-------
 #include
 -------*/
#include <windows.h>
#include "Sections.h"
```

continues

Listing 4.8. continued

```
/*----
 Menu
 ----*/
Sections  MENU
BEGIN
   POPUP  "&File"
      BEGIN
         MENUITEM "&Play",  IDM_PLAY
         MENUITEM "&Quit",  IDM_QUIT
         MENUITEM "&About", IDM_ABOUT
      END
   POPUP  "&Sections"
      BEGIN
         MENUITEM "&Hello",     IDM_HELLO
         MENUITEM "&Have",      IDM_HAVE
         MENUITEM "&A",         IDM_A
         MENUITEM "&Nice",      IDM_NICE
         MENUITEM "&Day",       IDM_DAY
         MENUITEM "&Good-Bye",  IDM_GOODBYE
      END
END


/*----------------------------------------
 Definition of the Cassette tape icon.
 Filename: Tape.ico
 Icon name: IconOfTape
 ----------------------------------------*/
IconOfTape ICON Tape.ico

/*--------------
 The dialog box.
 --------------*/
AboutBox DIALOG 81, 43, 160, 100
STYLE DS_MODALFRAME | WS_POPUP | WS_VISIBLE | WS_CAPTION | WS_SYSMENU
CAPTION "About this program"
FONT 8, "MS Sans Serif"
BEGIN
    PUSHBUTTON      "OK", IDOK, 64, 75, 40, 14
    CTEXT           "(C) Copyright Gurewich 1992, 1993", -1,
                     13, 47, 137, 18
    ICON            "IconOfTape", -1, 14, 12, 18, 20
    CTEXT           "The Sections program", -1, 48, 21, 83, 10
    CONTROL         "", -1, "Static", SS_BLACKFRAME, 46, 17, 83, 18
    ICON            "IconOfTape", -1, 138, 14, 18, 20
    ICON            "IconOfTape", -1, 132, 71, 18, 20
    ICON            "IconOfTape", -1, 14,  68, 18, 20

END
```

Listing 4.9. Sections.def.

```
;=======================================
; module-definition file for Sections.c
;=======================================

NAME          Sections

DESCRIPTION   'The Sections program. (C) Copyright Gurewich 1992, 1993'

EXETYPE       WINDOWS

STUB          'WINSTUB.EXE'

CODE   PRELOAD MOVEABLE DISCARDABLE

DATA   PRELOAD MOVEABLE MULTIPLE

HEAPSIZE      1024
STACKSIZE     8192
```

Listing 4.10. Sections.mak.

```
#=============
# Sections.mak
#=============

Sections.exe : Sections.obj Sections.h Sections.def Sections.res
    link /nod Sections.obj, Sections.exe, NUL, \
        slibcew.lib oldnames.lib libw.lib commdlg \
        c:\spSDK\TegoWlib\TegoWin.lib, \
        Sections.def
    rc -t Sections.res

Sections.obj : Sections.c Sections.h
    cl -c -G2sw -Ow -W3 -Zp Sections.c

Sections.res : Sections.rc Sections.h Tape.ico
    rc -r Sections.rc
```

The *WM_CREATE* Case

Under the WM_CREATE case we open the sound session with the Hello.ts sound file, and then obtain the lpfnDlgProc of the About dialog box:

```
case WM_CREATE:
    /*-----------------
    Open a sound session.
    ------------------*/
    sp_OpenSession ( "c:\\spSDK\\TSfiles\\Hello.ts",
                    SP_NON_STAND_ALONE,
                    0L,  /* Not applicable. */
                    SP_TS_TYPE);

    /*--------------------------------------------------
    Obtain the lpfnAboutDlgProc of the About dialog box.
    ---------------------------------------------------*/
    lpfnAboutDlgProc =
    MakeProcInstance (( FARPROC) AboutDlgProc, ghInst );
    return 0;
```

The session opens as a non-stand-alone program and as a TS-type.

Playing the Entire Sound File

If the user selects the Play option from the File menu, the IDM_PLAY case is executed. IDM_PLAY is #defined in Sections.h. Under this case we simply play the entire file:

```
case IDM_PLAY:
    /*----------------------------------------
    Play the sound file.
    Range to play: very beginning to end.
    Phrase: "Hello, have a nice day. Good-Bye".
    -----------------------------------------*/
    sp_PlayF ( SP_START_OF_FILE, SP_END_OF_FILE );
    return 0L;
```

Playing Sections from the Sound File

If the user selects any of the options from the Sections menu, the corresponding case is executed. The various menu options are #defined in Sections.h.

For example, if the Have option is selected, then the IDM_HAVE is executed:

```
case IDM_HAVE:
    /*-------------------------------------
    Play a section of the sound file.
    Range to play: 15,000 to 18,250.
    Phrase: "have".
    -------------------------------------*/
    sp_PlayF ( 15000L, 18250L );
    return 0L;
```

Similarly, the WndProc() function has cases that correspond to the following sound sections: Hello, A, Nice, Day, and Good-Bye.

The *WM_ABOUT* Case

The IDM_ABOUT case of the Sections program is identical to the IDM_ABOUT case of the Hello program, saying *Hello,* and then displaying the About dialog box:

```
case IDM_ABOUT :
    /*-------------------------------------
    Play a section of the sound file.
    Range to play: 0 to 10,000.
    Phrase: "Hello".
    -------------------------------------*/
    sp_PlayF ( SP_START_OF_FILE, 10000L );
    DialogBox ( ghInst,
    "AboutBox",
    hWnd,
    lpfnAboutDlgProc );
    return 0;
```

The *WM_DESTROY* Case

The WM_DESTROY case of the Sections program is identical to the WM_DESTROY case of the Hello program, saying *Good-Bye* and then quitting the program:

```
case WM_DESTROY:
    /*-------------------------------------
    Play a section of the sound file.
    Range to play: 30,000 to 40,000.
    Phrase: "Good-Bye".
    -------------------------------------*/
    sp_PlayF ( 30000L, 40000L );
    PostQuitMessage (0);
    return 0;
```

The Push2Say Program

The Push2Say program is very similar to the Sections program, except for its user-interface representation which is more appropriate for a Windows application.

The main window of the Push2Say program is shown in Figure 4.7. It consists of a single menu with three options: Push, Quit, and About.

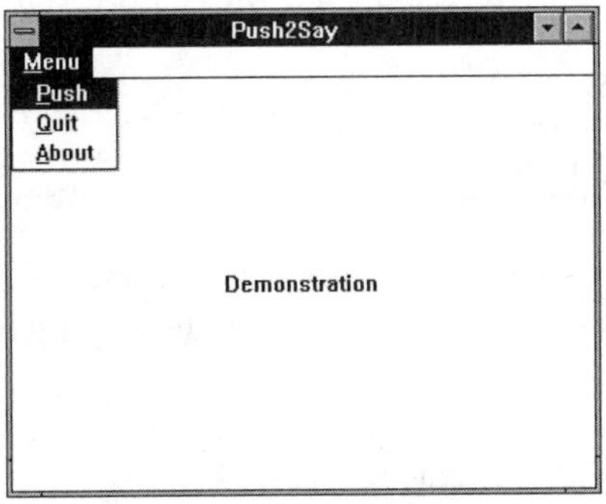

Figure 4.7. The main window of the Push2Say program.

When the user selects the About option, the program says *Hello* and then displays the About dialog box (see Figure 4.9). When the user selects the Quit option, the program says *Good-Bye* and terminates. When the user selects the Push option, the program displays a dialog box with several push buttons in it (see Figure 4.8). Each push button plays a different section of the sound file. Here the user may press P or click the Push Me to Play Entire File push button to hear the entire Hello.ts file. Similarly, the user may press H or click the Have push button to hear the word *Have*.

Compiling and Linking the Push2Say Program

To compile and link the Push2Say program with the Microsoft compiler:

- Make sure your PC is in a DOS-protected mode.
- Log into c:\spSDK\Samp4Win\.

- At the DOS prompt type

  `NMAKE Push2Say.mak` {Enter}

To compile and link the Push2Say program with the Borland compiler:

- Log into c:\spSDK\Samp4Win\.
- At the DOS prompt type

  `MAKE -f Push2Say.bmk` {Enter}

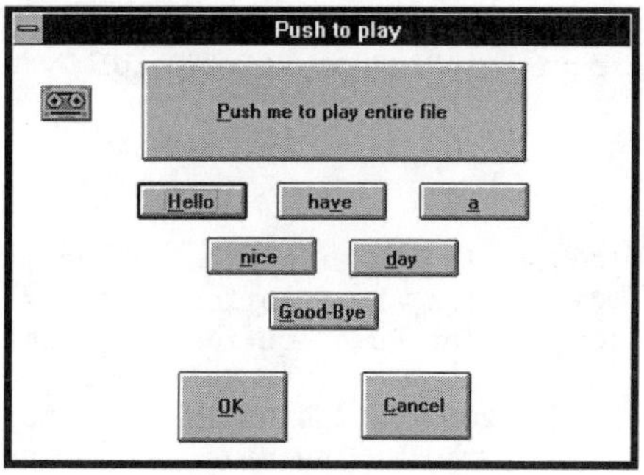

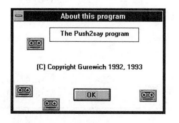

Figure 4.8. The PushBox dialog box of Push2Say.c.

Figure 4.9. The About dialog box of Push2Say.c.

The Files of the Push2Say Program

All the Push2Say files are provided for you in c:\spSDK\Samp4Win\.

A complete listing of the Push2Say files is shown in Listings 4.11 through 4.15.

Listing 4.11. Push2Say.h.

```
/*======================================================
 FILE NAME: Push2Say.h

 (C) Copyright Gurewich 1992, 1993
 ======================================================*/

/*---------
 prototypes
 ---------*/
long FAR PASCAL _export WndProc      ( HWND, UINT, UINT, LONG ) ;
BOOL FAR PASCAL _export AboutDlgProc ( HWND, UINT, UINT, LONG ) ;
BOOL FAR PASCAL _export PushDlgProc  ( HWND, UINT, UINT, LONG ) ;

/*------
 #define
 ------*/
#define IDM_QUIT  100  /* The Quit  option in the menu */
#define IDM_ABOUT 101  /* The About option in the menu */
#define IDM_PUSH  102  /* The Push  option in the menu */

#define  PB_HELLO        200  /* The Hello       push button. */
#define  PB_HAVE         201  /* The Have        push button. */
#define  PB_A            202  /* The A           push button. */
#define  PB_NICE         203  /* The Nice        push button. */
#define  PB_DAY          204  /* The Day         push button. */
#define  PB_GOODBYE      205  /* The Good-Bye    push button. */
#define  PB_ENTIRE_FILE  206  /* The Entire file push button. */

/*---------------
 Global variables
 ---------------*/
char      gszAppName[] = "Push2Say" ; /* Our application name. */
HINSTANCE ghInst;                     /* current instance.     */
```

Listing 4.12. Push2Say.c.

```
/*==========================================================
 PROGRAM: Push2Say.c
 -------
 (C) Copyright 1992, 1993 Gurewich. (R) All rights reserved.

 PROGRAM DESCRIPTION:
 -------------------
 User has to push Push buttons to play sound sections.
```

```
==========================================================*/

/*--------
 #include
 -------*/
/*------------------------------------------------
 windows.h required for all Windows applications.
 ----------------------------------------------*/
#include <windows.h>

/*-------------------------------------------------------
 sp4Win.h required so that sp_ functions, SP_ macros
 and #definitions from the TS C sound library may be used
 in this application.
 -----------------------------------------------------*/
#include "c:\spSDK\TegoWlib\sp4Win.h"

/*----------------------------------------------------
 Definitions & prototypes specific to this application.
 --------------------------------------------------*/
#include "c:\spSDK\Samp4WIN\Push2Say.h"

/*==================
 FUNCTION: WinMain()
 ==================*/
int PASCAL WinMain ( HANDLE hInstance,
                     HANDLE hPrevInstance,
                     LPSTR  lpszCmdLine,
                     int    nCmdShow )
{
/*-----------------------
 Local and static variables.
 -----------------------*/
HWND      hWnd; /* Handler to the window of our application.   */
MSG       msg;  /* Message to be processed by our application. */
WNDCLASS  wc;   /* Window class of our application.            */

/*----------------------------------------------
 Make the hInstance variable a global variable.
 --------------------------------------------*/
ghInst = hInstance;

/*----------------------------------------------
 Update the window class structure and register
 the window class.
 --------------------------------------------*/
if ( !hPrevInstance )
   {
```

continues

Listing 4.12. continued

```
/*-------------------------------------------
  The "if" is satisfied. This is the very 1st
  run of this application.
  -----------------------------------------*/
  wc.style            = CS_HREDRAW ¦ CS_VREDRAW ;
  wc.lpfnWndProc      = WndProc ;
  wc.cbClsExtra       = 0 ;
  wc.cbWndExtra       = 0 ;
  wc.hInstance        = ghInst ;
  wc.hIcon            = LoadIcon   ( ghInst, "IconOfTape" ) ;
  wc.hCursor          = LoadCursor ( NULL, IDC_ARROW      ) ;
  wc.hbrBackground    = GetStockObject ( WHITE_BRUSH );
  wc.lpszMenuName     = gszAppName ;
  wc.lpszClassName    = gszAppName ;

  /*-----------------
    Register the window.
    ---------------*/
  RegisterClass ( &wc );

  }/* end of if(!hPrevInstance) */

/*-------------------------------------
  Create the window of our application.
  -----------------------------------*/
hWnd = CreateWindow ( gszAppName,
                      gszAppName,
                      WS_OVERLAPPEDWINDOW,
                      CW_USEDEFAULT,
                      CW_USEDEFAULT,
                      CW_USEDEFAULT,
                      CW_USEDEFAULT,
                      NULL,
                      NULL,
                      ghInst,
                      NULL );

/*---------------------------------------------
  Show and update the window of our application.
  -------------------------------------------*/
ShowWindow   ( hWnd, nCmdShow );
UpdateWindow ( hWnd );

/*---------------
  The message loop.
  -------------*/
while ( GetMessage ( &msg, NULL, 0, 0 ) )
```

```
        {
        TranslateMessage ( &msg );
        DispatchMessage ( &msg );
        }

return msg.wParam ;

} /* end of function. */
/*======================= end of WinMain() ===================*/


/*=================
 FUNCTION: WndProc()
 =================*/
/*-----------------------------
 DESCRIPTION: Processes messages.
 -----------------------------*/
long FAR PASCAL _export WndProc ( HWND hWnd,
                                  UINT message,
                                  UINT wParam,
                                  LONG lParam )
{
/*-------------------------
 Local and static variables.
 -------------------------*/
HDC            hdc;        /* Needed for displaying text. */
PAINTSTRUCT    ps;         /* Needed for displaying text. */
RECT           rect;       /* Needed for displaying text. */

static FARPROC lpfnAboutDlgProc ;   /* For the About dialog box. */
static FARPROC lpfnPushBoxDlgProc ; /* For the Push  dialog box. */

switch ( message )
        {
        case WM_CREATE:
                /*-----------------
                Open a sound session.
                ------------------*/
                sp_OpenSession ( "c:\\spSDK\\TSfiles\\Hello.ts",
                            SP_NON_STAND_ALONE,
                            0L,   /* Not applicable. */
                            SP_TS_TYPE);


                /*---------------------------------------------
                Obtain the lpfnAboutDlgProc of the About dialog box.
                ---------------------------------------------*/
                lpfnAboutDlgProc =
                MakeProcInstance (( FARPROC) AboutDlgProc, ghInst );
```

continues

Listing 4.12. continued

```
              /*------------------------------------------------
              Obtain the lpfnPushBoxDlgProc of the Push dialog box.
              ------------------------------------------------*/
              lpfnPushBoxDlgProc =
              MakeProcInstance (( FARPROC) PushDlgProc, ghInst );
              return 0;

      case WM_PAINT:
              hdc = BeginPaint ( hWnd, &ps );
              GetClientRect ( hWnd, &rect );
              DrawText ( hdc,
                         "Demonstration",
                         -1,
                         &rect,
                         DT_SINGLELINE ¦ DT_CENTER ¦ DT_VCENTER );
              EndPaint ( hWnd, &ps );
              return 0;

      case WM_COMMAND:              /* Process menu items. */
              switch (wParam)
                   {
                   case IDM_PUSH:
                        DialogBox ( ghInst,
                                    "PushBox",
                                    hWnd,
                                    lpfnPushBoxDlgProc );
                        return 0L;

                   case IDM_QUIT: /* User clicked on Quit option. */
                        DestroyWindow (hWnd);
                        return 0L;

                   case IDM_ABOUT :
                        /*----------------------------
                        Play a section of the sound file.
                        Range to play: 0 to 10,000.
                        Phrase: "Hello".
                        -------------------------------*/
                        sp_PlayF ( SP_START_OF_FILE, 10000L );
                        DialogBox ( ghInst,
                                    "AboutBox",
                                    hWnd,
                                    lpfnAboutDlgProc );
                        return 0;
                   }/* end of switch(wParam) */
```

```
        case WM_DESTROY:
            /*-------------------------------
            Play a section of the sound file.
            Range to play: 30,000 to 40,000.
            Phrase: "Good-Bye".
            ------------------------------*/
            sp_PlayF ( 30000L, 40000L );
            PostQuitMessage (0);
            return 0;
        }/* end of switch(message) */

/*-----------------------
 Message was not processed.
 ----------------------*/
return DefWindowProc ( hWnd, message, wParam, lParam ) ;


}
/*================= end of WndProc() ===================*/

/*=======================
 FUNCTION: AboutDlgProc()
 ======================*/
/*--------------------------------------
 DESCRIPTION:
 This is the About dialog box procedure.
 -------------------------------------*/
BOOL FAR PASCAL _export AboutDlgProc ( HWND hDlg,
                                       UINT message,
                                       UINT wParam,
                                       LONG lParam )
{
switch ( message )
        {
        case WM_INITDIALOG :
            return TRUE;

        case WM_COMMAND :
            switch ( wParam )
                    {
                    case IDOK :
                    case IDCANCEL :
                        EndDialog ( hDlg, 0 );
                        return TRUE;
                    }
        }
return FALSE ;
}/* End of function. */
/*=============== end of AboutDlgProc() =============*/
```

continues

Listing 4.12. continued

```
/*=======================
 FUNCTION: PushDlgProc()
 =======================*/
/*-----------------------------------
 DESCRIPTION:
 This is the Push dialog box procedure.
 -----------------------------------*/
BOOL FAR PASCAL _export PushDlgProc ( HWND hDlg,
                                      UINT message,
                                      UINT wParam,
                                      LONG lParam )

{
switch ( message )
        {
        case WM_INITDIALOG :
              return TRUE;

        case WM_COMMAND :
              switch ( wParam )
                      {
                      case PB_HELLO:
                            /*---------------------------------------
                            Play a section of the sound file.
                            Range to play: 0 to 10,000.
                            Phrase: "Hello".
                            ---------------------------------------*/
                            sp_PlayF ( 0L, 10000L );
                            return TRUE;

                      case PB_HAVE:
                            /*---------------------------------------
                            Play a section of the sound file.
                            Range to play: 15,000 to 18,250.
                            Phrase: "have".
                            ---------------------------------------*/
                            sp_PlayF ( 15000L, 18250L );
                            return TRUE;

                      case PB_A:
                            /*---------------------------------------
                            Play a section of the sound file.
                            Range to play: 18,250 to 18,500.
                            Phrase: "a".
                            ---------------------------------------*/
                            sp_PlayF ( 18250L, 18500L );
                            return TRUE;
```

```
                case PB_NICE:
                    /*-------------------------------------
                    Play a section of the sound file.
                    Range to play: 19,000 to 23,000.
                    Phrase: "nice".
                    -------------------------------------*/
                    sp_PlayF ( 19000L, 23000L );
                    return TRUE;

                case PB_DAY:
                    /*-------------------------------------
                    Play a section of the sound file.
                    Range to play: 23,000 to 30,000.
                    Phrase: "day".
                    -------------------------------------*/
                    sp_PlayF ( 23000L, 30000L );
                    return TRUE;

                case PB_GOODBYE:
                    /*-------------------------------------
                    Play a section of the sound file.
                    Range to play: 30,000 to 40,000.
                    Phrase: "Good-Bye".
                    -------------------------------------*/
                    sp_PlayF ( 30000L, 40000L );
                    return TRUE;

                case PB_ENTIRE_FILE:
                    /*-------------------------------------
                    Play the sound file.
                    Range to play: very beginning to end.
                    Phrase: "Hello, have a nice day. Good-Bye".
                    -------------------------------------*/
                    sp_PlayF ( SP_START_OF_FILE, SP_END_OF_FILE );
                    return TRUE;

                case IDOK :
                case IDCANCEL :
                    EndDialog ( hDlg, 0 );
                    return TRUE;
                }/* end of switch(wParam) */

        }/* ennd of switch(message) */

return FALSE ;

}/* End of function. */
/*=============== end of PushDlgProc() ===============*/
```

Listing 4.13. Push2Say.rc.

```
/*=====================================================
FILE NAME: Push2Say.rc
. . . . . . . . . .

FILE DESCRIPTION:
. . . . . . . . . . . . . . . .
The resource file.

(C) Copyright Gurewich 1992, 1993


=====================================================*/

/*------
 #include
 ------*/
#include <windows.h>
#include "Push2Say.h"

/*--
 Menu
 --*/
Push2Say   MENU
BEGIN
    POPUP    "&Menu"
        BEGIN
            MENUITEM "&Push",   IDM_PUSH
            MENUITEM "&Quit",   IDM_QUIT
            MENUITEM "&About",  IDM_ABOUT
        END
END

/*-------------------------------------------
 Definition of the Cassette tape icon.
 File name: Tape.ico
 Icon name: IconOfTape
 -------------------------------------------*/
IconOfTape ICON Tape.ico

/*--------------
 The dialog box.
 --------------*/
AboutBox DIALOG 81, 43, 160, 100
STYLE DS_MODALFRAME ¦ WS_POPUP ¦ WS_VISIBLE ¦ WS_CAPTION ¦ WS_SYSMENU
CAPTION "About this program"
FONT 8, "MS Sans Serif"
BEGIN
    PUSHBUTTON       "OK", IDOK, 64, 75, 40, 14
```

```
    CTEXT              "(C) Copyright Gurewich 1992, 1993", -1,
                       13, 47, 137, 18
    ICON               "IconOfTape", -1, 14, 12, 18, 20
    CTEXT              "The Push2Say program", -1, 45, 9, 84, 14
    CONTROL            "", -1, "Static", SS_BLACKFRAME, 38, 7, 96, 16
    ICON               "IconOfTape", -1, 2, 65, 18, 20
    ICON               "IconOfTape", -1, 31, 80, 18, 20
    ICON               "IconOfTape", -1, 135, 70, 18, 20

END

/*----------------
 The Push dialog box
 ----------------*/
PushBox DIALOG 38, 29, 225, 158
STYLE DS_MODALFRAME ¦ WS_POPUP ¦ WS_VISIBLE ¦
                    WS_CAPTION ¦ WS_SYSMENU
CAPTION "Push to play"
FONT 8, "MS Sans Serif"
BEGIN
    ICON               "IconOfTape", -1,         10,   9, 18, 20
    PUSHBUTTON         "&Hello", PB_HELLO,        45,  52, 40, 14
    PUSHBUTTON         "&have",  PB_HAVE,         96,  52, 40, 14
    PUSHBUTTON         "&a",        PB_A,        148,  52, 40, 14
    PUSHBUTTON         "&nice",  PB_NICE,         70,  73, 40, 14
    PUSHBUTTON         "&day",   PB_DAY,         122,  74, 40, 14
    PUSHBUTTON         "&Good-Bye", PB_GOODBYE, 93,  94, 40, 14
    PUSHBUTTON         "&Push me to play entire file",
                       PB_ENTIRE_FILE, 47, 6, 140, 38
    PUSHBUTTON         "&OK",       IDOK,         60, 124, 40, 27
    PUSHBUTTON         "&Cancel", IDCANCEL,      127, 124, 40, 26
END
```

Listing 4.14. Push2Say.def.

```
;=======================================
; module-definition file for Push2Say.c
;=======================================

NAME       Push2Say

DESCRIPTION  'The Push2Say program. (C) Copyright Gurewich 1992,
1993'

EXETYPE    WINDOWS
```

continues

Listing 4.14. continued

```
STUB          'WINSTUB.EXE'

CODE   PRELOAD MOVEABLE DISCARDABLE

DATA   PRELOAD MOVEABLE MULTIPLE

HEAPSIZE      1024
STACKSIZE     8192
```

Listing 4.15. Push2Say.mak.

```
#=============
# Push2Say.mak
#=============

Push2Say.exe : Push2Say.obj Push2Say.h Push2Say.def Push2Say.res
    link /nod Push2Say.obj, Push2Say.exe, NUL, \
        slibcew.lib oldnames.lib libw.lib commdlg \
        c:\spSDK\TegoWlib\TegoWin.lib, \
        Push2Say.def
    rc -t Push2Say.res

Push2Say.obj : Push2Say.c Push2Say.h
    cl -c -G2sw -Ow -W3 -Zp Push2Say.c

Push2Say.res : Push2Say.rc Push2Say.h Tape.ico
    rc -r Push2Say.rc
```

The Push Buttons of the Push2Say Program

The Push dialog box of the Push2Say program was prepared using the Dialog Editor program that came with the SDK for Windows.

The push buttons are #defined in Push2Say.h, and the corresponding cases of those push buttons are handled under the WM_COMMAND case in the Push dialog box procedure. For example, the PB_DAY case that corresponds to clicking the Day button (or pressing **D** on the keyboard) looks as follows:

```
case PB_DAY:
       /*-------------------------------------
       Play a section of the sound file.
       Range to play: 23,000 to 30,000.
       Phrase: "day".
       -------------------------------------*/
       sp_PlayF ( 23000L, 30000L );
       return TRUE;
```

Note that the TSEngine responds instantaneously. The sound sections are played immediately without any delays.

Sound File Types

This chapter discusses and demonstrates the different sound file types that you can open with the sp_OpenSession() function. The chapter also discusses the returned value of the sp_OpenSession() function, which plays a very important role. It indicates whether the TSEngine was able to open the sound session.

This chapter also discusses bit-map files: how to create them and how to display them. The creation and display of bit maps is an important topic, and it is discussed extensively in the later chapters that introduce animation programs.

The FileType Program

The FileType.c program plays different types of sound files. Figure 5.1 shows the main window of the FileType program. As shown, the main window contains five push buttons: S file, TS file, WAV file, VOC file, and Exit.

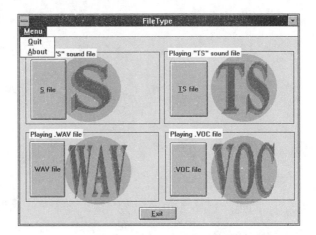

Figure 5.1. The main window of the FileType program.

When the user pushes a push button, the corresponding type of sound file plays. (For example, when the user pushes the S file push button, an .S sound file is played.) When the user pushes the Exit push button, the program terminates.

The FileType program menu contains two options: Quit and About. The About dialog box of FileType is shown in Figure 5.2.

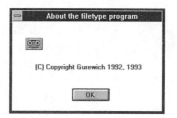

Figure 5.2. The About dialog box.

Compiling and Linking the FileType Program

To compile and link the FileType program with the Microsoft compiler:

- Make sure you are in a DOS-protected mode.

- Log into c:\spSDK\Samp4Win\.

- At the DOS prompt type

  NMAKE FileType.mak   {Enter}

To compile and link the FileType program with the Borland compiler:

- Log into c:\spSDK\Samp4Win\.

- At the DOS prompt type

  MAKE -f FileType.bmk   {Enter}

Executing the FileType Program

To execute the FileType program:

- Select Run from the File menu of the Program Manager of Windows.

- Use Browse to select the file

```
c:\spSDK\Samp4Win\FileType.exe
```

The Files of the FileType Program

The FileType program is a Generic-type-1-based program. It consists of the following files:

FileType.c	The C code of the program.
FileType.h	The #include file of the program.
FileType.rc	The resource file of the program.
FileType.def	The module definition file of the program.
FileType.mak	The make file of the program.
Tape.ico	The icon of the program.
S.bmp	A bit map for the S symbol.
TS.bmp	A bit map for the TS symbol.
WAV.bmp	A bit map for the WAV symbol.
VOC.bmp	A bit map for the VOC symbol.
BACKGND.bmp	The bit map used for the background of the main window.

These files are provided for you in c:\spSDK\Samp4Win\.

The complete listing of the FileType program is shown in Listings 5.1 through 5.5.

Listing 5.1. FileType.h.

```
/*===================================================
FILE NAME: FileType.h

(C) Copyright Gurewich 1992, 1993
===================================================*/

/*---------
 prototypes
 --------*/
long FAR PASCAL _export WndProc       ( HWND, UINT, UINT, LONG );
BOOL FAR PASCAL _export AboutDlgProc ( HWND, UINT, UINT, LONG );

/*------
 #define
 ------*/
```

```
#define IDM_QUIT   1  /* The Quit  option in the menu */
#define IDM_ABOUT  2  /* The About option in the menu */

#define EXIT_PB 101 /* The Exit     push button. */
#define S_PB    102 /* The S        push button. */
#define TS_PB   103 /* The TS       push button. */
#define WAV_PB  104 /* The WAV      push button. */
#define VOC_PB  105 /* The VOC      push button. */

/*---------------
 Global variables
 --------------*/
char       gszAppName[] = "FileType" ; /* Our application name. */
HINSTANCE  ghInst;                      /* current instance.     */
```

Listing 5.2. FileType.c.

```
/*============================================================
  PROGRAM: FileType.c
  -------
  (C) Copyright 1992, 1993 Gurewich. (R) All rights reserved.

  PROGRAM DESCRIPTION:
  ------------------
  This is a Generic type 1 based program.

  This program displays five push buttons:

      S    push button
      TS   push button
      WAV  push button
      VOC  push button
      Exit push button

  When the user pushes a push button, the corresponding sound file
  is played. That is, when the user pushes the TS push button, a
  TS sound file plays.

  When the user pushes the Exit push button, the program
  terminates.

  ============================================================*/
```

continues

Listing 5.2. continued

```
/*--------
 #include
 --------*/
/*----------------------------------------------------
 windows.h is required for all Windows applications.
 ----------------------------------------------*/
#include <windows.h>


/*--------------------------------------------------
 sp4Win.h is required so that sp_ functions,
 SP_ macros and #definitions from the TS C sound
 library may be used in this application.
 ------------------------------------------*/
#include "c:\spSDK\TegoWlib\sp4Win.h"


/*-----------------------------------------------------
 Definitions & prototypes specific to this application.
 ------------------------------------------------*/
#include "c:\spSDK\Samp4WIN\FileType.h"


/*---------------------------------------------------------
 For C functions that require the standard C #include files.
 ---------------------------------------------------------*/
#include <stdlib.h>
#include <stdio.h>



/*==================
 FUNCTION: WinMain()
 ==================*/
int PASCAL WinMain ( HANDLE hInstance,
                     HANDLE hPrevInstance,
                     LPSTR  lpszCmdLine,
                     int    nCmdShow )
{
/*------------------------
 Local and static variables.
 ------------------------*/
HWND     hWnd; /* Handler to the window of our application.   */
MSG      msg;  /* Message to be processed by our application. */
WNDCLASS wc;   /* Window class of our application.            */

HBITMAP  hBitmapOfBkGnd; /* Handle to the bit map of the background. */
HBRUSH   hBrushOfBkGnd;  /* Handle to the brush  of the background.  */
```

```
/*----------------------------------------------------
Make the hInstance variable a global variable.
----------------------------------------------*/
ghInst = hInstance;

/*----------------------------------------------------------------
Load the background Bitmap, and create a Brush.
"BkGndBitmap" is defined in the .rc file, and it is based on the
file: BACKGND.bmp.
----------------------------------------------------------*/
hBitmapOfBkGnd = LoadBitmap ( ghInst, "BkGndBitmap" );
hBrushOfBkGnd = CreatePatternBrush ( hBitmapOfBkGnd );

/*---------------------------------------------------
Update the window class structure and register
the window class.
----------------------------------------------*/
if ( !hPrevInstance )
    {
    /*-------------------------------------------
    The "if" is satisfied, this is the very 1st
    run of this application.
    ------------------------------------------*/
    wc.style         = CS_HREDRAW | CS_VREDRAW ;
    wc.lpfnWndProc   = WndProc ;
    wc.cbClsExtra    = 0 ;
    wc.cbWndExtra    = DLGWINDOWEXTRA ;  /* Dialog box as the */
                                         /* main window.      */
    wc.hInstance     = ghInst ;
    wc.hIcon         = LoadIcon   ( ghInst, "IconOfTape" ) ;
    wc.hCursor       = LoadCursor ( NULL, IDC_ARROW    ) ;

    wc.hbrBackground = hBrushOfBkGnd;  /* The brush that we created */
                                       /* with the bitmap.          */

    wc.lpszMenuName  = gszAppName ;
    wc.lpszClassName = "FileTypeClass" ; /* As appears in the CLASS */
                                         /* in the .rc file.        */

    /*-----------------
    Register the window.
    ----------------*/
    RegisterClass ( &wc );

    }/* end of if( !hPrevInstance ) */

/*-----------------------------------------------------------
Create the Modeless Dialog.
NOTE: In this application the main window is a dialog box.
```

continues

Listing 5.2. continued

```
"FileTypeBox" is the name of the dialog box as defined
in the .rc file preceding the DIALOG keyword.
----------------------------------------------------------*/
hWnd = CreateDialog ( ghInst, "FileTypeBox", 0, NULL );


/*----------------------------------------------
 Show and update the window of our application.
 -----------------------------------------------*/
ShowWindow   ( hWnd, nCmdShow );
UpdateWindow ( hWnd );

/*---------------
 The message loop.
 ---------------*/
while ( GetMessage ( &msg, NULL, 0, 0 ) )
     {
     TranslateMessage ( &msg );
     DispatchMessage ( &msg );
     }

/*----------------------------------------------
 Delete the background object that we created.
 ---------------------------------------------*/
DeleteObject ( hBrushOfBkGnd );

return msg.wParam ;

} /* end of function. */
/*========================= end of WinMain() ====================*/

/*==================
 FUNCTION: WndProc()
 ==================*/
/*------------------------------
 DESCRIPTION: Processes messages.
 ------------------------------*/
long FAR PASCAL _export WndProc ( HWND hWnd,
                                  UINT message,
                                  UINT wParam,
                                  LONG lParam )
{
/*-------------------------
 Local and static variables.
 -------------------------*/
```

```
static HDC              hdc;
static HDC              hMemDC;
static PAINTSTRUCT      ps;

static HBITMAP          hBitmapS;   /* For the S   bit map. */
static HBITMAP          hBitmapTS;  /* For the TS  bit map. */
static HBITMAP          hBitmapWAV; /* For the WAV bit map. */
static HBITMAP          hBitmapVOC; /* For the VOC bit map. */

static FARPROC lpfnAboutDlgProc ; /* For the About dialog box. */

static int iOpenResultS;  /* The result of opening the S  session. */
static int iOpenResultTS; /* The result of opening the TS session. */

switch ( message )
        {
    case WM_CREATE:
        /*----------------------------------------------------------
        Load the bit maps.
        Those bit maps are later destroyed in the WM_DESTROY case.
        ----------------------------------------------------------*/
        hBitmapS   = LoadBitmap ( ghInst, "SBitmap"   );
        hBitmapTS  = LoadBitmap ( ghInst, "TSBitmap"  );
        hBitmapWAV = LoadBitmap ( ghInst, "WAVBitmap" );
        hBitmapVOC = LoadBitmap ( ghInst, "VOCBitmap" );

        /*----------------------------------------------------------
        Obtain the lpfnAboutDlgProc of the About the dialog box.
        ----------------------------------------------------------*/
        lpfnAboutDlgProc =
        MakeProcInstance (( FARPROC) AboutDlgProc, ghInst);

        return 0;

    case WM_PAINT:
        hdc = BeginPaint ( hWnd, &ps );
        hMemDC = CreateCompatibleDC ( hdc );

        /*--------------
        Display the S.
        --------------*/
        SelectObject ( hMemDC, hBitmapS );
        BitBlt ( hdc,
                 68,
                 31,
                 125,
                 125,
                 hMemDC,
                 0,
```

continues

Listing 5.2. continued

```
                    0,
                    SRCCOPY );

            /*--------------
            Display the TS.
            ------------*/
            SelectObject ( hMemDC, hBitmapTS );
            BitBlt ( hdc,
                    360,
                    31,
                    125,
                    125,
                    hMemDC,
                    0,
                    0,
                    SRCCOPY );

            /*--------------
            Display the WAV.
            ----------------*/
            SelectObject ( hMemDC, hBitmapWAV );
            BitBlt ( hdc,
                    86,
                    180,
                    125,
                    125,
                    hMemDC,
                    0,
                    0,
                    SRCCOPY );

            /*--------------
            Display the VOC.
            ----------------*/
            SelectObject ( hMemDC, hBitmapVOC );
            BitBlt ( hdc,
                    360,
                    180,
                    125,
                    125,
                    hMemDC,
                    0,
                    0,
                    SRCCOPY );

            DeleteDC ( hMemDC );
            EndPaint ( hWnd, &ps );

            return 0L;
```

```
case WM_CHAR:
    /*----------------------------------------
    A character from the keyboard received.
    --------------------------------------*/
    /*----------------------------
    Convert to uppercase.
    ----------------------*/
    wParam = toupper ( wParam );

    switch ( wParam )
            {
            case 'S':
                    /*----------------------------------------
                    User pressed S for playing the .S file.
                    --------------------------------------*/
                    SendMessage ( hWnd,
                                  WM_COMMAND,
                                  S_PB,
                                  0);
                return 0;

            case 'T':
                    /*----------------------------------------
                    User pressed T for playing the .TS file.
                    --------------------------------------*/
                    SendMessage ( hWnd,
                                  WM_COMMAND,
                                  TS_PB,
                                  0);
                return 0;


            case 'W':
                    /*------------------------------------------
                    User pressed W for playing the .WAV file.
                    ----------------------------------------*/
                    SendMessage ( hWnd,
                                  WM_COMMAND,
                                  WAV_PB,
                                  0);
                return 0;

            case 'V':
                    /*------------------------------------------
                    User pressed V for playing the .VOC file.
                    ----------------------------------------*/
                    SendMessage ( hWnd,
                                  WM_COMMAND,
                                  VOC_PB,
                                  0);
                return 0;
```

continues

Listing 5.2. continued

```
                case 'E':
                    /*-------------------------------------------
                    User pressed E for Exit.
                    ---------------------------------------*/
                    SendMessage ( hWnd,
                                  WM_COMMAND,
                                  EXIT_PB,
                                  0);
                    return 0;


                default:
                    /*---------------------------------
                    Return to Windows if user press any
                    other key.
                    ------------------------------*/
                    return 0;
                }

    case WM_COMMAND:
        /*---------------------------------
        User selected an item from the menu or
        pushed a push button.
        -----------------------------*/
        /*----------------------------------------------
        Take away the focus from the just selected item back
        to hWnd (which is our main window).
        --------------------------------------------*/
        SetFocus ( hWnd );

        switch (wParam)
                {
                case EXIT_PB:
                    /*---------------------------------
                    User selected the Exit push button.
                    ------------------------------*/
                    DestroyWindow ( hWnd );
                    return 0;

                case S_PB:
                    /*---------------------------------
                    User selected the S push button.
                    ------------------------------*/
                    iOpenResultS =
                    sp_OpenSession ( "c:\\spSDK\\Sfiles\\Sfile.s",
                                     SP_NON_STAND_ALONE,
                                     0L,
                                     SP_S_TYPE );
```

```
    /*-----------------------------------------
    Play the S file.
    Range to play:
    From: Very beginning of the file.
    To: Last byte of the file.
    -------------------------------------------*/
    if ( iOpenResultS == SP_NO_ERRORS )
       {
       sp_PlayF ( SP_START_OF_FILE,
                  SP_END_OF_FILE );
       }
    else
       {
       MessageBox( NULL,
                   "Can't open the S session",
                   "Message from filetype.exe",
                    MB_ICONINFORMATION );
       }
    return 0;

case TS_PB:
    /*----------------------------------
    User selected the TS Push button.
    ---------------------------------*/
    iOpenResultTS =
    sp_OpenSession ( "c:\\spSDK\\TSfiles\\TSfile.ts",
                      SP_NON_STAND_ALONE,
                      0L,
                      SP_TS_TYPE );
    /*-------------------------------------------
    Play the TS file.
    Range to play:
    From: Very beginning of the file.
    To: Last byte of the file.
    -------------------------------------------*/
    if ( iOpenResultTS == SP_NO_ERRORS )
       {
       sp_PlayF ( SP_START_OF_FILE,
                  SP_END_OF_FILE );
       }
    else
       {
       MessageBox( NULL,
                   "Can't open the TS session",
                   "Message from filetype.exe",
                    MB_ICONINFORMATION );
       }
    return 0;
```

continues

Listing 5.2. continued

```
                case WAV_PB:
                        /*---------------------------------
                        User clicked the WAV push button.
                        ----------------------------------*/
                        MessageBox( NULL,
          "Short version of TS library does not support WAV files.",
                                "Message from filetype.exe",
                                MB_ICONINFORMATION );
                        return 0;

                case VOC_PB:
                        /*---------------------------------
                        User clicked the VOC push button.
                        ----------------------------------*/
                        MessageBox( NULL,
          "Short version of TS library does not support VOC files.",
                                "Message from filetype.exe",
                                MB_ICONINFORMATION );
                        return 0;

                case IDM_QUIT:
                        /*-------------------------
                        User clicked the Quit option.
                        -------------------------*/
                        DestroyWindow (hWnd);
                        return 0L;

                case IDM_ABOUT :
                        /*-------------------------
                        User clicked the About option.
                        -------------------------*/
                        DialogBox ( ghInst,
                                "AboutBox",
                                hWnd,
                                lpfnAboutDlgProc );
                        return 0;

                }/* end of switch(wParam) in the WM_COMMAND case */

        case WM_DESTROY:
                /*-----------------------
                Delete the bitmap objects.
                -----------------------*/
                DeleteObject ( hBitmapS   );
                DeleteObject ( hBitmapTS  );
                DeleteObject ( hBitmapWAV );
                DeleteObject ( hBitmapVOC );

                PostQuitMessage (0);
```

```
            return 0;
    }/* end of switch (message) */

/*-----------------------
 Message was not processed.
 ----------------------*/
return DefWindowProc ( hWnd, message, wParam, lParam ) ;


}
/*================= end of WndProc() ===================*/

/*======================
 FUNCTION: AboutDlgProc()
 ======================*/
/*---------------------------------------
 DESCRIPTION:
 This is the About dialog box procedure.
 -------------------------------------*/
BOOL FAR PASCAL _export AboutDlgProc ( HWND hDlg,
                                       UINT message,
                                       UINT wParam,
                                       LONG lParam )

{
switch ( message )
        {
        case WM_INITDIALOG :
                return TRUE;

        case WM_COMMAND :
                switch ( wParam )
                        {
                        case IDOK :
                        case IDCANCEL :
                            EndDialog ( hDlg, 0 );
                            return TRUE;
                        }
        }
return FALSE ;
}/* End of function. */
/*=============== end of AboutDlgProc() =============*/
```

Listing 5.3. FileType.rc.

```
/*======================================================
FILE NAME: FileType.rc
----------

FILE DESCRIPTION:
----------------
The resource file.

(C) Copyright Gurewich 1992, 1993

======================================================*/

/*------
 #include
 ------*/
#include <windows.h>
#include "FileType.h"

/*--
 Menu
 --*/
FileType    MENU
BEGIN
    POPUP    "&Menu"
        BEGIN
            MENUITEM "&Quit",   IDM_QUIT
            MENUITEM "&About",  IDM_ABOUT
        END
END

/*-----------------------------------------
 Definition of the Cassette tape icon.
 Filename: Tape.ico
 Icon name: IconOfTape
 -----------------------------------------*/
IconOfTape ICON Tape.ico

/*--------
 Bit maps.
 --------*/
SBitmap     BITMAP S.bmp
TSBitmap    BITMAP TS.bmp
WAVBitmap   BITMAP WAV.bmp
VOCBitmap   BITMAP VOC.bmp
BkGndBitmap BITMAP BACKGND.bmp /* Used for the background. */
```

```
/*----------------------------------------------------
 The About dialog box of the application.
 --------------------------------------------------*/
AboutBox DIALOG 81, 43, 160, 100
STYLE DS_MODALFRAME ¦ WS_POPUP ¦ WS_VISIBLE ¦
                    WS_CAPTION ¦ WS_SYSMENU
CAPTION "About the filetype program"
FONT 8, "MS Sans Serif"
BEGIN
    PUSHBUTTON      "OK", IDOK, 64, 75, 40, 14
    CTEXT           "(C) Copyright Gurewich 1992, 1993", -1,
                    13, 47, 137, 18
    ICON            "IconOfTape", -1, 14, 12, 18, 20
END


/*----------------------------------------------------
 The main dialog box.
 This dialog box appears upon starting the application.
 --------------------------------------------------*/
FileTypeBox DIALOG PRELOAD 28, 25, 299, 220
STYLE WS_MINIMIZEBOX ¦ WS_POPUP   ¦ WS_VISIBLE ¦
                     WS_CAPTION ¦ WS_SYSMENU ¦
                     WS_THICKFRAME
CAPTION "FileType"
FONT 8, "MS Sans Serif"
CLASS "FileTypeClass"
BEGIN
    PUSHBUTTON      "&Exit", EXIT_PB, 129, 190, 40, 14
    PUSHBUTTON      "&S file", S_PB, 12, 25, 39, 67
    PUSHBUTTON      "&TS file", TS_PB, 162, 27, 40, 62
    GROUPBOX        "Playing ""TS"" sound file", -1,
                    156, 12, 139, 85
    GROUPBOX        "Playing ""S"" sound file", -1,
                    6, 13, 145, 84
    GROUPBOX        "Playing .WAV sound file", WAV_PB,
                    6, 103, 144, 81
    GROUPBOX        "Playing .VOC sound file", VOC_PB,
                    157, 103, 138, 80
    PUSHBUTTON      "&WAV file", WAV_PB,
                    11, 116, 38, 63
    PUSHBUTTON      "&VOC file", VOC_PB,
                    162, 118, 39, 60
END
```

Listing 5.4. FileType.def.

```
;=======================================
; module-definition file for FileType.c
;=======================================

NAME          FileType

DESCRIPTION   'The FileType program. (C) Copyright Gurewich 1992, 1993'

EXETYPE       WINDOWS

STUB          'WINSTUB.EXE'

CODE  PRELOAD MOVEABLE DISCARDABLE

DATA  PRELOAD MOVEABLE MULTIPLE

HEAPSIZE      1024
STACKSIZE     8192
```

Listing 5.5. FileType.mak.

```
#=============
# FileType.mak
#=============

FileType.exe : FileType.obj FileType.h FileType.def FileType.res
    link /nod FileType.obj, FileType.exe, NUL, \
        slibcew.lib oldnames.lib libw.lib commdlg \
        c:\spSDK\TegoWlib\TegoWin.lib, \
        FileType.def
    rc -t FileType.res

FileType.obj : FileType.c FileType.h
    cl -c -G2sw -Ow -W3 -Zp FileType.c

FileType.res : FileType.rc FileType.h Tape.ico
    rc -r FileType.rc
```

Bit-Map Files

The five bit-map files (S.bmp, TS.bmp, WAV.bmp, VOC.bmp, and BACKGND.bmp) are shown in Figure 5.3.

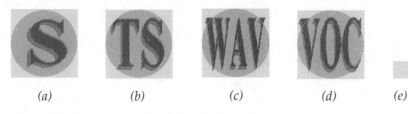

(a)   (b)   (c)   (d)   (e)

Figure 5.3. The bit-map files of the FileType program.
(a) The S.bmp file.
(b) The TS.bmp file.
(c) The WAV.bmp file.
(d) The VOC.bmp file.
(e) The BACKGND.bmp file.

Quick Overview of the FileType Program

The purpose of the FileType program is to demonstrate the various sound types supported by the TS C sound library. It also demonstrates how a program can use the returned value of sp_OpenSession().

A Dialog Box as the Main Window

Note that the FileType program does not have a main window. Instead, it has a main dialog box. As soon as the program starts, the main dialog box appears. This is accomplished in WinMain() by updating the element cbWndExtra of the structure wc with the value DLGWINDOWEXTRA:

```
wc.cbWndExtra = DLGWINDOWEXTRA;
```

and by executing the statement

```
hWnd = CreateDialog ( ghInst, "FileTypeBox", 0, NULL );
```

This statement creates the dialog in accordance with the window class as specified by the element lpszClassName of the wc structure. In WinMain() we updated this structure element as FileTypeClass:

```
wc.lpszClassName =  "FileTypeClass";
```

FileTypeClass is defined as the CLASS in FileType.rc:

```
FileTypeBox DIALOG PRELOAD 28, 25, 299, 220
STYLE WS_MINIMIZEBOX ¦ WS_POPUP ¦ WS_VISIBLE ¦ WS_CAPTION ¦
      WS_SYSMENU ¦ WS_THICKFRAME
CAPTION "FileType"
FONT 8, "MS Sans Serif"
CLASS "FileTypeClass"
BEGIN
    . . . . . . . . . . . .
    . . . . . . . . . . . .
    . . . . . . . . . . . .
END
```

Note that FileTypeBox is the name of the dialog box, and it appears as the second parameter in CreateDialog() in WinMain().

This main dialog box contains a menu by the name of FileType, as defined in WinMain() by updating the element lpszMenuName of the wc structure with gszAppName:

```
wc.lpszMenuName  = gszAppName ;
```

The outline of this menu is defined in FileType.rc:

```
FileType   MENU
BEGIN
    . . . . . . . . . .
    . . . . . . . . . .
    . . . . . . . . . .
END
```

Processing *WM_COMMAND* Messages

The push buttons are #defined as S_PB (the S push button), TS_PB (the TS push button), WAV_PB (the WAV push button), VOC_PB (the VOC push button), and EXIT_PB (the Exit push button) in FileType.h, and their positions are outlined in FileType.rc.

When using a dialog box as the main window of the program, the dialog procedure is the function WndProc(). We committed ourselves to the name WndProc in WinMain() when we updated the element lpfnWndProc of the wc structure with the following name:

```
wc.lpfnWndProc   = WndProc ;
```

All the events that are related to the options of this dialog box (for example, the push buttons) are processed within the WM_COMMAND case of WndProc():

```
case WM_COMMAND
    {
    case S_PB:
        /*-------------------------------------------
         Process here the response to pushing the
         S push button.
         -------------------------------------*/
         .........
         .........
         .........

    other push buttons and menu item cases...

    }
```

The sections code that corresponds to the S and TS push buttons opens a sound session and plays the sound file. Of course, the sp_OpenSession() of the S session has SP_S_TYPE as its fourth parameter, and the TS session has SP_TS_TYPE as its fourth parameter.

Here is the sp_OpenSession statement for the TS session:

```
iOpenResultTS =
sp_OpenSession ( "c:\\spSDK\\TSfiles\\TSfile.ts",
                 SP_NON_STAND_ALONE,
                 0L,
                 SP_TS_TYPE );
```

We assign the returned value of the sp_OpenSession() statements to the iOpenResultS and iOpenResultTS integers.

We then check the values of iOpenResultS and iOpenResultTS. Here is the if code that checks for the returned value of the TS session:

```
 if ( iOpenResultTS == SP_NO_ERRORS )
    {
    sp_PlayF ( SP_START_OF_FILE,
               SP_END_OF_FILE );
    }
else
```

```
         {
         MessageBox( NULL,
                     "Can't open the S session",
                     "Message from filetype.exe",
                      MB_ICONINFORMATION );
         }
```

A returned value of SP_NO_ERRORS from sp_OpenSession() indicates that the sound session opened successfully; thus we play the file by executing the sp_PlayF() function.

If, however, the returned value from the sp_OpenSession() is not equal to SP_NO_ERRORS, then an error occurred during the opening of the session. We then skip the playback, and display a message box.

It is very important to understand that your program should not issue the sp_PlayF() function if the sound session did not open successfully. In fact, if you try to play while there is no open sound session, the TSEngine simply ignores your request to play.

The full version of the TS C sound library enables you to open a sound session with .WAV files, .VOC files, and .SND files. However, the short version does not support sound files other than S or TS types. This is the reason for displaying a message box for the cases when the user pushes the WAV push button and the VOC push button. If you have a copy of the full version of the TS C Sound library, simply upgrade the program by including the appropriate code for the WAV case and the VOC case.

For the WAV_PB case the corresponding code is

```
iOpenResultWAV =
sp_OpenSession ( "c:\\spSDK\\WAVfiles\\WAVfile.wav",
                 SP_NON_STAND_ALONE,
                 0L,
                 SP_WAV_TYPE );

  if ( iOpenResultWAV == SP_NO_ERRORS )
     {
     sp_PlayF ( SP_START_OF_FILE,
                SP_END_OF_FILE );
     }
else
     {
     MessageBox( NULL,
                 "Can't open the WAV session",
                 "Message from filetype.exe",
                  MB_ICONINFORMATION );
     }
```

The corresponding code for the VOC_PB case is

```
iOpenResultVOC =
sp_OpenSession ( "c:\\spSDK\\VOCfiles\\VOCfile.voc",
                 SP_NON_STAND_ALONE,
                 0L,
                 SP_VOC_TYPE );

 if ( iOpenResultVOC == SP_NO_ERRORS )
    {
    sp_PlayF ( SP_START_OF_FILE,
               SP_END_OF_FILE );
    }
else
    {
    MessageBox( NULL,
                "Can't open the VOC session",
                "Message from filetype.exe",
                MB_ICONINFORMATION );
    }
```

The full version of the TS C Sound library also supports .SND sound files. For .SND files, substitute SP_SND_TYPE as the fourth parameter of sp_OpenSession().

Other Returned Values From *sp_OpenSession*

As noted previously, a returned value of SP_NO_ERRORS from sp_OpenSession indicates that the sound session opened successfully.

When a session does not open, your program can detect the exact reason for the failure. This might be useful during development time of the program. Here is the list of possible returned values:

Returned Value From sp_OpenSession()	Meaning
SP_NO_ERRORS	No errors. Sound session opened successfully.
SP_CANT_OPEN_FILE	Error. File cannot open. For example, sound file is supposed to be in the A drive, and there is no diskette in the A drive.

Returned Value From `sp_OpenSession()`	Meaning
SP_FILESIZE_ERROR	Error. TSEngine can't determine the file size. One reason for this error could be that it has a bad sector on the hard drive.
SP_ALLOC_FAILURE	Error. Not enough memory. This error is very rare, especially under the Windows operating system.
SP_READ_ERROR	Error. TSEngine can't read the file. It could have a bad sector on the hard drive, or the sound file could be corrupt.
SP_UNSUPPORTED_TYPE	Error. The TSEngine can't determine the type of the sound file.

NOTE   Usually, when the TSEngine fails to open a session, it is because the sound file that was specified does not exist, or the sound file that was specified is not a legal sound file.

Processing Keyboard Messages

The accelerator keys of the push buttons are processed within the WM_CHAR case of WndProc().

```
case WM_CHAR:
    wParam = toupper ( wParam );
    {
    case 'S':
        /*----------------------------------------
        Process here the response to pressing the
        S or s key.
        ----------------------------------------*/
        .........
        .........
        .........
```

```
       ...................................
       .... other cases for other keys: ....
       ...................................

     default: return 0;
     }
```

Note that we first convert the received character to uppercase with the `toupper()` function.

The default under the `WM_CHAR` case is `return 0`, because any time the user presses a key that is not E, S, T, W, or V we want the program to return to the Windows operating system, and we don't want the Windows operating system to do anything about it.

For each of the cases under the `WM_CHAR` case we execute the `SendMessage()` function, treating the case as if the corresponding push button was chosen. For example, the case that corresponds to pressing the **S** key sends the same message that is generated when the user pushes the S push button.

```
SendMessage ( hWnd,
              WM_COMMAND,
              S_PB,
              0);
```

The About Dialog Box

When you select the About option from the menu, the About dialog box appears. The outline of the About dialog box is defined in the FileType.rc file.

The selection of the About option from the menu is processed by the `WM_ABOUT` case within the `WM_COMMAND` case.

The *SetFocus()* Function

Note that the first thing executed under the `WM_COMMAND` case is the `SetFocus()` function:

```
SetFocus (hWnd);
```

The reason for using this statement is that after the user clicks a push button, that push button has the focus. This means that after clicking a push button, pressing **S**, **T**, or any other key will not be processed by `WndProc()`, because the push button has the focus, and its own internal WndProc() will process the keys pressed. By including the SetFocus(hWnd) statement, we return the focus back to our main dialog box. This way, pressing a key after clicking a push button will cause the Windows operating system to send a WM_CHAR message to WndProc(). The WM_CHAR message is sent with wParam equal to the value of the key pressed.

Displaying the Bit Maps

Later chapters will teach you how to write programs that perform animation (moving pictures simultaneously with the playback of sound). Thus, you should know how to create and display bit maps. This section discusses how we created the bit maps of FileType and how we displayed them. The discussion may serve as a quick review of bit maps, a topic which you'll use extensively in subsequent chapters.

The FileType program displays four bit maps: S.bmp, TS.bmp, WAV.bmp, and VOC.bmp. We display these bit maps under the WM_PAINT case. We get the hdc by using the BeginPaint() function, and we get the hMemDC by using the CreateCompatibleDC() function. Once we have hdc and hMemDC, we can use the BitBlt() function to actually display the bit map:

```
case WM_PAINT:
    hdc = BeginPaint ( hWnd, &ps );
    hMemDC = CreateCompatibleDC ( hdc );

    /*------------
    Display the S.
    -------------*/
    SelectObject ( hMemDC, hBitmapS );
    BitBlt ( hdc,
             68,
             31,
             125,
             125,
             hMemDC,
             0,
             0,
             SRCCOPY );


    ...................................
    .... display the other bitmaps....
    ...................................
```

```
DeleteDC ( hMemDC );
EndPaint ( hWnd, &ps );

return 0L;
```

The fourth and fifth parameters of `BitBlt()` are the width and height of the bit map. We supply 125 for the width and 125 for the height.

Here is how we created the S.bmp:

- Using Paintbrush, we drew the S picture (see Figure 5.3).

- We saved the picture as a bit-map file, S.bmp.

This process was repeated for creating the other bit-map files.

How did we determine the x,y coordinates of the bit maps? When we created the `FileTypeBox` dialog box, we used the Dialog Editor that comes with the SDK for Windows. We positioned the various push buttons in the dialog box, and also positioned four icons in it. These four icons were positioned at the places where we wanted the bit maps to appear. Later, we examined the corresponding .DLG file that the Dialog Editor created, and we noticed the x,y coordinates of these icons. When we created the FileType.rc file from the .DLG file, we removed the four icons (because we don't need them) and substituted the icon coordinates as the second and third parameters to the `BitBlt()` function.

The `BitBlt()` function does not use the name of the .BMP bit-map file. For example, it uses `hBitmapS` for the S.bmp. We updated `hBitmapS` (as well as all the other bit maps) in the `WM_CREATE` case of `WndProc()` as follows:

```
hBitmapS   = LoadBitmap ( ghInst, "SBitmap"   );
hBitmapTS  = LoadBitmap ( ghInst, "TSBitmap"  );
hBitmapWAV = LoadBitmap ( ghInst, "WAVBitmap" );
hBitmapVOC = LoadBitmap ( ghInst, "VOCBitmap" );
```

The names of the bit-map files are defined in FileType.rc:

```
SBitmap     BITMAP S.bmp
TSBitmap    BITMAP TS.bmp
WAVBitmap   BITMAP WAV.bmp
VOCBitmap   BITMAP VOC.bmp
```

The bit maps are removed from memory during the execution of the `WM_DESTROY` case:

```
case WM_DESTROY:
```

```
/*----------------------
Delete the bit-map objects.
----------------------*/
DeleteObject ( hBitmapS   );
DeleteObject ( hBitmapTS  );
DeleteObject ( hBitmapWAV );
DeleteObject ( hBitmapVOC );

PostQuitMessage (0);
return 0;
```

We deleted the bit maps from memory before terminating the program so other programs could use this memory. If you have a bad habit of not deleting memory used by your programs, sooner or later your users will notice that after using your programs they experience memory problems.

The Background of FileType

The FileTypeBox dialog box has a yellow background. To create this background we first created the BACKGND.bmp file with the Paintbrush program, saved it as a .BMP file, and included it in FileType.rc:

```
BkGndBitmap BITMAP BACKGND.bmp
```

In WinMain() we defined the handles of the background and the brush:

```
HBITMAP    hBitmapOfBkGnd; /* Handle to the bit map of the background. */
HBRUSH     hBrushOfBkGnd;  /* Handle to the brush  of the background.  */
```

We then updated the handle of the background brush as follows:

```
hBitmapOfBkGnd= LoadBitmap ( ghInst, "BkGndBitmap" );
hBrushOfBkGnd = CreatePatternBrush ( hBitmapOfBkGnd );
```

Finally we updated the element hBrushOfBkGnd of the wc structure:

```
wc.hbrBackground  = hBrushOfBkGnd;
```

At the end of WinMain() we removed the bit map from the memory:

```
DeleteObject ( hBrushOfBkGnd );
```

Although the BACKGND.bmp that FileType uses is a simple yellow square, the above method can be used to create more complex and fancy background patterns.

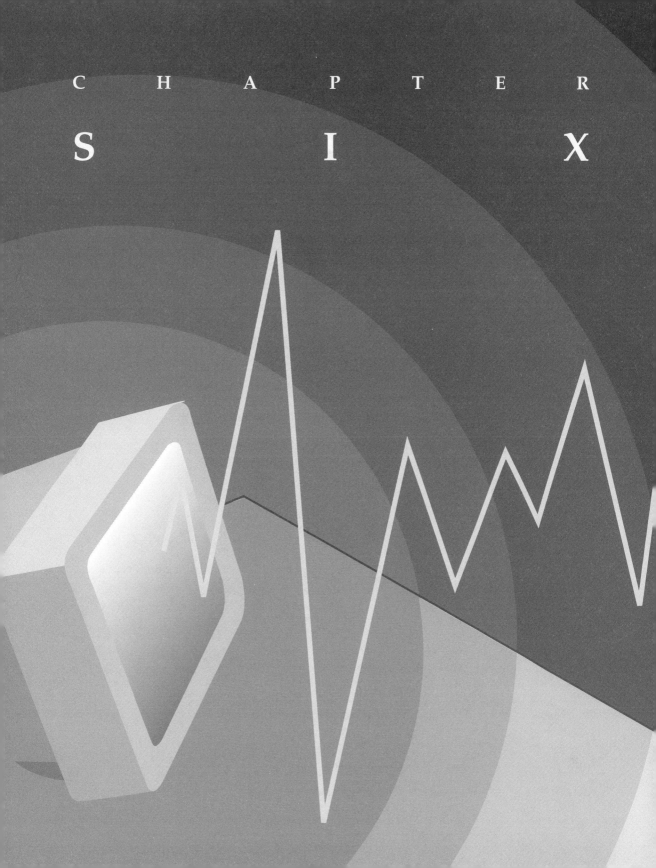

Animation

In this chapter, we will write a program that uses the returned value of the `sp_PlayF()` function. The returned value of `sp_PlayF()` is important, and it serves as the basic tool for accomplishing multimedia Windows applications.

The program presented in this chapter is called the Dog program. This program teaches how to write a program that displays a moving graphic object simultaneously with the playback of sound.

The Dog Program

We recommend that you compile, link, and execute the program before studying its code. This way you will gain a better understanding of what the program can do.

Compiling, Linking, and Executing the Dog Program

To compile and link the Dog program with the Microsoft compiler:

- Make sure your PC is in a DOS-protected mode.

- Log into c:\spSDK\Samp4Win\.

- At the DOS prompt type

    NMAKE Dog.mak   {Enter}

To compile and link the Dog program with the Borland compiler:

- Log into c:\spSDK\Samp4Win\.

- At the DOS prompt type

    MAKE -f Dog.bmk   {Enter}

To execute the Dog program:

- Select Run from the File menu of the Program Manager of Windows.

- Use Browse to select the file

  ```
  c:\spSDK\Samp4Win\Dog.exe
  ```

The main window appears, as shown in Figure 6.1.

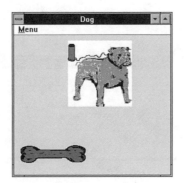

Figure 6.1. The main window of Dog.exe.

The main menu of Dog.exe (see Figure 6.2) contains three options: Quit, About, and Instructions. When the user selects the Quit option, the program says *Good-Bye* and quits. When the user selects the About option, the program displays the About dialog box, as shown in Figure 6.3. When the user selects the Instructions option, the program displays the Instructions dialog box as shown in Figure 6.4. The Instructions dialog box displays a message, telling the user to Click on the bone, or press B to make the dog crazy! If the user clicks the bone or presses **B**, the dog will start attacking, jumping, and barking.

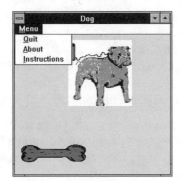

Figure 6.2. The main menu of Dog.exe.

Figure 6.3. The About dialog box of the Dog program.

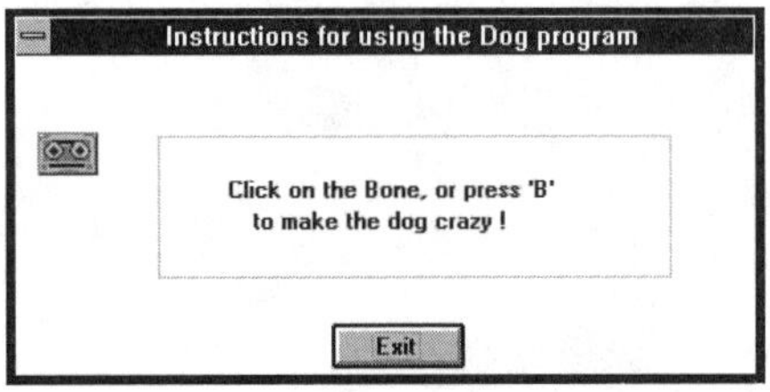

Figure 6.4. The Instructions dialog box of the Dog program.

What Is Animation?

Animation is the process of moving a two-dimensional picture and giving the impression that it is moving continuously in time. Animated movies display several frames each second, creating the illusion that objects are moving continuously.

You can, however, create animation with less frames per second than a real movie. For example, the familiar push button that is used in every Windows application is an example of animation that is composed of only two frames. One frame is the picture of the push button in its un-depressed position, and the other frame is the picture of the push button in its depressed position. When you click the push button, the built-in program of the push button displays the push button in its depressed position, thus giving you the feeling that the push button was pushed like a mechanical button.

The Dog program uses the same trick. There are only two frames: One frame is a picture of the dog with its mouth closed and its leash loose, and the other frame is a picture of the dog with its mouth open, water dripping out of its mouth, and its leash pulled. These two frames are shown in Figure 6.5. (The bone of the dog is shown in Figure 6.6.)

Figure 6.5. The two frames of the Dog program.

Figure 6.6. The Bone.bmp.

Creating the Bit Maps

We created the two dog pictures and the bone picture with the Image Editor that came with the SDK for Windows. Alternatively, you may draw the pictures with Paintbrush or another drawing software tool, and then copy and paste the image to the Image Editor of the SDK for Windows. When you set up the Image Editor for a new image, set the file that you create to a bit-map type such as .BMP. The Image Editor prompts you to enter the dimensions in pixels. These dimensions determine the size of the resultant .BMP file.

The dimensions we supplied for the dog pictures were 125 pixels for the width and 125 pixels for the height. These dimensions yielded dog bit-map files that are 8,188 bytes each. We specified the Bone.bmp at 125 × 32 pixels. The resultant bone bit-map file is 2,166 bytes.

The drawing process of the dog frames are quite simple. In fact, in most cases you can create impressive animations such as the dog even if you are not a professional artist. For the dog animation, we first displayed the dog with its mouth closed. We then changed this picture to create a new picture that shows the dog with its mouth opened. Other changes that we made to the picture were the moving of the dog's tail to a new position, coloring the inside of the mouth with a red vicious color, and redrawing the leash. We also added drops of water to the picture to create the illusion that there is water dripping out of the dog's mouth—that is, the Dog is angry.

The Dog Program Files

The Dog program consists of the following files:

Dog.c	The C code of the program.
Dog.h	The #include file of the program.
Dog.def	The module definition file of the program.
Dog.rc	The resource file of the program.
Dog.mak	The make file of the program.
DogOpen.bmp	The dog with its mouth open.
DogClose.bmp	The dog with its mouth closed.
Bone.bmp	The bone of the dog.
Tape.ico	The icon of the program.
BackGnd.bmp	The pattern used for the brush.

These files are provided for you in c:\spSDK\Samp4Win\.

The complete listing of the Dog program is shown in Listings 6.1 through 6.5.

Listing 6.1. Dog.h.

```
/*======================================================
 FILE NAME: Dog.h

 (C) Copyright Gurewich 1992, 1993
 ======================================================*/

/*----------
 prototypes
 ----------*/
long FAR PASCAL _export WndProc       ( HWND, UINT, UINT, LONG ) ;
BOOL FAR PASCAL _export AboutDlgProc ( HWND, UINT, UINT, LONG ) ;
BOOL FAR PASCAL _export InstDlgProc  ( HWND, UINT, UINT, LONG ) ;

void BarkingShow        ( HWND hWnd );
void PlayIt             ( HWND hWnd );
void DisplayDogWithOpen  ( HWND hWnd );
void DisplayDogWithClose ( HWND hWnd );

/*------
 #define
 ------*/
#define IDM_QUIT        1   /* The Quit        option in the menu. */
```

```
#define IDM_ABOUT        2   /* The About        option in the menu. */
#define IDM_INSTRUCTIONS 3   /* The Instructions option in the menu. */

#define EXIT_PB 100 /* The "Exit" push button in the instructions box. */

/*--------------
 Global variables
 --------------*/
char       gszAppName[] = "Dog" ; /* Our application name. */
HINSTANCE  ghInst;                /* current instance.     */
HBRUSH     ghBrushOfBkGnd;        /* For the brush.        */
HBITMAP    ghDogWithOpenMouth;    /* For the Dog bit map.  */
HBITMAP    ghDogWithCloseMouth;   /* For the Dog bit map.  */
```

Listing 6.2. Dog.c.

```
/*===============================================================
  PROGRAM: Dog.c
  -------
  (C) Copyright 1992, 1993 Gurewich. (R) All rights reserved.

  PROGRAM DESCRIPTION:
  -------------------
  This is the a Generic type 1 program.

  If the user clicks on the bone, the dog goes crazy !

  ===============================================================*/

/*--------
 #include
 --------*/
/*------------------------------------
 Required for all Windows applications.
 ------------------------------------*/
#include <windows.h>

/*-------------------------------------------------------------------
 Required so that sp_ functions, SP_ macros and #definitions
 from the TS C Sound library may be used in this applications.
 -------------------------------------------------------------------*/
#include "c:\spSDK\TegoWlib\sp4Win.h"
```

continues

Listing 6.2. continued

```
/*-------------------------------------------------------
  Definitions & prototypes specific to this application.
  -----------------------------------------------------*/
#include "c:\spSDK\Samp4WIN\Dog.h"


/*--------------------------------------------------
  For standard C functions used in this application.
  ------------------------------------------------*/
#include <stdlib.h>
#include <stdio.h>


/*==================
  FUNCTION: WinMain()
  ================*/
int PASCAL WinMain ( HANDLE hInstance,
                     HANDLE hPrevInstance,
                     LPSTR  lpszCmdLine,
                     int    nCmdShow )
{
/*------------------------
  Local and static variables.
  ------------------------*/
HWND      hWnd;   /* Handler to the window of our application.  */
MSG       msg;    /* Message to be processed by our application. */
WNDCLASS  wc;     /* Window class of our application.           */

HBITMAP   hBitmapOfBkGnd; /* For the background. */

/*-------------------------------------------------
  Make the hInstance variable a global variable.
  -----------------------------------------------*/
ghInst = hInstance;

/*--------------------------------
  Create the brush for the background.
  ------------------------------*/
hBitmapOfBkGnd = LoadBitmap ( ghInst, "BackGround"  );
ghBrushOfBkGnd = CreatePatternBrush ( hBitmapOfBkGnd );

/*-----------------------------------------------
  Update the window class structure and register
  the window class.
  ---------------------------------------------*/
if ( !hPrevInstance )
    {
```

```
/*----------------------------------------------
The "if" is satisfied, this is the very 1st
run of this application.
----------------------------------------*/
wc.style           = CS_HREDRAW ¦ CS_VREDRAW ;
wc.lpfnWndProc     = WndProc ;
wc.cbClsExtra      = 0 ;
wc.cbWndExtra      = 0 ;
wc.hInstance       = ghInst ;
wc.hIcon           = LoadIcon  ( ghInst, "IconOfTape" ) ;
wc.hCursor         = LoadCursor ( NULL, IDC_ARROW      ) ;
wc.hbrBackground   = ghBrushOfBkGnd; /* The brush that we created */
                                     /*  with the bitmap.         */
wc.lpszMenuName    = gszAppName ;
wc.lpszClassName   = gszAppName ;

/*------------------
Register the window.
------------------*/
RegisterClass ( &wc );

}/* end of if(!hPrevInstance) */


/*--------------------------------------
  Create the window of our application.
------------------------------------*/
hWnd = CreateWindow ( gszAppName,
                      gszAppName,
                      WS_OVERLAPPEDWINDOW,
                      10,
                      10,
                      300,
                      300,
                      NULL,
                      NULL,
                      ghInst,
                      NULL );

/*------------------------------------------------
  Show and update the window of our application.
--------------------------------------------*/
ShowWindow   ( hWnd, nCmdShow );
UpdateWindow ( hWnd );

/*----------------
  The message loop.
----------------*/
while ( GetMessage ( &msg, NULL, 0, 0 ) )
```

continues

Listing 6.2. continued

```
        {
        TranslateMessage ( &msg );
        DispatchMessage  ( &msg );
        }

/*------------------------------------------------------------
 Delete the memory and brush objects used for the background.
 ------------------------------------------------------------*/
DeleteObject ( hBitmapOfBkGnd );
DeleteObject ( ghBrushOfBkGnd );

return msg.wParam ;

} /* end of function. */
/*========================= end of WinMain() ===================*/


/*==================
 FUNCTION: WndProc()
 ==================*/
/*------------------------------
 DESCRIPTION: Processes messages.
 ------------------------------*/
long FAR PASCAL _export WndProc ( HWND hWnd,
                                  UINT message,
                                  UINT wParam,
                                  LONG lParam )

{
/*--------------------------
 Local and static variables.
 --------------------------*/
static HDC         hdc;      /* Needed for displaying.   */
static PAINTSTRUCT ps;       /* Needed for displaying.   */
static RECT        rect;     /* Needed for displaying.   */
static HDC         hMemDC;   /* Needed for displaying bit map. */
static HBITMAP     hBone;    /* For the bone bit map. */

static FARPROC lpfnAboutDlgProc;/* For the "About" dialog box.    */
static FARPROC lpfnInstDlgProc ;/* For the "Instructions" dialog. */

static int     iOpenBarkResult;
static int     iOpenHelloResult;

switch ( message )
        {
        case WM_CREATE:
            /*------------------------------
             Open the barking sound session.
             ------------------------------*/
```

```
iOpenBarkResult = sp_OpenSession (
                  "c:\\spSDK\\TSfiles\\Bark.ts",
                  SP_NON_STAND_ALONE,
                  0L,
                  SP_TS_TYPE );

/*-------------------------
Quit if can't open the file.
------------------------*/
if ( iOpenBarkResult != SP_NO_ERRORS )
   {
   MessageBox ( NULL,
                "Failed to open the sound session!",
                "Message from Dog.c",
                 MB_ICONINFORMATION );

   /*------------------
   Quit the application.
   -------------------*/
   SendMessage ( hWnd,
                 WM_DESTROY,
                 0,
                 0 );
   }

/*-------------------------------------------
Obtain the lpfnAboutDlgProc of the About
the dialog box.
--------------------------------------*/
lpfnAboutDlgProc =
MakeProcInstance (( FARPROC) AboutDlgProc, ghInst);

/*----------------------------------------------
Obtain the lpfnInstDlgProc of the Instructions
dialog box.
----------------------------------------*/
lpfnInstDlgProc =
MakeProcInstance (( FARPROC) InstDlgProc, ghInst);

/*---------------------------------------------
Obtain the handlers of the dog bit map and the
bone bit maps.
---------------------------------------------*/
ghDogWithCloseMouth = LoadBitmap ( ghInst,
                                   "DogCloseMouth" );

ghDogWithOpenMouth  = LoadBitmap ( ghInst,
                                   "DogOpenMouth"  );
```

continues

Listing 6.2. continued

```
            hBone                = LoadBitmap ( ghInst,
                                               "Bone" );
            return 0;

    case WM_PAINT:
            /*----------------------------------
            Paint the dog with its mouth closed.
            ---------------------------------*/
            hdc = BeginPaint ( hWnd, &ps );
            hMemDC = CreateCompatibleDC ( hdc );
            SelectObject ( hMemDC, ghDogWithCloseMouth );
            BitBlt ( hdc,
                     100,
                     10,
                     120,
                     120,
                     hMemDC,
                     0,
                     0,
                     SRCCOPY );
            DeleteDC ( hMemDC );
            /*--------------
            Paint the bone.
            -------------*/
            hMemDC = CreateCompatibleDC ( hdc );
            SelectObject ( hMemDC, hBone );
            BitBlt ( hdc,
                     10,
                     200,
                     125,
                     32,
                     hMemDC,
                     0,
                     0,
                     SRCCOPY );
            DeleteDC ( hMemDC );
            EndPaint ( hWnd, &ps );

            return 0;

    case WM_COMMAND:
            /*-----------------
            Process menu items.
            -----------------*/
            switch (wParam)
                    {
```

```
        case IDM_QUIT:
            /*------------------------
            User clicked on Quit option.
            ------------------------*/
            DestroyWindow (hWnd);
            return 0L;

        case IDM_ABOUT :
            /*-------------------------
            User clicked on About option.
            -------------------------*/
            DialogBox ( ghInst,
                        "AboutBox",
                        hWnd,
                        lpfnAboutDlgProc );
            return 0L;

        case IDM_INSTRUCTIONS :
            /*-----------------------------------
            User clicked on Instructions option.
            -----------------------------------*/
            DialogBox ( ghInst,
                        "InstructionsBox",
                        hWnd,
                        lpfnInstDlgProc );
            return 0L;

        }/* end of switch (wParam) */


case WM_CHAR:
    /*-----------------------------------
    User pressed a key on the keyboard.
    ---------------------------------*/

    /*-------------------
    Convert to uppercase.
    -------------------*/
    wParam = toupper ( wParam );

    switch ( wParam )
        {
        case 'B':
            /*---------------
            Make the dog bark.
            ---------------*/
            BarkingShow ( hWnd );
            return 0;
        }
```

continues

Listing 6.2. continued

```
case WM_LBUTTONDOWN:
        /*-----------------------------------------------
        This message was received because the user has the
        left button of the mouse down.
        -----------------------------------------------*/

        if (
            /*-----------
            The Bone area.
            -----------*/
            LOWORD ( lParam ) < 10 +  125   &&
            LOWORD ( lParam ) > 10          &&
            HIWORD ( lParam ) < 200 + 32    &&
            HIWORD ( lParam ) > 200
            )
            {
            /*----------------
            Make the dog bark.
            ----------------*/
            BarkingShow ( hWnd );
            }
        return 0L;


case WM_DESTROY:
        /*------------------------------
        Open the Hello.ts sound session.
        ------------------------------*/
        iOpenHelloResult =
        sp_OpenSession ( "c:\\spSDK\\TSfiles\\Hello.ts",
                          SP_NON_STAND_ALONE,
                          0L,
                          SP_TS_TYPE ) ;

        if ( iOpenHelloResult == SP_NO_ERRORS )
            {
            /*-------------------------------
            Play a section of the sound file.
            Range to play: 30,000 to 40,000
            phrase: "Good-Bye"
            -------------------------------*/
            sp_PlayF ( 30000L, 40000L ) ;
            }

        /*------------------
        Delete the bit maps.
        ------------------*/
```

```
                DeleteObject ( ghDogWithCloseMouth );
                DeleteObject ( ghDogWithOpenMouth  );
                DeleteObject ( hBone               );

                PostQuitMessage (0);
                return 0;
        }/* end of switch (message) */

/*------------------------
 Message was not processed.
 ----------------------*/
return DefWindowProc ( hWnd, message, wParam, lParam ) ;

}/* end of WndProc() */
/*================== end of WndProc() ===================*/

/*=====================
 FUNCTION: AboutDlgProc()
 =====================*/
/*---------------------------------------
 DESCRIPTION:
 This is the About dialog box procedure.
 ------------------------------------*/
BOOL FAR PASCAL _export AboutDlgProc ( HWND hDlg,
                                       UINT message,
                                       UINT wParam,
                                       LONG lParam )

{
switch ( message )
        {
        case WM_INITDIALOG :
                return TRUE;

        case WM_COMMAND :
            switch ( wParam )
                    {
                    case IDOK :
                    case IDCANCEL :
                        EndDialog ( hDlg, 0 );
                        return TRUE;
                    }
        }/* end of switch(message) */
return FALSE ;
}/* End of function. */
/*=============== end of AboutDlgProc() =============*/

/*=====================
 FUNCTION: InstDlgProc()
 =====================*/
```

continues

Listing 6.2. continued

```
/*------------------------------------------------
 DESCRIPTION:
 This is the Instructions dialog box procedure.
 ----------------------------------------------*/
BOOL FAR PASCAL _export InstDlgProc ( HWND hDlg,
                                      UINT message,
                                      UINT wParam,
                                      LONG lParam )

{
switch ( message )
        {
        case WM_INITDIALOG :
                return TRUE;

        case WM_COMMAND :
                switch ( wParam )
                        {
                        case EXIT_PB :
                        case IDOK :
                        case IDCANCEL :
                                EndDialog ( hDlg, 0 );
                                return TRUE;
                        }
        }
return FALSE ;
}/* End of function. */
/*=============== end of InstDlgProc() ==============*/

/*========
 FUNCTION
 ========*/
/*-------------------------------
 DESCRIPTION:
 -----------
 Make the dog bark.
 -------------------------------*/
void BarkingShow ( HWND hWnd )
{
int  iNumberOfPlays;

for ( iNumberOfPlays = 0; iNumberOfPlays < 4; iNumberOfPlays++)
    {
    PlayIt ( hWnd );
    }

DisplayDogWithClose ( hWnd );
```

```
}/* end of function. */
/*============ end of function ===========*/

/*========
 FUNCTION
 ========*/
/*--------------------------------
 DESCRIPTION:
 ----------
 Play the sound file 1 time.
 -------------------------------*/
void PlayIt ( HWND hWnd )
{
int  iMouthFlag    = 0;
long lCurrentByte = 0L;

while (1)
    {
    lCurrentByte = sp_PlayF ( lCurrentByte,
                              lCurrentByte + 2000L );

    if ( lCurrentByte == 0L )
        {
        break;
        }

    if ( iMouthFlag == 0 )
        {
        /*--------------------------------
        Display the dog with its mouth open.
        -------------------------------*/
        iMouthFlag = 1;
        DisplayDogWithOpen  ( hWnd );
        continue;
        }

    if ( iMouthFlag == 1 )
        {
        /*--------------------------------
        Display the dog with its mouth closed.
        --------------------------------*/
        iMouthFlag = 0;
        DisplayDogWithClose ( hWnd );
        continue;
        }

    }/* end of while(1) loop. */
```

continues

Listing 6.2. continued

```
}/* end of function. */
/*============ end of function ==========*/

/*========
 FUNCTION
 ========*/
/*-------------------------------
 DESCRIPTION:
 ----------
 Display the dog with its mouth open.
 -------------------------------*/
void DisplayDogWithOpen ( HWND hWnd )
{
HDC hdc;
HDC hMemDC;

/*-------------------------------
 Draw the dog with its mouth open.
 -------------------------------*/
hdc = GetDC ( hWnd );
hMemDC = CreateCompatibleDC ( hdc );
SelectObject ( hMemDC, ghDogWithOpenMouth );

BitBlt ( hdc,
         100,
         10,
         125,
         125,
         hMemDC,
         0,
         0,
         SRCCOPY );

DeleteDC ( hMemDC );
ReleaseDC ( hWnd, hdc   );
}
/*============ end of function ==========*/

/*========
 FUNCTION
 ========*/
/*-------------------------------------
 DESCRIPTION:
 ----------
 Display the dog with its mouth closed.
 -------------------------------------*/
void DisplayDogWithClose ( HWND hWnd )
```

```
{
static HDC hdc;
static HDC hMemDC;

/*----------------------------------
 Draw the dog with its mouth closed.
 --------------------------------*/
hdc = GetDC ( hWnd );
hMemDC = CreateCompatibleDC ( hdc );
SelectObject ( hMemDC, ghDogWithCloseMouth );

BitBlt ( hdc,
         100,
         10,
         125,
         125,
         hMemDC,
         0,
         0,
         SRCCOPY );

DeleteDC ( hMemDC );
ReleaseDC ( hWnd, hdc   );
}
/*============ end of function ===========*/
```

Listing 6.3. Dog.rc.

```
/*===================================================
 FILE NAME: Dog.rc
 ----------

 FILE DESCRIPTION:
 ----------------
 The resource file.

 (C) Copyright Gurewich 1992, 1993

 ==================================================*/

/*-------
 #include
 -------*/
#include <windows.h>
#include "Dog.h"
```

continues

Listing 6.3. continued

```
/*---
 Menu
 ---*/
Dog   MENU
BEGIN
    POPUP   "&Menu"
        BEGIN
            MENUITEM "&Quit",          IDM_QUIT
            MENUITEM "&About",         IDM_ABOUT
            MENUITEM "&Instructions", IDM_INSTRUCTIONS
        END
END


/*------------------------------------------
 Definition of the Cassette tape icon.
 File name: Tape.ico
 Icon name: IconOfTape
 ------------------------------------------*/
IconOfTape ICON Tape.ico



/*---------
 Bit maps.
 --------*/
BackGround     BITMAP BackGnd.bmp
DogOpenMouth   BITMAP DogOpen.bmp
DogCloseMouth  BITMAP DogClose.bmp
Bone           BITMAP Bone.bmp

/*--------------------
 The About dialog box.
 -------------------*/
AboutBox DIALOG 81, 43, 160, 100
STYLE DS_MODALFRAME ¦ WS_POPUP ¦ WS_VISIBLE ¦ WS_CAPTION ¦ WS_SYSMENU
CAPTION "About the Dog program"
FONT 8, "MS Sans Serif"
BEGIN
    PUSHBUTTON     "OK", IDOK, 64, 75, 40, 14
    CTEXT          "(C) Copyright Gurewich 1992, 1993",
                   -1, 13, 47, 137, 18
    ICON           "IconOfTape", -1, 14, 12, 18, 20
END


/*-------------------------
 The Instructions dialog box.
 ------------------------*/
InstructionsBox DIALOG 41, 45, 222, 100
```

```
STYLE DS_MODALFRAME ¦ WS_POPUP ¦ WS_VISIBLE ¦ WS_CAPTION ¦ WS_SYSMENU
CAPTION "Instructions for using the Dog program"
FONT 8, "MS Sans Serif"
BEGIN
    PUSHBUTTON      "Exit", EXIT_PB, 95, 84, 40, 14
    CTEXT           "Click on the Bone, or press 'B'",
                    -1, 37, 38, 152, 13
    CTEXT           "to make the dog crazy !", -1, 47, 48, 125, 8
    CONTROL         "", -1, "Static", SS_GRAYFRAME, 43, 25, 154, 45
    ICON            "IconOfTape", -1, 7, 18, 18, 20
END
```

Listing 6.4. Dog.def.

```
;=======================================
; module-definition file for Dog.c
;=======================================

NAME            Dog

DESCRIPTION     'The Dog program. (C) Copyright Gurewich 1992, 1993'

EXETYPE         WINDOWS

STUB            'WINSTUB.EXE'

CODE    PRELOAD MOVEABLE DISCARDABLE

DATA    PRELOAD MOVEABLE MULTIPLE

HEAPSIZE        1024
STACKSIZE       8192
```

Listing 6.5. Dog.mak.

```
#=============
# Dog.mak
#=============

Dog.exe : Dog.obj Dog.h Dog.def Dog.res
```

continues

Listing 6.5. continued

```
link /nod Dog.obj, Dog.exe, NUL, \
    slibcew.lib oldnames.lib libw.lib commdlg \
    c:\spSDK\TegoWlib\TegoWin.lib, \
    Dog.def
rc -t Dog.res

Dog.obj : Dog.c Dog.h
    cl -c -G2sw -Ow -W3 -Zp  Dog.c

Dog.res : Dog.rc Dog.h Tape.ico
    rc -r Dog.rc
```

Using the Returned Value of *sp_PlayF()*

The sp_PlayF() function returns a long integer. This long integer specifies the last byte played by the TSEngine. For example, the returned value from

```
sp_PlayF ( 0L, 3000L );
```

is 3000L, because the last byte played is byte location 3,000.

Sometimes, the coordinates supplied to the sp_PlayF() function do not make sense. For example, suppose the sound file to be played is 40,000 bytes long, and that you supplied the value 50000L as the second parameter to the sp_PlayF() function:

```
sp_PlayF ( 0L, 50000L );
```

In this case, the TSEngine plays from byte 0 to byte 40,000, and the returned value becomes 0L, an indication that the sound file reached the end of the file.

If the parameters don't make sense (such as supplying 30000L as the first parameter and 20000L as the second parameter), then the sp_PlayF() function returns 0L and no sound plays, but no harm is done (that is, the program will not crash).

> **NOTE**   The returned value of sp_PlayF() is a long integer that represents the last byte played by the TSEngine.
>
> If the second parameter of sp_PlayF() is larger then the size of the sound file, then the returned value of sp_PlayF is 0L. In this case, the TSEngine plays up to the last byte of the sound file.
>
> If the byte coordinates supplied to sp_PlayF() are invalid, then the TSEngine will not be able to play, and the returned value of sp_PlayF() will be 0L.

The *WinMain()* of Dog.c

The WinMain() of Dog.c loads the bit map of the background pattern and creates the brush:

```
hBitmapOfBkGnd = LoadBitmap ( ghInst, "BackGround"  );
ghBrushOfBkGnd = CreatePatternBrush ( hBitmapOfBkGnd );
```

Then the element hbrBackground of the wc structure is updated with the value of ghBrushOfBkGnd:

```
wc.hbrBackground = ghBrushOfBkGnd;
```

The CreateWindow() function defines the main window as a window that starts at pixel location (10,10) as specified by the fourth and fifth parameters of CreateWindow(). The width and height of the window are defined as 300 pixels long and 300 pixels wide as specified by the sixth and seventh parameters of CreateWindow():

```
hWnd = CreateWindow ( gszAppName,
                      gszAppName,
                      WS_OVERLAPPEDWINDOW,
                      10,
                      10,
                      300,
                      300,
                      NULL,
                      NULL,
                      ghInst,
                      NULL );
```

The *WndProc( )* of Dog.c.

The WndProc() function handles the cases that correspond to the events during the program execution. We will now discuss each of these cases.

The *WM_CREATE* Case

Under the WM_CREATE case we open the sound session as a TS sound file with the sound file c:\spSDK\TSfiles\Bark.ts. If the session does not open successfully, then the program terminates:

```
/*----------------------------
Open the barking sound session.
-------------------------*/
iOpenBarkResult = sp_OpenSession (
                    "c:\\spSDK\\TSfiles\\Bark.ts",
                    SP_NON_STAND_ALONE,
                    0L,
                    SP_TS_TYPE);

/*------------------------
Quit if can't open the file.
-----------------------*/
if ( iOpenBarkResult != SP_NO_ERRORS )
    {
    MessageBox ( NULL,
                "Failed to open the sound session!",
                "Message from Dog.c",
                MB_ICONINFORMATION );

    /*-----------------
    Quit the application.
    -----------------*/
    SendMessage ( hWnd,
                WM_DESTROY,
                0,
                0 );
    }
```

We then obtain the lpfn of the About dialog box and the lpfn of the Instructions dialog box:

```
lpfnAboutDlgProc =
MakeProcInstance (( FARPROC) AboutDlgProc, ghInst);

lpfnInstDlgProc =
MakeProcInstance (( FARPROC) InstDlgProc, ghInst);
```

Next we load the bit maps for the dog with the open mouth, the dog with the closed mouth, and the bone:

```
ghDogWithClosedMouth = LoadBitmap ( ghInst, "DogClosedMouth" );
ghDogWithOpenMouth   = LoadBitmap ( ghInst, "DogOpenMouth"  );
hBone                = LoadBitmap ( ghInst, "Bone"          );
```

The *WM_PAINT* Case

Under the WM_PAINT we paint the dog bone and the dog with its mouth closed. We use the BitBlt() function to display those bit-map files:

```
    hdc = BeginPaint ( hWnd, &ps );
    hMemDC = CreateCompatibleDC ( hdc );
    SelectObject ( hMemDC, ghDogWithClosedMouth );
    BitBlt ( hdc,
             100,
             10,
             120,
             120,
             hMemDC,
             0,
             0,
             SRCCOPY );
    DeleteDC ( hMemDC );

hMemDC = CreateCompatibleDC ( hdc );
SelectObject ( hMemDC, hBone );
BitBlt ( hdc,
         10,
         200,
         125,
         32,
         hMemDC,
         0,
         0,
         SRCCOPY );
    DeleteDC ( hMemDC );
    EndPaint ( hWnd, &ps );
```

The *WM_DESTROY* Case

Under the WM_DESTROY case we open a sound session with the c:\spSDK\TSfiles\Hello.ts sound file, and play the sound section that corresponds to the phrase *Good-Bye*. If the session cannot open, playback is skipped:

```
/*----------------------------
Open the Hello.ts sound session.
---------------------------*/
iOpenHelloResult =
sp_OpenSession ( "c:\\spSDK\\TSfiles\\Hello.ts",
                 SP_NON_STAND_ALONE,
                 0L,
                 SP_TS_TYPE ) ;

if ( iOpenHelloResult == SP_NO_ERRORS )
   {
   /*----------------------------
   Play a section of the sound file.
   Range to play: 30,000 to 40,000
   phrase: "Good-Bye"
   ------------------------------*/
   sp_PlayF ( 30000L, 40000L ) ;
   }
```

The last section of the WM_DESTROY case deletes the memory objects created under the WM_CREATE case:

```
DeleteObject ( ghDogWithClosedMouth );
DeleteObject ( ghDogWithOpenMouth  );
DeleteObject ( hBone               );
```

Note that under the WM_CREATE case we check that the Bark.ts sound session opened successfully. If not, we quit the program by sending the WM_DESTROY message:

```
SendMessage ( hWnd,
              WM_DESTROY,
              0,
              0 );
```

The WM_CHAR Case

The WM_CHAR message is received whenever the user presses a key on the keyboard. Under the WM_CHAR case we first convert the character to an uppercase, and then check to see if the character is the **B** character. If the received character is the **B** or **b** character, we execute the BarkingShow() function:

```
/*--------------------
Convert to uppercase.
-------------------*/
wParam = toupper ( wParam );

switch ( wParam )
```

```
{
case 'B':
        /*--------------
        Make the dog bark.
        ----------------*/
        BarkingShow ( hWnd );
        return 0;
```

The *WM_LBUTTONDOWN* Case

The WM_LBUTTONDOWN message is received whenever the user presses the left mouse button. The lParam of this message is the x,y pixel coordinates of the mouse location at the time of clicking. The low byte of lParam is the x coordinate, and the high byte of lParam is the y coordinate. Under the WM_LBUTTONDOWN case we check if the left button was clicked within the rectangular of the bone bit map. Because in the WM_CREATE case we displayed the bone at pixel location (10,10), and the length and width of the bone is 32 × 125 pixels, the following if statement is satisfied if the bone was clicked (see Figure 6.7):

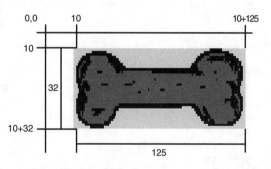

Figure 6.7. The pixel coordinates of the bone.

```
if (
    /*------------
    The Bone area.
    ------------*/
    LOWORD ( lParam ) < 10 +  125   &&
    LOWORD ( lParam ) > 10          &&
    HIWORD ( lParam ) < 200 + 32    &&
    HIWORD ( lParam ) > 200
    )
```

```
{
/*-------------
Make the dog bark.
---------------*/
BarkingShow ( hWnd );
}
return 0L;
```

The *BarkingShow()* Function

The BarkingShow() function causes the dog to bark, and to open and close its mouth. It is accomplished in a for() loop:

```
for ( iNumberOfPlays = 0; iNumberOfPlays < 4; iNumberOfPlays++)
    {
    PlayIt ( hWnd );
    }
```

The for() loop simply executes the PlayIt() function four times.

After completing the for() loop, we execute the DisplayDogWithClose() function:

```
DisplayDogWithClose ( hWnd );
```

The DisplayDogWithClose() function simply displays the dog with its mouth closed, because at the end of the barking, we want the dog to remain on-screen with its mouth closed.

The *PlayIt()* Function

The PlayIt() function uses a while(1) loop as its main component:

```
long lCurrentByte = 0L;

while (1)
     {
     lCurrentByte = sp_PlayF ( lCurrentByte,
                               lCurrentByte + 2000L );

     if ( lCurrentByte == 0L )
        {
        break;
        }
```

```
..............................
.......... The animation ..........
..............................
}
```

The body of the while(1) loop plays the sound file starting at location 0L. The file plays in groups of 2,000 bytes each. Here is how it works:

Recall that the sp_PlayF() function returns the last byte played. This means that the variable lCurrentByte is updated with the value of 2000L after the playback of the first 2,000 bytes.

The next play plays the next 2,000 bytes, from byte location 2,000 to byte location 4,000.

This process continues until the complete file is played.

In fact, eventually the second parameter of sp_PlayF() will exceed the size of the sound file, and as previously discussed, the TSEngine will play up to the last byte of the sound file and sp_PlayF() will return 0L.

The while(1) loop is terminated upon discovering that the sp_PlayF() function returned 0L:

```
if ( lCurrentByte == 0L )
    {
    break; /* break from the while(1) loop. */
    }
```

So where is the animation? The animation is accomplished after the playback of each 2,000 group. Of course, when users execute the dog program they get the impression that the dog moves and barks simultaneously. We know, however, that the PC has a single CPU and can only perform one task at a time. Yet we insert the animation between the playback of groups, giving users the illusion that the barking and the dog's movement are done simultaneously.

Is 2,000 bytes per group a good number? Lets do the calculations:

The Bark.ts sound file was recorded at a sampling rate of 8,000 hertz. Using the formula for TS-type

$$[\text{ \# of seconds }] = \frac{[\text{ Number of bytes }]}{[\text{Sampling rate in Hertz}]}$$

the number of seconds it takes to play 2,000 bytes is

$$[\text{ \# of seconds }] = \frac{[\text{ 2,000 }]}{[\text{ 8,000 }]} = 0.25 \text{ sec.} = 250 \text{ milliseconds.}$$

Considering that the displaying process takes less than 1 millisecond, to the human brain, the whole process (the movement of the images and the playback of the sound) appears simultaneously.

It is important to remember that the animation code is done in real-time, between playback of groups. As such, your animation code should be as efficient as possible. The less time the program spends between playback of groups, the better.

Here is the animation code of the Dog program:

```
if ( iMouthFlag == 0 )
    {
    /*---------------------------------
    Display the dog with its mouth open.
    ----------------------------------*/
    iMouthFlag = 1;
    DisplayDogWithOpen  ( hWnd );
    continue;
    }

if ( iMouthFlag == 1 )
    {
    /*----------------------------------
    Display the dog with its mouth closed.
    ----------------------------------*/
    iMouthFlag = 0;
    DisplayDogWithClose ( hWnd );
    continue;
    }
```

We have a flag called iMouthFlag that indicates the current position of the dog's mouth. A value of 1 indicates that the dog's mouth is closed, and a value of 0 indicates that the dog's mouth is open.

When you enter the while(1) loop for the first time, the value of iMouthFlag is 0. We detect this fact with the if statement. We then change the value of the flag to 1, and display the dog with its mouth open by executing the function:

```
DisplayDogWithOpen  ( hWnd );
```

Then we use the continue statement to return to the beginning of the while(1) loop.

The body of the while(1) loop is executed again, playing the next 2,000 bytes, and because now the flag is equal to 1, the second if statement is satisfied, changing the flag back to 0, displaying the dog with its mouth open, and returning to the beginning of the while(1) loop by executing the continue statement.

This process continues until the returned value from sp_PlayF() is 0L, indicating that the whole file played.

The *DisplayDogWithOpen()* and *DisplayDogWithClose()* Functions

The functions that are responsible for displaying the dog with its mouth open and closed are the DisplayDogWithOpen() and DisplayDogWithClose(). These two functions simply utilize the BitBlt() function to display the dog with the appropriate bit map.

The HearMe Program

The HearMe program is a simple program that displays a push button and a picture of a man in its main window. When the user pushes the push button (or presses the **H** keys), the program says *Press any key to continue.*

As the PC speaks, the mouth of the person is moving as if the voice is coming out of his mouth. (The man also blinks from time to time as he speaks.)

This program just says *Press any key to continue....* You can upgrade it to say any sound file. As such, the program may replace your usual README.TXT files. That is, if you have something to say to your users, then send them a HearMe file rather then a ReadMe file. No doubt, your HearMe file will receive more attention and respect than a ReadMe file.

The Files of the HearMe Program

The HearMe program consists of the following files:

HearMe.h	The #include file of the program.
HearMe.c	The C code of the program.
HearMe.rc	The resource file of the program.
HearMe.def	The module definition file of theprogram.
HearMe.mak	The make file of the program.
Tape.ico	The icon of the program.

FaceOpen.bmp	The Face bit map with open mouth.
FaceClose.bmp	The Face bit map with closed mouth.
FaceMid.bmp	The Face bit map with different facial expressions.

These files are provided for you in c:\spSDK\Samp4Win\.

We recommend that you compile, link, and execute the HearMe program before going over its code. This way you'll gain a better understanding of what the program is supposed to do.

Compiling, Linking, and Executing the HearMe Program

To compile and link the program with the Microsoft compiler:

- Make sure your PC is in a DOS-protected mode.

- Log into c:\spSDK\Samp4Win\.

- At the DOS prompt type

  `NMAKE HearMe.mak`   {Enter}

To execute the HearMe program:

- Select Run from the File menu of the Program Manager of Windows.

- Use Browse to select the file

  `C:\spSDK\Samp4Win\HearHe.exe`

The main window appears, as shown in Figure 6.8. The main menu is shown in Figure 6.9.

Figure 6.8. The main window of HearMe.

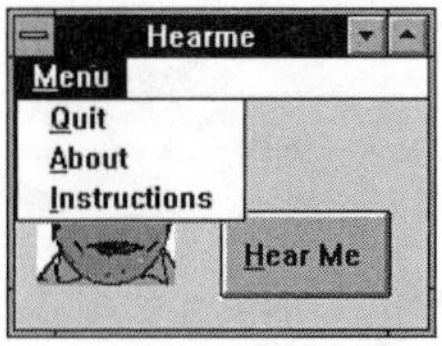

Figure 6.9. The main menu of the HearMe window.

When the user selects the About option from the menu, the About dialog box appears, as shown in Figure 6.10. When the user selects the Instructions option, the Instructions dialog box appears, as shown in Figure 6.11.

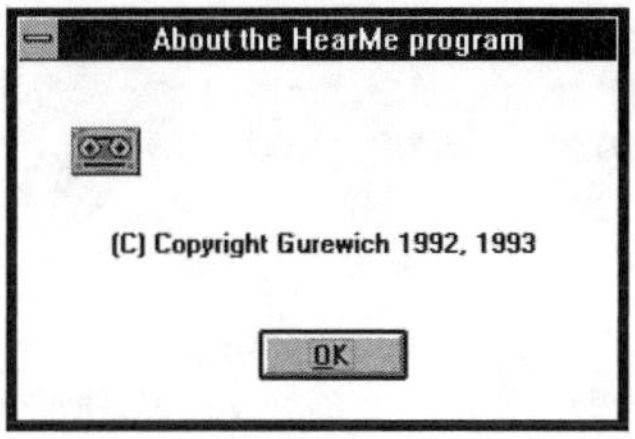

Figure 6.10. The About dialog box of the HearMe program.

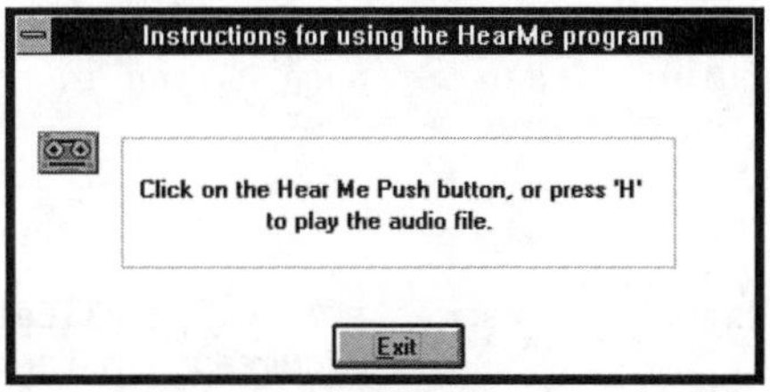

Figure 6.11. The Instructions dialog box of the HearMe program.

When the user pushes the Hear Me push button that appears in the main window, the man starts saying *Press any key to continue....* While speaking, the man opens and closes his mouth, and blinks.

A complete listing of the HearMe program is shown in Listings 6.6 through 6.10.

Listing 6.6. HearMe.h.

```c
/*=====================================================
 FILE NAME: Hearme.h

 (C) Copyright Gurewich 1992, 1993
 =====================================================*/

/*---------
 prototypes
 ---------*/
long FAR PASCAL _export WndProc      ( HWND, UINT, UINT, LONG ) ;
BOOL FAR PASCAL _export AboutDlgProc ( HWND, UINT, UINT, LONG ) ;
BOOL FAR PASCAL _export InstDlgProc  ( HWND, UINT, UINT, LONG ) ;

void SpeakShow            ( HWND hWnd );
void DisplayFaceWithOpen  ( HWND hWnd );
void DisplayFaceWithClose ( HWND hWnd );
void DisplayFaceWithMid   ( HWND hWnd );

/*------
 #define
 ------*/
#define IDM_QUIT          1  /* The Quit option in the menu. */
#define IDM_ABOUT         2  /* The About option in the menu. */
#define IDM_INSTRUCTIONS  3  /* The Instructions option in the menu.*/


#define EXIT_PB    100 /* "Exit" push button in the instructions box.*/
#define HEARME_PB  101 /* "Hear Me" push button in the main window.   */

/*---------------
 Global variables
 ---------------*/
char       gszAppName[] = "Hearme" ; /* Our application name. */
HINSTANCE  ghInst;                   /* current instance.      */
HBRUSH     ghBrushOfBkGnd;           /* For the brush.         */
HBITMAP    ghFaceWithOpenMouth;  /* For the FaceOpen  bit map.  */
HBITMAP    ghFaceWithCloseMouth; /* For the FaceClose bit map.  */
HBITMAP    ghFaceWithMidMouth;   /* For the FaceMid   bit map.  */
```

Listing 6.7. HearMe.c.

```c
/*===============================================================
  PROGRAM: Hearme.c
  -------
  (C) Copyright 1992, 1993 Gurewich. (R) All rights reserved.

  PROGRAM DESCRIPTION:
  -------------------
  This is a Generic type 1 program.

  This is a visual-audio HearMe file.

  =============================================================*/

/*---------
  #include
  --------*/
/*------------------------------------
  Required for all Windows applications.
  ------------------------------------*/
#include <windows.h>

/*-----------------------------------------------------------------
  Required so that sp_ functions, SP_ macros and #definitions
  from the TS C sound library may be used in this applications.
  ---------------------------------------------------------------*/
#include "c:\spSDK\TegoWlib\sp4Win.h"

/*--------------------------------------------------------
  Definitions & prototypes specific to this application.
  ------------------------------------------------------*/
#include "c:\spSDK\Samp4WIN\Hearme.h"

/*------------------------------------------------
  For standard C functions used in this application.
  ----------------------------------------------*/
#include <stdlib.h>
#include <stdio.h>

/*==================
  FUNCTION: WinMain()
  ==================*/
int PASCAL WinMain ( HANDLE hInstance,
                     HANDLE hPrevInstance,
                     LPSTR  lpszCmdLine,
                     int    nCmdShow )
```

continues

Listing 6.7. continued

```
{
/*-------------------------
Local and static variables.
-------------------------*/
HWND      hWnd;    /* Handler to the window of our application.  */
MSG       msg;     /* Message to be processed by our application. */
WNDCLASS  wc;      /* Window class of our application.           */

HBITMAP   hBitmapOfBkGnd; /* For the background. */

/*--------------------------------------------
 Make the hInstance variable a global variable.
----------------------------------------------*/
ghInst = hInstance;

/*----------------------------------
Create the brush for the background.
----------------------------*/
hBitmapOfBkGnd = LoadBitmap ( ghInst, "BackGround"  );
ghBrushOfBkGnd = CreatePatternBrush ( hBitmapOfBkGnd );

/*---------------------------------------------
Update the window class structure and register
the window class.
----------------------------------------------*/
if ( !hPrevInstance )
    {
    /*---------------------------------------------
    The "if" is satisfied, this is the very 1st
    run of this application.
    ----------------------------------------*/
    wc.style         = CS_HREDRAW ¦ CS_VREDRAW ;
    wc.lpfnWndProc   = WndProc ;
    wc.cbClsExtra    = 0 ;
    wc.cbWndExtra    = 0 ;
    wc.hInstance     = ghInst ;
    wc.hIcon         = LoadIcon   ( ghInst, "IconOfTape" ) ;
    wc.hCursor       = LoadCursor ( NULL, IDC_ARROW       ) ;
    wc.hbrBackground = ghBrushOfBkGnd; /* The brush that we created */
                                       /*  with the bit map.        */
    wc.lpszMenuName  = gszAppName ;
    wc.lpszClassName = gszAppName ;
```

```
    /*------------------
    Register the window.
    ----------------*/
    RegisterClass ( &wc );

    }/* end of if(!hPrevInstance) */


/*-----------------------------------
  Create the window of our application.
  -----------------------------------*/
hWnd = CreateWindow ( gszAppName,
                      gszAppName,
                      WS_OVERLAPPEDWINDOW,
                      50,
                      50,
                      50+150,
                      50+100,
                      NULL,
                      NULL,
                      ghInst,
                      NULL );
/*---------------------------------------------
  Show and update the window of our application.
  ---------------------------------------------*/
ShowWindow    ( hWnd, nCmdShow );
UpdateWindow  ( hWnd );

/*---------------
  The message loop.
  ---------------*/
while ( GetMessage ( &msg, NULL, 0, 0 ) )
     {
     TranslateMessage ( &msg );
     DispatchMessage  ( &msg );
     }

/*------------------------------------------------------------
  Delete the memory and brush objects used for the background.
  ------------------------------------------------------------*/
DeleteObject ( hBitmapOfBkGnd );
DeleteObject ( ghBrushOfBkGnd );

return msg.wParam ;

} /* end of function. */
/*========================= end of WinMain() ====================*/
```

continues

Listing 6.7. continued

```
/*==================
 FUNCTION: WndProc()
 =================*/
/*-----------------------------
 DESCRIPTION: Processes messages.
 -----------------------------*/
long FAR PASCAL _export WndProc ( HWND hWnd,
                                  UINT message,
                                  UINT wParam,
                                  LONG lParam )

{
/*--------------------------
 Local and static variables.
 --------------------------*/
HDC          hdc;      /* Needed for displaying. */
PAINTSTRUCT ps;        /* Needed for displaying. */
HDC          hMemDC;   /* For the Face bit map.  */

static FARPROC lpfnAboutDlgProc; /* For the About        dialog box.*/
static FARPROC lpfnInstDlgProc ; /* For the Instructions dialog box.*/

int     iOpenFaceResult;
int     iOpenHelloResult;

static HWND      hButton;

switch ( message )
        {
        case WM_CREATE:
            /*---------------------------
            Open the HearMe sound session.
            --------------------------*/
            iOpenFaceResult = sp_OpenSession (
                                "c:\\spSDK\\Sfiles\\Press.s",
                                SP_NON_STAND_ALONE,
                                0L,
                                SP_S_TYPE);
            /*------------------------
            Quit if can't open the file.
            ------------------------*/
            if ( iOpenFaceResult != SP_NO_ERRORS )
                {
```

```
      MessageBox ( NULL,
               "Failed to open the sound session!",
               "Message from Hearme.c",
                MB_ICONINFORMATION );

   /*------------------
   Quit the application.
   ------------------*/
   SendMessage ( hWnd, WM_DESTROY, 0, 0 );
   }

/*---------------------------------------------------------
Obtain the lpfnAboutDlgProc of the About the dialog box.
---------------------------------------------------------*/
lpfnAboutDlgProc =
MakeProcInstance (( FARPROC) AboutDlgProc, ghInst);

/*----------------------------------------------------------
Obtain the lpfnInstDlgProc of the Instructions dialog box.
----------------------------------------------------------*/
lpfnInstDlgProc =
MakeProcInstance (( FARPROC) InstDlgProc, ghInst);

/*------------------------------------
Obtain the handler of the Face bit maps.
------------------------------------*/
ghFaceWithOpenMouth  = LoadBitmap ( ghInst, "FaceOpen"  );
ghFaceWithCloseMouth = LoadBitmap ( ghInst, "FaceClose" );
ghFaceWithMidMouth   = LoadBitmap ( ghInst, "FaceMid"   );

/*----------------------------
Create the Hear Me push button.
----------------------------*/
hButton = CreateWindow ( "BUTTON",
                    "&Hear Me",
                    WS_CHILD|WS_VISIBLE|BS_PUSHBUTTON,
                    10 + 85,
                    50,
                    80,
                    40,
                    hWnd,
                    HEARME_PB,
                    ghInst,
                    NULL);
```

continues

Listing 6.7. continued

```
            ShowWindow ( hButton, SW_SHOW );

            return 0;

    case WM_PAINT:
            /*---------------------------------
            Paint the face with its mouth closed.
            --------------------------------*/
            hdc = BeginPaint ( hWnd, &ps );
            hMemDC = CreateCompatibleDC ( hdc );
            SelectObject ( hMemDC, ghFaceWithCloseMouth );
            BitBlt ( hdc,
                    10,
                    20,
                    10+64,
                    10+64,
                    hMemDC,
                    0,
                    0,
                    SRCCOPY );
            DeleteDC ( hMemDC );
            EndPaint ( hWnd, &ps );

            return 0;

    case WM_COMMAND:
            /*----------------
            Process menu items.
            ----------------*/
            switch (wParam)
                    {
                    case HEARME_PB:
                            SetFocus  ( hWnd );
                            SpeakShow ( hWnd );
                            return 0;

                    case IDM_QUIT:
                            /*-----------------------
                            User clicked on Quit option.
                            -----------------------*/
                            DestroyWindow (hWnd);
                            return 0L;
```

```
                    case IDM_ABOUT :
                            /*-------------------------
                            User clicked on About option.
                            ------------------------*/
                            DialogBox ( ghInst,
                                        "AboutBox",
                                        hWnd,
                                        lpfnAboutDlgProc );

                            return 0L;

                    case IDM_INSTRUCTIONS :
                            /*--------------------------------
                            User clicked on Instructions option.
                            -------------------------------*/
                            DialogBox ( ghInst,
                                        "InstructionsBox",
                                        hWnd,
                                        lpfnInstDlgProc );
                            return 0L;

                    }/* end of switch (wParam) */


        case WM_CHAR:
            /*---------------------------------
            User pressed a key on the keyboard.
            --------------------------------*/

            /*--------------------
            Convert to uppercase.
            -------------------*/
            wParam = toupper ( wParam );

            switch ( wParam )
                    {
                    case 'H':
                            /*----------------
                            Make the face speak.
                            -----------------*/
                            SpeakShow ( hWnd );
                            return 0;
                    }
            return 0L;
```

continues

Listing 6.7. continued

```
                    case WM_DESTROY:
            /*-------------------------------
            Open the Hello.ts sound session.
            ------------------------------*/
            iOpenHelloResult =
               sp_OpenSession ( "c:\\spSDK\\TSfiles\\Hello.ts",
                                SP_NON_STAND_ALONE,
                                0L,
                                SP_TS_TYPE ) ;

            if ( iOpenHelloResult == SP_NO_ERRORS )
               {
               /*-------------------------------
               Play a section of the sound file.
               Range to play: 30,000 to 40,000
               phrase: "Good-Bye"
               -------------------------------*/
               sp_PlayF ( 30000L, 40000L ) ;
               }

            /*-----------------
            Delete the bit maps.
            ------------------*/
            DeleteObject ( ghFaceWithCloseMouth );
            DeleteObject ( ghFaceWithMidMouth   );
            DeleteObject ( ghFaceWithOpenMouth  );

            PostQuitMessage (0);
            return 0;
      }/* end of switch (message) */

/*-----------------------
 Message was not processed.
 ----------------------*/
return DefWindowProc ( hWnd, message, wParam, lParam ) ;

}/* end of WndProc() */
/*=================== end of WndProc() ====================*/

/*=======================
 FUNCTION: AboutDlgProc()
 ======================*/
/*----------------------------------------
 DESCRIPTION:
 This is the About dialog box procedure.
 ---------------------------------------*/
BOOL FAR PASCAL _export AboutDlgProc ( HWND hDlg,
                                       UINT message,
```

```
                                              UINT wParam,
                                              LONG lParam )
{
switch ( message )
        {
        case WM_INITDIALOG :
               return TRUE;

        case WM_COMMAND :
              switch ( wParam )
                     {
                     case IDOK :
                     case IDCANCEL :
                          EndDialog ( hDlg, 0 );
                          return TRUE;
                     }
        }/* end of switch(message) */
return FALSE ;
}/* End of function. */
/*============== end of AboutDlgProc() ==============*/


/*=====================
 FUNCTION: InstDlgProc()
 ====================*/
/*---------------------------------------------
 DESCRIPTION:
 This is the Instructions dialog box procedure.
 ---------------------------------------------*/
BOOL FAR PASCAL _export InstDlgProc ( HWND hDlg,
                                      UINT message,
                                      UINT wParam,
                                      LONG lParam )

{
switch ( message )
        {
        case WM_INITDIALOG :
              return TRUE;

        case WM_COMMAND :
              switch ( wParam )
                     {
                     case EXIT_PB :
                     case IDOK :
                     case IDCANCEL :
                          EndDialog ( hDlg, 0 );
                          return TRUE;
                     }
        }
return FALSE ;
}/* End of function. */
/*============== end of InstDlgProc() ==============*/
```

continues

Listing 6.7. continued

```c
/*========
 FUNCTION
 ========*/
/*--------------------------------
 DESCRIPTION:
 -----------
 Make the face speak.
 -------------------------------*/
void SpeakShow ( HWND hWnd )
{
int  iMouthFlag  = 0;
long lCurrentByte = 0L;

while (1)
    {
    lCurrentByte = sp_PlayF ( lCurrentByte,
                              lCurrentByte + 2000L );

    if ( lCurrentByte == 0L )
        {
        break;
        }

    if ( iMouthFlag == 0 )
        {
        /*-----------------------------------
        Display the face with its mouth open.
        -----------------------------------*/
        iMouthFlag = 1;
        DisplayFaceWithOpen  ( hWnd );
        continue;
        }

    if ( iMouthFlag == 1 )
        {
        /*-----------------------------------
        Display the face with its mouth closed.
        -----------------------------------*/
        iMouthFlag = 2;
        DisplayFaceWithClose ( hWnd );
        continue;
        }

    if ( iMouthFlag == 2 )
        {
```

```
          /*----------------------------------------
          Display the face with its mouth closed.
          ----------------------------------------*/
          iMouthFlag = 0;
          DisplayFaceWithMid ( hWnd );
          continue;
          }

     }/* end of the while() loop. */

DisplayFaceWithClose ( hWnd );

}/* end of function. */
/*============ end of function ===========*/

/*========
 FUNCTION
 ========*/
/*-----------------------------------
 DESCRIPTION:
 -----------
 Display the face with its mouth open.
 -------------------------------*/
void DisplayFaceWithOpen ( HWND hWnd )
{
HDC hdc;
HDC hMemDC;

/*---------------------------------
 Draw the face with its mouth open.
 -------------------------------*/
hdc = GetDC ( hWnd );
hMemDC = CreateCompatibleDC ( hdc );
SelectObject ( hMemDC, ghFaceWithOpenMouth );

BitBlt ( hdc,
         10,
         20,
         10+64,
         10+64,
         hMemDC,
         0,
         0,
         SRCCOPY );

DeleteDC ( hMemDC );
ReleaseDC ( hWnd, hdc   );
}
/*============ end of function ===========*/
```

continues

Listing 6.7. continued

```c
/*========
 FUNCTION
 ========*/
/*------------------------------------
 DESCRIPTION:
 ----------
 Display the face with its mouth closed.
 ------------------------------------*/
void DisplayFaceWithClose ( HWND hWnd )
{
static HDC hdc;
static HDC hMemDC;

/*------------------------------------
 Draw the face with its mouth closed.
 ----------------------------------*/
hdc = GetDC ( hWnd );
hMemDC = CreateCompatibleDC ( hdc );
SelectObject ( hMemDC, ghFaceWithCloseMouth );

BitBlt ( hdc,
         10,
         20,
         10+64,
         10+64,
         hMemDC,
         0,
         0,
         SRCCOPY );

DeleteDC ( hMemDC );
ReleaseDC ( hWnd, hdc   );
}
/*============ end of function ==========*/

/*========
 FUNCTION
 ========*/
/*------------------------------------
 DESCRIPTION:
 ----------
 Display the face with mouth half open.
 ------------------------------------*/
void DisplayFaceWithMid ( HWND hWnd )
{
HDC hdc;
HDC hMemDC;
```

```
/*---------------------------------------
 Draw the face with its mouth half open.
 ---------------------------------------*/
hdc = GetDC ( hWnd );
hMemDC = CreateCompatibleDC ( hdc );
SelectObject ( hMemDC, ghFaceWithMidMouth );

BitBlt ( hdc,
         10,
         20,
         10+64,
         10+64,
         hMemDC,
         0,
         0,
         SRCCOPY );

DeleteDC ( hMemDC );
ReleaseDC ( hWnd, hdc   );
}
/*============ end of function ===========*/
```

Listing 6.8. HearMe.rc.

```
/*===================================================
 FILE NAME: Hearme.rc
 ---------

 FILE DESCRIPTION:
 ---------------
 The resource file.

 (C) Copyright Gurewich 1992, 1993


 ===================================================*/

/*-------
 #include
 -------*/
#include <windows.h>
#include "Hearme.h"

/*----
 Menu
 ----*/
HearMe   MENU
```

continues

Listing 6.8. continued

```
BEGIN
   POPUP   "&Menu"
      BEGIN
         MENUITEM "&Quit",          IDM_QUIT
         MENUITEM "&About",         IDM_ABOUT
         MENUITEM "&Instructions", IDM_INSTRUCTIONS
      END
END

/*-----------------------------------------
 Definition of the Cassette tape icon.
 File name: Tape.ico
 Icon name: IconOfTape
 -----------------------------------------*/
IconOfTape ICON Tape.ico

/*---------
 Bit maps.
 --------*/
FaceOpen       BITMAP FaceOpen.bmp
FaceClose      BITMAP FaceClos.bmp
FaceMid        BITMAP FaceMid.bmp
BackGround     BITMAP BackGnd.bmp

/*-------------------
 The About dialog box.
 -----------------*/
AboutBox DIALOG 81, 43, 160, 100
STYLE DS_MODALFRAME | WS_POPUP | WS_VISIBLE |
                     WS_CAPTION | WS_SYSMENU
CAPTION "About the HearMe program"
FONT 8, "MS Sans Serif"
BEGIN
    PUSHBUTTON      "&OK", IDOK, 64, 75, 40, 14
    CTEXT           "(C) Copyright Gurewich 1992, 1993",
                    -1, 13, 47, 137, 18
    ICON            "IconOfTape", -1, 14, 12, 18, 20
END

/*--------------------------
 The Instructions dialog box.
 -------------------------*/
InstructionsBox DIALOG 41, 45, 222, 100
STYLE DS_MODALFRAME | WS_POPUP | WS_VISIBLE |
                     WS_CAPTION | WS_SYSMENU
CAPTION "Instructions for using the HearMe program"
FONT 8, "MS Sans Serif"
```

```
BEGIN
    PUSHBUTTON      "&Exit", EXIT_PB, 95, 84, 40, 14
    CTEXT           "Click on the Hear Me Push button, or press 'H'",
                    -1, 37, 38, 152, 13
    CTEXT           "to play the audio file.", -1, 47, 48, 125, 8
    CONTROL         "", -1, "Static", SS_GRAYFRAME, 32, 26, 166, 41
    ICON            "IconOfTape", -1, 7, 18, 18, 20
END
```

Listing 6.9. HearMe.def.

```
;======================================
; module-definition file for HearMe.c
;======================================

NAME            HearMe

DESCRIPTION     'The HearMe program. (C) Copyright Gurewich 1992, 1993'

EXETYPE         WINDOWS

STUB            'WINSTUB.EXE'

CODE   PRELOAD MOVEABLE DISCARDABLE

DATA   PRELOAD MOVEABLE MULTIPLE

HEAPSIZE        1024
STACKSIZE       8192
```

Listing 6.10. HearMe.mak.

```
#=============
# Hearme.mak
#=============

Hearme.exe : Hearme.obj Hearme.h Hearme.def Hearme.res
    link /nod Hearme.obj, Hearme.exe, NUL, \
        slibcew.lib oldnames.lib libw.lib commdlg \
        c:\spSDK\TegoWlib\TegoWin.lib, \
        Hearme.def
    rc -t Hearme.res
```

continues

Listing 6.10. continued

```
Hearme.obj : Hearme.c Hearme.h
    cl -c -G2sw -Ow -W3 -Zp  Hearme.c

Hearme.res : Hearme.rc Hearme.h Tape.ico
    rc -r Hearme.rc
```

Saying Good-Bye and Quitting the Program

When the user selects Close from the system menu, or Quit from the program menu, the program says *Good-Bye* and quits. Note that we play the *Good-Bye* only if the session of the sound file c:\spSDK\TSfiles\Hello.ts opens success-fully.

Facial Expressions of the HearMe Program

The HearMe program contains three bit maps for the different facial expres-sions:

1. The FaceOpen.bmp (see Figure 6.12) shows the man with his mouth open.

2. The FaceClose.bmp (see Figure 6.13) shows the man with his mouth closed.

3. The FaceMid.bmp (see Figure 6.14) shows the man with his mouth open in a different way (more teeth show), and his eyes half closed.

Figure 6.12. The FaceOpen.bmp.

Figure 6.13. The FaceClose.bmp.

Figure 6.14. The FaceMid.bmp.

Playing and Animating

The SpeakShow() function is called whenever the user pushes the Hear Me push button (under the HEARME_PB case), and whenever the user presses the H key (under the WM_CHAR case).

The SpeakShow() function uses a while(1) loop as its main component:

```
long lCurrentByte = 0L;

while (1)
    {
    lCurrentByte = sp_PlayF ( lCurrentByte,
                              lCurrentByte + 2000L );

    if ( lCurrentByte == 0L )
        {
        break;
        }
```

```
. . . . . . . . . . . . . . . . . . . . . . . . . . . . . . . . .
. . . . . . . . . . The animation . . . . . . . . . .
. . . . . . . . . . . . . . . . . . . . . . . . . . . . . . . . .
    }/* end of the while() loop. */
```

The body of the while(1) loop plays the sound file starting at location 0L. The file plays in groups of 2,000 bytes each. Here is how it works:

The sp_PlayF() function returns the last byte played. This means that the variable lCurrentByte is updated with the value of 2000L after the playback of the first 2,000 bytes. The next play plays the next 2,000 bytes, from byte location 2,000 to byte location 4,000. This process continues until the complete file is played.

When the second parameter of sp_PlayF() exceeds the size of the sound file, the TSEngine plays up to last byte of the sound file and sp_PlayF() returns 0L. The while(1) loop is terminated upon discovering that sp_PlayF() returned 0L:

```
if ( lCurrentByte == 0L )
  {
  break; /* break from the while(1) loop. */
  }
```

To give the illusion that the playback of the sound occurs simultaneously with the animation, we must make sure that the playback time of each group is small enough. So let's calculate the playback time of each 2,000 bytes.

The Press.s sound file was recorded at a sampling rate of 40,000 hertz. Using the formula for S sound type

$$[\text{\# of seconds}] = \frac{[\text{Number of bytes}] \times 8}{[\text{Sampling rate in Hertz}]}$$

the number of seconds it takes to play 2,000 bytes is

$$[\text{\# of seconds}] = \frac{[2,000] \times 8}{[40,000]} = 0.4 \text{ sec.} = 400 \text{ milliseconds.}$$

Considering that the displaying process takes less than 1 millisecond to the human brain, the whole process (the movement of the images and the playback of the sound) appears simultaneously.

Remember that the animation code is done in real-time, between playback of groups. As such, the animation code should be as efficient as possible. The less time the program spends between playback of groups, the better.

Let's take a look at the animation code of the HearMe program:

```
if ( iMouthFlag == 0 )
    {
    /*----------------------------------
    Display the face with its mouth open.
    ----------------------------------*/
    iMouthFlag = 1;
    DisplayFaceWithOpen  ( hWnd );
    continue;
    }

if ( iMouthFlag == 1 )
    {
    /*----------------------------------
    Display the face with its mouth closed.
    ----------------------------------*/
    iMouthFlag = 2;
    DisplayFaceWithClose ( hWnd );
    continue;
    }

if ( iMouthFlag == 2 )
    {
    /*----------------------------------
    Display the face with its mouth closed.
    ----------------------------------*/
    iMouthFlag = 0;
    DisplayFaceWithMid ( hWnd );
    continue;
    }
```

We have a flag called iMouthFlag that indicates the current position of the man's mouth. A value of 0 indicates that the man's mouth should open, a value of 1 indicates that the man's mouth should close, and a value of 2 indicates that the man's mouth should half open.

When you enter the while(1) loop for the first time, the value of iMouthFlag is 0. We detect this fact with the if statement. We then change the value of the flag to 1, and display the man with his mouth open by executing the function

```
DisplayFaceWithOpen  ( hWnd );
```

Then we use the continue statement to return to the beginning of the while(1) loop.

The body of the while(1) loop is executed again, playing the next 2,000 bytes. The flag is now equal to 1, the second if statement is satisfied, changing the flag to 2 and displaying the man with his mouth closed, and returning to the beginning of the while(1) loop by executing the continue statement.

The body of the while(1) loop is executed again, playing the next 2,000 bytes, and because the flag is now equal to 2, the third if statement is satisfied, changing the flag back to 0, displaying the man with his mouth half open, and returning to the beginning of the while(1) loop by executing the continue statement.

This process continues until the returned value from sp_PlayF() is 0L, indicating that the whole file played. Upon discovering that the whole sound file played, we break from the while(1) loop:

```
if ( lCurrentByte == 0L )
   {
   break;
   }
```

The *DisplayFaceWithOpen()*, *DisplayFaceWithClose()*, and *DisplayFaceWithMid()* Functions

The functions responsible for displaying the man with his mouth open, closed, and half open are DisplayFaceWithOpen(), DisplayFaceWithClose(), and DisplayFaceWithMid(). These three functions simply utilize the BitBlt() function to display the man with the appropriate facial expression bit map.

Note that the SpeakShow() function terminates with the execution of DisplayFaceWithClose(); now, at the end of the show, the man remains onscreen with his mouth closed.

Improving the HearMe Program

You can even improve the HearMe program. For example, you can generate HearMe files that play your own voice as well as display your own face. This is accomplished by using an off-the-shelf, inexpensive scanner device that transforms a picture of your face from a paper picture to a .BMP file. Of course, you'll have to scan several pictures of yourself: one picture with your mouth closed, another picture with your mouth opened, and maybe several other pictures showing your face with raised eyebrows, closed eyes, and any other facial expressions that may be appropriate.

You can also improve the program by synchronizing the facial expression with the words spoken. For example, when the program says *I*, the face opens its mouth; when the program says *Up*, the face opens and immediately closes its mouth, and so on. To accomplish this, you need to synchronize the phonemes with the animation.

The Dance Program

The Dance program is a small show that shows a couple dancing to music. This program puts to use many of the topics that we have already covered.

Compiling, Linking, and Executing the Dance Program

To compile and link the Dance program with the Microsoft compiler:

- Make sure your PC is in a DOS-protected mode.
- Log into c:\spSDK\Samp4Win\.
- At the DOS prompt type

  `NMAKE  Dance.mak` {Enter}

To compile and link the Dance program with the Borland compiler:

- Log into c:\spSDK\Samp4Win.
- At the DOS prompt type

  `MAKE -f Dance.bmk` {Enter}

To execute the Dance program:

- Select Run from the File menu of the Program Manager of Windows.
- Click Browse and select the file

  `c:\spSDK\Samp4Win\Dance.exe`

The main window appears, as shown in Figure 6.15. As you can see, it displays a picture of a couple ready to perform a dance act; it also displays the Dance push button.

The Dance program menu (see Figure 6.16) contains three options: Quit, About, and Instructions. When you select the Quit option, the program says *Good-Bye* and terminates. When you select the About option, the About dialog box appears. When you select the Instructions option, the Instructions dialog box appears as shown in Figure 6.17. When you select the Dance push button, the couple dances to music.

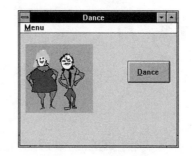

Figure 6.15. The main window of the Dance program.

Figure 6.16. The main menu of the Dance program.

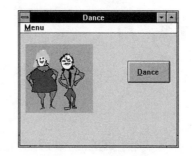

Figure 6.17. The Instructions dialog box of the Dance program.

The Files of the Dance Program

The Dance program consists of the following files:

Dance.h	The #include file of the program.
Dance.c	The C code of the program.
Dance.rc	The resource file of the program.
Dance.def	The module definition file of the program.
Dance.mak	The make file of the program.
Tape.ico	The icon of the program.
BackGnd.bmp	The bit map used for the background of the main window.
Dance0.bmp	Position #0 of the dance.
Dance1.bmp	Position #1 of the dance.
Dance2.bmp	Position #2 of the dance.
Dance3.bmp	Position #3 of the dance.
Dance4.bmp	Position #4 of the dance.
Dance5.bmp	The Credit frame.

These files are provided for you in c:\spSDK\Samp4Win\.

The complete listing of the Dance program is shown in Listings 6.11 through 6.15.

Listing 6.11. Dance.h.

```
/*====================================================
FILE NAME: Dance.h

(C) Copyright Gurewich 1992, 1993
====================================================*/

/*..........
prototypes
..........*/
long FAR PASCAL _export WndProc       ( HWND, UINT, UINT, LONG ) ;
BOOL FAR PASCAL _export AboutDlgProc ( HWND, UINT, UINT, LONG ) ;
BOOL FAR PASCAL _export InstDlgProc  ( HWND, UINT, UINT, LONG ) ;
```

continues

Listing 6.11. continued

```
void DanceShow          ( HWND hWnd );
void DisplayDanceAct0   ( HWND hWnd );
void DisplayDanceAct1   ( HWND hWnd );
void DisplayDanceAct2   ( HWND hWnd );
void DisplayDanceAct3   ( HWND hWnd );
void DisplayDanceAct4   ( HWND hWnd );
void DisplayDanceAct5   ( HWND hWnd );

/*------
 #define
 ------*/
#define IDM_QUIT         1 /* The Quit         option in the menu. */
#define IDM_ABOUT        2 /* The About        option in the menu. */
#define IDM_INSTRUCTIONS 3 /* The Instructions option in the menu. */


#define EXIT_PB   100 /*Exit  push button in the instructions box.*/
#define Dance_PB 101  /*Dance push button in the main window.      */

/*---------------
 Global variables
 ---------------*/
char        gszAppName[] = "Dance" ; /* Our application name.    */
HINSTANCE   ghInst;                  /* Current instance.        */
HBRUSH      ghBrushOfBkGnd;          /* For the brush.    */
HBITMAP     ghDanceAct0;             /* For the dance.    */
HBITMAP     ghDanceAct1;             /* For the dance.    */
HBITMAP     ghDanceAct2;             /* For the dance.    */
HBITMAP     ghDanceAct3;             /* For the dance.    */
HBITMAP     ghDanceAct4;             /* For the dance.    */
HBITMAP     ghDanceAct5;             /* For the dance.    */
```

Listing 6.12. Dance.c.

```
/*============================================================
  PROGRAM: Dance.c
  -------
  (C) Copyright 1992, 1993 Gurewich. (R) All rights reserved.

  PROGRAM DESCRIPTION:
  -------------------
  This is a Generic type 1 program.

  This is a visual-audio Dance file.
```

```
===============================================================*/

/*--------
 #include
 --------*/
/*----------------------------------
 Required for all Windows applications.
 ----------------------------------*/
#include <windows.h>

/*-------------------------------------------------------------------
 Required so that sp_ functions, SP_ macros and #definitions
 from the TS C sound library may be used in this applications.
 ---------------------------------------------------------------*/
#include "c:\spSDK\TegoWlib\sp4Win.h"

/*-------------------------------------------------------
 Definitions & prototypes specific to this application.
 ---------------------------------------------------*/
#include "c:\spSDK\Samp4WIN\Dance.h"

/*-----------------------------------------------
 For standard C functions used in this application.
 ----------------------------------------------*/
#include <stdlib.h>
#include <stdio.h>

/*==================
 FUNCTION: WinMain()
 ==================*/
int PASCAL WinMain ( HANDLE hInstance,
                     HANDLE hPrevInstance,
                     LPSTR  lpszCmdLine,
                     int    nCmdShow )
{
/*------------------------
 Local and static variables.
 ------------------------*/
HWND      hWnd;   /* Handler to the window of our application.   */
MSG       msg;    /* Message to be processed by our application. */
WNDCLASS  wc;     /* Window class of our application.            */

HBITMAP   hBitmapOfBkGnd; /* For the background. */

/*------------------------------------------
 Make the hInstance variable a global variable.
 ----------------------------------------*/
ghInst = hInstance;
```

continues

Listing 6.12. continued

```
/*---------------------------------
Create the brush for the background.
-------------------------------*/
hBitmapOfBkGnd = LoadBitmap ( ghInst, "BackGround"   );
ghBrushOfBkGnd = CreatePatternBrush ( hBitmapOfBkGnd );

/*------------------------------------------------
Update the window class structure and register
the window class.
---------------------------------------------*/
if ( !hPrevInstance )
    {
    /*------------------------------------------
    The "if" is satisfied, this is the very 1st
    run of this application.
    -----------------------------------------*/
    wc.style          = CS_HREDRAW | CS_VREDRAW ;
    wc.lpfnWndProc    = WndProc ;
    wc.cbClsExtra     = 0 ;
    wc.cbWndExtra     = 0 ;
    wc.hInstance      = ghInst ;
    wc.hIcon          = LoadIcon   ( ghInst, "IconOfTape" ) ;
    wc.hCursor        = LoadCursor ( NULL, IDC_ARROW      ) ;
    wc.hbrBackground  = ghBrushOfBkGnd; /* The brush that we created  */
                                        /*  with the bit map.         */
    wc.lpszMenuName   = gszAppName ;
    wc.lpszClassName  = gszAppName ;

    /*------------------
    Register the window.
    ----------------*/
    RegisterClass ( &wc );

    }/* end of if(!hPrevInstance) */


/*------------------------------------
Create the window of our application.
----------------------------------*/
hWnd = CreateWindow ( gszAppName,
                      gszAppName,
                      WS_OVERLAPPEDWINDOW,
                      50,
                      50,
                      300,
```

```
                        250,
                        NULL,
                        NULL,
                        ghInst,
                        NULL );

/*-----------------------------------------------
 Show and update the window of our application.
 -------------------------------------------*/
ShowWindow   ( hWnd, nCmdShow );
UpdateWindow ( hWnd );

/*----------------
 The message loop.
 ---------------*/
while ( GetMessage ( &msg, NULL, 0, 0 ) )
      {
      TranslateMessage ( &msg );
      DispatchMessage  ( &msg );
      }

/*-------------------------------------------------------------
 Delete the memory and brush objects used for the background.
 ----------------------------------------------------------*/
DeleteObject ( hBitmapOfBkGnd );
DeleteObject ( ghBrushOfBkGnd );

return msg.wParam ;

} /* end of function. */
/*========================= end of WinMain() ====================*/

/*==================
 FUNCTION: WndProc()
 ==================*/
/*----------------------------
 DESCRIPTION: Processes messages.
 ----------------------------*/
long FAR PASCAL _export WndProc ( HWND hWnd,
                                  UINT message,
                                  UINT wParam,
                                  LONG lParam )
{
/*-------------------------
 Local and static variables.
 -------------------------*/
HDC         hdc;    /* Needed for displaying.  */
PAINTSTRUCT ps;     /* Needed for displaying.  */
HDC         hMemDC; /* For the Face bit map.   */
```

continues

Listing 6.12. continued

```
static FARPROC lpfnAboutDlgProc; /* For the About         dialog box. */
static FARPROC lpfnInstDlgProc ; /* For the Instructions dialog box. */

int     iOpenDanceResult;
int     iOpenHelloResult;

static HWND    hButton;

switch ( message )
        {
        case WM_CREATE:
             /*---------------------------
             Open the Dance sound session.
             ---------------------------*/
             iOpenDanceResult = sp_OpenSession (
                             "c:\\spSDK\\TSfiles\\Music.ts",
                             SP_NON_STAND_ALONE,
                             0L,
                             SP_TS_TYPE);
             /*-------------------------
             Quit if can't open the file.
             -------------------------*/
             if ( iOpenDanceResult != SP_NO_ERRORS )
                {
                MessageBox ( NULL,
                             "Failed to open the sound session!",
                             "Message from Dance.c",
                             MB_ICONINFORMATION );

                 /*-----------------
                 Quit the application.
                 -------------------*/
                 SendMessage ( hWnd, WM_DESTROY, 0, 0 );
                 }

             /*----------------------------------------------------------
             Obtain the lpfnAboutDlgProc of the About the dialog box.
             ----------------------------------------------------------*/
             lpfnAboutDlgProc =
             MakeProcInstance (( FARPROC) AboutDlgProc, ghInst);

             /*----------------------------------------------------------
             Obtain the lpfnInstDlgProc of the Instructions dialog box.
             ----------------------------------------------------------*/
             lpfnInstDlgProc =
             MakeProcInstance (( FARPROC) InstDlgProc, ghInst);
```

```
        /*----------------------------------------
        Obtain the handler of the Face bit maps.
        ----------------------------------------*/
        ghDanceAct0  = LoadBitmap ( ghInst, "Dance0"  );
        ghDanceAct1  = LoadBitmap ( ghInst, "Dance1"  );
        ghDanceAct2  = LoadBitmap ( ghInst, "Dance2"  );
        ghDanceAct3  = LoadBitmap ( ghInst, "Dance3"  );
        ghDanceAct4  = LoadBitmap ( ghInst, "Dance4"  );
        ghDanceAct5  = LoadBitmap ( ghInst, "Dance5"  );

        /*----------------------------
        Create the Hear Me push button.
        ----------------------------*/
        hButton = CreateWindow ( "BUTTON",
                                 "&Dance",
                                 WS_CHILD¦WS_VISIBLE¦BS_PUSHBUTTON,
                                 200,
                                 50,
                                 80,
                                 40,
                                 hWnd,
                                 Dance_PB,
                                 ghInst,
                                 NULL);

        ShowWindow ( hButton, SW_SHOW );

        return 0;

case WM_PAINT:
        /*----------------------------------
        Paint the face with its mouth closed.
        ----------------------------------*/
        hdc = BeginPaint ( hWnd, &ps );
        hMemDC = CreateCompatibleDC ( hdc );
        SelectObject ( hMemDC, ghDanceAct0 );
        BitBlt ( hdc,
                 10,
                 20,
                 135,
                 135,
                 hMemDC,
                 0,
                 0,
                 SRCCOPY );
        DeleteDC ( hMemDC );
        EndPaint ( hWnd, &ps );

        return 0;
```

continues

Listing 6.12. continued

```
case WM_COMMAND:
        /*-----------------
        Process menu items.
        -----------------*/
        switch (wParam)
                {
                case Dance_PB:
                        SetFocus  ( hWnd );
                        DanceShow ( hWnd );
                        return 0;

                case IDM_QUIT:
                        /*-----------------------
                        User clicked on Quit option.
                        -----------------------*/
                        DestroyWindow (hWnd);
                        return 0L;

                case IDM_ABOUT :
                        /*-----------------------
                        User clicked on About option.
                        -----------------------*/
                        DialogBox ( ghInst,
                                    "AboutBox",
                                    hWnd,
                                    lpfnAboutDlgProc );

                        return 0L;

                case IDM_INSTRUCTIONS :
                        /*-------------------------------
                        User clicked on Instructions option.
                        -------------------------------*/
                        DialogBox ( ghInst,
                                    "InstructionsBox",
                                    hWnd,
                                    lpfnInstDlgProc );
                        return 0L;

                }/* end of switch (wParam) */


case WM_CHAR:
        /*-------------------------------
        User pressed a key on the keyboard.
        -------------------------------*/
```

```
        /*-------------------
        Convert to uppercase.
        -------------------*/
        wParam = toupper ( wParam );

        switch ( wParam )
                {
                case 'D':
                        /*-----------------
                        Make the face speak.
                        -----------------*/
                        DanceShow ( hWnd );
                        return 0;
                }
        return 0L;


    case WM_DESTROY:
        /*------------------------------
        Open the Hello.ts sound session.
        ------------------------------*/
        iOpenHelloResult =
        sp_OpenSession ( "c:\\spSDK\\TSfiles\\Hello.ts",
                        SP_NON_STAND_ALONE,
                        0L,
                        SP_TS_TYPE ) ;

        if ( iOpenHelloResult == SP_NO_ERRORS )
            {
            /*-----------------------------
            Play a section of the sound file.
            Range to play: 30,000 to 40,000
            phrase: "Good-Bye"
            -----------------------------*/
            sp_PlayF ( 30000L, 40000L ) ;
            }

        /*-----------------
        Delete the bit maps.
        -------------------*/
        DeleteObject ( ghDanceAct0 );
        DeleteObject ( ghDanceAct1 );
        DeleteObject ( ghDanceAct2 );
        DeleteObject ( ghDanceAct3 );
        DeleteObject ( ghDanceAct4 );

        PostQuitMessage (0);
        return 0;
}/* end of switch (message) */
```

continues

Listing 6.12. continued

```c
/*-----------------------
 Message was not processed.
 -----------------------*/
return DefWindowProc ( hWnd, message, wParam, lParam ) ;

}/* end of WndProc() */
/*================= end of WndProc() ====================*/

/*======================
 FUNCTION: AboutDlgProc()
======================*/
/*----------------------------------------
 DESCRIPTION:
 This is the About dialog box procedure.
 ----------------------------------------*/
BOOL FAR PASCAL _export AboutDlgProc ( HWND hDlg,
                                       UINT message,
                                       UINT wParam,
                                       LONG lParam )
{
switch ( message )
      {
      case WM_INITDIALOG :
            return TRUE;

      case WM_COMMAND :
            switch ( wParam )
                  {
                  case IDOK :
                  case IDCANCEL :
                      EndDialog ( hDlg, 0 );
                      return TRUE;
                  }
      }/* end of switch(message) */
return FALSE ;
}/* End of function. */
/*=============== end of AboutDlgProc() =============*/

/*======================
 FUNCTION: InstDlgProc()
======================*/
/*----------------------------------------
 DESCRIPTION:
 This is the Instructions dialog box procedure.
 ----------------------------------------*/
```

```c
BOOL FAR PASCAL _export InstDlgProc ( HWND hDlg,
                                      UINT message,
                                      UINT wParam,
                                      LONG lParam )
{
switch ( message )
        {
        case WM_INITDIALOG :
             return TRUE;

        case WM_COMMAND :
             switch ( wParam )
                     {
                     case EXIT_PB :
                     case IDOK :
                     case IDCANCEL :
                          EndDialog ( hDlg, 0 );
                          return TRUE;
                     }
        }
return FALSE ;
}/* End of function. */
/*=============== end of InstDlgProc() ==============*/

/*========
 FUNCTION
 ========*/
/*--------------------------------
 DESCRIPTION:
 -----------
 Make the couple dance.
 -------------------------------*/
void DanceShow ( HWND hWnd )
{
int    iActFlag    = 0;
long   lCurrentByte = 0L;
DWORD  dwStart;
DWORD  dwFinish;

while (1)
    {
    lCurrentByte = sp_PlayF ( lCurrentByte,
                              lCurrentByte + 5000L );

    if ( lCurrentByte == 320000L )
        {
        break;
        }
```

continues

Listing 6.12. continued

```
    if ( iActFlag == 0 )
        {
        /*--------------------------------
        Display Dance Act #1.
        --------------------------------*/
        iActFlag = 1;
        DisplayDanceAct1 ( hWnd );
        continue;
        }

    if ( iActFlag == 1 )
        {
        /*--------------------------------
        Display Dance Act #2.
        --------------------------------*/
        iActFlag = 2;
        DisplayDanceAct2 ( hWnd );
        continue;
        }

    if ( iActFlag == 2 )
        {
        /*--------------------------------
        Display Dance Act #3.
        --------------------------------*/
        iActFlag = 0;
        DisplayDanceAct3 ( hWnd );
        continue;
        }

    }/* end of the while() loop. */


DisplayDanceAct0 ( hWnd );

/*--------------------------------
Play Bravoooooooooooooooooooooooooo
--------------------------------*/
sp_PlayF ( 321144L, SP_END_OF_FILE );

DisplayDanceAct4 ( hWnd );

/*--------------------------------
Play Bravoooooooooooooooooooooooooo
--------------------------------*/
sp_PlayF ( 321144L, SP_END_OF_FILE );

DisplayDanceAct0 ( hWnd );
```

```
DisplayDanceAct0 ( hWnd );

/*-----------------------------
 Play Bravooooooooooooooooooooooooo
 -------------------------------*/
sp_PlayF ( 321144L, SP_END_OF_FILE );

/*------
 Credit
 --------*/
DisplayDanceAct5 ( hWnd );

    /*-------------------
    Delay.
    --------------------*/
    dwStart = GetTickCount ();
    while ( 1 )
            {
            dwFinish = GetTickCount ();
            if ( dwFinish >= dwStart + 4000 )
                break;
            }

DisplayDanceAct0 ( hWnd );

}/* end of function. */
/*============ end of function ===========*/

/*========
 FUNCTION
 ========*/
/*--------------------------------
 DESCRIPTION:
 ----------
 Display Dance Act #0.
 --------------------------------*/
void DisplayDanceAct0 ( HWND hWnd )
{
HDC hdc;
HDC hMemDC;

hdc = GetDC ( hWnd );
hMemDC = CreateCompatibleDC ( hdc );
SelectObject ( hMemDC, ghDanceAct0 );

BitBlt ( hdc,
        10,
        20,
```

continues

Listing 6.12. continued

```
                135,
                135,
                hMemDC,
                0,
                0,
                SRCCOPY );

DeleteDC ( hMemDC );
ReleaseDC ( hWnd, hdc    );
}
/*============ end of function ==========*/

/*========
 FUNCTION
 ========*/
/*---------------------------------
 DESCRIPTION:
 ----------
 Display Dance Act #1.
 ---------------------------------*/
void DisplayDanceAct1 ( HWND hWnd )
{
HDC hdc;
HDC hMemDC;

hdc = GetDC ( hWnd );
hMemDC = CreateCompatibleDC ( hdc );
SelectObject ( hMemDC, ghDanceAct1 );

BitBlt ( hdc,
        10,
        20,
        135,
        135,
        hMemDC,
        0,
        0,
        SRCCOPY );

DeleteDC ( hMemDC );
ReleaseDC ( hWnd, hdc    );
}
/*============ end of function ==========*/

/*========
 FUNCTION
 ========*/
```

```
/*-----------------------------------
 DESCRIPTION:
 ----------
 Display Dance Act #2.
-----------------------------------*/
void DisplayDanceAct2 ( HWND hWnd )
{
HDC hdc;
HDC hMemDC;

hdc = GetDC ( hWnd );
hMemDC = CreateCompatibleDC ( hdc );
SelectObject ( hMemDC, ghDanceAct2 );

BitBlt ( hdc,
         10,
         20,
         135,
         135,
         hMemDC,
         0,
         0,
         SRCCOPY );

DeleteDC ( hMemDC );
ReleaseDC ( hWnd, hdc   );
}
/*============ end of function ===========*/

/*========
 FUNCTION
 ========*/
/*-----------------------------------
 DESCRIPTION:
 ----------
 Display Dance Act #3.
-----------------------------------*/
void DisplayDanceAct3 ( HWND hWnd )
{
HDC hdc;
HDC hMemDC;

hdc = GetDC ( hWnd );
hMemDC = CreateCompatibleDC ( hdc );
SelectObject ( hMemDC, ghDanceAct3 );

BitBlt ( hdc,
         10,
```

continues

Listing 6.12. continued

```
            20,
            135,
            135,
            hMemDC,
            0,
            0,
            SRCCOPY );

DeleteDC ( hMemDC );
ReleaseDC ( hWnd, hdc   );
}
/*============ end of function ==========*/

/*========
 FUNCTION
 ========*/
/*--------------------------------
 DESCRIPTION:
 ----------
 Display Dance Act #4.
 --------------------------------*/
void DisplayDanceAct4 ( HWND hWnd )
{
HDC hdc;
HDC hMemDC;

hdc = GetDC ( hWnd );
hMemDC = CreateCompatibleDC ( hdc );
SelectObject ( hMemDC, ghDanceAct4 );

BitBlt ( hdc,
         10,
         20,
         135,
         135,
         hMemDC,
         0,
         0,
         SRCCOPY );

DeleteDC ( hMemDC );
ReleaseDC ( hWnd, hdc   );
}
/*============ end of function ==========*/
```

```
/*========
 FUNCTION
 =======*/
/*---------------------------------
 DESCRIPTION:
 ----------
 Display Dance Act #5.
 --------------------------------*/
void DisplayDanceAct5 ( HWND hWnd )
{
HDC hdc;
HDC hMemDC;

hdc = GetDC ( hWnd );
hMemDC = CreateCompatibleDC ( hdc );
SelectObject ( hMemDC, ghDanceAct5 );

BitBlt ( hdc,
         10,
         20,
         135,
         135,
         hMemDC,
         0,
         0,
         SRCCOPY );

DeleteDC ( hMemDC );
ReleaseDC ( hWnd, hdc   );
}
/*============ end of function ==========*/
```

Listing 6.13. Dance.rc.

```
/*==================================================
 FILE NAME: Dance.rc
 ---------

 FILE DESCRIPTION:
 ----------------
 The resource file.

 (C) Copyright Gurewich 1992, 1993

 =================================================*/
```

continues

Listing 6.13. continued

```
/*------
 #include
 ------*/
#include <windows.h>
#include "Dance.h"

/*--
 Menu
 --*/
Dance  MENU
BEGIN
    POPUP   "&Menu"
        BEGIN
            MENUITEM "&Quit",          IDM_QUIT
            MENUITEM "&About",         IDM_ABOUT
            MENUITEM "&Instructions", IDM_INSTRUCTIONS
        END
END

/*-----------------------------------------
 Definition of the Cassette tape icon.
 File name: Tape.ico
 Icon name: IconOfTape
 -----------------------------------------*/
IconOfTape ICON Tape.ico

/*---------
 Bit maps.
 --------*/
Dance0          BITMAP Dance0.bmp
Dance1          BITMAP Dance1.bmp
Dance2          BITMAP Dance2.bmp
Dance3          BITMAP Dance3.bmp
Dance4          BITMAP Dance4.bmp
Dance5          BITMAP Dance5.bmp
BackGround      BITMAP BackGnd.bmp

/*--------------------
 The About dialog box.
 ------------------*/
AboutBox DIALOG 81, 43, 160, 100
STYLE DS_MODALFRAME ¦ WS_POPUP ¦ WS_VISIBLE ¦
                    WS_CAPTION ¦ WS_SYSMENU
CAPTION "About the Dance program"
FONT 8, "MS Sans Serif"
```

```
BEGIN
    PUSHBUTTON       "&OK", IDOK, 64, 75, 40, 14
    CTEXT            "(C) Copyright Gurewich 1992, 1993",
                     -1, 13, 47, 137, 18
    ICON             "IconOfTape", -1, 14, 12, 18, 20
END

/*------------------------
 The Instructions dialog box.
 ------------------------*/
InstructionsBox DIALOG 41, 45, 222, 100
STYLE DS_MODALFRAME ¦ WS_POPUP ¦ WS_VISIBLE ¦
                    WS_CAPTION ¦ WS_SYSMENU
CAPTION "Instructions for using the Dance program"
FONT 8, "MS Sans Serif"
BEGIN
    PUSHBUTTON       "&Exit", EXIT_PB, 95, 84, 40, 14
    CTEXT            "Click on the Dance Push button, or press 'D'",
                     -1, 37, 38, 152, 13
    CTEXT            "to play and dance.", -1, 47, 48, 125, 8
    CONTROL          "", -1, "Static", SS_GRAYFRAME, 32, 26, 166, 41
    ICON             "IconOfTape", -1, 7, 18, 18, 20
END
```

Listing 6.14. Dance.def.

```
;=======================================
; module-definition file for Dance.c
;=======================================

NAME          Dance

DESCRIPTION   'The Dance program. (C) Copyright Gurewich 1992, 1993'

EXETYPE       WINDOWS

STUB          'WINSTUB.EXE'

CODE   PRELOAD MOVEABLE DISCARDABLE

DATA   PRELOAD MOVEABLE MULTIPLE

HEAPSIZE       1024
STACKSIZE      8192
```

Listing 6.15. Dance.mak.

```
#============
# Dance.mak
#============

Dance.exe : Dance.obj Dance.h Dance.def Dance.res
    link /nod Dance.obj, Dance.exe, NUL, \
        slibcew.lib oldnames.lib libw.lib commdlg \
        c:\spSDK\TegoWlib\TegoWin.lib, \
        Dance.def
    rc -t Dance.res

Dance.obj : Dance.c Dance.h
    cl -c -G2sw -Ow -W3 -Zp  Dance.c

Dance.res : Dance.rc Dance.h Tape.ico
    rc -r Dance.rc
```

The *WndProc()* of the Dance Program

The following sections discuss the various cases that appear in the WndProc()
function.

Opening the Sound Session

Under the WM_CREATE case we open a sound session of type TS with the file
c:\spSDK\Samp4Win\Music.ts as a Non-Stand-Alone program:

```
case WM_CREATE:
    /*---------------------------
    Open the Dance sound session.
    ---------------------------*/
    iOpenDanceResult = sp_OpenSession (
                    "c:\\spSDK\\TSfiles\\Music.ts",
                    SP_NON_STAND_ALONE,
                    0L,
                    SP_TS_TYPE);
    /*-------------------------
    Quit if can't open the file.
    -------------------------*/
    if ( iOpenDanceResult != SP_NO_ERRORS )
```

```
     {
     MessageBox ( NULL,
                 "Failed to open the sound session!",
                 "Message from Dance.c",
                  MB_ICONINFORMATION );

     /*------------------
     Quit the application.
     ------------------*/
     SendMessage ( hWnd, WM_DESTROY, 0, 0 );
     }
..............
..............
..............
return 0;
```

The Dance Show

The code of the dance show is located in the function DanceShow(). WndProc() calls this function whenever the user pushes the Dance push button or presses the D key.

The *DANCE_PB* Case

Under the DANCE_PB case we detect the fact that the user pushed the Dance push button, and we execute the DanceShow() function:

```
case Dance_PB:
    SetFocus  ( hWnd );
    DanceShow ( hWnd );
    return 0;
```

The *WM_CHAR* Case

Under the WM_CHAR case we detect the fact that the user pressed the D key, and we execute the DanceShow() function:

```
case WM_CHAR:
    /*------------------
    Convert to uppercase.
    ------------------*/
    wParam = toupper ( wParam );
```

```
switch ( wParam )
        {
        case 'D':
            /*----------------
            Make the face speak.
            ----------------*/
            DanceShow ( hWnd );
            return 0;
        }
    return 0L;
```

The *DanceShow()* Function

The DanceShow() function executes the show as follows:

```
void DanceShow ( hWnd )
{
while (1)
        {
        ............................
        ...... The dance show .......
        ............................
        }

.......................................
........ Final acts of the show ........
.......................................
}
```

The *while(1)* Loop of the *DanceShow()*

The DanceShow() utilizes the sound file Music.ts.

To create the sound file music.ts, we used the TS Sound Editor to add two sound files. Because we assume that you do not have a copy of the TS Sound Editor, here is the result of the file addition:

```
========================     ==================
Byte coordinates             Sound section
========================     ==================

0 - 321,144                  Music.

321,144 - SP_END_OF_FILE     Audience claps hands and
                             shouts Bravo.
```

The while(1) loop plays the music in groups of 5,000 bytes each:

```
lCurrentByte = sp_PlayF ( lCurrentByte,
                          lCurrentByte + 5000L );
```

If the last byte played is byte coordinate 320,000, then we break from the while(1) loop:

```
if ( lCurrentByte == 320000L )
    {
    break;
    }
```

Actually, we should break from the loop when the last byte played is byte coordinate 321,144. We decided, however, not to play the last 1,144 bytes of the music section because we are playing in groups of 5,000 bytes each.

The dance show is composed of three frames: Act1, Act2, and Act3. The bit-map files that correspond to these acts are Dance1.bmp, Dance2.bmp, and Dance3.bmp. These bit-map files are shown in Figure 6.18.

a) Dance1.bmp   b) Dance2.bmp   c) Dance3.bmp

Figure 6.18. Three bit-map files for the Dance program.

We have a flag called iActFlag that indicates which frame to display next. When the flag is equal to zero, the frame to be displayed is Act1. When the flag is equal to 1, the frame to be displayed is Act2. And when the frame is equal to 2, the frame to be displayed is Act3. The flag changes after the playback of every 5,000 bytes. We implemented this process by using three if statements:

```
if ( iActFlag == 0 )
    {
    /*--------------------------------
    Display Dance Act #1.
    --------------------------------*/
    iActFlag = 1;
    DisplayDanceAct1 ( hWnd );
    continue;
    }
```

```
if ( iActFlag == 1 )
    {
    /*---------------------------------
    Display Dance Act #2.
    ---------------------------------*/
    iActFlag = 2;
    DisplayDanceAct2 ( hWnd );
    continue;
    }

if ( iActFlag == 2 )
    {
    /*---------------------------------
    Display Dance Act #3.
    ---------------------------------*/
    iActFlag = 0;
    DisplayDanceAct3 ( hWnd );
    continue;
    }
```

Upon breaking from the while(1) loop we display the couple in a stand-up position by executing the DisplayDanceAct0() function:

```
DisplayDanceAct0 ( hWnd );
```

The DisplayDanceAct0() function displays the bit-map file Dance0.bmp (see Figure 6.19).

Figure 6.19. The Dance0.bmp bit-map file.

We then cause the audience to shout *Bravo* by playing the sound section that corresponds to *Bravo:*

```
/*---------------------------------
Play Bravooooooooooooooooooooooooo
---------------------------------*/
sp_PlayF ( 321144L, SP_END_OF_FILE );
```

Naturally, the dancers appreciate the *Bravo,* and thank the audience. This gratitude is implemented by executing the `DisplayDanceAct4()` function:

```
DisplayDanceAct4 ( hWnd );
```

The `DisplayDanceAct4()` function displays the bit-map file Dance4.bmp (see Figure 6.20).

Figure 6.20. The Dance4.bmp bit-map file.

We play the *Bravo* again, and then execute the `DisplayDanceAct0()` function, making the dancers stand up.

Finally, we display a frame that shows who owns the copyright of the show and who created the show (like in a real movie). This is done by executing the `DisplayDanceAct5()` function:

```
/*------
Credit
--------*/
DisplayDanceAct5 ( hWnd );
```

The `DisplayDanceAct5()` function displays the bit-map file Dance5.bmp (see Figure 6.21).

Figure 6.21. The Dance5.bmp bit-map file.

We leave the credit frame on-screen for four seconds by implementing a four-second delay:

```
/*--------------------
Delay.
--------------------*/
dwStart = GetTickCount ();
while ( 1 )
      {
      dwFinish = GetTickCount ();
      if ( dwFinish >= dwStart + 4000 )
          break;
      }
```

The show is terminated by executing the `DisplayDanceAct0()` function, causing the dancers to reappear in their stand-up position, ready for the next show.

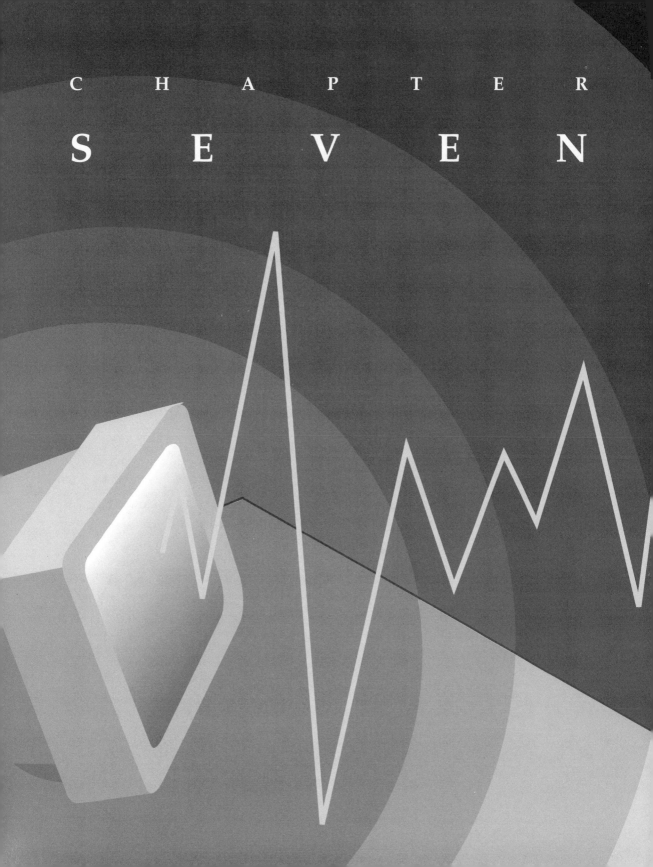

Synchronizing Moving Text with Speech

This chapter illustrates how to move text simultaneously with the playback of speech.

The Press Program

The Press program displays a push button in its main window. The push button is marked `Push for an audio instruction`.

When you press the push button, the program plays the phrase *Press any key to continue* simultaneously with the displaying of the text `Press any key to continue`. The display of the text is synchronized with the audio. (That is, the word *Press* is played while the word `Press` appears, then the word *any* is played while the word `any` appears, and so on.)

We recommend that you compile, link, and execute the program prior to studying its code. This way you'll gain a better understanding of what the program can do.

Compiling, Linking, and Executing the Press Program

To compile and link the Press program with the Microsoft compiler:

- Make sure your PC is in a DOS-protected mode.
- Log into C:\spSDK\Samp4Win\.
- At the DOS prompt type

   NMAKE Press.mak   {Enter}

To compile and link the Press program with the Borland compiler:

- Log into c:\spSDK\Samp4Win\.
- At the DOS prompt type

   MAKE -f Press.bmk   {Enter}

To execute the Press program:

- Select Run from the File menu of the Program Manager of Windows.
- Click Browse and select the file

   c:\spSDK\Samp4Win\Press.exe

The main window appears, as shown in Figure 7.1. As you can see, it contains the push button Push for an audio instruction.

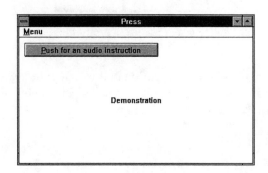

Figure 7.1. The main window of the Press program.

The Press program menu contains two options: Quit and About (see Figure 7.2). When the user selects the About option, the About dialog box appears (see Figure 7.3). When the user selects the Quit option, the program says *Good-Bye* and terminates.

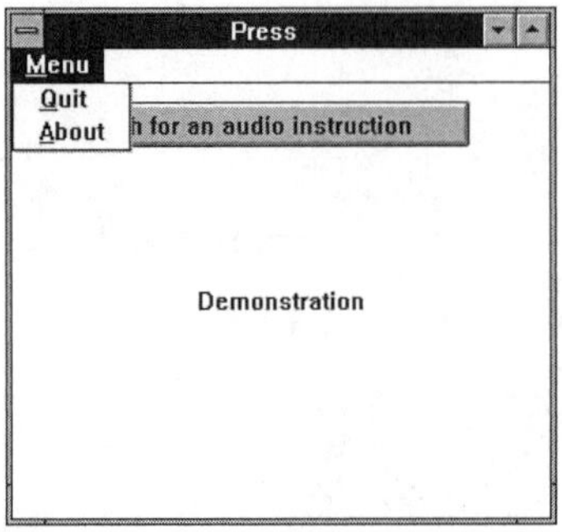

Figure 7.2. The Press program menu.

Figure 7.3. The About dialog box of the Press program.

When the user clicks the push button in the main window (or presses the **P** key), the program says *Press any key to continue* in synchronization with the displaying of the words.

The Files of the Press Program

The Press program consists of the following files:

Press.h	The #include file of the program.
Press.c	The C code of the program.
Press.rc	The resource file of the program.

Press.def	The module definition file of the program.
Press.mak	The make file of the program.
Tape.ico	The icon of the program.

These files are provided for you in c:\spSDK\Samp4Win\.

The *WndProc()* Function of Press.c

The WndProc() function of Press.c handles the various messages that are generated during the program execution.

The *WM_CREATE* Case

Under the WM_CREATE case we open a type S Non-Stand-Alone sound session with the C:\spSDK\SFiles\Press.s file:

```
iOpenResult = sp_OpenSession (
               "c:\\spSDK\\Sfiles\\Press.s",
               SP_NON_STAND_ALONE,
               0L,
               SP_S_TYPE);
```

If the opening of the sound session fails, we terminate the program:

```
if ( iOpenResult != SP_NO_ERRORS )
   {
   MessageBox ( NULL,
               "Failed to open the sound session!",
               "Message from Press.exe",
               MB_ICONINFORMATION );

   SendMessage ( hWnd,
               WM_DESTROY,
               0,
               0 );
   }
```

We obtain the lpfn of the About dialog box and then create and show the push button of the main window:

```
hButton =
CreateWindow ( "BUTTON",
               "&Push for an audio instruction",
               WS_CHILD | WS_VISIBLE | BS_PUSHBUTTON,
               10,
               10,
```

```
        250,
        25,
        hWnd,
        INSTRUCTION_PB,
        ghInst,
        NULL);

ShowWindow ( hButton, SW_SHOW );
```

The ninth parameter of CreateWindow() of the push button, INSTRUCTION_PB, is #defined in Press.h.

The WM_CHAR Case

The WM_CHAR message is received whenever the user presses a key on the keyboard. Under the WM_CHAR case we convert the received key to uppercase, and investigate which key was pressed:

```
switch ( wParam )
        {
        case 'P':
                /*-----------------
                Play the instruction.
                -----------------*/
                PlayInstruction ( hWnd );
                return 0L;
        }
```

If it is the P key that was pressed, we execute the PlayInstruction() function.

Similarly, if the user clicks the INSTRUCTION_PB push button, we detect it under the INSTRUCTION_PB case and execute the PlayInstruction() function:

```
case INSTRUCTION_PB:
        /*------------------------------------
        User pushed the Instruction push button.
        ------------------------------------*/
        PlayInstruction ( hWnd );

        return 0L;
```

The *PlayInstruction()* Function

The prototype of `PlayInstruction()` is declared in Press.h:

```
void PlayInstruction ( HWND hWnd );
```

We pass `hWnd` to this function because this function does some text drawing inside the main window. Therefore, it needs to know the value of `hWnd` of the main window.

Within `PlayInstruction()` we first initialize a string variable `sSpaces[]` with all spaces. This string will be used later to erase a line of text:

```
/*--------------------------
 Create a string with spaces.
--------------------------*/
 for ( i=0; i<100; i++ )
     sSpaces[i] = ' ';
 sSpaces[i] = '\0';
```

The `PlayInstruction()` function uses `TextOut()` to display text. Therefore, we need to extract several variables that are used by `TextOut()`:

We get the `hDC` with the `GetDC()` function:

```
hDC = GetDC ( hWnd );
```

We update the `tm` structure (the `tm` structure contains the dimensions of the current text font):

```
GetTextMetrics ( hDC, &tm );
```

The horizontal dimension of the characters are given in the `tmAveCharWidth` element of the `tm` structure, and the vertical dimensions of the characters are given as the `tmWeight` and `tmExternalLeading` elements of the `tm` structure:

```
cxChar = tm.tmAveCharWidth ;
cyChar = tm.tmWeight + tm.tmExternalLeading ;
```

Press does not make use of the vertical dimension `cyChar`. However, the value of `cyChar` is important when the text is displayed on several lines.

The value of `cxChar` is used later when the `TextOut()` function is executed.

Now that we have all the variables needed for the `TextOut()` function, we can display the word `Press`:

```
TextOut ( hDC,
          50,
          50,
          "Press ",
          6 );
```

and play the word *Press:*

```
sp_PlayF ( 0L, 3896L ); /* Press */
```

How did we know that the Press sound section in the C:\spSDK\SFiles\Press.s file has the byte coordinates (0,3896)? We used the TS Editor. Because we assume that you do not have a copy of the TS Editor program, here are the various sound sections of the Press.s sound file:

Byte Coordinates	Audio Phrase
0 - 3,896	*Press*
3,896 - 6,224	*any*
6,224 - 10,137	*key*
10,137 - 11,228	*to*
11,228 - SP_END_OF_FILE	*continue*

You might have noticed that the byte coordinate 3,896 is used as the last byte of *Press,* as well as the first byte of *any.* Indeed, the first byte of *any* should be 3,897, however, one sound byte is negligible. The following is the playback length of one byte in a type S file:

$$[\text{Length in seconds for "S" type}] = \frac{[\text{ Number of bytes }] \times 8}{[\text{ Sampling rate }]}$$

The Press.s sound file was recorded at a sampling rate of 40,000 hertz. Using the above formula, the number of seconds that it takes to play 1 byte in the Press.s file is:

$$[\text{Length in seconds for "S" type}] = \frac{1 \times 8}{40,000} = 0.0002 \text{ seconds} =$$

$$= 0.2 \text{ milliseconds.}$$

As you can see, overlapping one byte is negligible.

The rest of the code in the `PlayInstruction()` function simply repeats the process, displaying and playing the words: *any, key, to,* and *continue.*

Finally, we erase the text by displaying spaces over the location of the displayed text:

```
TextOut ( hDC,
          50,
          50,
          sSpaces,
          lstrlen( sSpaces) );
```

The *WM_DESTROY* Case

Upon terminating the program we play *Good-Bye:*

```
case WM_DESTROY:
    iOpenResult =
    sp_OpenSession ( "c:\\spSDK\\TSfiles\\Hello.ts",
                     SP_NON_STAND_ALONE,
                     0L,
                     SP_TS_TYPE );

    if ( iOpenResult == SP_NO_ERRORS )
        {
        /*-------------------------------------
        Play a section of the sound file.
        Range to play: 30,000 to 40,000
        phrase: "Good-Bye"
        ---------------------------------------*/
        sp_PlayF ( 30000L, 40000L );
        }
    PostQuitMessage (0);
    return 0;
```

Programs Similar to Press

The technique introduced in the Press program can be used in programs that provide audio-visual help prompts. For example, your program may display a dialog box with an audio-visual push button to provide the appropriate help.

In some programs, you may want to output the audio-visual prompt without the need to push a push button. For example, you may write a program that causes the printer to print. If your program detects that there is no paper in the printer, then the program could shout and display: *No paper! Please feed the printer with paper.*

The PlzWait Program

We will now examine another program that performs playback in synchronization with moving text—the PlzWait program. Unlike the Press program, PlzWait displays and moves the text by using bit-map files.

The PlzWait program plays and displays the phrase `Please Wait`. The program starts saying *Please Wait* when the user pushes the Hear Me push button.

Compiling and Linking the PlzWait Program

To compile and link the PlzWait program with the Microsoft compiler:

- Make sure your PC is in a DOS-protected mode.
- Log into C:\spSDK\Samp4Win\.
- At the DOS prompt type

```
NMAKE PlzWait.mak   {Enter}
```

To compile and link the PlzWait program with the Borland compiler:

- Log into c:\spSDK\Samp4Win\.
- At the DOS prompt type

```
MAKE -f PlzWait.bmk   {Enter}
```

Executing the PlzWait Program

To execute the PlzWait program:

- Select Run from the File menu of the File Manager of Windows.

- Click Browse and select the file

```
c:\spSDK\Samp4Win\PlzWait.exe.
```

The main window appears, as shown in Figure 7.4. The PlzWait program menu contains three options: Quit, About, and Instructions (see Figure 7.5).

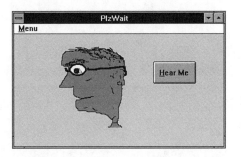

Figure 7.4. The PlzWait main window.

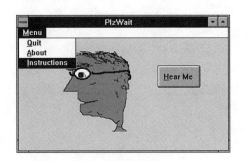

Figure 7.5. The PlzWait program menu.

When the user selects the About option, the About dialog box appears (see Figure 7.6). When the user selects the Instructions option, the Instructions dialog box appears (see Figure 7.7).

Figure 7.6. The About dialog box of PlzWait.

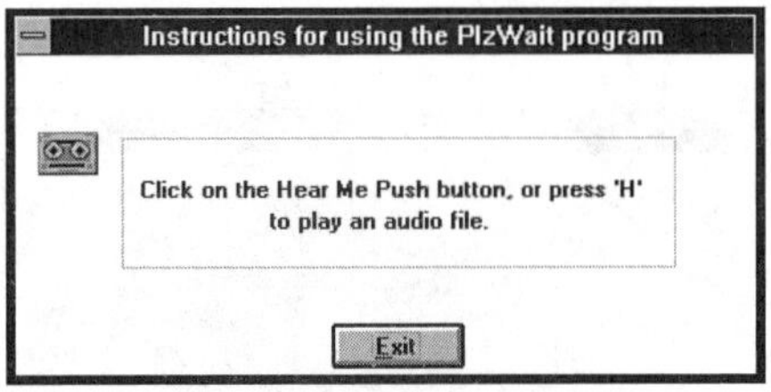

Figure 7.7. The Instruction dialog box of PlzWait.

The main window of PlzWait contains the Hear Me push button. When the user pushes this button, the man in the main window opens his mouth, the word Please shoots out of his mouth, the word *Please* is played, the word Wait shoots out of his mouth, and finally the word *Wait* is played (see Figure 7.8). While this process goes on, the man opens and closes his mouth. This process is repeated twice (that is, you hear the phrase *Please Wait* twice).

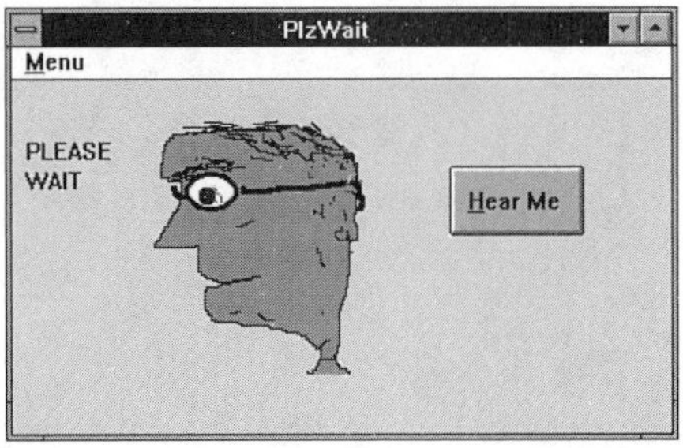

Figure 7.8. Displaying the bit maps of the PlzWait program.

A similar audio-visual `Please Wait` prompt can be inserted in a program that is about to perform a long operation. In this program, you'll omit the Hear Me push button, and execute the *Please Wait* code prior to performing the long operation.

The Files of the PlzWait Program

The Press program consists of the following files:

PlzWait.h	The `#include` file of the program.
PlzWait.c	The C code of the program.
PlzWait.rc	The resource file of the program.
PlzWait.def	The module definition file of the program.
PlzWait.mak	The make file of the program.
Tape.ico	The icon of the program.
Wait1.bmp	The bit map of the man.
Wait2.bmp	The bit map of the man's closed mouth.
Wait3.bmp	The bit map of the man's opened mouth.
Wait4.bmp	The bit map of the *Please* text.
Wait5.bmp	The bit map of the *Wait* text.
BackGnd.bmp	The bit-map file used for the background of the program.

These files are provided for you in c:\spSDK\Samp4Win\.

The *WndProc()* of PlzWait

The `WndProc()` function of PlzWait handles the various cases that are generated during the program execution.

The *WM_CREATE* Case

Under the `WM_CREATE` case we open a sound session with the sound file C:\spSDK\Samp4Win\Wait.s as non-stand-alone, and as type S:

```
case WM_CREATE:
    iOpenFaceResult = sp_OpenSession (
                        "c:\\spSDK\\Sfiles\\Wait.s",
                        SP_NON_STAND_ALONE,
                        0L,
                        SP_S_TYPE);
```

If the sound session does not open successfully, we terminate the program:

```
if ( iOpenFaceResult != SP_NO_ERRORS )
    {
    MessageBox ( NULL,
                "Failed to open the sound session!",
                "Message from PlzWait.c",
                MB_ICONINFORMATION );
    SendMessage ( hWnd, WM_DESTROY, 0, 0 );
    }
```

We obtain the lpfn of the About dialog box and the lpfn of the Instruction dialog box by using the MakeProcInstance() function.

We obtain the handlers of all the bit-map files that are used in the program:

```
ghFullFace      = LoadBitmap ( ghInst, "FullFace" );
ghMouthClosed   = LoadBitmap ( ghInst, "MouthClosed" );
ghMouthOpen     = LoadBitmap ( ghInst, "MouthOpen" );
ghPlease        = LoadBitmap ( ghInst, "Please" );
ghWait          = LoadBitmap ( ghInst, "Wait" );
```

The bit-map files are specified in the PlzWait.rc file:

```
FullFace      BITMAP Wait1.bmp
MouthClosed   BITMAP Wait2.bmp
MouthOpen     BITMAP Wait3.bmp
Please        BITMAP Wait4.bmp
Wait          BITMAP Wait5.bmp
BackGround    BITMAP BackGnd.bmp
```

The last thing we do under the WM_CREATE case is create and show the Hear Me push button.

The WM_PAINT Case

Under the WM_PAINT case we display the Wait1.bmp file (see Figure 7.9) inside the main window:

```
case WM_PAINT:
     /*----------------------------------
     Paint the Face with its mouth closed.
     --------------------------------*/
     hdc = BeginPaint ( hWnd, &ps );
     hMemDC = CreateCompatibleDC ( hdc );
     SelectObject ( hMemDC, ghFullFace );
     BitBlt ( hdc,
              10,
              20,
              200,
              150,
              hMemDC,
              0,
              0,
              SRCCOPY );
     DeleteDC ( hMemDC );
     EndPaint ( hWnd, &ps );

     return 0;
```

Figure 7.9. The Wait1.bmp file.

The *HEARME_PB* and *WM_CHAR* Cases

When the user pushes the Hear Me push button, the message WM_COMMAND with wParam equal to HEARME_PB is received. Under this case we set the focus back to the main window by using SetFocus(), and execute the SpeakShow() function:

```
case HEARME_PB:
     SetFocus  ( hWnd );
     SpeakShow ( hWnd );
     return 0;
```

Similarly, when the user presses the **H** key, we convert the received character to uppercase, and execute the `SpeakShow()` function:

```
case WM_CHAR:
    /*-------------------
    Convert to uppercase.
    -------------------*/
    wParam = toupper ( wParam );

    switch ( wParam )
        {
        case 'H':
            /*---------------
            Make the face speak.
            ----------------*/
            SpeakShow ( hWnd );
            return 0;
        }

    return 0;
```

The *SpeakShow()* Function

The fun part of the program is the `SpeakShow()` function, where you can apply your imagination and creativity.

The prototype of `SpeakShow()` is declared in PlzWait.h:

```
void SpeakShow ( HWND hWnd );
```

`SpeakShow()` needs the parameter `hWnd` because it displays bit maps inside the main window; therefore, it needs the handler of the main window.

Because we want the show to repeat itself twice, we write the code of `SpeakShow()` within a `for()` loop:

```
for ( iCounter = 0; iCounter < 2; iCounter++ )
    {
    ....................................
    ........ The code of the show ........
    ....................................

    DisplayFace ( hWnd );
    }
```

The `DisplayFace()` function is executed after each show. `DisplayFace()` displays the bit map Wait1.bmp (see Figure 7.9). As shown in Figure 7.9, the man's mouth is closed. The reason for executing `DisplayFace()` upon terminating the show in each loop iteration is that we want the man to appear with his mouth closed and without the `Please Wait` text when the show is completed.

The Code of the Show

The show starts by displaying the man's mouth in an open position. We do this by executing the `DisplayOpenMouth()` function:

```
/*---------------------
Open the man's open mouth.
--------------------*/
DisplayOpenMouth ( hWnd);
```

To save disk space, the `DisplayOpenMouth()` function displays a very small bit-map file—the Wait3.bmp (see Figure 7.10). This bit-map file is the portion of the man's face with his mouth open.

We play the phrase *Please:*

```
/*---------------------
Play the phrase "Please".
--------------------*/
sp_PlayF ( SP_START_OF_FILE, 4700L );
```

and then display the bit-map file Wait4.bmp by executing the `DisplayPlease()` function:

```
/*---------------------
 Display the word "Please"
--------------------*/
DisplayPlease ( hWnd );
```

Bit-map file Wait4.bmp is the text `Please`, as shown in Figure 7.10.

Once we complete the display of `Please`, we close the man's mouth by executing the `DisplayCloseMouth()` function:

```
/*--------------------------------
Display the man's closed mouth.
-------------------------------*/
DisplayClosedMouth ( hWnd );
```

The `DisplayCloseMouth()` function executes the `BitBlt()` function with the Wait2.bmp bit-map file. This bit-map file is a small section of the man's face that shows the mouth in a closed position (see Figure 7.10).

We pause for half a second (500 milliseconds) by executing a small delay loop:

```
/*--------------------
Delay.
--------------------*/
dwStart = GetTickCount ();
while ( 1 )
      {
      dwFinish = GetTickCount ();
      if ( dwFinish >= dwStart + 500 )
          break;
      }
```

We are now ready to display and play the *Wait* word. We start by opening the man's mouth by executing the `DisplayOpenMouth()` function:

```
/*---------------------------------
Display the man's open mouth.
-----------------------------------*/
DisplayOpenMouth ( hWnd );
```

and then play the word *Wait:*

```
/*----------------------
Play the phrase "Wait".
----------------------*/
sp_PlayF ( 4700L, SP_END_OF_FILE );
```

Finally, we display the text `Wait` (Wait5.bmp) by executing the `DisplayWait()` function:

```
/*----------------------
 Display the word "Wait"
 ----------------------*/
DisplayWait ( hWnd );
```

Wait5.bmp is the bit map of the word *Wait* (see Figure 7.10).

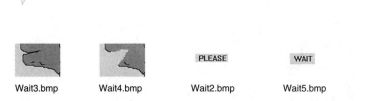

Wait3.bmp   Wait4.bmp   Wait2.bmp   Wait5.bmp

Figure 7.10. The bit-map files of the PlzWait program.

Before returning to the beginning of the `for()` loop we close the man's mouth

```
/*--------------------------------
Display the man's closed mouth.
----------------------------------*/
DisplayClosedMouth ( hWnd );
```

and create a small delay of 500 milliseconds:

```
/*-------------------
Delay.
--------------------*/
dwStart = GetTickCount ();

while ( 1 )
     {
     dwFinish = GetTickCount ();
     if ( dwFinish >= dwStart + 500 )
        break;
     }
```

The *DisplayPlease()* Function

The `DisplayPlease()` function is responsible for displaying `Please`.

The function starts by preparing the various overhead variables that are needed for the `SelectObject()` function, and then executing the `SelectObject()` function:

```
hdc = GetDC ( hWnd );
hMemDC = CreateCompatibleDC ( hdc );
SelectObject ( hMemDC, ghPlease );
```

The object that was selected by the `SelectObject()` function is the *Please* bit map, as indicated by the second parameter of `SelectObject()`.

This `DisplayPlease()` function creates the illusion that the word *Please* is shooting out of the man's mouth, going horizontally to the left, and then climbing vertically upward. We accomplish this by using two `for()` loops. The first `for()` loop moves the word *Please* horizontally to the left:

```
iYStep = 110;
for ( iXStep = 50;
      iXStep >= 10;
      iXStep-- )
    {
    BitBlt ( hdc,
             iXStep,
             iYStep,
             60,
             40,
             hMemDC,
             0,
             0,
             SRCCOPY );

}/* end of for() loop. */
```

The initial pixel coordinates of the Wait5.bmp (the *Please* word) is: $x = 50$ and $y = 110$. The `for()` loop keeps displaying the bit map one pixel to the left by decreasing the x pixel coordinate. By examining Figure 7.11, you can see that the initial pixel coordinates (50,110) indicate the place in the picture that is a little bit to the left of the man's mouth.

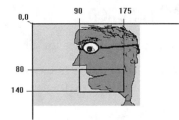

Figure 7.11. Pixel coordinates of the mouth area.

The second `for()` loop takes the bit map *Please* (Wait4.bmp) and moves it vertically upward. We accomplish this by executing the `BitBlt()` function, decreasing the value of the y pixel coordinate in each loop iteration:

```
iXStep = 10 + 0 ;
for ( iYStep  = 20 + 90;
      iYStep >= 20 +25;
      iYStep-- )
   {
   BitBlt ( hdc,
            iXStep,
            iYStep,
            60,
            40,
            hMemDC,
            0,
            0,
            SRCCOPY );

   }/* end of for() loop. */
```

In each loop iteration, Please moves to a new location (either one pixel to the left, or one pixel upward). As Please moves, we do not have to restore the original section of the picture that Please covered. The reason for this is that the bit map Wait4.bmp has a yellow background, and it is surrounded by yellow margins. We deliberately created Wait4.bmp this way. When moving Please pixel by pixel, the yellow margin of Please repaints the previous Please with a yellow background. This way, we do not have to write code that stores the area that we are about to cover with Please, and we do not have to write code that restores the original area.

Alternative Methods for Implementing the Show

You may experiment with the code of SpeakShow() by changing the sequence of events. For example, you may decide that the man should first say the word, and only after saying the word the text should appear. There are no rules regarding the sequence, it is basically a question of which sequence yields the best show for your taste.

Using Paintbrush

All the bit maps that PlzWait uses were created with the Paintbrush program that comes with Windows. Because the pixel coordinates of the various bit maps are important, we selected the Cursor position option in the View menu of Paintbrush. This causes the cursor pixel coordinates to appear at the top of the Paintbrush window as the cursor moves. When cutting, pasting, and doing other drawing manipulations, we use the keyboard arrow keys to place the cursor at the precise pixel coordinates.

Before saving the bit maps, we made sure that the files are saved as .BMP files. We also limited the sizes of the bit-map files by specifying the desired width and height of each .BMP file. This is done by selecting the Image Attributes menu option of the Options menu, and then specifying the width and height of the .BMP file in units of pixels (pels) in the dialog box that appears.

General Suggestions for Creating Shows

As you develop your shows, it is best to first write high-level functions such as `DisplayCloseMouth()`, `DisplayOpenMouth()`, and so on. Once these high-level functions are written, you can use them in your show. The code of the show will consist of these high-level functions. This way the code of the show is very easy to read and understand. It will also be very easy to experiment with the show, changing the order of these high-level functions until you are satisfied with the results.

Controls

This chapter illustrates how to combine Windows controls, such as the scroll bar, with the TS sound library. This chapter also introduces several new sp_ functions from the TS library.

A Windows control such as the scroll bar is an important tool for implementing applications that incorporate sound. For example, you can use a scroll bar to vary the playback speed, the playback volume, or the current position of the playback.

The Rotate Program

We recommend that you compile, link, and execute the program before studying its code. This way you'll gain a better understanding of what the program can do.

Compiling, Linking, and Executing the Rotate Program

To compile and link the Rotate program with the Microsoft compiler:

- Make sure your PC is in a DOS-protected mode.
- Log into C:\spSDK\Samp4Win\.
- At the DOS prompt type

  `NMAKE Rotate.mak` {Enter}

To compile and link the Rotate program with the Borland compiler:

- Log into C:\spSDK\Samp4Win\.

- At the DOS prompt type

  NMAKE -f Rotate.bmk   {Enter}

To execute the Rotate program:

- Select Run from the File menu of the Program Manager of Windows.

- Click Browse and select the file

  c:\spSDK\Samp4Win\Rotate.exe

The main window appears, as shown in Figure 8.1.

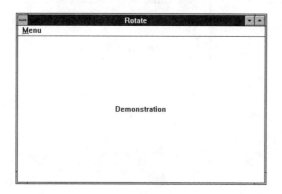

Figure 8.1. The main window of the Rotate program.

The Rotate program menu (see Figure 8.2) contains three options: Quit, About, and Rotate. When the user selects the Quit option, the program says *Good-bye* and terminates. When the user selects the About option, the About dialog box appears (see Figure 8.3). When the user selects the Rotate option, the Rotate dialog box appears (see Figure 8.4).

The Rotate dialog box has a scroll bar and three push buttons: Play, Play Backward, and Exit. When the user selects the Exit push button, the Rotate dialog box closes. When the user selects the Play push button, the phrase *Press any key to continue* is played. When the user selects the Play Backward push button, the phrase *Press any key to continue* is played backward. The user may also change the playback speed by changing the position of the Speed scroll bar.

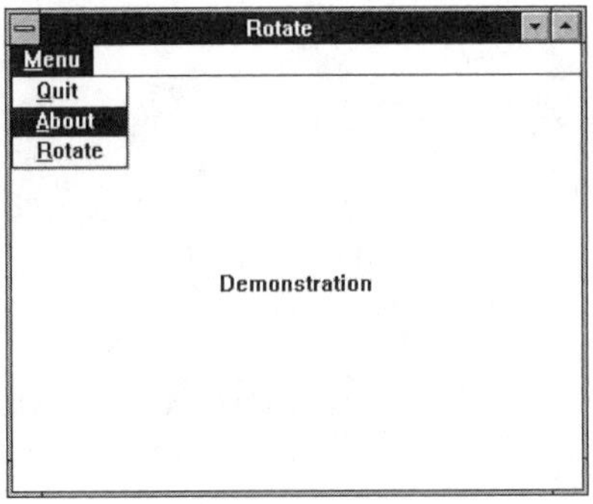

Figure 8.2. The Rotate program menu.

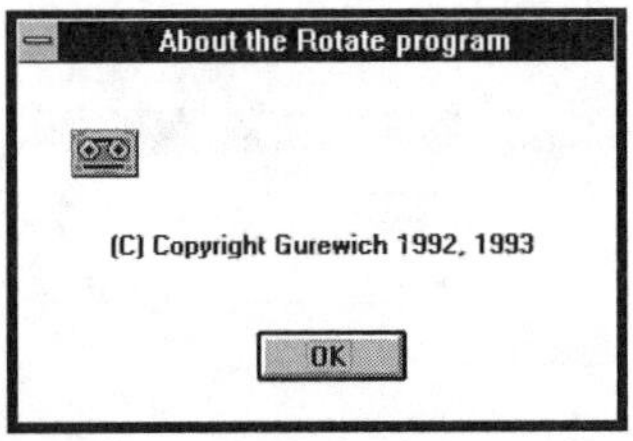

Figure 8.3. The About dialog box of the Rotate program.

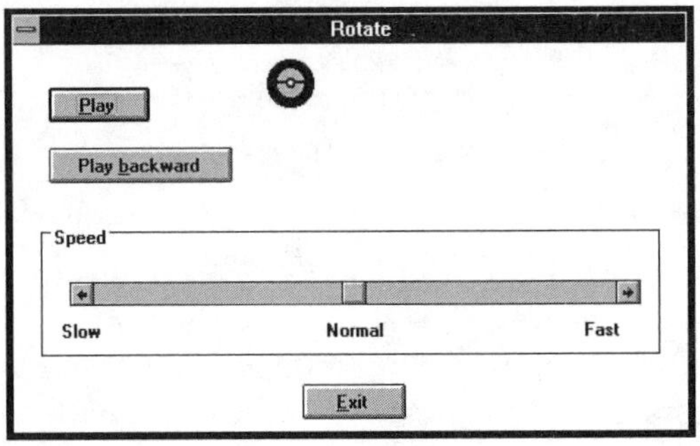

Figure 8.4. The Rotate dialog box.

The Rotate Program Files

The Rotate program consists of the following files:

Rotate.h	The #include file of the program.
Rotate.c	The C code of the program.
Rotate.rc	The resource file of the program.
Rotate.def	The module definition file of the program.
Rotate.mak	The make file of the program.
Tape.ico	The icon of the program.
Axis1.bmp	Position #1 of the wheel.
Axis2.bmp	Position #2 of the wheel.
Axis3.bmp	Position #3 of the wheel.
Axis4.bmp	Position #4 of the wheel.

These files are provided for you in C:\spSDK\Samp4Win\.

The complete listing of the Rotate program is shown in Listings 8.1 through 8.5.

Listing 8.1. Rotate.h.

```
/*=====================================================
FILE NAME: Rotate.h

(C) Copyright Gurewich 1992, 1993
=====================================================*/

/*..........
 prototypes
 ..........*/
long FAR PASCAL _export WndProc          ( HWND, UINT, UINT, LONG ) ;
BOOL FAR PASCAL _export AboutDlgProc     ( HWND, UINT, UINT, LONG ) ;
BOOL FAR PASCAL _export RotateDlgProc    ( HWND, UINT, UINT, LONG ) ;

void ChangeSpeedWasRequested ( HWND ) ;
void RotateRight             ( HWND ) ;
void RotateLeft              ( HWND ) ;
void DisplayAxis             ( HWND, HBITMAP ) ;
```

continues

Listing 8.1. continued

```
/*------
 #define
 ------*/
#define IDM_QUIT    1  /* The Quit   option in the menu */
#define IDM_ABOUT   2  /* The About  option in the menu */
#define IDM_ROTATE 3  /* The Rotate option in the menu */

#define PLAY_PB            101  /* The Play push button.        */
#define SPEED_CHANGE_SB   102  /* The change speed scroll bar.  */
#define EXIT_PB           103  /* The Exit push button.         */
#define PLAY_BACKWARD_PB 104  /* The Play backward push button */

/*----------------
 Speed Scroll Bar.
 ----------------*/
#define NAT_SPEED_SCROLL    0
#define MIN_SPEED_SCROLL -100
#define MAX_SPEED_SCROLL  100

/*--------------
 Global variables
 --------------*/
char      gszAppName[] = "Rotate" ; /* Our application name. */
HINSTANCE ghInst;                    /* current instance.     */

int       giSpeedScroll;             /* Speed scroll bar position. */

HBITMAP   ghAxis1;
HBITMAP   ghAxis2;
HBITMAP   ghAxis3;
HBITMAP   ghAxis4;
```

Listing 8.2. Rotate.c.

```
/*============================================================
 PROGRAM: Rotate.c
 --------
 (C) Copyright 1992, 1993 Gurewich. (R) All rights reserved.

 PROGRAM DESCRIPTION:
 -------------------
 This is a Generic type 1 based program.
```

The program has a scroll bar that lets the user change the
playing speed.

Upon pushing the Play push button, a sound file is played
together with the displaying of a rotating axis.

Upon pushing the Playback push button, a sound file is played
backward together with the displaying of a backward
rotating axis.

```
===========================================================*/

/*--------
 #include
 --------*/
/*-----------------------------------
 Required for all Windows applications.
 -----------------------------------*/
#include <windows.h>

/*------------------------------------------------------------------
 Required so that sp_ functions and SP_ macros and #definitions
 from the TS sound library may be used in this applications.
 ----------------------------------------------------------------*/
#include "c:\spSDK\TegoWlib\sp4Win.h"

/*--------------------------------------------------------
 Definitions & prototypes specific to this application.
 ----------------------------------------------------*/
#include "c:\spSDK\Samp4WIN\Rotate.h"

/*==================
 FUNCTION: WinMain()
 ==================*/
int PASCAL WinMain ( HANDLE hInstance,
                     HANDLE hPrevInstance,
                     LPSTR  lpszCmdLine,
                     int    nCmdShow )
{
/*-------------------------
 Local and static variables.
 -------------------------*/
HWND      hWnd;   /* Handler to the window of our application.  */
MSG       msg;    /* Message to be processed by our application. */
WNDCLASS  wc;     /* Window class of our application.            */
```

continues

Listing 8.2. continued

```
/*---------------------------------------------
Make the hInstance variable a global variable.
---------------------------------------------*/
ghInst = hInstance;

/*---------------------------------------------
Update the window class structure and register
the window class.
---------------------------------------------*/
if ( !hPrevInstance )
    {
    /*---------------------------------------------
    The "if" is satisfied, this is the very 1st
    run of this application.
    ---------------------------------------------*/
    wc.style         = CS_HREDRAW ¦ CS_VREDRAW ;
    wc.lpfnWndProc   = WndProc ;
    wc.cbClsExtra    = 0 ;
    wc.cbWndExtra    = 0 ;
    wc.hInstance     = ghInst ;
    wc.hIcon         = LoadIcon   ( ghInst, "IconOfTape" ) ;
    wc.hCursor       = LoadCursor ( NULL, IDC_ARROW      ) ;
    wc.hbrBackground = GetStockObject ( WHITE_BRUSH );
    wc.lpszMenuName  = gszAppName ;
    wc.lpszClassName = gszAppName ;

    /*-----------------
    Register the window.
    -----------------*/
    RegisterClass ( &wc );

    }/* end of if(!hPrevInstance) */

/*---------------------------------------------
 Create the window of our application.
---------------------------------------------*/
hWnd = CreateWindow ( gszAppName,
                      gszAppName,
                      WS_OVERLAPPEDWINDOW,
                      CW_USEDEFAULT,
                      CW_USEDEFAULT,
                      CW_USEDEFAULT,
                      CW_USEDEFAULT,
                      NULL,
                      NULL,
                      ghInst,
                      NULL );
```

```
/*------------------------------------------------
 Show and update the window of our application.
 ----------------------------------------------*/
ShowWindow   ( hWnd, nCmdShow );
UpdateWindow ( hWnd );

/*-----------------
 The message loop.
 ----------------*/
while ( GetMessage ( &msg, NULL, 0, 0 ) )
      {
      TranslateMessage ( &msg );
      DispatchMessage  ( &msg );
      }

return msg.wParam ;

} /* end of function. */
/*========================= end of WinMain() ====================*/

/*==================
 FUNCTION: WndProc()
 =================*/
/*------------------------------
 DESCRIPTION: Processes messages.
 -----------------------------*/
long FAR PASCAL _export WndProc ( HWND hWnd,
                                  UINT message,
                                  UINT wParam,
                                  LONG lParam )
{
/*--------------------------
 Local and static variables.
 --------------------------*/
HDC          hdc;      /* Needed for displaying text. */
PAINTSTRUCT  ps;       /* Needed for displaying text. */
RECT         rect;     /* Needed for displaying text. */

int          iOpenHelloResult; /* Open Hello session result. */
int          iOpenPressResult; /* Open Press session result. */

static FARPROC lpfnAboutDlgProc  ; /* For the About  dialog box. */
static FARPROC lpfnRotateDlgProc ; /* For the Rotate dialog box. */

switch ( message )
      {
      case WM_CREATE:
```

continues

Listing 8.2. continued

```
            /*---------------------------
            Open the Press sound session.
            --------------------------*/
            iOpenPressResult = sp_OpenSession (
                            "c:\\spSDK\\Sfiles\\Press.s",
                            SP_NON_STAND_ALONE,
                            0L,
                            SP_S_TYPE);
            /*-------------------------
            Quit if can't open the file.
            ------------------------*/
            if ( iOpenPressResult != SP_NO_ERRORS )
               {
               MessageBox ( NULL,
                            "Failed to open the sound session!",
                            "Message from Rotate.exe",
                            MB_ICONINFORMATION );

               /*-------------------
               Quit the application.
               ------------------*/
               SendMessage ( hWnd, WM_DESTROY, 0 ,0 );
               }

            /*--------------------------------------------
            Obtain the lpfnAboutDlgProc of the About
            dialog box.
            -------------------------------------------*/
            lpfnAboutDlgProc =
            MakeProcInstance (( FARPROC) AboutDlgProc, ghInst);

            /*--------------------------------------------
            Obtain the lpfnAboutDlgProc of the Rotate
            dialog box.
            -------------------------------------------*/
            lpfnRotateDlgProc =
            MakeProcInstance (( FARPROC) RotateDlgProc, ghInst);

            return 0;

     case WM_PAINT:
            hdc = BeginPaint ( hWnd, &ps );
            GetClientRect ( hWnd, &rect );
            DrawText ( hdc,
                       "Demonstration",
                       -1,
```

```
                    &rect,
                      DT_SINGLELINE ¦ DT_CENTER ¦ DT_VCENTER );
        EndPaint ( hWnd, &ps );
        return 0;

case WM_COMMAND:
        /*----------------
        Process menu items.
        -----------------*/
        switch (wParam)
                {
                case IDM_QUIT:
                        /*---------------------------
                        User clicked on Quit option.
                        --------------------------*/
                        DestroyWindow (hWnd);
                        return 0L;

                case IDM_ABOUT :
                        /*---------------------------
                        User clicked on About option.
                        --------------------------*/
                        DialogBox ( ghInst,
                                    "AboutBox",
                                    hWnd,
                                    lpfnAboutDlgProc );
                        return 0;

                case IDM_ROTATE :
                        /*---------------------------
                        User clicked on Rotate option.
                        --------------------------*/
                        DialogBox ( ghInst,
                                    "RotateBox",
                                    hWnd,
                                    lpfnRotateDlgProc );
                        return 0;

                }/* end of switch (wParam) */

case WM_DESTROY:
        iOpenHelloResult =
        sp_OpenSession ( "c:\\spSDK\\TSfiles\\Hello.ts",
                         SP_NON_STAND_ALONE,
                         0L,
                         SP_TS_TYPE);
```

continues

Listing 8.2. continued

```
                /*-----------------------------------------
                Don't play if the session was not opened.
                ------------------------------------*/
                if ( iOpenHelloResult == SP_NO_ERRORS )
                    {
                    /*-----------------------------------------
                    Play a section of the sound file.
                    Range to play: 30,000 to 40,000
                    phrase: "Good-Bye"
                    ------------------------------------------*/
                    sp_PlayF ( 30000L, 40000L );
                    }

                PostQuitMessage (0);
                return 0;
            }/* end of switch (message) */

/*------------------------
 Message was not processed.
 ------------------------*/
return DefWindowProc ( hWnd, message, wParam, lParam ) ;

}/* end of WndProc() */
/*================= end of WndProc() ====================*/


/*=======================
 FUNCTION: AboutDlgProc()
 =====================*/
/*-----------------------------------------
 DESCRIPTION:
 This is the About dialog box procedure.
 ------------------------------------*/
BOOL FAR PASCAL _export AboutDlgProc ( HWND hDlg,
                                        UINT message,
                                        UINT wParam,
                                        LONG lParam )
{
switch ( message )
        {
        case WM_INITDIALOG :
                return TRUE;

        case WM_COMMAND :
                switch ( wParam )
                        {
                        case IDOK :
```

```
                    case IDCANCEL :
                            EndDialog ( hDlg, 0 );
                            return TRUE;
                    }
          }
return FALSE ;
}/* End of function. */
/*=============== end of AboutDlgProc() =============*/


/*========================
 FUNCTION: RotateDlgProc()
 =======================*/
/*-----------------------------------------
 DESCRIPTION:
 This is the Rotate dialog box procedure.
 ------------------------------------*/
BOOL FAR PASCAL _export RotateDlgProc ( HWND hDlg,
                                        UINT message,
                                        UINT wParam,
                                        LONG lParam )
{
static HDC          hdc;     /* Needed for displaying.  */
static PAINTSTRUCT  ps;      /* Needed for displaying.  */
static HDC          hMemDC;  /* Needed for displaying bit map. */


HWND hWndCtrl;
long lCurrentByte;

switch ( message )
        {
        case WM_INITDIALOG :
              /*---------------------------------------------------
              Set the max. and min. values of the Speed scroll bar.
              --------------------------------------------------*/
              hWndCtrl = GetDlgItem ( hDlg, SPEED_CHANGE_SB );
              SetScrollRange ( hWndCtrl,
                              SB_CTL,
                              MIN_SPEED_SCROLL,
                              MAX_SPEED_SCROLL,
                              TRUE );

              /*-----------------------------------
              Position the Speed scroll bar at its
              natural speed posistion.
              --------------------------------*/
              SetScrollPos ( hWndCtrl,
                              SB_CTL,
```

continues

Listing 8.2. continued

```
                                 NAT_SPEED_SCROLL,
                                 TRUE );

          giSpeedScroll = NAT_SPEED_SCROLL ;


          ghAxis1 = LoadBitmap ( ghInst, "Axis1" );
          ghAxis2 = LoadBitmap ( ghInst, "Axis2" );
          ghAxis3 = LoadBitmap ( ghInst, "Axis3" );
          ghAxis4 = LoadBitmap ( ghInst, "Axis4" );

          return TRUE;

    case WM_PAINT:

          hdc = BeginPaint ( hDlg, &ps );

          hMemDC = CreateCompatibleDC ( hdc );
          SelectObject ( hMemDC, ghAxis1 );

          BitBlt ( hdc,
                   175,
                   10,
                   32,
                   32,
                   hMemDC,
                   0,
                   0,
                   SRCCOPY );
          DeleteDC ( hMemDC );
          EndPaint ( hDlg, &ps );

          return TRUE;

    case WM_HSCROLL:
          /*----------------------------------------------
          User changed the horizontal scroll bar position.
          ----------------------------------------------*/

          switch ( wParam )
                {
                case SB_PAGEUP:
                case SB_LINEUP:
                      /*------------------------------
                      The scroll bar was decremented.
                      ----------------------------*/
                      giSpeedScroll--;
```

```
                    ChangeSpeedWasRequested ( hDlg );
                    return TRUE;

              case SB_PAGEDOWN:
              case SB_LINEDOWN:
                    /*----------------------------
                    The scroll bar was incremented.
                    ----------------------------*/
                    giSpeedScroll++;
                    ChangeSpeedWasRequested ( hDlg );
                    return TRUE;

              case SB_THUMBPOSITION:
                    /*------------------------
                    The scroll bar was dragged.
                    ------------------------*/
                    giSpeedScroll = LOWORD ( lParam );
                    ChangeSpeedWasRequested ( hDlg );
                    return TRUE;

              } /* end of switch(wParam) */


    case WM_COMMAND :
         switch ( wParam )
              {
              case PLAY_PB:
                    lCurrentByte = 0L;
                    while ( 1 )
                          {
                          lCurrentByte =
                          sp_PlayF ( lCurrentByte,
                                      lCurrentByte + 2000L );

                          RotateRight ( hDlg );

                          if ( lCurrentByte == 0L )
                             break;

                          }/* end of while (1) */

                    return TRUE;

              case PLAY_BACKWARD_PB:
                    lCurrentByte = 16000L;
                    while ( 1 )
```

continues

Listing 8.2. continued

```
                                 {
                                 lCurrentByte =
                                 sp_PlayB ( lCurrentByte,
                                            lCurrentByte - 2000L );

                                 RotateLeft ( hDlg );

                                 if ( lCurrentByte == 0L )
                                    break;

                                 }/* end of while (1) */


                        return TRUE;

                    case EXIT_PB:
                    case IDOK :
                    case IDCANCEL :
                        /*----------------------------------
                        Set the TSEngine playback speed to
                        the natural speed.
                        ---------------------------------*/
                        giSpeedScroll = NAT_SPEED_SCROLL ;
                        sp_SetNewSpeed ( MAX_SPEED_SCROLL,
                                         NAT_SPEED_SCROLL,
                                         NAT_SPEED_SCROLL );

                        DeleteObject ( ghAxis1 );
                        DeleteObject ( ghAxis2 );
                        DeleteObject ( ghAxis3 );
                        DeleteObject ( ghAxis4 );

                        EndDialog ( hDlg, 0 );
                        return TRUE;
                    }/* end of switch(wParam) */

            }/* end of switch(wParam) */

    return FALSE ;

    }/* End of function. */
    /*=============== end of RotateDlgProc() ==============*/
```

```
/*========
 FUNCTION
 ======*/
 /*-----------------------------------------
  User changed the Speed scroll bar position.
  ----------------------------------------*/
void ChangeSpeedWasRequested ( HWND hWnd )
{

HWND  hWndCtrl;

if ( giSpeedScroll >  MAX_SPEED_SCROLL )
   giSpeedScroll = MAX_SPEED_SCROLL;

if ( giSpeedScroll <  MIN_SPEED_SCROLL )
   giSpeedScroll = MIN_SPEED_SCROLL;

sp_SetNewSpeed ( MAX_SPEED_SCROLL,
                 NAT_SPEED_SCROLL,
                 giSpeedScroll );

hWndCtrl = GetDlgItem ( hWnd, SPEED_CHANGE_SB );
SetScrollPos ( hWndCtrl, SB_CTL, giSpeedScroll, TRUE );

}/* end of function. */
/*=================== end of function ==============*/

/*========
 FUNCTION
 ======*/
void RotateRight ( HWND hWnd )
{
static int iRotateFlag = 1;
static HDC hdc;
static HDC hMemDC;

if ( iRotateFlag == 1 )
   {
   DisplayAxis ( hWnd, ghAxis1 );
   iRotateFlag = 2;
   return;
   }

if ( iRotateFlag == 2 )
   {
   DisplayAxis ( hWnd, ghAxis2 );
   iRotateFlag = 3;
   return;
   }
```

continues

Listing 8.2. continued

```c
if ( iRotateFlag == 3 )
    {
    DisplayAxis ( hWnd, ghAxis3 );
    iRotateFlag = 4;
    return;
    }

if ( iRotateFlag == 4 )
    {
    DisplayAxis ( hWnd, ghAxis4 );
    iRotateFlag = 1;
    return;
    }

}/* end of function. */
/*============ end of function: RotateRight() ===========*/

/*========
 FUNCTION
 =======*/
void RotateLeft ( HWND hWnd )
{
static int iRotateFlag = 1;
static HDC hdc;
static HDC hMemDC;

if ( iRotateFlag == 1 )
    {
    DisplayAxis ( hWnd, ghAxis1 );
    iRotateFlag = 4;
    return;
    }

if ( iRotateFlag == 4 )
    {
    DisplayAxis ( hWnd, ghAxis4 );
    iRotateFlag = 3;
    return;
    }
```

```
if ( iRotateFlag == 3 )
   {
   DisplayAxis ( hWnd, ghAxis3 );
   iRotateFlag = 2;
   return;
   }

if ( iRotateFlag == 2 )
   {
   DisplayAxis ( hWnd, ghAxis2 );
   iRotateFlag = 1;
   return;
   }

}/* end of function. */
/*============ end of function: RotateLeft() ===========*/

/*========
 FUNCTION
 =======*/
void DisplayAxis ( HWND hWnd, HBITMAP hAxis)
{
static HDC hdc;
static HDC hMemDC;

hdc = GetDC ( hWnd );
hMemDC = CreateCompatibleDC ( hdc );
SelectObject ( hMemDC, hAxis );

BitBlt ( hdc,
         175,
         10,
         32,
         32,
         hMemDC,
         0,
         0,
         SRCCOPY );

DeleteDC ( hMemDC );
ReleaseDC ( hWnd, hdc   );

}/* end of function. */
/*============ end of function ===========*/
```

Listing 8.3. Rotate.rc.

```
/*=====================================================
FILE NAME: Rotate.rc
- - - - - - - - -

FILE DESCRIPTION:
- - - - - - - - - - - - - - - -
The resource file.

(C) Copyright Gurewich 1992, 1993

=====================================================*/

/*------
 #include
 ------*/
#include <windows.h>
#include "Rotate.h"

/*--
 Menu
 --*/
Rotate   MENU
BEGIN
    POPUP   "&Menu"
        BEGIN
            MENUITEM "&Quit",    IDM_QUIT
            MENUITEM "&About",   IDM_ABOUT
            MENUITEM "&Rotate", IDM_ROTATE
        END
END

/*---------------------------------------
 Definition of the Cassette tape icon.
 File name: Tape.ico
 Icon name: IconOfTape
 ---------------------------------------*/
IconOfTape ICON Tape.ico

/*---------
 Bit maps.
 ---------*/
Axis1 BITMAP Axis1.bmp
Axis2 BITMAP Axis2.bmp
Axis3 BITMAP Axis3.bmp
Axis4 BITMAP Axis4.bmp
```

```
/*--------------------
 The About dialog box.
 -------------------*/
AboutBox DIALOG 81, 43, 160, 100
STYLE DS_MODALFRAME ¦ WS_POPUP ¦ WS_VISIBLE ¦ WS_CAPTION ¦ WS_SYSMENU
CAPTION "About the Rotate program"
FONT 8, "MS Sans Serif"
BEGIN
    PUSHBUTTON      "OK", IDOK, 64, 75, 40, 14
    CTEXT           "(C) Copyright Gurewich 1992, 1993",
                    -1, 13, 47, 137, 18
    ICON            "IconOfTape", -1, 14, 12, 18, 20
END

/*--------------------
 The Rotate dialog box.
 -------------------*/
RotateBox DIALOG 33, 28, 263, 157
STYLE DS_MODALFRAME ¦ WS_POPUP ¦ WS_VISIBLE ¦ WS_CAPTION
                    ¦ WS_SYSMENU
CAPTION "Rotate"
FONT 8, "MS Sans Serif"
BEGIN
    PUSHBUTTON      "&Play", PLAY_PB, 14, 17, 40, 14
    SCROLLBAR       SPEED_CHANGE_SB, 22, 96, 222, 10
    PUSHBUTTON      "&Exit", EXIT_PB, 113, 138, 40, 14
    GROUPBOX        "Speed", -1, 11, 72, 241, 54
    LTEXT           "Normal", -1, 122, 112, 27, 8
    LTEXT           "Fast",   -1, 222, 112, 20, 8
    LTEXT           "Slow",   -1, 19, 112, 20, 8
    PUSHBUTTON      "Play &backward", PLAY_BACKWARD_PB,
                    14, 42, 72, 14
END
```

Listing 8.4. Rotate.def.

```
;=======================================
; module-definition file for Rotate.c
;=======================================

NAME        Rotate

DESCRIPTION 'The Rotate program. (C) Copyright Gurewich 1992, 1993'

EXETYPE     WINDOWS
```

continues

Listing 8.4. continued

```
STUB          'WINSTUB.EXE'

CODE   PRELOAD MOVEABLE DISCARDABLE

DATA   PRELOAD MOVEABLE MULTIPLE

HEAPSIZE      1024
STACKSIZE     8192
```

Listing 8.5. Rotate.mak.

```
#=============
# Rotate.mak
#=============

Rotate.exe : Rotate.obj Rotate.h Rotate.def Rotate.res
    link /nod Rotate.obj, Rotate.exe, NUL, \
        slibcew.lib oldnames.lib libw.lib commdlg \
        c:\spSDK\TegoWlib\TegoWin.lib, \
        Rotate.def
   rc -t Rotate.res

Rotate.obj : Rotate.c Rotate.h
   cl -c -G2sw -Ow -W3 -Zp Rotate.c

Rotate.res : Rotate.rc Rotate.h Tape.ico
   rc -r Rotate.rc
```

Opening the Sound Session

Under the WM_CREATE case we open a sound session for the S-type
C:\spSDK\Sfiles\Press.s sound file as a non-stand-alone program:

```
application:
      case WM_CREATE:
            /*-------------------------
            Open the Press sound session.
            -------------------------*/
```

```
          iOpenPressResult = sp_OpenSession (
                          "c:\\spSDK\\Sfiles\\Press.s",
                          SP_NON_STAND_ALONE,
                          0L,
                          SP_S_TYPE);
          /*-------------------------
          Quit if can't open the file.
          -----------------------*/
          if ( iOpenPressResult != SP_NO_ERRORS )
             {
             MessageBox ( NULL,
                       "Failed to open the sound session!",
                       "Message from Rotate.exe",
                        MB_ICONINFORMATION );

             /*------------------
             Quit the application.
             ------------------*/
             SendMessage ( hWnd, WM_DESTROY, 0 ,0 );
             }
          .............
          .............
          .............
          return 0;
```

Executing the Rotate Dialog Box

We detect that the user selected the Rotate option from the program menu with the IDM_ROTATE case. Under this case we call the DialogBox() function, which causes the Rotate dialog box to appear.

```
case IDM_ROTATE :
     /*---------------------------
     User clicked on Rotate option.
     ---------------------------*/
     DialogBox ( ghInst,
               "RotateBox",
               hWnd,
               lpfnRotateDlgProc );
     return 0;
```

Initializing the Rotate Dialog Box

We initialize the Rotate dialog box under the WM_INITDIALOG case of the Rotate dialog box function:

```
case WM_INITDIALOG :
        .......................................
        ...... Set the maximum and minimum    ....
        ...... values of the Speed scroll bar....
        .......................................

        .......................................
        ......... Position the Speed Scroll .....
        ......... Bar at its natural speed  .....
        ......... position.                 .....
        .......................................

        .......................................
        ...... Save the value of the current ....
        ........ scroll bar position.         ....
        .......................................

        .......................................
        ....... Load the bit maps that are  .....
        ....... used by the Rotating wheel. .....
        .......................................
        return TRUE;
```

Setting the Minimum and Maximum Values of the Speed Scroll Bar

The Speed scroll bar is #defined in Rotate.h as SPEED_CHANGE_SB, and its screen location inside the Rotate dialog box is outlined in Rotate.rc. We also #defined in Rotate.h three constants:

```
#define NAT_SPEED_SCROLL    0
#define MIN_SPEED_SCROLL  -100
#define MAX_SPEED_SCROLL   100
```

These constants define the natural playback speed as zero, the maximum playback speed as 100, and the minimum playback speed as –100. The division of the scroll bar to 200 parts allows the user to adjust the playback speed in small increments.

The maximum and minimum values of the Speed scroll bar are set by extracting the handler `hWndCtrl` of the Speed scroll bar, and then using the `SetScrollRange()` function:

```
/*-------------------------------------------------
Set the max. and min. values of the Speed scroll bar.
-----------------------------------------------------*/
hWndCtrl = GetDlgItem ( hDlg, SPEED_CHANGE_SB );
SetScrollRange ( hWndCtrl,
                 SB_CTL,
                 MIN_SPEED_SCROLL,
                 MAX_SPEED_SCROLL,
                 TRUE );
```

Positioning the Speed Scroll Bar at Its Natural Position

The Speed scroll bar is set at the middle. As you will see shortly, this will result in a natural playback speed. To set the Speed scroll bar at the middle, we use the `SetScrollPos()` function:

```
/*----------------------------------
Position the Speed scroll bar at its
natural speed position.
--------------------------------*/
SetScrollPos ( hWndCtrl,
               SB_CTL,
               NAT_SPEED_SCROLL,
               TRUE );
```

Saving the Current Position of the Speed Scroll Bar

Throughout the program, we keep track of the current position of the Speed scroll bar by saving its current position value to the variable `giSpeedScroll`. Currently, the Speed scroll bar is in its natural position, so we update the `giSpeedScroll` variable accordingly:

```
giSpeedScroll = NAT_SPEED_SCROLL ;
```

Loading Bit-Map Files Used in the Rotate Dialog Box

Four bit maps are used in the Rotate dialog box. Each bit-map file shows a wheel in a different position. These bit-map files are shown in Figure 8.5. We load the bit-map files by using the LoadBitmap() function:

```
ghAxis1 = LoadBitmap ( ghInst, "Axis1" );
ghAxis2 = LoadBitmap ( ghInst, "Axis2" );
ghAxis3 = LoadBitmap ( ghInst, "Axis3" );
ghAxis4 = LoadBitmap ( ghInst, "Axis4" );
```

a) Wheel position 1.   b) Wheel position 2.   c) Wheel position 3.   d) Wheel position 4.

Figure 8.5. The four bit maps used in the Rotate dialog box.

The *WM_PAINT* Case of the Rotate Dialog Box

Under the WM_PAINT case of the Rotate dialog box we display the wheel in its Axis1 position. We do that using the BitBlt() function:

```
case WM_PAINT:

        hdc = BeginPaint ( hDlg, &ps );

        hMemDC = CreateCompatibleDC ( hdc );
        SelectObject ( hMemDC, ghAxis1 );

        BitBlt ( hdc,
                175,
                10,
                32,
                32,
                hMemDC,
                0,
                0,
                SRCCOPY );
        DeleteDC ( hMemDC );
        EndPaint ( hDlg, &ps );

        return TRUE;
```

The *WM_HSCROLL* Case

Whenever the user changes the position of the Speed scroll bar, the WM_HSCROLL message is received. The WM_HSCROLL message is generated whenever the user decrements the Speed scroll bar, increments the Speed scroll bar, or moves the thumb of the Speed scroll bar:

```
case WM_HSCROLL:
    switch ( wParam )
        {
        case SB_PAGEUP:
        case SB_LINEUP:
                ....................................
                .... Scroll bar was incremented ....
                ....................................
                return TRUE;

        case SB_PAGEDOWN:
        case SB_LINEDOWN:
                ....................................
                .... Scroll bar was decremented ....
                ....................................
                return TRUE;

        case SB_THUMBPOSITION:
                ....................................
                .... The thumb of the speed   ....
                .... scroll bar was dragged.  ....
                ....................................
                return TRUE;

        } /* end of switch(wParam) */
```

Incrementing and Decrementing the Speed Scroll Bar

If wParam equals to either SB_PAGEUP or SB_LINEUP, it means that the user decremented the scroll bar by one. Upon discovering that our scroll bar was decremented, we decrement the variable giSpeedScroll and then execute the ChangeSpeedWasRequested() function.

The preceeding code is repeated when the user increments the scroll bar. The only difference is that in that case we increment the variable giSpeedScroll.

Dragging the Speed Scroll Bar

When the user drags the thumb position of the Speed scroll bar, the SB_THUMBPOSITION message is received. Under the SB_THUMBPOSITION case we update the variable giSpeedScroll with the new position of the scroll bar. The new position of the scroll bar is given by the low word of lParam that comes with the message. The last thing that we do under this case is execute the ChangeSpeedWasRequested() function.

The *ChangeSpeedWasRequested()* Function

We execute the ChangeSpeedWasRequested() function whenever the scroll bar is modified (that is, incremented, decremented, or dragged). This function checks that the new value of the variable giSpeedScroll is within a valid range:

```
if ( giSpeedScroll >  MAX_SPEED_SCROLL )
   giSpeedScroll = MAX_SPEED_SCROLL;

if ( giSpeedScroll <  MIN_SPEED_SCROLL )
   giSpeedScroll = MIN_SPEED_SCROLL;
```

After validating giSpeedScroll we tell the TSEngine to change the playback speed with the sp_SetNewSpeed() function:

```
sp_SetNewSpeed ( MAX_SPEED_SCROLL,
                 NAT_SPEED_SCROLL,
                 giSpeedScroll );
```

We then set the scroll bar to its new position:

```
hWndCtrl = GetDlgItem ( hWnd, SPEED_CHANGE_SB );
SetScrollPos ( hWndCtrl, SB_CTL, giSpeedScroll, TRUE );
```

The *sp_SetNewSpeed()* Function

The sp_SetNewSpeed() function tells the TSEngine to set a new playback speed. The prototype of sp_SetNewSpeed() is declared in the c:\spSDK\TegoWlib\sp4Win.h file as

```
int sp_SetNewSpeed ( int, int, int );
```

This function returns an integer, but its value has no meaning. The function takes three parameters. The first parameter is an integer that represents the maximum speed; the second parameter is an integer that represents the natural speed; and the third parameter is an integer that represents the new speed setting.

For example, the execution of

```
sp_SetNewSpeed ( 10, 5, 6 );
```

means that the maximum speed is 10, the natural speed is 5, and the new value of the speed should be changed to 6, which is greater than 5 and, therefore, faster.

In our program we execute the sp_SetNewSpeed() as follows:

```
sp_SetNewSpeed ( MAX_SPEED_SCROLL,
                 NAT_SPEED_SCROLL,
                 giSpeedScroll );
```

This means that the maximum speed is MAX_SPEED_SCROLL (which we #defined as 100), the natural speed is NAT_SPEED_SCROLL (which we #defined as 0), and the new speed is giSpeedScroll (which we limited to be in the range −100 to +100).

NOTE The sp_SetNewSpeed() function takes three parameters:

First parameter: Integer. Specifies the maximum speed.

Second parameter: Integer. Specifies the natural speed.

Third parameter: Integer. Specifies the new speed.

The sp_OpenSession() function must be executed prior to executing the sp_SetNewSpeed() function.

The *PLAY_PB* Push Button of the Rotate Dialog Box

Whenever the user pushes the Play push button, the code under the PLAY_PB case is executed. Under the PLAY_PB case we play the sound file in groups of 2,000 bytes each. Between groups we execute the RotateRight() function:

```
case PLAY_PB:
    lCurrentByte = 0L;
    while ( 1 )
            {
            lCurrentByte =
            sp_PlayF ( lCurrentByte,
                      lCurrentByte + 2000L );

            RotateRight ( hDlg );
            if ( lCurrentByte == 0L )
                break;

            }/* end of while (1) */

            return TRUE;
```

The RotateRight() function is responsible for rotating the wheel in the clockwise direction.

The *PLAY_BACKWARD_PB* Case of the Rotate Dialog Box

Whenever the user pushes the Play backward push button, the code under the PLAY_BACKWARD_PB is executed:

```
case PLAY_BACKWARD_PB:
    lCurrentByte = 16000L;
    while ( 1 )
            {
            lCurrentByte =
            sp_PlayB ( lCurrentByte,
                      lCurrentByte - 2000L );

            RotateLeft ( hDlg );

            if ( lCurrentByte == 0L )
                break;

            }/* end of while (1) */
    return TRUE;
```

The *sp_PlayB()* Function

The sp_PlayB() function is a TS C sound library function (you can tell by the first three characters: sp_).

The prototype of this function is declared in c:\spSDK\TegoWlib\sp4Win.h as

```
long sp_PlayB( long lStartPoint,
               long lEndPoint );
```

The sp_PlayB() function is very similar to the sp_PlayF() function. (The *F* stands for Forward, and the *B* stands for Backward.)

The function returns a long integer, which represents the last byte played. The first parameter is a long integer that represents the first byte to play; the second parameter is a long integer that represents the last byte to play. Because the sp_PlayB() function plays the sound in the backward direction, the first parameter should be larger than the second parameter. Otherwise, the sp_PlayF() and sp_PlayB() functions are alike.

NOTE The sp_PlayB() function takes two parameters:

First parameter: Long integer. Specifies the first byte coordinate of the section to be played.

Second parameter: Long integer. Specifies the last byte coordinate of the section to be played.

Returns: The return value is a long integer that represents the last byte played.

The sp_OpenSession() function must be executed prior to executing the sp_PlayB() function.

Because the function plays the sound in the backward direction, the value of its first parameter should be greater than its second parameter.

The *ROTATERIGHT()* and *ROTATELEFT()* Functions

The RotateRight() function causes the wheel to rotate in the clockwise direction, and the RotateLeft() function causes the wheel to rotate in the counterclockwise direction.

The RotateRight() function is called between the forward playback of 2,000 bytes, and the RotateLeft() function is called between the backward playback of 2,000 bytes.

The RotateRight() function uses a static variable iRotateFlag. This flag indicates which wheel position should be displayed next. Initially, the iRotateFlag flag is set to 1. Upon calling the RotateRight() function, the first if statement detects the flag is equal to 1, and the DisplayAxis() function is executed:

```
if ( iRotateFlag == 1 )
   {
   DisplayAxis ( hWnd, ghAxis1 );
   iRotateFlag = 2;
   return;
   }
```

The second parameter of DisplayAxis() is ghAxis1, which causes the display of the wheel in position 1.

Within the if statement we also set the value of iRotateFlag to 2 so that the next time RotateRight() is executed, the second if statement will be satisfied.

The following is the second if statement:

```
if ( iRotateFlag == 2 )
   {
   DisplayAxis ( hWnd, ghAxis2 );
   iRotateFlag = 3;
   return;
   }
```

This time the second parameter of DisplayAxis() is ghAxis2, which causes the display of the wheel in position 2.

The flag iRotateFlag is defined as a static variable so that its value is not reinitialized after each execution of the RotateRight() function.

The iRotateFlag flag goes through the sequence of

1 -> 2 -> 3 -> 4 -> 1 -> 2 -> ...

which gives the illusion that the wheel is rotating in the clockwise direction.

The RotateLeft() function is identical to the RotateRight() function, but the iRotateFlag flag goes through the sequence of

1 -> 4 -> 3 -> 2 -> 1 -> 4-> ...

which gives the illusion that the wheel is rotating in the counterclockwise direction.

More About the *sp_PlayB()* Function

In the Rotate program, we execute the sp_PlayB() function to play a type S sound file in the backward direction. The sp_PlayB() function can be applied to other types of sound files (for example, TS, WAV, VOC, SND). However, the short version of the TS library supports the sp_PlayB() function only for S-type sound files.

There are many practical uses for the sp_PlayB() function. For example, you may write a program that displays a tape-recorder machine with all the regular tape-recorder buttons: Pause, Rewind, Fast Forward, and Play. When implementing the Rewind button, your program should cause the tape to rewind; while the tape is rewinding, your program may also play the tape in the backward direction. The sp_PlayB() function can also be used to verify or dispute the rumors that certain rock and roll records have hidden messages in them. The rumors claim that sections of the record (usually toward the end of the record) contain audio messages that are played backward. You may verify (or dispute) these rumors by using the sp_PlayB() function to play the suspected reversed sections in reverse. (When playing an already reversed recording in the backward direction, you hear the original recording.)

Exiting From the Rotate Dialog Box

When the user exits from the Rotate dialog box, we use the sp_SetNewSpeed() function to set the TSEngine playback speed back to its natural speed. We also delete the bit maps that were used in the Rotate dialog box:

```
case EXIT_PB:
case IDOK :
case IDCANCEL :
    /*--------------------------------
    Set the TSEngine playback speed to
    the natural speed.
    --------------------------------*/
```

```
giSpeedScroll = NAT_SPEED_SCROLL ;
sp_SetNewSpeed ( MAX_SPEED_SCROLL,
                 NAT_SPEED_SCROLL,
                 giSpeedScroll );

DeleteObject ( ghAxis1 );
DeleteObject ( ghAxis2 );
DeleteObject ( ghAxis3 );
DeleteObject ( ghAxis4 );

EndDialog ( hDlg, 0 );
return TRUE;
```

The reason for setting the TSEngine playback speed to its natural speed is that the user may have changed the Speed scroll bar from the natural speed, and then exited the Rotate dialog box without changing the Speed scroll bar back to the natural speed. We want to make sure that when the user pushes the Exit push button and exits from the Rotate dialog box, the TSEngine playback speed is at the natural speed.

The Controls Program

The Controls program plays a sound file and lets the user control the various playback parameters. The user can change the speed of the playback (even during the playback), rewind, fast forward, and pause the playback. Several new sp_ functions are used in this program.

We recommend that you compile, link, and execute the program before studying its code. This way you'll gain a better understanding of what the program can do.

Compiling, Linking, and Executing the Controls Program

To compile and link the Controls program from the Microsoft compiler:

- Make sure your PC is in a DOS-protected mode.

- Log into C:\spSDK\Samp4Win\.

- At the DOS prompt type

  `NMAKE Controls.mak   {Enter}`

To compile and link the Controls program from the Borland compiler:

- Log into c:\spSDK\Samp4Win\.

- At the DOS prompt type

  `NMAKE -f Controls.bmk   {Enter}`

To execute the Controls program:

- Select Run from the File menu of the Program Manager of Windows.

- Click Browse and select the file

  `c:\spSDK\Samp4Win\Controls.exe`

The main window appears, as shown in Figure 8.6.

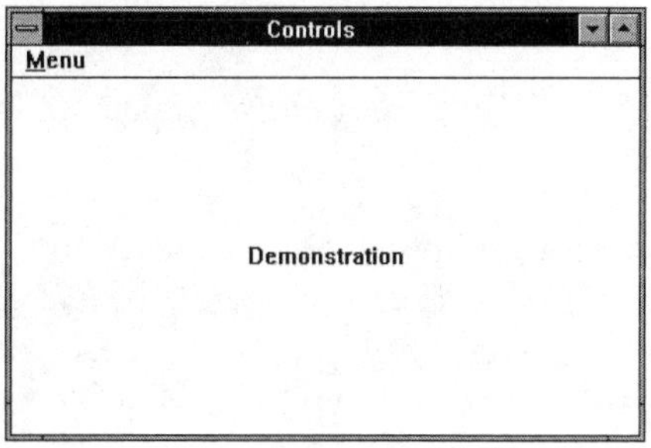

Figure 8.6. The main window of the Controls program.

The Controls program menu (see Figure 8.7) contains three options: Quit, About, and Controls.

When the user selects the Quit option, the program says *Good-bye* and terminates. When the user selects the About option, the About dialog box appears as shown in Figure 8.8. When the user selects the Controls option, the Controls dialog box appears, as shown in Figure 8.9. As shown, the dialog box contains several push buttons, scroll bars, and text.

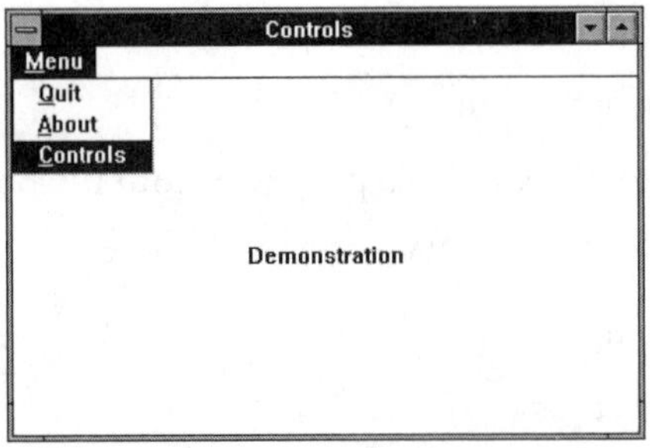

Figure 8.7. The Controls program menu.

Figure 8.8. The About dialog box of the Controls program.

When the user pushes the Play push button, a sound file is played. While the sound file is playing, the user may change the playback speed by pressing **F** to play the sound file ,faster, or by pressing **L** to play the sound file slower. The user may also press **S** to stop the playback.

There are several things moving and changing during the playback. The text inside the Position in Seconds box indicates the current position of the playback. The Controls dialog box has a rewind/forward scroll bar. This scroll bar also indicates the current position of the playback. The thumb of this scroll bar moves during the playback.

When the file is not played, the user may rewind and fast forward the rewind/forward scroll bar, positioning the current position of the sound file to any desired position.

The upper-left text box of the dialog box displays the sampling rate of the sound file. The right text box displays the total length in seconds of the sound file.

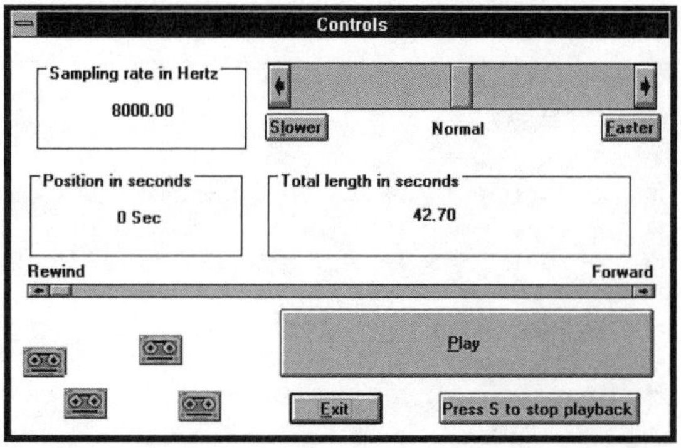

Figure 8.9. The Controls dialog box.

The Files of the Controls Program

The Control program consists of the following files:

Controls.h	The #include file of the program.
Controls.c	The C code of the program.
Controls.rc	The resource file of the program.
Controls.def	The module definition file of the program.
Controls.mak	The make file of the program.
Tape.ico	The icon of the program.

These files are provided for you in c:\spSDK\Samp4Win\. All the Controls files are found in Listings 8.6 through 8.10.

Listing 8.6. Controls.h.

```
/*===================================================
FILE NAME: Controls.h

(C) Copyright Gurewich 1992, 1993
===================================================*/
```

continues

Listing 8.6. continued

```
/*---------
  prototypes
  --------*/
long FAR PASCAL _export WndProc           ( HWND, UINT, UINT, LONG ) ;
BOOL FAR PASCAL _export AboutDlgProc      ( HWND, UINT, UINT, LONG ) ;
BOOL FAR PASCAL _export ControlsDlgProc ( HWND, UINT, UINT, LONG ) ;

void ChangeSpeedWasRequested    ( HWND );
void ChangePositionWasRequested ( HWND );
void DisplayLocation            ( HWND, long );
void DisplayFileSize            ( HWND );
void DisplaySamplingRate        ( HWND hDlg);

/*------
  #define
  ------*/
#define IDM_QUIT     1  /* The Quit     option in the menu */
#define IDM_ABOUT    2  /* The About    option in the menu */
#define IDM_CONTROLS 3  /* The Controls option in the menu */

#define PLAY_PB        101 /* The Play push button.        */
#define SPEED_SB       102 /* The change speed    scroll bar. */
#define POSITION_SB    103 /* The change position scroll bar. */
#define POSITION_TEXT 104 /* The position text.      */
#define SAMPLING_TEXT 105 /* The sampling text.      */
#define TOTAL_TEXT    106 /* Total length text.      */
#define FAST_PB       107 /* The Faster speed push button.   */
#define SLOW_PB       108 /* The Slower speed push button.   */
#define EXIT_PB       109 /* The Exit push button. */

/*----------------
  Speed Scroll Bar.
  ---------------*/
#define NAT_SPEED_SCROLL    0
#define MIN_SPEED_SCROLL -100
#define MAX_SPEED_SCROLL  100


/*------------------
  Position Scroll Bar.
  -----------------*/
#define MIN_POSITION_SCROLL 0
#define MAX_POSITION_SCROLL 100
```

```
/*---------------
 Global variables
 --------------*/
char       gszAppName[] = "Controls" ; /* Our application name.  */
HINSTANCE  ghInst;                     /* current instance.      */

int        giSpeedScroll;       /* Location of speed scroll bar.   */
int        giPositionScroll;    /* Location of position scroll bar.*/
long       glFileSizeInBytes;   /* Sound file size.      */
long       glCurrentByte;       /* Sound file position. */
long       glSamplingRate;      /* The sampling rate.    */
```

Listing 8.7. Controls.c.

```
/*============================================================
 PROGRAM: Controls.c
 -------
 (C) Copyright 1992, 1993 Gurewich. (R) All rights reserved.

 PROGRAM DESCRIPTION:
 ------------------
 This is a Generic type 1 based program.

 The program has scroll bars that let the user change the
 playing speed and the sound file position.

 Upon pushing the Play push button, a sound file is played
 together with the displaying of the file position.

 This program also illustrates how the sampling rate and the
 file size may be extracted from the TSEngine.
 ============================================================*/


/*--------
 #include
 --------*/
/*------------------------------------
 Required for all Windows applications.
 ------------------------------------*/
#include <windows.h>
```

continues

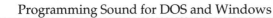

Listing 8.7. continued

```c
/*-------------------------------------------------------------
Required so that sp_ functions and SP_ macros and #definitions
from the TS sound library may be used in this application.
-----------------------------------------------------------*/
#include "c:\spSDK\TegoWlib\sp4Win.h"

/*-------------------------------------------------------
Definitions & prototypes specific to this application.
-----------------------------------------------------*/
#include "c:\spSDK\Samp4WIN\Controls.h"

/*----------------------------------------------------------
For C functions that require the standard C #include files.
--------------------------------------------------------*/
#include <stdlib.h>
#include <stdio.h>
#include <string.h>


/*==================
FUNCTION: WinMain()
==================*/
int PASCAL WinMain ( HANDLE hInstance,
                     HANDLE hPrevInstance,
                     LPSTR  lpszCmdLine,
                     int    nCmdShow )
{
/*------------------------
Local and static variables.
------------------------*/
HWND      hWnd;   /* Handler to the window of our application.  */
MSG       msg;    /* Message to be processed by our application. */
WNDCLASS  wc;     /* Window class of our application.            */

/*-------------------------------------------------
Make the hInstance variable a global variable.
-----------------------------------------------*/
ghInst = hInstance;

/*-------------------------------------------------
Update the window class structure and register
the window class.
-----------------------------------------------*/
if ( !hPrevInstance )
    {
```

```
/*------------------------------------------
The "if" is satisfied, this is the very 1st
run of this application.
----------------------------------------*/
wc.style          = CS_HREDRAW ¦ CS_VREDRAW ;
wc.lpfnWndProc    = WndProc ;
wc.cbClsExtra     = 0 ;
wc.cbWndExtra     = 0 ;
wc.hInstance      = ghInst ;
wc.hIcon          = LoadIcon   ( ghInst, "IconOfTape" ) ;
wc.hCursor        = LoadCursor ( NULL, IDC_ARROW        ) ;
wc.hbrBackground  = GetStockObject ( WHITE_BRUSH );
wc.lpszMenuName   = gszAppName ;
wc.lpszClassName  = gszAppName ;

/*-----------------
Register the window.
-----------------*/
RegisterClass ( &wc );

}/* end of if(!hPrevInstance) */

/*------------------------------------
 Create the window of our application.
 ------------------------------------*/
hWnd = CreateWindow ( gszAppName,
                      gszAppName,
                      WS_OVERLAPPEDWINDOW,
                      CW_USEDEFAULT,
                      CW_USEDEFAULT,
                      CW_USEDEFAULT,
                      CW_USEDEFAULT,
                      NULL,
                      NULL,
                      ghInst,
                      NULL );

/*-----------------------------------------------
 Show and update the window of our application.
 ---------------------------------------------*/
ShowWindow   ( hWnd, nCmdShow );
UpdateWindow ( hWnd );

/*----------------
 The message loop.
 ---------------*/
while ( GetMessage ( &msg, NULL, 0, 0 ) )
    {
```

continues

Listing 8.7. continued

```
        TranslateMessage ( &msg );
        DispatchMessage  ( &msg );
        }

return msg.wParam ;

} /* end of function. */
/*========================= end of WinMain() ====================*/

/*==================
 FUNCTION: WndProc()
 ==================*/
/*-----------------------------
 DESCRIPTION: Processes messages.
 ----------------------------*/
long FAR PASCAL _export WndProc ( HWND hWnd,
                                  UINT message,
                                  UINT wParam,
                                  LONG lParam )
{
/*--------------------------
 Local and static variables.
 -------------------------*/
HDC          hdc;       /* Needed for displaying text. */
PAINTSTRUCT  ps;        /* Needed for displaying text. */
RECT         rect;      /* Needed for displaying text. */

int          iOpenHelloResult; /* Open Hello session result. */
int          iOpenMusicResult; /* Open Music session result. */

static FARPROC lpfnAboutDlgProc;    /* For the About    dialog box. */
static FARPROC lpfnControlsDlgProc;/* For the Controls dialog box. */

switch ( message )
        {
        case WM_CREATE:

                /*---------------------------
                 Open the Music sound session.
                 --------------------------*/
                iOpenMusicResult = sp_OpenSession (
                            "c:\\spSDK\\TSfiles\\Music.ts",
                            SP_NON_STAND_ALONE,
                            0L,
                            SP_TS_TYPE);
```

```
          /*--------------------------
          Quit if can't open the file.
          -------------------------*/
          if ( iOpenMusicResult != SP_NO_ERRORS )
              {
              MessageBox ( NULL,
                        "Failed to open the sound session!",
                        "Message from Controls.exe",
                         MB_ICONINFORMATION );

              /*-------------------
              Quit the application.
              -------------------*/
              SendMessage ( hWnd, WM_DESTROY, 0 ,0 );
              }

          /*----------------------------------------
          Obtain the lpfnAboutDlgProc of the About
          dialog box.
          ----------------------------------------*/
          lpfnAboutDlgProc =
          MakeProcInstance (( FARPROC) AboutDlgProc, ghInst);

          /*----------------------------------------
          Obtain the lpfnAboutDlgProc of the Controls
          dialog box.
          ----------------------------------------*/
          lpfnControlsDlgProc =
          MakeProcInstance (( FARPROC) ControlsDlgProc, ghInst);

          return 0;

   case WM_PAINT:
          hdc = BeginPaint ( hWnd, &ps );
          GetClientRect ( hWnd, &rect );
          DrawText ( hdc,
                   "Demonstration",
                   -1,
                   &rect,
                    DT_SINGLELINE | DT_CENTER | DT_VCENTER );
          EndPaint ( hWnd, &ps );
          return 0;

   case WM_COMMAND:
          /*----------------
          Process menu items.
          ----------------*/
```

continues

Listing 8.7. continued

```
            switch (wParam)
                    {
                    case IDM_QUIT:
                            /*---------------------------
                            User clicked on Quit option.
                            --------------------------*/
                            DestroyWindow (hWnd);
                            return 0L;

                    case IDM_ABOUT :
                            /*---------------------------
                            User clicked on About option.
                            --------------------------*/
                            DialogBox ( ghInst,
                                        "AboutBox",
                                        hWnd,
                                        lpfnAboutDlgProc );
                            return 0;

                    case IDM_CONTROLS:
                            /*----------------------------
                            User clicked on Controls option.
                            ---------------------------*/
                            DialogBox ( ghInst,
                                        "ControlsBox",
                                        hWnd,
                                        lpfnControlsDlgProc );
                            return 0;

                    }/* end of switch (wParam) */

        case WM_DESTROY:
            iOpenHelloResult =
            sp_OpenSession ( "c:\\spSDK\\TSfiles\\Hello.ts",
                            SP_NON_STAND_ALONE,
                            0L,
                            SP_TS_TYPE);

        /*----------------------------------------
        Don't play if the session was not opened.
        --------------------------------------*/
        if ( iOpenHelloResult == SP_NO_ERRORS )
            {
            /*----------------------------------------
            Play a section of the sound file.
            Range to play: 30,000 to 40,000
```

```
                 phrase: "Good-Bye"
                 ----------------------------------------*/
                 sp_PlayF ( 30000L, 40000L );
                 }

           PostQuitMessage (0);
           return 0;
      }/* end of switch (message) */

/*------------------------
 Message was not processed.
 -----------------------*/
return DefWindowProc ( hWnd, message, wParam, lParam ) ;

}/* end of WndProc() */
/*================== end of WndProc() ====================*/

/*=======================
 FUNCTION: AboutDlgProc()
 =======================*/
/*---------------------------------------
 DESCRIPTION:
 This is the About dialog box procedure.
 ---------------------------------------*/
BOOL FAR PASCAL _export AboutDlgProc ( HWND hDlg,
                                       UINT message,
                                       UINT wParam,
                                       LONG lParam )
{
switch ( message )
      {
      case WM_INITDIALOG :
           return TRUE;

      case WM_COMMAND :
           switch ( wParam )
                 {
                 case IDOK :
                 case IDCANCEL :
                     EndDialog ( hDlg, 0 );
                     return TRUE;
                 }
      }
return FALSE ;
}/* End of function. */
/*=============== end of AboutDlgProc() ==============*/
```

continues

Listing 8.7. continued

```
/*========================
 FUNCTION: ControlsDlgProc()
 ========================*/
/*----------------------------------------
 DESCRIPTION:
 This is the Controls dialog box procedure.
 ----------------------------------------*/
BOOL FAR PASCAL _export ControlsDlgProc ( HWND hDlg,
                                          UINT message,
                                          UINT wParam,
                                          LONG lParam )

{
MSG   msg;

HWND  hWndCtrl;
HWND  hWndCtrlSpeed;
HWND  hWndCtrlPosition;

switch ( message )
        {
        case WM_INITDIALOG :
                /*----------------------------------------
                Get the sampling rate from the TSEngine
                and display it.
                ----------------------------------------*/
                DisplaySamplingRate ( hDlg);

                /*----------------------------------------
                Initialize the current byte counter
                to the beginning of the sound file.
                ----------------------------------------*/
                glCurrentByte = 0L;

                /*----------------------------------------
                Find the size (in bytes) of the sound file.
                ----------------------------------------*/
                glFileSizeInBytes = sp_GetFileSizeInBytes ();

                /*----------------------------------------
                Find and display the size (in seconds) of
                the sound file.
                ----------------------------------------*/
                DisplayFileSize ( hDlg );

                /*----------------------------------------
                Set the max. and min. values of the Speed scroll bar.
                ----------------------------------------*/
```

```
hWndCtrlSpeed = GetDlgItem ( hDlg, SPEED_SB );
SetScrollRange ( hWndCtrlSpeed,
                 SB_CTL,
                 MIN_SPEED_SCROLL,
                 MAX_SPEED_SCROLL,
                 TRUE );

/*---------------------------------------------------------
Set the max. and min. values of the Position scroll bar.
---------------------------------------------------------*/
hWndCtrlPosition = GetDlgItem ( hDlg, POSITION_SB );
SetScrollRange ( hWndCtrlPosition,
                 SB_CTL,
                 MIN_POSITION_SCROLL,
                 MAX_POSITION_SCROLL,
                 TRUE );

/*---------------------------------------
Position the Speed scroll bar at its
natural speed position.
---------------------------------*/
SetScrollPos ( hWndCtrlSpeed,
               SB_CTL,
               NAT_SPEED_SCROLL,
               TRUE );

/*---------------------------------------
The variable giSpeedScroll is updated.
This variable reflects the position of
the Speed scroll bar.
-----------------------------------*/
giSpeedScroll = NAT_SPEED_SCROLL ;

/*---------------------------------------
Position the Position scroll bar at its
beginning point.
-------------------------------------*/
SetScrollPos ( hWndCtrlPosition,
               SB_CTL,
               MIN_POSITION_SCROLL,
               TRUE );

/*-----------------------------------------
The variable giPositionScroll is updated.
This variable reflects the position of
the Position Scroll bar.
---------------------------------------*/
giPositionScroll = MIN_SPEED_SCROLL ;
return TRUE;
```

continues

Listing 8.7. continued

```
case WM_HSCROLL:
    /*----------------------------------------------------
    User changed the position of one of the scroll bars.
    ----------------------------------------------------*/
    /*----------------------------------------------------
    Extracting the window handler of the scroll bar that
    caused this message to arrive.
    ----------------------------------------------------*/
    hWndCtrl = HIWORD ( lParam );

    switch ( wParam )
        {
        case SB_PAGEUP:
        case SB_LINEUP:
            if ( GetDlgItem ( hDlg, SPEED_SB )
                == hWndCtrl )
                {
                /*----------------------------------------
                The Speed scroll bar was decremented.
                ----------------------------------*/
                giSpeedScroll--;
                ChangeSpeedWasRequested ( hDlg );
                return TRUE;
                }
            else
                {
                /*----------------------------------------
                The Position scroll bar was decremented.
                ----------------------------------*/
                giPositionScroll-=2;
                ChangePositionWasRequested ( hDlg );
                return TRUE;
                }

        case SB_PAGEDOWN:
        case SB_LINEDOWN:
            if ( GetDlgItem ( hDlg, SPEED_SB )
                == hWndCtrl )
                {
                /*----------------------------------------
                The Speed scroll bar was incremented.
                ----------------------------------*/
                giSpeedScroll++;
                ChangeSpeedWasRequested ( hDlg );
                return TRUE;
                }
```

```
            else
                {
                /*-------------------------------------
                The Position scroll bar was incremented.
                ------------------------------------*/
                giPositionScroll+=2;
                ChangePositionWasRequested ( hDlg );
                return TRUE;
                }

        case SB_THUMBPOSITION:
            if ( GetDlgItem ( hDlg, SPEED_SB )
                == hWndCtrl )
                {
                /*------------------------------
                The Speed scroll bar was dragged.
                -----------------------------*/
                giSpeedScroll = LOWORD ( lParam );
                ChangeSpeedWasRequested ( hDlg );
                return TRUE;
                }
            else
                {
                /*----------------------------------
                The Position scroll bar was dragged.
                --------------------------------*/
                giPositionScroll = LOWORD ( lParam );
                ChangePositionWasRequested ( hDlg );
                return TRUE;
                }

        } /* end of switch(wParam) */


case WM_COMMAND :
    SetFocus ( hDlg );

    switch ( wParam )
        {
        case FAST_PB:
            /*------------------------------------------
            User pushed the Faster push button to
            increase the playback speed.
            ------------------------------------------*/
            giSpeedScroll++;
            ChangeSpeedWasRequested ( hDlg );
            return TRUE;
```

continues

Listing 8.7. continued

```
            case SLOW_PB:
                /*-----------------------------------------
                User pushed the Slow push button to
                decrease the playback speed.
                -----------------------------------------*/
                giSpeedScroll--;
                ChangeSpeedWasRequested ( hDlg );
                return TRUE;

            case PLAY_PB:
                /*-----------------------------------------
                User pushed the Play push button to start
                the playback.
                -----------------------------------------*/
                while ( 1 )
                        {
                        glCurrentByte =
                        sp_PlayF ( glCurrentByte,
                                glCurrentByte + 7000L );

                        DisplayLocation ( hDlg, glCurrentByte );

                        if ( glCurrentByte == 0L )
                            break;

                        /*----------------------------
                        Check if the user pressed a key
                        during the playback.
                        ----------------------------*/
                        if ( PeekMessage ( &msg,
                                        hDlg,
                                        0,
                                        0,
                                        PM_REMOVE ) )
                            {
                            TranslateMessage ( &msg );
                            if ( msg.message == WM_CHAR &&
                                toupper(msg.wParam) == 'S')
                                {
                                /*----------------------------
                                User pressed 'S' or 's' during
                                the playback to stop.
                                ----------------------------*/
                                return TRUE;
                                }
```

```
                              if ( msg.message == WM_CHAR &&
                                   toupper(msg.wParam) == 'L')
                              {
                              /*-----------------------------
                              User pressed 'L' or 'l' during
                              the playback to decrease speed.
                              ---------------------------*/
                              giSpeedScroll-=5;
                              ChangeSpeedWasRequested ( hDlg );
                              continue;
                              }

                              if ( msg.message == WM_CHAR &&
                                   toupper(msg.wParam) == 'F')
                              {
                              /*-----------------------------
                              User pressed 'F' or 'f' during
                              the playback to increase speed.
                              ---------------------------*/
                              giSpeedScroll+=5;
                              ChangeSpeedWasRequested ( hDlg );
                              continue;
                              }

                          }/* end of if(PeekMessage()) */
                     }/* end of while (1) */

                return TRUE;

            case EXIT_PB:
            case IDOK :
            case IDCANCEL :
                giSpeedScroll = NAT_SPEED_SCROLL;
                sp_SetNewSpeed ( MAX_SPEED_SCROLL,
                                 NAT_SPEED_SCROLL,
                                 giSpeedScroll );

                EndDialog ( hDlg, 0 );
                return TRUE;
            }/* end of switch(wParam) */

        }/* end of switch(wParam) */

    return FALSE ;

}/* End of function. */
/*=============== end of ControlsDlgProc() ==============*/
```

continues

Listing 8.7. continued

```
/*========
 FUNCTION
 =======*/
 /*----------------------------------------------
  User changed the Speed scroll bar position.
  ---------------------------------------------*/
void ChangeSpeedWasRequested ( HWND hDlg )
{

HWND  hWndCtrl;

if ( giSpeedScroll >  MAX_SPEED_SCROLL )
   giSpeedScroll = MAX_SPEED_SCROLL;

if ( giSpeedScroll <  MIN_SPEED_SCROLL )
   giSpeedScroll = MIN_SPEED_SCROLL;

sp_SetNewSpeed ( MAX_SPEED_SCROLL,
                 NAT_SPEED_SCROLL,
                 giSpeedScroll );

hWndCtrl = GetDlgItem ( hDlg, SPEED_SB );
SetScrollPos ( hWndCtrl, SB_CTL, giSpeedScroll, TRUE );


}/* end of function. */
/*==================== end of function ==============*/

/*========
 FUNCTION
 =======*/
 /*----------------------------------------
  User changed the Position scroll bar.
  ---------------------------------------*/
void ChangePositionWasRequested ( HWND hDlg )
{

HWND  hWndCtrl;

if ( giPositionScroll >  MAX_POSITION_SCROLL )
   giPositionScroll = MAX_POSITION_SCROLL;

if ( giPositionScroll <  MIN_POSITION_SCROLL )
   giPositionScroll = MIN_POSITION_SCROLL;
```

```
/*-------------------------------------------
   Calculate the new current byte based on the
   Position scroll bar.
   -------------------------------------*/
glCurrentByte = (long)
(( glFileSizeInBytes * giPositionScroll ) / MAX_POSITION_SCROLL );

/*-------------------------------------------
  Set the Position scroll bar to the new position.
  ---------------------------------------------*/
hWndCtrl = GetDlgItem ( hDlg, POSITION_SB );
SetScrollPos ( hWndCtrl,
               SB_CTL,
               giPositionScroll,
               TRUE );

DisplayLocation ( hDlg, glCurrentByte );

}/* end of function. */
/*=================== end of function ==============*/

/*========
 FUNCTION
 ========*/
/*----------------------------------------------
 DESCRIPTION:
 This function updates the Position scroll bar
 and updates the Position text.
 ---------------------------------------------*/
void DisplayLocation ( HWND hDlg, long lCurrentBytePosition )
{
HWND    hWndCtrl;
float   fCurrentPositionInSec;
char    sPositionInSeconds[15];

hWndCtrl = GetDlgItem ( hDlg, POSITION_SB );

/*----------------------------------
 Get from the TSEngine the current
 position in seconds.
 ----------------------------------*/
fCurrentPositionInSec =
sp_GetCurrentPosInSeconds ( lCurrentBytePosition );

/*-----------------------------
 Display the position in seconds.
 -------------------------------*/
sprintf ( sPositionInSeconds,
          "%.2f",
          fCurrentPositionInSec );
SetDlgItemText (hDlg, POSITION_TEXT, sPositionInSeconds );
```

continues

Listing 8.7. continued

```
/*--------------------------------------------------------
 Calculate the new position of the Position scroll bar.
 ------------------------------------------------------*/
giPositionScroll =
(int)(( MAX_POSITION_SCROLL * lCurrentBytePosition )/
       glFileSizeInBytes);

/*-----------------------------------------------------
 Set the Position scroll bar to the new position.
 --------------------------------------------------*/
SetScrollPos ( hWndCtrl,
               SB_CTL,
               giPositionScroll,
               TRUE );
}/* end of function. */
/*================ end of function ====================*/


/*========
 FUNCTION
 ========*/
/*=========================================================
 DESCRIPTION:
 This function displays the size of the file in seconds.
 =======================================================*/
void DisplayFileSize ( HWND hDlg)
{
char sLengthInSeconds[15];

sprintf ( sLengthInSeconds,
          "%.2f",
          sp_GetFileSizeInSeconds() );

SetDlgItemText ( hDlg,
                 TOTAL_TEXT,
                 sLengthInSeconds );

}/* end of function. */
/*============ end of function ========*/


/*========
 FUNCTION
 ========*/
/*=========================================================
 DESCRIPTION:
 This function displays the sampling rate of the file.
 =======================================================*/
```

```
void DisplaySamplingRate ( HWND hDlg)
{
char sSamplingRate[15];


sprintf ( sSamplingRate,
          "%.2f",
          (float)sp_GetSamplingRate() );

SetDlgItemText ( hDlg,
                 SAMPLING_TEXT,
                 sSamplingRate );

}/* end of function. */
/*============ end of function ========*/
```

Listing 8.8. Controls.rc.

```
/*===================================================
FILE NAME: Controls.rc
.........

FILE DESCRIPTION:
................
The resource file.

(C) Copyright Gurewich 1992, 1993

===================================================*/

/*-------
 #include
 -------*/
#include <windows.h>
#include "Controls.h"

/*---
 Menu
 ---*/
Controls  MENU
BEGIN
   POPUP   "&Menu"
       BEGIN
```

continues

Listing 8.8. continued

```
            MENUITEM "&Quit",     IDM_QUIT
            MENUITEM "&About",    IDM_ABOUT
            MENUITEM "&Controls", IDM_CONTROLS
        END
END

/*----------------------------------------
 Definition of the Cassette tape icon.
 Filename: Tape.ico
 Icon name: IconOfTape
 ----------------------------------------*/
IconOfTape ICON Tape.ico

/*--------
 Bit maps.
 --------*/
Axis1 BITMAP Axis1.bmp
Axis2 BITMAP Axis2.bmp
Axis3 BITMAP Axis3.bmp
Axis4 BITMAP Axis4.bmp

/*------------------
 The About dialog box.
 ------------------*/
AboutBox DIALOG 81, 43, 160, 100
STYLE DS_MODALFRAME ¦ WS_POPUP ¦ WS_VISIBLE ¦ WS_CAPTION ¦ WS_SYSMENU
CAPTION "About the Controls program"
FONT 8, "MS Sans Serif"
BEGIN
    PUSHBUTTON      "OK", IDOK, 64, 75, 40, 14
    CTEXT           "(C) Copyright Gurewich 1992, 1993",
                    -1, 13, 47, 137, 18
    ICON            "IconOfTape", -1, 14, 12, 18, 20
END

/*---------------------
 The Controls dialog box.
 ---------------------*/
ControlsBox DIALOG 32, 34, 280, 178
STYLE DS_MODALFRAME ¦ WS_POPUP ¦ WS_VISIBLE ¦
                    WS_CAPTION ¦ WS_SYSMENU
CAPTION "Controls"
FONT 8, "MS Sans Serif"
BEGIN
    PUSHBUTTON      "&Exit", EXIT_PB, 118, 159, 40, 14
    GROUPBOX        "Sampling rate in Hertz", -1,
                    11, 10, 89, 40
```

```
        GROUPBOX        "Position in seconds", -1
                        8, 58, 90, 40
        SCROLLBAR       POSITION_SB, 7, 110, 267, 6
        SCROLLBAR       SPEED_SB, 109, 11, 165, 21
        PUSHBUTTON      "Press S to stop playback", -1,
                        182, 159, 85, 14
        PUSHBUTTON      "&Play", PLAY_PB, 114, 121, 159, 31
        CTEXT           "0 Sec", POSITION_TEXT, 29, 76, 50, 8
        ICON            "IconOfTape", -1, 5, 132, 18, 20
        ICON            "IconOfTape", -1, 22, 151, 18, 20
        ICON            "IconOfTape", -1, 54, 127, 18, 20
        ICON            "IconOfTape", -1, 71, 152, 18, 20
        PUSHBUTTON      "S&lower", SLOW_PB, 108, 34, 27, 12
        PUSHBUTTON      "&Faster", FAST_PB, 251, 34, 25, 12
        LTEXT           "Normal", -1, 179, 36, 28, 8
        LTEXT           "Rewind", -1, 7, 100, 34, 8
        LTEXT           "Forward", -1, 247, 100, 32, 8
        CTEXT           "0  Hertz", SAMPLING_TEXT, 33, 28, 45, 8
        LTEXT           "Unknown", TOTAL_TEXT, 171, 75, 32, 8
        GROUPBOX        "Total length in seconds", -1, 109, 58, 154, 40
END
```

Listing 8.9. Controls.def.

```
;=======================================
; module-definition file for Controls.c
;=======================================

NAME            Controls

DESCRIPTION     'The Controls program. (C) Copyright Gurewich 1992, 1993'

EXETYPE         WINDOWS

STUB            'WINSTUB.EXE'

CODE   PRELOAD MOVEABLE DISCARDABLE

DATA   PRELOAD MOVEABLE MULTIPLE

HEAPSIZE        1024
STACKSIZE       8192
```

Listing 8.10. Controls.mak.

```
#=============
# Controls.mak
#=============

Controls.exe : Controls.obj Controls.h Controls.def Controls.res
    link /nod Controls.obj, Controls.exe, NUL, \
        slibcew.lib oldnames.lib libw.lib commdlg \
        c:\spSDK\TegoWlib\TegoWin.lib, \
        Controls.def
    rc -t Controls.res

Controls.obj : Controls.c Controls.h
    cl -c -G2sw -Ow -W3 -Zp Controls.c

Controls.res : Controls.rc Controls.h Tape.ico
    rc -r Controls.rc
```

New *sp_* Functions in the Controls Program

The Controls program includes several new sp_ functions. This section discusses these functions in detail.

The *sp_GetFileSizeInBytes()* Function

The size of the sound file in bytes may be extracted from the TSEngine by utilizing the sp_GetFileSizeInBytes() function:

```
glFileSizeInBytes = sp_GetFileSizeInBytes ();
```

The prototype of sp_GetFileSizeInBytes() is declared in c:\spSDK\ TegoWlib\sp4Win.h as

```
long sp_GetFileSizeInBytes ( void );
```

This function takes no parameters, and it returns a long integer that represents the size of the opened sound file in bytes.

> **NOTE** The sp_GetFileSizeInBytes() function takes no parameters.
>
> *Returns:* The return value is a long integer that represents the size of the opened sound file in bytes.
>
> The sp_OpenSession() function must be executed prior to executing the sp_GetFileSizeInBytes() function.

The *sp_GetCurrentPosInSeconds()* Function

The current position (in seconds) of the opened sound file may be extracted from the TSEngine by using the sp_GetCurrentPosInSeconds() function.

The prototype of sp_GetCurrentPosInSeconds() function is declared in c:\spSDK\TegoWlib\sp4Win.h as

```
float sp_GetCurrentPosInSeconds (long );
```

The function takes one parameter—a long integer. This long integer represents the current byte location of the sound file in bytes.

The function returns a float number. This float number represents the current position of the sound file in seconds.

> **NOTE** The sp_GetCurrentPosInSeconds() function takes one parameter:
>
> *Parameter:* Long integer. Specifies the current byte coordinate of the sound file.
>
> *Returns:* The function returns a float number. This float number represents the current position of the sound file in seconds.

The *sp_GetSamplingRate()* Function

The sampling rate of the opened sound file may be extracted from the TSEngine by using sp_GetSamplingRate() function.

The prototype of sp_GetSamplingRate() is declared in c:\spSDK\ TegoWlib\sp4Win.h as

```
long sp_GetSamplingRate ( void );
```

The function does not take any parameters; it returns a long integer. This long integer represents the sampling rate of the opened sound file.

> **NOTE**   The sp_GetSamplingRate() function takes no parameters.
>
> *Returns:* The return value is a long integer that represents the sampling rate of the opened sound file. The sp_OpenSession() function must be executed prior to executing the sp_GetSamplingRate() function.

About the Controls Program

The Controls program is similar to the Rotate program. However, there are two major differences:

1. The Controls program has more controls (that is, more push buttons, more scroll bars, and so on).

2. The Controls program enables the user to stop the playback. It also enables the user to change the playback speed during playback. (See the following section for more information.)

Displaying the Sound File Position During Playback

Under the PLAY_PB case we start a while(1) loop that plays the sound file in groups of 7,000 bytes each:

```
case PLAY_PB:
    /*----------------------------------------
    User pushed the Play push button to start
    the playback.
    ----------------------------------------*/
```

```
while ( 1 )
        {
        glCurrentByte =
        sp_PlayF ( glCurrentByte,
                    glCurrentByte + 7000L );

        DisplayLocation ( hDlg, glCurrentByte );

        if ( glCurrentByte == 0L )
            break;

        .......................................
        ... Check if the user pressed a key ...
        ... during the playback.            ...
        .......................................
        } /* end of while(1) loop. */

    return TRUE;
```

After playing 7,000 bytes, the DisplayLocation() function is called. This function moves the thumb of the Position scroll bar to a new location, and displays the current position of the file in seconds.

Within the body of the DisplayLocation() function we use the sp_GetCurrentPosInSeconds() function to extract the current position of the sound file in seconds:

```
fCurrentPositionInSec =
sp_GetCurrentPosInSeconds ( lCurrentBytePosition );
```

Then we display the following value:

```
sprintf ( sPositionInSeconds,
          "%.2f",
          fCurrentPositionInSec );

SetDlgItemText (hDlg,
                POSITION_TEXT,
                sPositionInSeconds );
```

DisplayLocation() moves the thumb of the Position scroll bar to its new location by calculating the new value of the variable giPositionScroll. Then it uses the SetScrollPos() function:

```
giPositionScroll =
(int)(( MAX_POSITION_SCROLL * lCurrentBytePosition )/
      glFileSizeInBytes);
```

```
SetScrollPos ( hWndCtrl,
               SB_CTL,
               giPositionScroll,
               TRUE );
```

Enabling the User to Stop Playback

It is important to understand that during the playback of the groups, the playback cannot be interrupted.

If during the while(1) loop execution the user pushes the **s** key, the Windows operating system deposits the message that corresponds to this event into the message buffer of our program. Upon completing playing the group, our program checks to see if there is a message for our program by executing the PeekMessage() function:

```
if ( PeekMessage ( &msg,
                   hDlg,
                   0,
                   0,
                   PM_REMOVE ) )
   {
   TranslateMessage ( &msg );

   ...............................
   ... Analyze the message.    ...
   ...............................
   }
```

If there is no message for our program, it starts executing the while(1) loop all over again, playing the next group of bytes.

If there is a message for our program, we analyze the message with a series of if statements. (We could analyze the message with a switch(msg.message) as well.)

The following if statement determines if the user pressed the **S** or **s** key to stop the playback:

```
if ( msg.message == WM_CHAR &&
        toupper(msg.wParam) == 'S')
```

```
{
/*---------------------------
User pressed 'S' or 's' during
the playback to stop.
----------------------------*/
return TRUE;
}
```

Enabling the User to Change the Playback Speed During Playback

Similarly, we use if statements to check whether the user pressed the L key to slow down the speed, or pressed the F key to increase the playback speed:

```
if ( msg.message == WM_CHAR &&
        toupper(msg.wParam) == 'L')
    {
    /*----------------------------
    User pressed 'L' or 'l' during
    the playback to decrease speed.
    ----------------------------*/
    giSpeedScroll-=5;
    ChangeSpeedWasRequested ( hDlg );
    continue;
    }

if ( msg.message == WM_CHAR &&
        toupper(msg.wParam) == 'F')
    {
    /*----------------------------
    User pressed 'F' or 'f' during
    the playback to increase speed.
    ----------------------------*/
    giSpeedScroll+=5;
    ChangeSpeedWasRequested ( hDlg );
    continue;
    }
```

Choosing the Size of the Playback Group

The size of the playback group determines how fast the program responds to the keys that are pressed during the playback. In our program, we used 7,000 bytes in each group.

Using the formula for a TS-type sound file:

$$[\text{Amount of time in seconds}] = \frac{[\text{Number of bytes}]}{[\text{Sampling rate}]}$$

The sound file was recorded at a sampling rate of 8,000 hertz, so it will take 0.875 seconds to play 7,000 bytes:

$$[\text{Amount of time in seconds}] = \frac{7{,}000}{8{,}000} = 0.875 \text{ seconds.}$$

This means that if the user presses the **s** key at the beginning of a group playback, then the user will have to wait a maximum of 0.875 seconds before the playback stops.

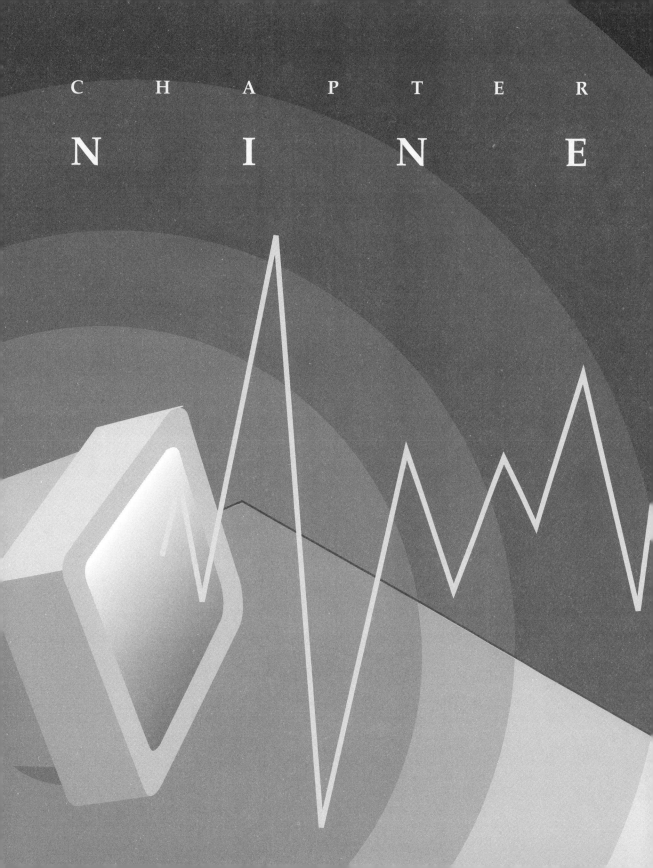

C H A P T E R

NINE

Generic2-Based Programs— Multitasking

Until now we have been writing Windows applications that are Generic1-based. As you probably noticed, the Generic1-based programs do not take advantage of the powerful multitasking capability of the Windows operating system. In fact, the technique that Generic1-based programs use is not different from the technique used by C programs for DOS.

On the other hand, the Generic2-based programs do take advantage of the powerful multitasking capability of the Windows operating system.

The Windows Operating System Operation

The Windows operating system is capable of executing several applications at the same time. We'll now review how this is accomplished.

The Message Loop of Generic1

This section offers a quick review of the operation of the message loop of Generic1.

Every Windows application must have a `WinMain()` function. For our discussion, we'll assume that we are in a Windows session, and that there are currently three open programs: App1, App2, and App3. Furthermore, we'll assume that these three programs utilize the `GetMessage()` function in their message loop as follows:

```
while ( GetMessage ( &msg, NULL, 0, 0 ) )
    {
    TranslateMessage ( &msg );
    DispatchMessage  ( &msg );
    }
```

When the `GetMessage()` function of App1 is executed, control is given to the Windows operating system. The Windows operating system returns control to App1 ONLY when there is a message for App1 (for example, the user clicked the mouse inside the window of App1). When there is a message for App1, control returns to App1, and the instruction following the `GetMessage()` function is executed. Usually, the instructions following the `GetMessage()` function are the `TranslateMessage()` and `DispatchMessage()` functions. The `TranslateMessage()` function translates the message, and the `DispatchMessage()` function sends the message back to the Windows operating system. The Windows operating system executes the `WndProc()` function of App1. When the program completes the execution of `WndProc()`, control is given back to the Windows operating system, which returns control back to the statement following the `DispatchMessage()` statement. In our message loop, the next statement to be executed is the beginning of the `while()` loop, which is the `GetMessage()` function. If there is no message for App1, Windows does not return the control to App1, but rather returns control to the message loop of App2 (or App3) if they have any messages. The next time control is given back to App1 will be when there is a message for App1.

It is important to understand that if there are no messages for either App1, App2, or App3, the Windows operating system maintains control. Control will remain with the Windows operating system until there is a message for either App1, App2 or App3. At that time, Windows will give control to the program that owns that message.

The `while()` loop is terminated when the `GetMessage()` function returns FALSE. The only time `GetMessage()` returns FALSE is when the message is the `WM_QUIT` message. This causes the `while()` loop to break, and the program to terminate.

The Message Loop of Generic2

Now we assume that the message loop of App1 is modified as follows:

```
while (TRUE)
    {
    if ( PeekMessage ( &msg, NULL, 0, 0, PM_REMOVE ) )
        {
        /*----------------------------------------------
        There is a message in the message queue.
        Check if the message is the WM_QUIT message.
        ----------------------------------------------*/
        if ( msg.message == WM_QUIT )
            {
            /*--------------------------
            A WM_QUIT message received.
            -------------------------*/
            break; /* Terminate the application. */
            }
        /*-----------------------------------
        A message received.
        The received message is not WM_QUIT.
        ----------------------------------*/
        TranslateMessage ( &msg );
        DispatchMessage  ( &msg );
        }
    else
        {
        ..............................................
        ........ Perform here a "No Message" Task ....
        ..............................................
        }
    }/* end of while (TRUE) */
```

This message loop is the one used in Generic2-based programs. It is similar to the Generic1 message loop, but it uses the PeekMessage() function, not the GetMessage() function.

When the PeekMessage() of App1 is executed, control is given to the Windows operating system. The Windows operating system checks if there are any messages for App2 and App3; if so, control returns to the message loop of App2 and App3.

Here is the big difference between the GetMessage() function and the PeekMessage() function:

If App1 uses the GetMessage() function, then the Windows operating system executes the statement that follows GetMessage() *only if there is a message* for the program. On the other hand, when using the `PeekMessage()` function, the Windows operating system returns control to the statement that follows `PeekMessage()` *in any case,* whether there is or isn't a message. Thus, the statement that follows `PeekMessage()` is *always* executed. The returned value of `PeekMessage()` is an indication, whether there was or wasn't a message for the program. The message loop of App1 checks the returned value of `PeekMessage()`, and if there is a message, the message is examined to see whether the message is the `WM_QUIT` message. If it is the `WM_QUIT` message, the `while(TRUE)` loop is broken, and the program terminates. If the received message is not the `WM_QUIT` message, then the `TranslateMessage()` and `DispatchMessage()` functions are executed. The `TranslateMessage()` function translates the message, and the `DispatchMessage()` function sends the message back to the Windows operating system. The Windows operating system then executes the `WndProc()` of the App1 program. When the execution of `WndProc()` is complete, control is given back to the Windows operating system, and the Windows operating system returns control to the statement that follows the `DispatchMessage()` function. In our case, the statement after the `DispatchMessage()` function is the beginning of the `while(TRUE)` loop. This means that the next statement to be executed is the `PeekMessage()` function, and the whole process repeats itself.

As you can see, because we use the `PeekMessage()` function, and therefore the Windows operating system gives control to our program whether there is or isn't a message, we also need to take care of the case when there isn't a message for our program. Indeed, we took care of this case in the `else` of `if(PeekMessage())`. In this `else` we put the code that we want to execute when there isn't a message for our program.

The Generic2 Program

The Generic2 program utilizes the `PeekMessage()` function in its message loop. The main window of Generic2 is shown in Figure 9.1.

The Generic2 program menu (see Figure 9.2) contains six options: Quit, About, Enable Background Playback, Disable Background Playback, Disable Mouse During Playback, and Enable Mouse During Playback. The About dialog box of Generic2 is shown in Figure 9.3.

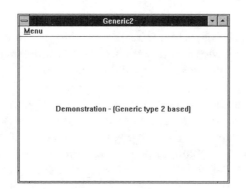

Figure 9.1. The main window of Generic2.

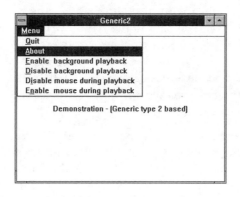

Figure 9.2. The Generic2 program menu.

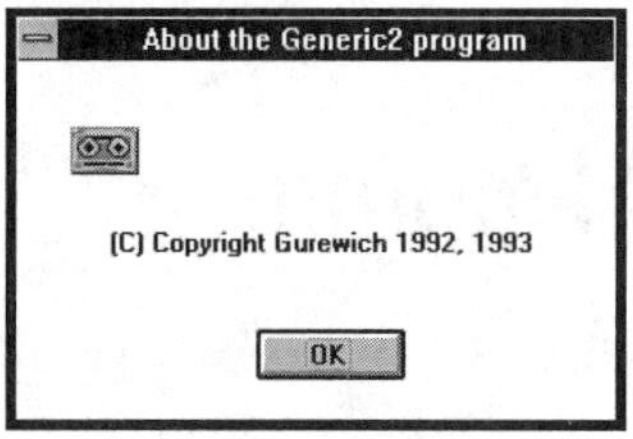

Figure 9.3. The About dialog box of the Generic2 program.

Compiling and Linking the Generic2 Program

To compile and link the Generic2 program with the Microsoft compiler:

- Make sure your PC is in a DOS-protected mode.
- Log into c:\spSDK\Samp4Win.
- At the DOS prompt type

  `NMAKE Generic2.mak` {Enter}

To compile and link the Generic2 program with the Borland compiler:

- Log into c:\spSDK\Samp4Win.
- At the DOS prompt type

  `NMAKE -f Generic2.bmk` {Enter}

Executing the Generic2 Program

To execute the Generic2 program:

- Select Run from the File menu of the Program Manager of Windows.
- Click Browse and select the file

  `c:\spSDK\Samp4Win\Generic2.exe`

The main window appears and a background sound file plays.

To disable the background playback, press Alt-M, and then use the arrow keys to select the Disable Background Playback option.

To enable the background playback, press Alt-M, and then use the arrow keys to select the Enable Background Playback option.

The mouse may be made enabled or disabled during the playback by pressing Alt-M and then using the arrow keys to select the Enable Mouse During Playback option or the Disable Mouse During Playback option.

You may now switch to the Program Manager and execute Paintbrush. While working with Paintbrush, the background sound file still plays. You may select the MS-DOS icon in the Main group of icons and execute the DOS shell. Depending on your computer, it may take several seconds for the MS-DOS shell to execute. Eventually, the PC will be in a DOS shell, and the background sound file will still play. You may execute a DOS program, and still hear the background sound file play.

To return to Windows, type **Exit** at the DOS prompt.

The Files of Generic2

The Generic2 program consists of the following files:

Generic2.h	The #include file of the program.
Generic2.c	The C code of the program.
Generic2.rc	The resource file of the program.
Generic2.def	The module definition file of the program.
Generic2.mak	The make file of the program.
Tape.ico	The icon of the program.

These files are provided for you in c:\spSDK\Samp4Win\. All the Generic2 files are found in Listings 9.1 through 9.5.

Listing 9.1. Generic2.h.

```
/*====================================================
FILE NAME: Generic2.h

(C) Copyright Gurewich 1992, 1993
====================================================*/

/*----------
 prototypes
 ----------*/
long FAR PASCAL _export WndProc          ( HWND, UINT, UINT, LONG ) ;
BOOL FAR PASCAL _export AboutDlgProc     ( HWND, UINT, UINT, LONG ) ;

/*------
 #define
 ------*/
#define IDM_QUIT          1  /* The Quit     option in the menu */
#define IDM_ABOUT         2  /* The About    option in the menu */
#define IDM_ENABLE_PLAY   3  /* Enable play  option in the menu */
#define IDM_DISABLE_PLAY  4  /* Disable play option in the menu */
```

```
#define IDM_ENABLE_MOUSE  5  /* Enable mouse  option in the menu */
#define IDM_DISABLE_MOUSE 6  /* Disable mouse option in the menu */


/*--------------
 Global variables
 --------------*/
char       gszAppName[] = "Generic2" ; /* Our application name. */
HINSTANCE  ghInst;                     /* current instance.     */
int        giPlayEnable;
long       glCurrentBackGndByte;
```

Listing 9.2. Generic2.c.

```
/*===============================================================
  PROGRAM: Generic2.c
  -------
  (C) Copyright 1992, 1993 Gurewich. (R) All rights reserved.

  PROGRAM DESCRIPTION:
  -------------------
  This is the Generic type 2 program.

  This program plays sound in the background (in an endless loop).

  User can execute other Windows applications, as well as
  DOS applications, and the PC will keep playing the sound
  in the background.

  ==============================================================*/


/*---------
 #include
 --------*/
/*--------------------------------------------------
 windows.h is required for all Windows applications.
 -------------------------------------------------*/
#include <windows.h>

/*-------------------------------------------------
 sp4Win.h is required so that sp_ functions,
 SP_ macros and #definitions from the TS C sound
 library may be used in this applications.
 ---------------------------------------------*/
#include "c:\spSDK\TegoWlib\sp4Win.h"
```

continues

Listing 9.2. continued

```
/*----------------------------------------------------
  Definitions & prototypes specific to this application.
  ------------------------------------------------*/
#include "c:\spSDK\Samp4WIN\Generic2.h"


/*------------------------------------------------------------
  For C functions that require the standard C #include files.
  ------------------------------------------------------------*/
#include <stdlib.h>
#include <stdio.h>


/*==================
  FUNCTION: WinMain()
  ==================*/
int PASCAL WinMain ( HANDLE hInstance,
                     HANDLE hPrevInstance,
                     LPSTR  lpszCmdLine,
                     int    nCmdShow )
{
/*------------------------
  Local and static variables.
  ------------------------*/
HWND      hWnd; /* Handler to the window of our application.    */
MSG       msg;  /* Message to be processed by our application. */
WNDCLASS wc;    /* Window class of our application.             */

int       iOpenResult; /* Result of opening the sound session. */

/*----------------------------------------------
  Make the hInstance variable a global variable.
  ----------------------------------------------*/
ghInst = hInstance;


/*----------------------------------------------
  Update the window class structure and register
  the window class.
  ----------------------------------------------*/
if ( !hPrevInstance )
    {
    /*----------------------------------------------
      The "if" is satisfied, this is the very 1st
      run of this application.
      ----------------------------------------------*/
    wc.style         = CS_HREDRAW | CS_VREDRAW ;
    wc.lpfnWndProc   = WndProc ;
    wc.cbClsExtra    = 0 ;
    wc.cbWndExtra    = 0 ;
```

```
    wc.hInstance     = ghInst ;
    wc.hIcon         = LoadIcon   ( ghInst, "IconOfTape" ) ;
    wc.hCursor       = LoadCursor ( NULL, IDC_ARROW      ) ;
    wc.hbrBackground = GetStockObject ( WHITE_BRUSH ) ;
    wc.lpszMenuName  = gszAppName ;
    wc.lpszClassName = gszAppName ;


    /*-----------------
    Register the window.
    -----------------*/
    RegisterClass ( &wc );

    }/* end of if( !hPrevInstance ) */

/*-----------------------
 Open the sound session.
 -----------------------*/
iOpenResult =
sp_OpenSession ( "c:\\spSDK\\Sfiles\\Day.s",
                 SP_NON_STAND_ALONE,
                 0L,
                 SP_S_TYPE );
/*-------------------------
 Quit if can't open the file.
 -------------------------*/
if ( iOpenResult != SP_NO_ERRORS )
   {
   MessageBox ( NULL,
                "Failed to open the sound session!",
                "Message from WM_CREATE",
                MB_ICONINFORMATION );

    /*-------------------
    Quit the application.
    -------------------*/
    SendMessage ( hWnd,
                  WM_DESTROY,
                  0,
                  0 );

    }/* end of if(iOpenResult!=SP_NO_ERRORS) */

/*----------------------------------------
 Enable mouse operation during playback.
 ----------------------------------------*/
sp_EnableMouseDuringPlay ();
```

continues

Listing 9.2. continued

```
/*----------------------------------
   Create the window of our application.
   ----------------------------------*/
hWnd = CreateWindow ( gszAppName,
                      gszAppName,
                      WS_OVERLAPPEDWINDOW,
                      CW_USEDEFAULT,
                      CW_USEDEFAULT,
                      CW_USEDEFAULT,
                      CW_USEDEFAULT,
                      NULL,
                      NULL,
                      ghInst,
                      NULL );

   /*---------------------------------------------
    Show and update the window of our application.
    --------------------------------------------*/
ShowWindow   ( hWnd, nCmdShow );
UpdateWindow ( hWnd );

   /*---------------------------------------------
    Set the giPlayEnable variable so that playback
    is enabled.
    --------------------------------------------*/
giPlayEnable = 1;

   /*-----------------------------------------------
    Initialize the current played byte counter to the
    beginning of the sound file.
    ----------------------------------------------*/
glCurrentBackGndByte = 0L;

   /*-----------------------------------
    The message loop (type Generic2).
    ----------------------------------*/
while (TRUE)
      {
      if ( PeekMessage ( &msg, NULL, 0, 0, PM_REMOVE ) )
         {
         /*---------------------------------------------
          There is a message in the message queue.
          Check if the message is the WM_QUIT message.
          --------------------------------------------*/
```

```
            if ( msg.message == WM_QUIT )
                {
                /*--------------------------
                A WM_QUIT message received.
                ------------------------*/
                break; /* Terminate the application. */
                }
            /*----------------------------------
            A message received.
            The received message is not WM_QUIT
            ---------------------------------*/
            TranslateMessage ( &msg );
            DispatchMessage  ( &msg );
            }
        else
            {
            /*-----------------------------------------
            There is no message in the message queue.
            ---------------------------------------*/
            if ( giPlayEnable == 1 )
                {
                /*----------------
                It is Ok to play.
                ---------------*/
                glCurrentBackGndByte =
                sp_PlayF ( glCurrentBackGndByte,
                        glCurrentBackGndByte + 2000L );
                }
            }
        }/* end of while (TRUE) */


return msg.wParam ;

} /* end of function. */
/*========================= end of WinMain() ===================*/

/*==================
 FUNCTION: WndProc()
 =================*/
/*----------------------------
 DESCRIPTION: Processes messages.
 ----------------------------*/
long FAR PASCAL _export WndProc ( HWND hWnd,
                                  UINT message,
                                  UINT wParam,
                                  LONG lParam )
```

continues

Listing 9.2. continued

```
{
/*-------------------------
 Local and static variables.
-------------------------*/
HDC           hdc;       /* Needed for displaying text. */
PAINTSTRUCT   ps;        /* Needed for displaying text. */
RECT          rect;      /* Needed for displaying text. */

static FARPROC lpfnAboutDlgProc ; /* For the About dialog box. */

switch ( message )
       {
       case WM_CREATE:
              /*------------------------------------------------------
              Obtain the lpfnAboutDlgProc of the About the dialog box.
              ------------------------------------------------------*/
              lpfnAboutDlgProc =
              MakeProcInstance (( FARPROC) AboutDlgProc, ghInst);

              return 0;

       case WM_PAINT:
              hdc = BeginPaint ( hWnd, &ps );
              GetClientRect ( hWnd, &rect );
              DrawText ( hdc,
                        "Demonstration - (Generic type 2 based)",
                        -1,
                        &rect,
                         DT_SINGLELINE ¦ DT_CENTER ¦ DT_VCENTER );
              EndPaint ( hWnd, &ps );
              return 0;

       case WM_COMMAND:
              SetFocus ( hWnd );
              /*------------------------------------
              User selected an item from the menu or
              pushed a push button.
              ------------------------------------*/

              switch (wParam)
                     {
                     case IDM_ENABLE_PLAY:
                          giPlayEnable = 1 ;
                          return 0L;
```

```
            case IDM_DISABLE_PLAY:
                 giPlayEnable = 0 ;
                 return 0L;

            case IDM_ENABLE_MOUSE:
                 /*-------------------------------------
                 Enable mouse operation during playback.
                 -------------------------------------*/
                 sp_EnableMouseDuringPlay ();
                 return 0L;

            case IDM_DISABLE_MOUSE:
                 /*-------------------------------------
                 Disable mouse operation during playback.
                 -------------------------------------*/
                 sp_DisableMouseDuringPlay ();
                 return 0L;

            case IDM_QUIT:
                 /*-------------------------
                 User clicked on Quit option.
                 -------------------------*/
                 DestroyWindow (hWnd);
                 return 0L;

            case IDM_ABOUT :
                 /*-------------------------
                 User clicked on About option.
                 -------------------------*/
                 DialogBox ( ghInst,
                             "AboutBox",
                             hWnd,
                             lpfnAboutDlgProc );
                 return 0;


        }/* end of switch(wParam) in the WM_COMMAND case */

    case WM_DESTROY:
         PostQuitMessage (0);
         return 0;
    }/* end of switch (message) */

/*-----------------------
 Message was not processed.
 -----------------------*/
return DefWindowProc ( hWnd, message, wParam, lParam ) ;
```

continues

Listing 9.2. continued

```
}
/*================= end of WndProc() ====================*/

/*=======================
 FUNCTION: AboutDlgProc()
 =======================*/
/*---------------------------------------
 DESCRIPTION:
 This is the About dialog box procedure.
 ---------------------------------------*/
BOOL FAR PASCAL _export AboutDlgProc ( HWND hDlg,
                                       UINT message,
                                       UINT wParam,
                                       LONG lParam )
{
switch ( message )
      {
      case WM_INITDIALOG :
            return TRUE;

      case WM_COMMAND :
            switch ( wParam )
                  {
                  case IDOK :
                  case IDCANCEL :
                      EndDialog ( hDlg, 0 );
                      return TRUE;
                  }
      }
return FALSE ;
}/* End of function. */
/*=============== end of AboutDlgProc() ==============*/
```

Listing 9.3. Generic2.rc.

```
/*====================================================
 FILE NAME: Generic2.rc
 ---------

 FILE DESCRIPTION:
 ----------------
 The resource file.
```

```
(C) Copyright Gurewich 1992, 1993

================================================*/

/*-------
 #include
 -------*/
#include <windows.h>
#include "Generic2.h"

/*---
 Menu
 ---*/
Generic2  MENU
BEGIN
  POPUP  "&Menu"
    BEGIN
      MENUITEM "&Quit",  IDM_QUIT
      MENUITEM "&About", IDM_ABOUT
      MENUITEM "&Enable  background playback", IDM_ENABLE_PLAY
      MENUITEM "&Disable background playback", IDM_DISABLE_PLAY
      MENUITEM "D&isable mouse during playback", IDM_DISABLE_MOUSE
      MENUITEM "E&nable  mouse during playback", IDM_ENABLE_MOUSE
    END
END

/*---------------------------------------
 Definition of the Cassette tape icon.
 File name: Tape.ico
 Icon name: IconOfTape
 --------------------------------------*/
IconOfTape ICON Tape.ico


/*----------------------------------------------------
 The About dialog box of the application.
 ---------------------------------------------------*/
AboutBox DIALOG 81, 43, 160, 100
STYLE DS_MODALFRAME ¦ WS_POPUP ¦ WS_VISIBLE ¦
                    WS_CAPTION ¦ WS_SYSMENU
CAPTION "About the Generic2 program"
FONT 8, "MS Sans Serif"
BEGIN
    PUSHBUTTON      "OK", IDOK, 64, 75, 40, 14
    CTEXT           "(C) Copyright Gurewich 1992, 1993", -1,
                    13, 47, 137, 18
    ICON            "IconOfTape", -1, 14, 12, 18, 20
END
```

Listing 9.4. Generic2.def.

```
;=====================================
; module-definition file for Generic2.c
;=====================================

NAME          Generic2

DESCRIPTION   'The Generic2 program. (C) Copyright Gurewich 1992, 1993'

EXETYPE       WINDOWS

STUB          'WINSTUB.EXE'

CODE   PRELOAD MOVEABLE DISCARDABLE

DATA   PRELOAD MOVEABLE MULTIPLE

HEAPSIZE      1024
STACKSIZE     8192
```

Listing 9.5. Generic2.mak.

```
#=============
# Generic2.mak
#=============

Generic2.exe : Generic2.obj Generic2.h Generic2.def Generic2.res
    link /nod Generic2.obj, Generic2.exe, NUL, \
        slibcew.lib oldnames.lib libw.lib commdlg \
        c:\spSDK\TegoWlib\TegoWin.lib, \
        Generic2.def
    rc -t Generic2.res

Generic2.obj : Generic2.c Generic2.h
    cl -c -G2sw -Ow -W3 -Zp Generic2.c

Generic2.res : Generic2.rc Generic2.h Tape.ico
    rc -r Generic2.rc
```

The *WinMain( )* of Generic2

WinMain() of Generic2 opens a sound session as a non-stand-alone session with
the type S sound file c:\spSDK\Sfiles\Day.s. If the session cannot open, the
program terminates:

```
/*-----------------------
Open the sound session.
------------------------*/
iOpenResult =
sp_OpenSession ( "c:\\spSDK\\Sfiles\\Day.s",
                 SP_NON_STAND_ALONE,
                 0L,
                 SP_S_TYPE );

/*-------------------------
Quit if can't open the file.
-------------------------*/
if ( iOpenResult != SP_NO_ERRORS )
   {
   MessageBox ( NULL,
                "Failed to open the sound session!",
                "Message from WM_CREATE",
                MB_ICONINFORMATION );

   /*--------------------
   Quit the application.
   --------------------*/
   SendMessage ( hWnd,
                 WM_DESTROY,
                 0,
                 0 );

   }/* end of if(iOpenResult!=SP_NO_ERRORS) */
```

Enabling the Mouse

The mouse device can be disabled or enabled during the playback of the sound
file. Depending on the type of computer that you have, the sound quality may
degrade somewhat during the movement of the mouse device.

In `WinMain()` we enabled the mouse by using the `sp_EnableMouseDuringPlay()` function:

```
/*----------------------------------
Enable mouse operation during playback.
----------------------------------*/
sp_EnableMouseDuringPlay ();
```

The prototype of the `sp_EnableMouseDuringPlay()` function is declared in the file c:\spSDK\TegoWlib\sp4Win.h as

```
int sp_EnableMouseDuringPlay ( void );
```

The returned value of `sp_EnableMouseDuringPlay()` has no meaning.

NOTE   The `sp_EnableMouseDuringPlay()` function causes the enabling of the mouse during playback.

Parameters: None.

Returns: Integer. This integer has no meaning.

Initialization Before the Message Loop

In Generic2.h we declared the global variable `giPlayEnable` as

```
int giPlayEnable;
```

Prior to executing the message loop in `WinMain()`, we set the `giPlayEnable` variable to 1:

```
/*----------------------------------------------
Set the giPlayEnable variable so that playback
is enabled.
--------------------------------------------*/
giPlayEnable = 1;
```

This variable is examined later within the message loop.

Similarly, we declared a global variable `glCurrentBackGndByte` in Generic2.h as

```
long glCurrentBackGndByte;
```

This variable is used in the message loop as the counter of the current byte location of the background sound file. We initialized the value of this variable to 0 because we want the playback to start from the beginning of the sound file:

```
/*-----------------------------------------------
Initialize the current played byte counter to the
beginning of the sound file.
-----------------------------------------------*/
glCurrentBackGndByte = 0L;
```

Playing Sound Sections Within the Message Loop

The following is the Generic2 message loop:

```
/*--------------------------------
The message loop (type Generic2).
--------------------------------*/
while (TRUE)
     {
     if ( PeekMessage ( &msg, NULL, 0, 0, PM_REMOVE ) )
        {
        /*-----------------------------------------
        There is a message in the message queue.
        Check if the message is the WM_QUIT message.
        -----------------------------------------*/
        if ( msg.message == WM_QUIT )
           {
           /*---------------------------
           A WM_QUIT message received.
           ---------------------------*/
           break; /* Terminate the application. */
           }
        /*---------------------------------
        A message received.
        The received message is not WM_QUIT
        ---------------------------------*/
        TranslateMessage ( &msg );
        DispatchMessage  ( &msg );
        }
     else
        {
        /*-----------------------------------------
        There is no message in the message queue.
        -----------------------------------------*/
        if ( giPlayEnable == 1 )
```

```
      {
      /*---------------
      It is Ok to play.
      ---------------*/
      glCurrentBackGndByte =
      sp_PlayF ( glCurrentBackGndByte,
              glCurrentBackGndByte + 2000L );
      }
  }/* end of else */
}/* end of while (TRUE) */
```

The code in the else of if(PeekMessage()) will play 2,000 bytes of the sound file. This code is executed when the PeekMessage() function finds that there are no messages for our program. The sp_PlayF() function is executed provided that the variable giPlayEnable is 1. This variable serves as a disable and enable flag.

The glCurrentBackGndByte variable is updated so that the next time sp_PlayF() is executed, the next 2,000 bytes will play.

The *WndProc( )* of Generic2

The WndProc() of the Generic2 program is not different from the WndProc() of the Generic1 program. Under the WM_CREATE case we obtain the lpfn of the About dialog box, and under the WM_COMMAND case we process the menu options.

The Enable Play and Disable Play cases set the value of the giPlayEnable variable:

```
case IDM_ENABLE_PLAY:
    giPlayEnable = 1 ;
    return 0L;

case IDM_DISABLE_PLAY:
    giPlayEnable = 0 ;
    return 0L;
```

Remember that the giPlayEnable variable is used in the message loop in WinMain().

The Enable Mouse case and the Disable Mouse case execute the sp_EnableMouseDuringPlay() and sp_DisableMouseDuringPlay() functions, respectively:

```
case IDM_ENABLE_MOUSE:
    /*------------------------------------
    Enable mouse operation during playback.
    ------------------------------------*/
    sp_EnableMouseDuringPlay ();
    return 0L;

case IDM_DISABLE_MOUSE:
    /*------------------------------------
    Disable mouse operation during playback.
    ------------------------------------*/
    sp_DisableMouseDuringPlay ();
    return 0L;
```

Disabling the Mouse

The mouse device is disabled temporarily during the playback if the sp_DisableMouseDuringPlay() function is called prior to calling the sp_PlayF() function:

```
/*------------------------------------
Disable mouse operation during playback.
------------------------------------*/
sp_DisableMouseDuringPlay ();
```

The prototype of the sp_DisableMouseDuringPlay() function is declared in the file c:\spSDK\TegoWlib\sp4Win.h as

```
int sp_DisableMouseDuringPlay ( void );
```

The returned value of sp_DisableMouseDuringPlay() has no meaning.

NOTE   The sp_DisableMouseDuringPlay() function causes the disabling of the mouse during playback.

Parameters: None.

Returns: Integer. This integer has no meaning.

Multi-Instances

Because we put no restrictions on the number of instances that the Generic2 program may have, you may execute the Generic2 program more than once. You do that by executing Generic2, enabling the mouse, and then switching to the Program Manager and executing the Generic2 for the second time.

What you'll hear is the two background sound files being played simultaneously. However, because the playback groups are 2,000 bytes each, you can distinguish between the two instances. To make the background playbacks sound more simultaneous, you need to decrease the size of the playback group in the message loop.

As you can imagine, there are plenty of interesting and amazing programs to such multi-tasking, multi-instances type of programs. In particular, you may put a flag that determines the instance of the program, and based on the instance, play a different section of the sound file.

The SayName Program

The SayName program is a Generic2-type program. This program runs in the background, constantly monitoring the Windows session, and detecting certain events that occur during the Windows session. When the user executes another Windows program, the SayName program announces the name of the newly executed program. Upon quitting the Windows session, the SayName program prompts the user with an audio announcement: *Are you sure you want to exit Windows?*

Compiling and Linking the SayName Program

To compile and link the SayName program with the Microsoft compiler:

- Make sure your PC is in a DOS-protected mode.
- Log into c:\spSDK\Samp4Win.

- At the DOS prompt type

  `NMAKE SayName.mak` {Enter}

To compile and link the SayName program with the Borland compiler:

- Log into c:\spSDK\Samp4Win.

- At the DOS prompt type

  `NMAKE -f SayName.bmk` {Enter}

Executing the SayName Program

To execute the SayName program:

- Select Run from the File menu of the Program Manager of Windows.

- Click Browse and select the file

  `c:\spSDK\Samp4Win\SayName.exe`

The main window appears, as shown in Figure 9.4.

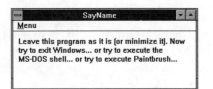

Figure 9.4. The main window of the SayName program.

The SayName program menu (see Figure 9.5) contains two options: Quit and About. The About dialog box of SayName is shown in Figure 9.6.

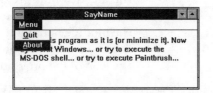

Figure 9.5. The SayName program menu.

Figure 9.6. The About dialog box of the SayName program.

When the user executes the SayName program, the program starts monitoring the Windows session, trying to detect certain events. In particular, the events being detected and the action taken by SayName are outlined in the following table:

Event	Action Taken by SayName
User starts the Paintbrush program for the first time.	SayName plays the audio prompt: *Welcome to Paintbrush*
User starts the MS-DOS shell.	SayName plays the audio prompt: *Welcome to MS-DOS*
User requests to exit Windows.	SayName plays the audio prompt: *Are you sure you want to quit Windows?*

The Files of SayName

The SayName program consists of the following files:

SayName.h	The #include file of the program.
SayName.c	The C code of the program.
SayName.rc	The resource file of the program.
SayName.def	The module definition file of the program.
SayName.mak	The make file of the program.
Tape.ico	The icon of the program.

These files are provided for you in c:\spSDK\Samp4Win\. All the SayName files are found in Listings 9.6 through 9.10.

Listing 9.6. SayName.h.

```
/*====================================================
 FILE NAME: SayName.h

 (C) Copyright Gurewich 1992, 1993
 ===================================================*/

/*---------
 prototypes
 ---------*/
long FAR PASCAL _export WndProc        ( HWND, UINT, UINT, LONG ) ;
BOOL FAR PASCAL _export AboutDlgProc   ( HWND, UINT, UINT, LONG ) ;

void  AnnounceTheApplication ( void );

/*------
 #define
 ------*/
#define IDM_QUIT        1  /* The Quit  option in the menu */
#define IDM_ABOUT       2  /* The About option in the menu */

/*--------------
 Global variables
 --------------*/
char       gszAppName[] = "SayName" ; /* Our application name. */
HINSTANCE  ghInst;                    /* current instance.     */
```

Listing 9.7. SayName.c.

```
/*===========================================================
  PROGRAM: SayName.c
  -------
  (C) Copyright 1992, 1993 Gurewich. (R) All rights reserved.

  PROGRAM DESCRIPTION:
  -------------------
  This is the Generic type 2 program.

  This program plays a welcome message whenever the user
  starts a particular Windows application, and plays a Good-Bye
  message when the user terminates the application.

  ==========================================================*/
```

continues

Listing 9.7. continued

```
/*-------
 #include
 -------*/
/*--------------------------------------------------
 windows.h is required for all Windows applications.
 -----------------------------------------------*/
#include <windows.h>

/*----------------------------------------------
 sp4Win.h is required so that sp_ functions,
 SP_ macros and #definitions from the TS C sound
 library may be used in this applications.
 ---------------------------------------------*/
#include "c:\spSDK\TegoWlib\sp4Win.h"

/*---------------------------------------------------
 Definitions & prototypes specific to this application.
 -------------------------------------------------*/
#include "c:\spSDK\Samp4WIN\SayName.h"

/*-------------------------------------------------------
 For C functions that require the standard C #include files.
 ----------------------------------------------------------*/
#include <stdlib.h>
#include <stdio.h>

/*==================
 FUNCTION: WinMain()
 ==================*/
int PASCAL WinMain ( HANDLE hInstance,
                     HANDLE hPrevInstance,
                     LPSTR  lpszCmdLine,
                     int    nCmdShow )
{
/*-------------------------
 Local and static variables.
 -------------------------*/
HWND     hWnd; /* Handler to the window of our application.   */
MSG      msg;  /* Message to be processed by our application. */
WNDCLASS wc;   /* Window class of our application.            */

int      iOpenResult; /* Result of opening the sound session. */

/*----------------------------------------------
 Make the hInstance variable a global variable.
 ---------------------------------------------*/
ghInst = hInstance;
```

```
/*-----------------------------------------------
 Update the window class structure and register
 the window class.
 ---------------------------------------------*/
if ( !hPrevInstance )
    {
    /*-------------------------------------------
    The "if" is satisfied, this is the very 1st
    run of this application.
    -----------------------------------------*/
    wc.style         = CS_HREDRAW ¦ CS_VREDRAW ;
    wc.lpfnWndProc   = WndProc ;
    wc.cbClsExtra    = 0 ;
    wc.cbWndExtra    = 0 ;
    wc.hInstance     = ghInst ;
    wc.hIcon         = LoadIcon  ( ghInst, "IconOfTape" ) ;
    wc.hCursor       = LoadCursor ( NULL, IDC_ARROW      ) ;
    wc.hbrBackground = GetStockObject ( WHITE_BRUSH ) ;
    wc.lpszMenuName  = gszAppName ;
    wc.lpszClassName = gszAppName ;


    /*------------------
    Register the window.
    -----------------*/
    RegisterClass ( &wc );

    }/* end of if( !hPrevInstance ) */

/*---------------------
 Open the sound session.
 --------------------*/
iOpenResult =
sp_OpenSession ( "c:\\spSDK\\TSfiles\\SayName.ts",
                 SP_NON_STAND_ALONE,
                 0L,
                 SP_TS_TYPE );
/*--------------------------
 Quit if can't open the file.
 -------------------------*/
if ( iOpenResult != SP_NO_ERRORS )
   {
   MessageBox ( NULL,
                "Failed to open the sound session!",
                "Message",
                MB_ICONINFORMATION );
```

continues

Listing 9.7. continued

```
/*-------------------
Quit the application.
------------------*/
SendMessage ( hWnd,
              WM_DESTROY,
              0,
              0 );

    }/* end of if(iOpenResult!=SP_NO_ERRORS) */

/*--------------------------------------
  Create the window of our application.
  ----------------------------------*/
hWnd = CreateWindow ( gszAppName,
                      gszAppName,
                      WS_OVERLAPPEDWINDOW,
                      CW_USEDEFAULT,
                      CW_USEDEFAULT,
                      350,
                      100,
                      NULL,
                      NULL,
                      ghInst,
                      NULL );

/*----------------------------------------------
  Show and update the window of our application.
  --------------------------------------------*/
ShowWindow   ( hWnd, nCmdShow );
UpdateWindow ( hWnd );

/*--------------------------------
  The message loop (type Generic2).
  ------------------------------*/
while (TRUE)
    {
    if ( PeekMessage ( &msg, NULL, 0, 0, PM_REMOVE ) )
        {
        /*-------------------------------------------
        There is a message in the message queue.
        Check if the message is the WM_QUIT message.
        ------------------------------------------*/
        if ( msg.message == WM_QUIT )
            {
            /*------------------------
            A WM_QUIT message received.
            ------------------------*/
```

```
            break; /* Terminate the application. */
            }
        /*-----------------------------------
        A message received.
        The received message is not WM_QUIT
        ---------------------------------*/
        TranslateMessage ( &msg );
        DispatchMessage  ( &msg );
        }
    else
        {
        /*-----------------------------------------
        There is no message in the message queue.
        ----------------------------------------*/
        AnnounceTheApplication();
        }
    }/* end of while (TRUE) */


return msg.wParam ;

} /* end of function. */
/*========================= end of WinMain() ====================*/

/*==================
 FUNCTION: WndProc()
 ==================*/
/*-----------------------------
 DESCRIPTION: Processes messages.
 ----------------------------*/
long FAR PASCAL _export WndProc ( HWND hWnd,
                                  UINT message,
                                  UINT wParam,
                                  LONG lParam )
{
/*-------------------------
 Local and static variables.
 ------------------------*/
HDC          hdc;      /* Needed for displaying text. */
PAINTSTRUCT  ps;       /* Needed for displaying text. */
RECT         rect;     /* Needed for displaying text. */

static FARPROC lpfnAboutDlgProc ; /* For the About dialog box. */

switch ( message )
        {
        case WM_CREATE:
```

continues

Listing 9.7. continued

```
            /*-----------------------------------------------------
            Obtain the lpfnAboutDlgProc of the About the dialog box.
            ------------------------------------------------------*/
            lpfnAboutDlgProc =
            MakeProcInstance (( FARPROC) AboutDlgProc, ghInst);

            return 0;

    case WM_PAINT:
            hdc = BeginPaint ( hWnd, &ps );
            GetClientRect ( hWnd, &rect );
            DrawText ( hdc,
                    "Demonstration - (Generic type 2 based)",
                    -1,
                    &rect,
                     DT_SINGLELINE ¦ DT_CENTER ¦ DT_VCENTER );
            EndPaint ( hWnd, &ps );
            return 0;

    case WM_COMMAND:
            SetFocus ( hWnd );
            /*-------------------------------------
            User selected an item from the menu or
            pushed a push button.
            ----------------------------------*/

            switch (wParam)
                    {
                    case IDM_QUIT:
                            /*------------------------
                            User clicked on Quit option.
                            ------------------------*/
                            DestroyWindow (hWnd);
                            return 0L;

                    case IDM_ABOUT :
                            /*------------------------
                            User clicked on About option.
                            ------------------------*/
                            DialogBox ( ghInst,
                                    "AboutBox",
                                    hWnd,
                                    lpfnAboutDlgProc );
                            return 0;
```

```
                    }/* end of switch(wParam) in the WM_COMMAND case */

          case WM_DESTROY:
                PostQuitMessage (0);
                return 0;
          }/* end of switch (message) */

/*------------------------
 Message was not processed.
 ------------------------*/
return DefWindowProc ( hWnd, message, wParam, lParam ) ;

}
/*================= end of WndProc() ====================*/

/*=======================
 FUNCTION: AboutDlgProc()
 =======================*/
/*---------------------------------------
 DESCRIPTION:
 This is the About dialog box procedure.
 ---------------------------------------*/
BOOL FAR PASCAL _export AboutDlgProc ( HWND hDlg,
                                       UINT message,
                                       UINT wParam,
                                       LONG lParam )

{
switch ( message )
        {
        case WM_INITDIALOG :
                return TRUE;

        case WM_COMMAND :
                switch ( wParam )
                        {
                        case IDOK :
                        case IDCANCEL :
                            EndDialog ( hDlg, 0 );
                            return TRUE;
                        }
        }
return FALSE ;
}/* End of function. */
/*=============== end of AboutDlgProc() ==============*/
```

continues

Listing 9.7. continued

```c
/*==================================
 FUNCTION: AnnounceTheApplication()
 ================================*/
void AnnounceTheApplication ( void )
{
HWND hWindow;

static iPaintbrush = 0;
static iExitWindows   = 0;
static iDOSshell      = 0;

if ( iPaintbrush == 0 )
    {
    /*-------------------------
    Was Paintbrush just started?
    ------------------------*/
    hWindow = FindWindow ( NULL, "Paintbrush - (Untitled)" );
    if ( hWindow )
        {
        iPaintbrush = 1;
        sp_PlayF ( 0L, 18153L );
        }
    }
else
    {
    hWindow = FindWindow ( NULL, "Paintbrush - (Untitled)" );
    if ( !hWindow )
        iPaintbrush = 0;
    }

if ( iExitWindows == 0 )
    {
    /*--------------------
    Exit Windows requested?
    -------------------*/
    hWindow = FindWindow ( NULL, "Exit Windows") ;
    if ( hWindow )
        {
        iExitWindows = 1;
        sp_PlayF ( 18153L, 42672L );
        }
    }
else
    {
    hWindow = FindWindow ( NULL, "Exit Windows" );
    if ( !hWindow )
        iExitWindows = 0;
    }
```

```
if ( iDOSshell == 0 )
   {
   /*-------------------------
   Was DOS shell just started?
   -------------------------*/
   hWindow = FindWindow ( NULL, "MS-DOS Prompt" );
   if ( hWindow )
      {
      iDOSshell = 1;
      sp_PlayF ( 42672L, SP_END_OF_FILE );
      }
   }
else
   {
   hWindow = FindWindow ( NULL, "MS-DOS Prompt" );
   if ( !hWindow )
      iDOSshell = 0;
   }

}/* end of function. */
/*=========== End of function =============*/
```

Listing 9.8. SayName.rc.

```
/*===================================================
FILE NAME: SayName.rc
---------

FILE DESCRIPTION:
----------------
The resource file.

(C) Copyright Gurewich 1992, 1993


===================================================*/

/*-------
 #include
 -------*/
#include <windows.h>
#include "SayName.h"
```

continues

Listing 9.8. continued

```
/*---
 Menu
 ---*/
SayName   MENU
BEGIN
  POPUP   "&Menu"
    BEGIN
      MENUITEM "&Quit",   IDM_QUIT
      MENUITEM "&About",  IDM_ABOUT
    END
END

/*-----------------------------------------
 Definition of the Cassette tape icon.
 File name: Tape.ico
 Icon name: IconOfTape
 ---------------------------------------*/
IconOfTape ICON Tape.ico


/*-------------------------------------------------
 The About dialog box of the application.
 -----------------------------------------------*/
AboutBox DIALOG 81, 43, 160, 100
STYLE DS_MODALFRAME ¦ WS_POPUP ¦ WS_VISIBLE ¦
                    WS_CAPTION ¦ WS_SYSMENU
CAPTION "About the SayName program"
FONT 8, "MS Sans Serif"
BEGIN
    PUSHBUTTON      "OK", IDOK, 64, 75, 40, 14
    CTEXT           "(C) Copyright Gurewich 1992, 1993", -1,
                    13, 47, 137, 18
    ICON            "IconOfTape", -1, 14, 12, 18, 20
END
```

Listing 9.9. SayName.def.

```
;=======================================
; module-definition file for SayName.c
;=======================================

NAME        SayName

DESCRIPTION 'The SayName program. (C) Copyright Gurewich 1992, 1993'
```

```
EXETYPE     WINDOWS

STUB        'WINSTUB.EXE'

CODE   PRELOAD MOVEABLE DISCARDABLE

DATA   PRELOAD MOVEABLE MULTIPLE

HEAPSIZE    1024
STACKSIZE   8192
```

Listing 9.10. SayName.mak.

```
#=============
# SayName.mak
#=============

SayName.exe : SayName.obj SayName.h SayName.def SayName.res
    link /nod SayName.obj, SayName.exe, NUL, \
        slibcew.lib oldnames.lib libw.lib commdlg \
        c:\spSDK\TegoWlib\TegoWin.lib, \
        SayName.def
    rc -t SayName.res

SayName.obj : SayName.c SayName.h
    cl -c -G2sw -Ow -W3 -Zp SayName.c

SayName.res : SayName.rc SayName.h Tape.ico
    rc -r SayName.rc
```

The *WinMain( )* of SayName

In `WinMain()` we open a sound session with the sound file c:\spSDK\
TSfiles\SayName.ts:

```
/*---------------------
Open the sound session.
----------------------*/
iOpenResult =
```

```
sp_OpenSession ( "c:\\spSDK\\TSfiles\\SayName.ts",
                 SP_NON_STAND_ALONE,
                 0L,
                 SP_TS_TYPE );

/*-------------------------
Quit if can't open the file.
-------------------------*/
if ( iOpenResult != SP_NO_ERRORS )
  {
  MessageBox ( NULL,
               "Failed to open the sound session!",
               "Message",
               MB_ICONINFORMATION );

  /*--------------------
  Quit the application.
  -------------------*/
  SendMessage ( hWnd,
                WM_DESTROY,
                0,
                0 );

}/* end of if(iOpenResult!=SP_NO_ERRORS) */
```

The SayName.ts sound file is made up of three sections. Because we assume that you do not have a copy of the TS Sound Editor, here is the breakdown of the SayName.ts sound file:

From Byte Location	To Byte Location	Audio Prompt
0	18,153	Welcome to Paintbrush
18,153,	42,672	Are you sure you want to quit Windows?
42,672L	SP_END_OF_FILE	Welcome to MS-DOS

The Message Loop of SayName

Because SayName is a Generic Type 2 program, its message loop is the same message loop as that of the Generic2 program:

```
/*--------------------------------
The message loop (type Generic2).
 ------------------------------*/
while (TRUE)
      {
      if ( PeekMessage ( &msg, NULL, 0, 0, PM_REMOVE ) )
         {
         /*-------------------------------------------
         There is a message in the message queue.
         Check if the message is the WM_QUIT message.
         -----------------------------------------*/
         if ( msg.message == WM_QUIT )
            {
            /*--------------------------
            A WM_QUIT message received.
            -------------------------*/
            break; /* Terminate the application. */
            }
         /*----------------------------------
         A message received.
         The received message is not WM_QUIT
         --------------------------------*/
         TranslateMessage ( &msg );
         DispatchMessage  ( &msg );
         }
      else
         {
         /*-------------------------------------------
         There is no message in the message queue.
         -----------------------------------------*/
         AnnounceTheApplication();
         }
    }/* end of while (TRUE) */
```

Whenever there is no message for SayName, the AnonunceTheApplication()
function is executed.

Monitoring the Windows Session

We monitor the Windows session by using the AnnounceTheApplication() function. Because the SayName program is a Generic2-type program, and because
we call the AnnounceTheApplication() function from the message loop of
WinMain(), the AnnounceTheApplication() function is being executed continuously, even when the user is working with other programs.

The `AnnounceTheApplication()` function defines three static variables:

```
static iPaintbrush    = 0;
static iExitWindows   = 0;
static iDOSshell      = 0;
```

These static variables are used as flags to indicate whether or not a particular program is open. For example, if the Paintbrush program is open, then the flag variable `iPaintbrush` should be 1.

In the declaration of these static variables we initialized them to 0 (that is, we assume that none of these programs is open).

The purpose of the `AnnounceTheApplication()` function is to announce that a program has just started. For example, if Paintbrush has just been started, then the `AnnounceTheApplication()` function should play the audio prompt: *Welcome to Paintbrush.*

We verify that a program has just started by checking for two conditions:

1. The flag of the program is equal to 0.

2. The `FindWindow()` function indicates that the program is open.

For example, to check if Paintbrush was just started, we check for these two conditions by using the following nested `if` statements:

```
if ( iPaintbrush == 0 )
   {
   /*--------------------------
   Was Paintbrush just started?
   ----------------------*/
   hWindow = FindWindow ( NULL, "Paintbrush - (Untitled)" );
   if ( hWindow )
      {
      iPaintbrush = 1;
      sp_PlayF ( 0L, 18153L );
      }
   }
else
   {
   hWindow = FindWindow ( NULL, "Paintbrush - (Untitled)" );
   if ( !hWindow )
      iPaintbrush = 0;
   }
```

Upon detecting that Paintbrush was just started by the user, we set the `iPaintbrush` flag to 1, and play the audio prompt: *Welcome to Paintbrush.*

If the `else` of the `if(iPaintbrush==0)` statement is satisfied, then it means that the Paintbrush program was already opened and that the user just closed it. In this case we reinitialize the `iPaintbrush` flag to 0.

Similarly, we use `if-else` statements to detect if the user just started the MS-DOS shell or if the user just tried to exit Windows.

The Organ Program

The Organ program is a Generic2-type program. As its name implies, this program implements an Organ.

Compiling, Linking, and Executing the Organ Program

To compile and link the Organ program with the Microsoft compiler:

- Make sure your PC is in a DOS-protected mode.
- Log into c:\spSDK\Samp4Win.
- At the DOS prompt type

  `NMAKE Organ.mak` {Enter}

To compile and link the Organ program with the Borland compiler:

- Log into c:\spSDK\Samp4Win.
- At the DOS prompt type

  `NMAKE -f Organ.bmk` {Enter}

To execute the Organ program:

- Select Run from the File menu of the Program Manager of Windows.
- Click Browse and select the file

  `c:\spSDK\Samp4Win\Organ.exe`

The main window appears, as shown in Figure 9.7.

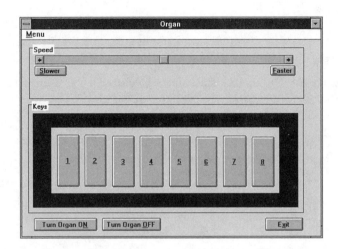

Figure 9.7. The main window of the Organ program.

The Organ program menu (see Figure 9.8) contains three options: Quit, About, and Instructions. The About dialog box is shown in Figure 9.9, and the Instructions dialog box is shown in Figure 9.10. This dialog box includes an Audio Instructions push button. The user obtains audio instructions by pushing this push button.

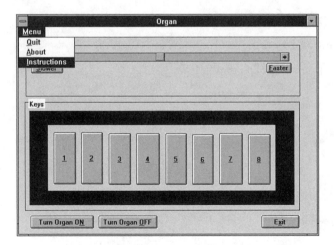

Figure 9.8. The Organ program menu.

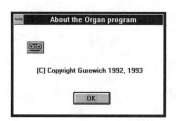

Figure 9.9. The About dialog box of the Organ program.

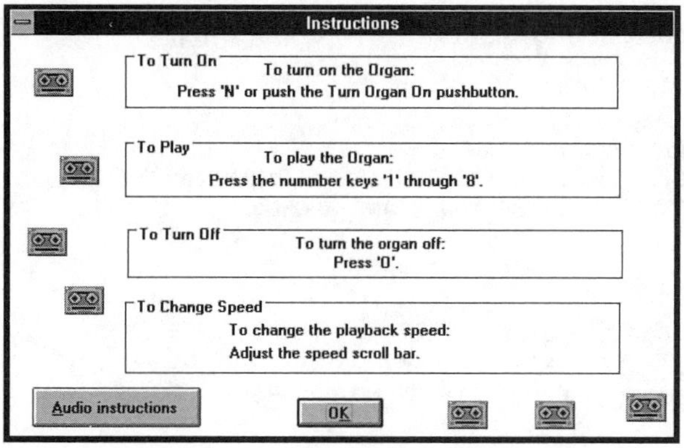

Figure 9.10. The Instructions dialog box of the Organ program.

The actual organ is displayed in the main window (see Figure 9.7). To turn the organ on, press **N**, or push the Turn Organ On push button. To turn the organ off, press **O**, or push the Turn Organ Off push button.

To try different chords on the organ, press number keys 1 through 8.

While the organ is on, you may change the playback speed by pressing **F** to speed up the playback, or by pressing **S** to slow down the playback.

The Files of Organ

The Organ program consists of the following files:

Organ.h	The #include file of the program.
Organ.c	The C code of the program.

Organ.rc   The resource file of the program.
Organ.def   The module definition file of the program.
Organ.mak   The make file of the program.
Tape.ico   The icon of the program.

These files are provided for you in c:\spSDK\Samp4Win\.

The *WinMain( )* of Organ

WinMain() opens a sound session with the sound file:

c:\spSDK\TSfiles\Notes:

```
iOpenOrganResult =
sp_OpenSession ( "c:\\spSDK\\TSfiles\\Notes.ts",
                 SP_NON_STAND_ALONE,
                 0L,
                 SP_TS_TYPE );
/*--------------------------
Quit if can't open the file.
-----------------------*/
if ( iOpenOrganResult != SP_NO_ERRORS )
   {
   MessageBox ( NULL,
                "Failed to open the sound session!",
                "Message from Organ.exe",
                MB_ICONINFORMATION );

   /*-------------------
   Quit the application.
   ------------------*/
   SendMessage ( hWnd,
                 WM_DESTROY,
                 0,
                 0 );
   }/* end of if() */
```

The sound file Notes.ts includes all the sound sections needed by the Organ program. Because we assume that you don't have a copy of the TS Sound Editor, here is the breakdown of the sound sections:

From Byte Location	To Byte Location	Sound Section
0	19,049	Organ background sound
19,049	38,606	Organ Do note.
38,606	57,603	Organ Re note.
57,603	76,560	Organ Me note.
76,560	95,435	Organ Fa note.
95,435	114,074	Organ So note.
114,074	130,791	Organ La note.
130,791	147,624	Organ Ti note.
147,624	167,681	Organ Higher Do note.
167,681	(end of file)	Audio Instructions

The Message Loop of Organ

The message loop of the Organ program is a Generic2-type loop.

```
while (TRUE)
    {
    if ( PeekMessage ( &msg, NULL, 0, 0, PM_REMOVE ) )
        {
        /*-------------------------------------------
        There is a message in the message queue.
        Check if the message is the WM_QUIT message.
        -------------------------------------------*/
        if ( msg.message == WM_QUIT )
            {
            /*-------------------------
            A WM_QUIT message received.
            -------------------------*/
            break; /* Terminate the application. */
            }
        /*-------------------------------
        A message received.
        The received message is not WM_QUIT
        -------------------------------*/
        TranslateMessage ( &msg );
        DispatchMessage  ( &msg );
        }
    else
        PlayBackground ();
    }/* end of while (TRUE) */
```

When there are no messages for the program, the PlayBackground() function is executed.

The *PlayBackground( )* Function

The PlayBackground() function plays the background organ music in groups of 2,000 bytes. Each time PlayBackground() is called, the next 2,000 bytes play. We execute the playback only if the giOrganIsOn flag is 1:

```
if ( giOrganIsOn == 1)
   {
   /*------------------------------------------------
   Since the Organ is ON, play the background music.
   --------------------------------------------*/
   glCurrentBackGndByte =
   sp_PlayF ( glCurrentBackGndByte,
             glCurrentBackGndByte + 2000L );

 if ( glCurrentBackGndByte >= 18000L )
    {
    sp_PlayF ( glCurrentBackGndByte, 19049L );
    glCurrentBackGndByte = 0L;
    }
}
```

The background sound coordinates are from byte coordinate 0 to byte coordinate 19,049. In WinMain() we initialized glCurrentBackGndByte to 0, so that initially, the playback starts from byte coordinate 0.

Each time the PlayBackground() is called, a new section of 2,000 bytes plays. Because the glCurrentBackGndByte variable is declared as a global (public) variable, its value is maintained throughout the program's life.

Because the playback is done in groups of 2,000 bytes each, we detect the fact that glCurrentBackGndByte reaches a value of 18,000 with an if statement, and then we play the rest of the sound section (that is, from byte coordinate 18,000 to byte coordinate 19,049).

Initializing the Scroll Bar

Because the Organ program contains a scroll bar, we need to set the range of the scroll bar and position the thumb of the scroll bar in its initial position.

This is done under the WM_PAINT case by executing the SetNotesScrollBar() function:

```
case WM_PAINT:
    hdc = BeginPaint ( hWnd, &ps );
    SetNotesScrollBar ( hWnd );
    EndPaint ( hWnd, &ps );
    return 0;
```

Responding to Scroll Bar Changes

Under the WM_HSCROLL case we take care of the scroll bar changes. If the user decremented, incremented, or dragged the thumb of the scroll bar, we change the value of giNotesSpeedScroll accordingly, and execute the ChangeNotesSpeedWasRequested() function.

Processing Keyboard Keys

Under the WM_CHAR case we process the messages that were generated as responses to pressing keys on the keyboard. The toupper() function converts the received wParam to uppercase, and then wParam is analyzed.

Terminating the Program by Pressing the X Key

If the user pressed the x key, the code under the case x is executed, causing the program to terminate:

```
switch ( wParam )
    {
    case 'X':
        /*-----------------------
        User pressed 'X' to exit.
        ----------------------*/
        DestroyWindow (hWnd);
        return 0L;
```

Turning the Organ On and Off by Using the Keyboard

If the user presses the **N** key or the **O** key, the flag giOrganIsOn is updated:

```
case 'N':
    /*-----------------------
    User pressed 'N' to turn
    the Organ ON.
    -----------------------*/
    giOrganIsOn = 1;
    return 0L;

case 'O':
    /*-----------------------
    User pressed 'O' to turn
    the Organ OFF.
    -----------------------*/
    giOrganIsOn = 0;
    return 0L;
```

Speeding Up and Slowing Down the Playback Speed by Using the Keyboard

While the organ is playing (the organ is on), the user may speed up the play-back speed by pressing the **F** key:

```
case 'F':
    /*-----------------------
    User pressed 'F' to speed up
    the playback (Faster).
    -----------------------*/
    giNotesSpeedScroll++;
    ChangeNotesSpeedWasRequested ( hWnd );
    return 0L;
```

Similarly, the user may slow down the playback by pressing the **S** key:

```
case 'S':
    /*-----------------------
    User pressed 'S' to slow down
    the playback (Slower).
    -----------------------*/
    giNotesSpeedScroll--;
    ChangeNotesSpeedWasRequested ( hWnd );
    return 0L;
```

Playing the Organ

To play the organ, the user may press keys 1 through 8. These keys correspond to the notes Do, Re, Me, Fa, So, La, Ti, Do.

To play a note, the corresponding play function is executed. For example, to play the Do note, the `PlayDO()` function is executed:

```
case '1':
    /*----------------
    User is pressing '1'
    ----------------*/
    if ( giOrganIsOn == 1 )
        PlayDO();
    return 0L;
```

The other play functions are `PlayRE()`, `PlayME()`, `PlayFA()`, `PlaySO()`, `PlayLA()`, `PlayTI()`, and `PlayDO2nd()`.

Each of these play functions use the `sp_PlayF()` function to play the corresponding sound section.

Processing Push Buttons

The push buttons are processed under the `WM_COMMAND` case of the `WndProc()` function.

Under the `FAST_NOTES_PB` case we process the Faster push button. Pushing this push button causes the playback speed to increase:

```
case FAST_NOTES_PB:
    /*---------------------------------
    User pressed the Faster push button
    to speed up the playback (Faster).
    ---------------------------------*/
    giNotesSpeedScroll++;
    ChangeNotesSpeedWasRequested ( hWnd );
    return 0L;
```

Similarly, we process the `SLOW_NOTES_PB` push button, the `TURN_ON_PB` push button, and the `TURN_OFF_PB` push button.

The Instructions Dialog Box

The Instructions dialog box contains an Audio Instructions push button. The user obtains audio instructions by pushing this push button.

Because the user might have changed the playback speed before opening the Instructions dialog box, we must return the playback speed to the natural speed so that the audio instructions play at the natural speed. Under the AUDIO_PB case, we set the playback speed to the natural speed, then play the instructions section, and finally return the playback speed to its original value:

```
case AUDIO_PB:
    /*---------------------------------
    User pushed the Audio Instructions.
    ---------------------------------*/
    sp_SetNewSpeed ( MAX_NOTES_SPEED_SCROLL,
                     NAT_NOTES_SPEED_SCROLL,
                     NAT_NOTES_SPEED_SCROLL);

    sp_PlayF ( 167681L, SP_END_OF_FILE);

    sp_SetNewSpeed ( MAX_NOTES_SPEED_SCROLL,
                     NAT_NOTES_SPEED_SCROLL,
                     giNotesSpeedScroll);
    return TRUE;
```

Upgrading the Organ Program

The Organ program demonstrates how a simple organ may be implemented. Of course, you may improve the Organ by adding more features to it. For example, each note is played from beginning to end, without letting the user produce shorter notes. To allow the user to produce shorter notes, play the note in small groups; and, between the playback of these groups, execute the PeekMessage() function to see if the user released the key (that is, check to see if the WM_KEYUP message was generated).

The Control2 Program

In a previous chapter, we discussed the Controls program as a Generic1-based program. In this chapter, we rewrite the Controls program as a Generic2-based program. This new program is called Control2.

Compiling, Linking, and Executing the Control2 Program

To compile and link the Control2 program with the Microsoft compiler:

- Make sure your PC is in a DOS-protected mode.

- Log into c:\spSDK\Samp4Win.

- At the DOS prompt type

  NMAKE Control2.mak   {Enter}

To compile and link the Control2 program with the Borland compiler:

- Log into c:\spSDK\Samp4Win.

- At the DOS prompt type

  NMAKE -f Control2.bmk   {Enter}

To execute the Control2 program:

- Select Run from the File menu of the Program manager of Windows.

- Click Browse and select the file

  c:\spSDK\Samp4Win\Control2.exe

The main window of appears, as shown in Figure 9.11.

The Control2 program menu (see Figure 9.12) contains four options: Quit, About, Enable Mouse, and Disable Mouse. The About dialog box is shown in Figure 9.13.

Clicking the Play push button causes the sound file to play. While the sound file plays, the Rewind/Forward scroll bar changes its thumb position, and the Position in seconds text changes as well.

Control2 enables the user to pause the playback by either pushing the Pause push button or by pressing **P**.

The user can play the sound file backward by pushing the Play Backward push button or by pressing the **b** key.

The user can change the playback speed by using the speed scroll bar or by using the Slower, Normal, and Faster push buttons.

The user can run the program with or without the mouse during the playback by pressing Alt-M, and then selecting the appropriate menu option.

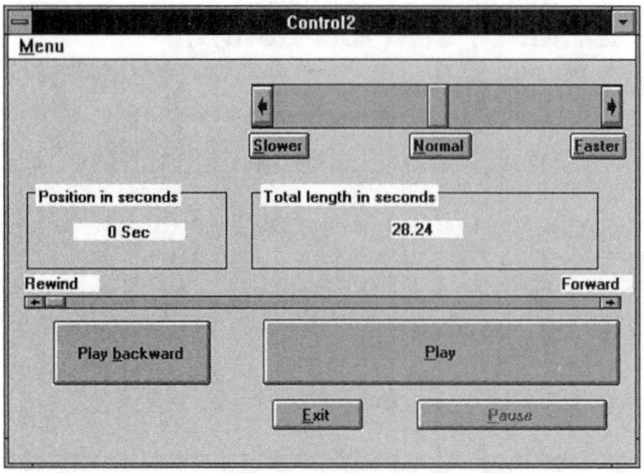

Figure 9.11. The main window of the Control2 program.

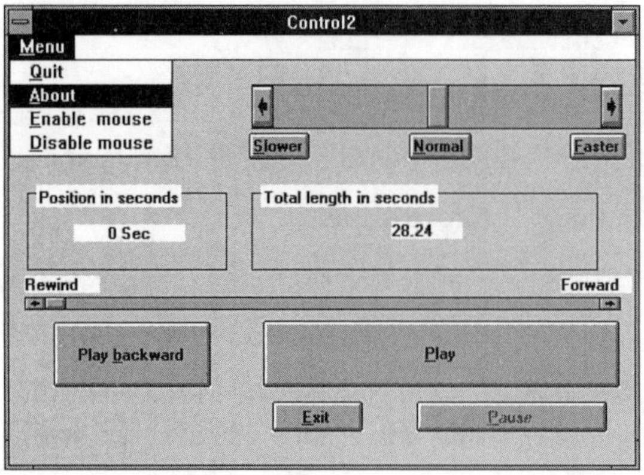

Figure 9.12. The Control2 program menu.

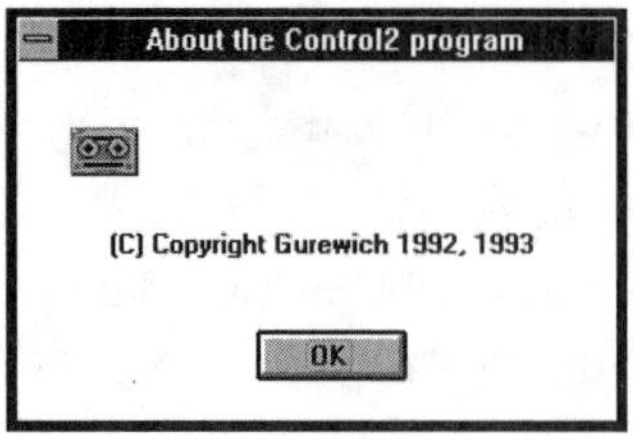

Figure 9.13. The About dialog box of the Control2 program.

The Files of Control2

The Control2 program consists of the following files:

Control2.h	The #include file of the program.
Control2.c	The C code of the program.
Control2.rc	The resource file of the program.
Control2.def	The module definition file of the program.
Control2.mak	The make file of the program.
Tape.ico	The icon of the program.

These files are provided for you in C:\spSDK\Samp4Win\.

A Dialog Box as the Program's Main Window

The Control2 program uses a dialog box as its main window. This is done by updating the cbWndExtra element of the wc structure with DLGWINDOWEXTRA:

```
wc.cbWndExtra    = DLGWINDOWEXTRA ;
```

and by creating the dialog box with the CreateDialog() function. The second parameter of CreateDialog() is Control2Box:

```
hWnd = CreateDialog ( ghInst, "Control2Box", 0, NULL );
```

Control2Box is defined in Control2.rc as the name of the dialog box.

Opening the Sound Session

The sound session opens as a non-stand-alone program. The S-type sound file c:\spSDK\Sfiles\Day.s opens:

```
iOpenResult =
sp_OpenSession ( "c:\\spSDK\\Sfiles\\Day.s",
                 SP_NON_STAND_ALONE,
                 0L,
                 SP_S_TYPE );
```

```
/*-------------------------
Quit if can't open the file.
------------------------*/
if ( iOpenResult != SP_NO_ERRORS )
   {
   MessageBox ( NULL,
                "Failed to open the sound session!",
                "Message from Control2.exe",
                MB_ICONINFORMATION );

   /*-------------------
   Quit the application.
   ------------------*/
   SendMessage ( hWnd,
                 WM_DESTROY,
                 0,
                 0 );

   }/* end of if(iOpenResult!=SP_NO_ERRORS) */
```

In order to use the mouse during playback, we execute the sp_EnableMouseDuringPlay() function:

```
sp_EnableMouseDuringPlay ();
```

The Message Loop of Control2

The message loop of Control2 is a Generic2 message loop. The ThePlay() function is executed whenever there is no message for the program:

```
while (TRUE)
     {
     if ( PeekMessage ( &msg, NULL, 0, 0, PM_REMOVE ) )
        {
        /*-----------------------------------------
        There is a message in the message queue.
        Check if the message is the WM_QUIT message.
        -----------------------------------------*/
        if ( msg.message == WM_QUIT )
           {
           /*-------------------------
           A WM_QUIT message received.
           ------------------------*/
           break; /* Terminate the application. */
           }
```

```
        /*---------------------------------
        A message received.
        The received message is not WM_QUIT
        --------------------------------*/
        TranslateMessage ( &msg );
        DispatchMessage  ( &msg );
        }
      else
        {
        /*----------------------------------------
        There is no message in the message queue.
        ----------------------------------------*/
        ThePlay(hWnd);
        }
    }/* end of while (TRUE) */
```

The *ThePlay()* Function

The `ThePlay()` function plays the sound file in groups of 2,000 bytes each. Throughout the program we maintain a variable `giPlayEnable`. This variable serves as a flag to indicate whether the sound file should be played in the forward direction, in the backward direction, or not played at all:

```
if ( giPlayEnable == 1 )
    {
    glCurrentByte =
    sp_PlayF ( glCurrentByte,
               glCurrentByte + 2000L );
    DisplayLocation ( hWnd, glCurrentByte );
    }

if ( giPlayEnable == -1 )
    {
    glCurrentByte =
    sp_PlayB ( glCurrentByte,
               glCurrentByte - 2000L );
    DisplayLocation ( hWnd, glCurrentByte );

    if ( glCurrentByte == 0 )
        {
        /*----------------------------
        Beginning of file encountered.
        ---------------------------*/
        SendMessage ( hWnd,
                      WM_COMMAND,
                      PAUSE_PB,
                      0);
    }
```

After the playback of each group, the DisplayLocation() function is executed, updating the Rewind/Forward scroll bar, and updating the Position in seconds text.

When playing in the forward direction, the sound file is played in an endless loop. Remember that when the playback reaches the end of the sound file, sp_PlayF() returns 0. Therefore, after the last group of 2,000 bytes is completed, sp_PlayF() returns 0 and glCurrentByte is updated with 0, so that the next playback group will start at the beginning of the sound file.

When playing in the backward direction, we detect the file reached its beginning position with the if(glCurrentByte==0) statement. If the file reached its beginning point, we stop the playback by executing the SendMessage() function. We send the WM_COMMAND message with wParam equal to PAUSE_PB. Sending this message is the same as pushing the Pause push button.

The *WM_CREATE* Case of Control2

Under the WM_CREATE case we obtain the lpfn of the About dialog box, extract the size of the sound file, and initialize the variables that hold the current thumb positions of the Speed scroll bar and the Rewind/Forward scroll bar:

```
case WM_CREATE:
     /*-----------------------------------------------------
     Obtain the lpfnAboutDlgProc of the About dialog box.
     -----------------------------------------------------*/
     lpfnAboutDlgProc =
     MakeProcInstance (( FARPROC) AboutDlgProc, ghInst);


     /*---------------------------------------------
     Find the size (in bytes) of the sound file.
     ---------------------------------------*/
     glFileSizeInBytes = sp_GetFileSizeInBytes ();


     /*----------------------------------------
     The variable giPositionScroll is updated.
     This variable reflects the position of
     the Position Scroll bar.
     ------------------------------------*/
     giPositionScroll = MIN_SPEED_SCROLL ;
```

```
/*-------------------------------------
The variable giSpeedScroll is updated.
This variable reflects the position of
the speed scroll bar.
-----------------------------------*/
giSpeedScroll = NAT_SPEED_SCROLL ;

return 0;
```

The *WM_PAINT* Case of Control2

Under the WM_PAINT case we display the size of the sound file in seconds by using the DisplayFileSize() function; we disable the Pause push button if there is no playback; and we initialize the scroll bars by using the InitScrollBars() function:

```
case WM_PAINT:
    hdc = BeginPaint ( hWnd, &ps );

    /*---------------------------------------
    Find and display the size (in seconds) of
    the sound file.
    ---------------------------------------*/
    DisplayFileSize ( hWnd );

    if ( giPlayEnable == 0 )
        {
        /*---------------------------
        Disable the Pause push button.
        ---------------------------*/
        hWndCtrl = GetDlgItem ( hWnd, PAUSE_PB );
        EnableWindow ( hWndCtrl, 0 );
        }

    /*--------------------------
    Initialize the scroll bars.
    --------------------------*/
    InitScrollBars ( hWnd );

    EndPaint ( hWnd, &ps );
    return 0;
```

The *WM_CHAR* Case of Control2

The WM_CHAR case processes all the messages that result when the user presses the keyboard. Because each key has a corresponding push button, we respond to the key pressed by using the SendMessage() function, sending the push button's message that corresponds to the key pressed. For example, upon detecting that the user pressed the **B** key, we send the WM_COMMAND message with wParam equal to PLAY_BACK_PB (PLAY_BACK_PB is the Play Backward push button):

```
case 'B':
    /*----------------------------------
    User pressed 'B' for Backward playback.
    ---------------------------------*/
    SendMessage ( hWnd,
                  WM_COMMAND,
                  PLAY_BACK_PB,
                  0);
    return 0L;
```

For easy operation, we use the **P** key for both the Play push button and the Pause push button. This enables the user to play and pause by simply pressing the **P** key. Under the **P** case we check for the value of the giPlayEnable variable. This variable indicates whether we are playing or pausing. If we are playing, then the pressing of the **P** key should cause a pause; if we are pausing, the pressing of the **P** key should start the playback:

```
case 'P':
    /*----------------------
    User pressed 'P' to Play,
    or 'P' to Pause.
    ---------------------*/
    if ( giPlayEnable == 1 )
        {
        SendMessage ( hWnd,
                      WM_COMMAND,
                      PAUSE_PB,
                      0);
        }
    else
        {
        SendMessage ( hWnd,
                      WM_COMMAND,
                      PLAY_PB,
                      0);
        }
    return 0L;
```

The *WM_HSCROLL* Case of Control2

Under the WM_HSCROLL case we process the scroll bar messages. The variables giSpeedScroll and giPositionScroll hold the current thumb positions of the scroll bars. When the user increments, decrements, or drags the thumb of the scroll bars, we update the giSpeedScroll variable (or the giPositionScroll variable), and execute the ChangePositionWasRequested() function. For example, when the user decrements the scroll bar, the code under the SB_PAGEUP and SB_LINEUP is executed:

```
case SB_PAGEUP:
case SB_LINEUP:
    if ( GetDlgItem ( hWnd, SPEED_SB )
        == hWndCtrl )
        {
        /*------------------------------------
        The Speed scroll bar was decremented.
        ---------------------------------*/
        giSpeedScroll--;
        ChangeSpeedWasRequested ( hWnd );
        return 0L;
        }
    else
        {
        /*------------------------------------
        The Position scroll bar was decremented.
        ---------------------------------*/
        giPositionScroll-=2;
        ChangePositionWasRequested ( hWnd );
        return 0L;
        }
```

Processing the Push Buttons

The push button messages are processed under the WM_COMMAND case. The giPlayEnable variable is maintained throughout the program. Its value indicates the current status of the playback. A value of +1 indicates that playback is in progress in the forward direction, a value of -1 means that the playback is in progress in the backward direction, and a value of 0 means that there is no playback.

When the user pushes the Play push button, the code under the PLAY_PB case is executed. This code updates the giPlayEnable variable, disables the Play push button, and enables the Play Backward and Pause push buttons (that is, once the user pushes the Play push button, playback should start, the Play push button should be disabled, and the Play Backward and Pause push buttons should be enabled):

```
switch (wParam)
        {
        case PLAY_PB:
                /*----------------------------------------
                User pushed the Play push button to start
                the playback.
                ----------------------------------------*/
                giPlayEnable = 1;

                /*--------------------------------
                Disable the Play push button.
                --------------------------*/
                hWndCtrl = GetDlgItem ( hWnd, PLAY_PB );
                EnableWindow ( hWndCtrl, 0 );

                /*----------------------------------------
                Enable the Play backward push button.
                ------------------------------------*/
                hWndCtrl = GetDlgItem ( hWnd, PLAY_BACK_PB );
                EnableWindow ( hWndCtrl, 1 );

                /*--------------------------------
                Enable the Pause push button.
                --------------------------*/
                hWndCtrl = GetDlgItem ( hWnd, PAUSE_PB );
                EnableWindow ( hWndCtrl, 1 );

                return 0L;
```

Similarly, we take the appropriate actions when the user pushes the Play Backward or Pause push buttons.

When the user pushes the Slower, Faster, or Normal push buttons, the variable giSpeedScroll is updated, and then the ChangeSpeedWasRequested() function is executed. For example, when the user pushes the Slower push button, the code under the SLOW_PB case is executed:

```
case SLOW_PB:
        /*--------------------------------
        User selected the Slow push button.
        --------------------------------*/
        giSpeedScroll--;
        ChangeSpeedWasRequested ( hWnd );
        return 0L;
```

Enabling and Disabling the Mouse Device

The user may enable or disable the mouse device by selecting the Disable Mouse or Enable Mouse menu options. The cases which correspond to the user selection of these menu options are the `IDM_ENABLE_MOUSE` and `IDM_DISABLE_MOUSE` cases (under the `WM_COMMAND` case). To enable the mouse during the playback, we use the `sp_EnableMouseDuringPlay()` function. To disable the mouse, we use the `sp_DisableMouseDuringPlay()` function:

```
case IDM_ENABLE_MOUSE:
    sp_EnableMouseDuringPlay();
    return 0;

case IDM_DISABLE_MOUSE:
    sp_DisableMouseDuringPlay();
    return 0;
```

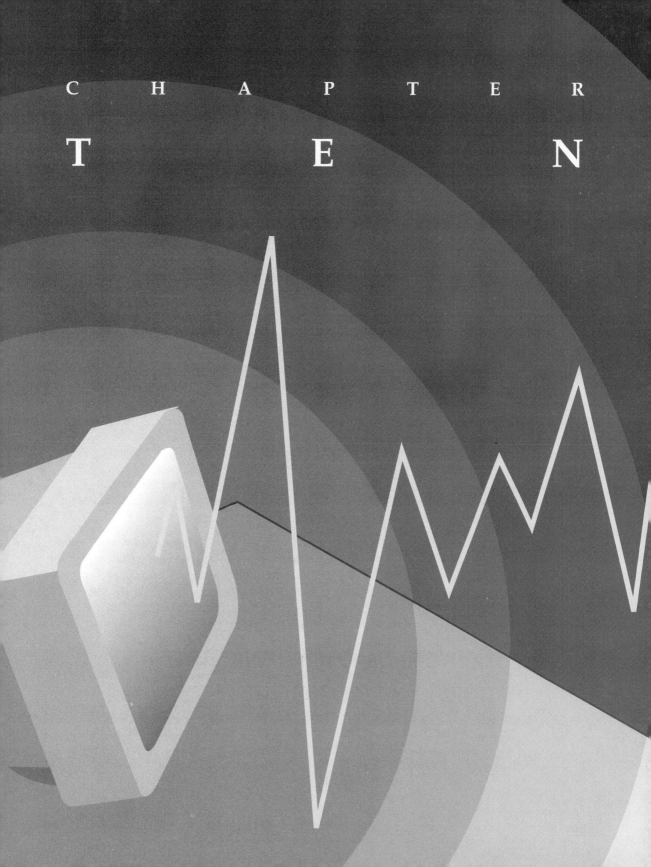

Stand-Alone Programs

So far, all the programs we have developed have been non-stand-alone sound programs. This means that the distribution disk (the disk that contains all the files of the complete program) of each of these programs must contain the .EXE program, as well as the sound file(s) that are used in the program. For example, the distribution disk of the Dog program must contain the following files:

1. Dog.exe

2. Bark.ts

3. Hello.ts

In addition to the inconvenience of having to distribute three separate files, the sound files have to reside in the directory specified by the first parameter of the sp_OpenSession() function.

To overcome this inconvenience, you may convert a non-stand-alone program to a stand-alone program. For example, after converting the Dog program to a stand-alone program, the distribution disk will consist of a single executable (.EXE) file. This file includes the sound file the program needs.

Converting the Dog Program to a Stand-Alone Program

As an exercise, we will now convert the non-stand-alone dog program (discussed in an earlier chapter) to a stand-alone program.

To convert Dog.c to a stand-alone program, perform the following steps:

Step 1

If you are using the Microsoft C compiler, add the following statement to the Dog.c file:

```
extern char ** __argv;
```

If you are using the Borland C compiler, add the following statement to the Dog.c file:

```
extern char ** _argv;
```

This statement should be added after the #include statements:

```
/*--------
 #include
 --------*/
/*-----------------------------------
 Required for all Windows applications.
 ---------------------------------*/
#include <windows.h>

/*------------------------------------------------------------------
 Required so that sp_ functions, SP_ macros and #definitions
 from the TS C Sound library may be used in this applications.
 ----------------------------------------------------------------*/
#include "c:\spSDK\TegoWlib\sp4Win.h"

/*--------------------------------------------------------
 Definitions & prototypes specific to this application.
 ------------------------------------------------------*/
#include "c:\spSDK\Samp4WIN\DogAlone.h"

/*--------------------------------------------------
 For standard C functions used in this application.
 ------------------------------------------------*/
#include <stdlib.h>
#include <stdio.h>

/*--------------------------------------------------------
        *** For the Microsoft C compiler ***
 SINCE THIS IS A STAND ALONE SOUND APPLICATION, __argv
 IS NEEDED.
 ------------------------------------------------------*/
extern char ** __argv;
```

```
/*----------------------------------------------------------
           *** For the Borland C compiler ***
SINCE THIS IS A STAND ALONE SOUND APPLICATION, _argv
IS NEEDED.
--------------------------------------------------------*/
extern char ** _argv;
```

Step 2

If you are using the Microsoft C compiler, change the sp_OpenSession() state-ment under the WM_CREATE case as follows:

```
case WM_CREATE:
      /*--------------------
      Open the sound session.
      -------------------*/
      iOpenBarkResult = sp_OpenSession (
                    __argv[0],
                    SP_STAND_ALONE,
                    0L,
                    SP_TS_TYPE);
```

If you are using the Borland C compiler, change the sp_OpenSession() state-ment under the WM_CREATE case as follows:

```
case WM_CREATE:
      /*----------------------------
      Open the barking sound session.
      ---------------------------*/
      iOpenBarkResult = sp_OpenSession (
                    _argv[0],
                    SP_STAND_ALONE,
                    0L,
                    SP_TS_TYPE);
```

In the above sp_OpenSession() function, we supplied __argv[0] (or _argv[0]) as the first parameter, and supplied SP_STAND_ALONE as the second parameter.

These are all the changes that have to be made to the source code in order to convert it to a stand-alone program.

Step 3

In this step we compile and link the stand-alone Dog program.

To compile and link with the Microsoft C compiler:

- Make sure your PC is in a DOS-protected mode.

- Log into c:\spSDK\Samp4Win\.

- At the DOS prompt type

    NMAKE Dog.mak   {Enter}

To compile and link with the Borland C compiler:

- Log into c:\spSDK\Samp4Win\.

- At the DOS prompt type

    MAKE -f Dog.bmk   {Enter}

Step 4

The last step is to link the Dog.exe file (generated in step 3) with the sound file c:\spSDK\SFiles\Bark.ts.

The Dog program uses two sound files: Bark.ts and Hello.ts. To perform the linking of the two sound files with the .EXE file, we need to use the TS Sound Editor. The TS Sound Editor program enables you to link an unlimited amount of sound files to an .EXE file. The sound files may be type S, TS, WAV, VOC, or SND.

Because we assume that you don't have a copy of the TS Sound Editor, we'll use the TSlink.exe utility. This utility lets you link only one sound file.

The TSlink Utility

The TSlink utility resides in c:\spSDK\Util\. This utility enables you to link an .EXE file with a single sound file (the sound file may be a type S sound file or a type TS sound file).

To use the TSlink utility:

- Log into c:\spSDK\Samp4Win\.

- At the DOS prompt type

    c:\spSDK\Util\TSlink Dog.exe c:\spSDK\TSFiles\Bark.ts DogAlone.exe

The first parameter of the TSlink utility is the name of the .EXE file to be linked; the second parameter is the name of the sound file that will be linked to the .EXE file; the third parameter is the name of the resultant Stand-Alone .EXE file. You must provide the file extensions. That is, the first parameter must be Dog.exe, not Dog. The second parameter must be Bark.ts, not Bark. And the third parameter must be DogAlone.exe, not DogAlone.

NOTE The TSlink.exe utility links an .EXE file with a sound file.

Syntax: `TSlink <1st parameter> <2nd parameter> <3rd parameter>`

First parameter: The name of the .EXE file to be linked.

Second parameter: The name of the sound file to be linked.

Third parameter: The name of the resultant .EXE file.

Executing the Stand-Alone Dog Program

You may now execute the stand-along Dog program.

To execute the program from Windows:

- Select Run from the File menu in the Program Manager of Windows.
- Click Browse and select the file

  `c:\spSDK\Samp4Win\DogAlone.exe.`

To execute the program from the DOS prompt:

- Exit Windows.
- Log into c:\spSDK\Samp4Win\.
- At the DOS prompt type

  WIN DogAlone {Enter}

The stand-alone program consists of a single file, DogAlone.exe. This file may reside in any drive and any directory.

The TSlink utility linked the sound file Bark.ts with the Dog.exe file, and created a new file called DogAlone.exe. The size of DogAlone.exe is approximately the sum of the sizes of the Dog.exe and Bark.ts files. The distribution disk will consist of a single file, the DogAlone.exe file. There is no need to distribute the sound file Bark.ts.

Using TSLabels

The short version of the TSlink utility enables you to link only one sound file. We did not, therefore, link the Hello.ts file. If, however, you have a copy of the TS Sound Editor, you may create a single sound file that is the sum of the Bark.ts file, and the Good-Bye sound section of the Hello.ts file. You may insert sound labels around the Good-Bye sound section, such as GoodBye starts here, and GoodBye ends here. To play the Good-Bye section, the following statement is used:

```
sp_PlayLabelF ( "GoodBye starts here", "GoodBye ends here" );
```

The sp_PlayLabelF() is not included in the short version of the TS C Sound library that comes with the book's diskette.

The __argv{} Parameter

The __argv[] variable that was used in the atand-alone program serves the same role as argv[] does in C programs for DOS. It contains the parameters that were typed when executing the program. In a stand-alone program, the first parameter of sp_OpenSession() should contain __argv[0], because __argv[0] contains the path and name of the program that is being executed. For example, if you execute the DogAlone.exe program from c:\spSDK\Samp4Win\, then __argv[0] is equal to c:\spSDK\Samp4Win\DogAlone.exe.

As previously discussed, when using the Microsoft C compiler, you have to use __argv. When using the Borland C compiler, you have to use _argv.

The Third Parameter of *sp_OpenSession()*

In the short version of the TS C Sound library, the third parameter of the sp_OpenSession() function does not have any meaning, so you may supply the value 0L for this parameter.

Converting Other Programs

You may now convert all the other non-stand-alone programs that are presented in this book to stand-alone sound programs in the same manner.

The WhoAmI Program

Our last program for this chapter is the WhoAmI program, a program that declares its path and name, and then plays itself.

When the user selects the Play option from the menu, a message box that contains the value of argv[0] appears, and then the linked sound file plays.

Here is the complete listing of the WhoAmI program:

Listing 10.1. WhoAmI.h.

```
/*====================================================
 FILE NAME: WhoAmI.h

 (C) Copyright Gurewich 1992, 1993
 ====================================================*/

/*---------
 prototypes
 ---------*/
long FAR PASCAL _export WndProc       ( HWND, UINT, UINT, LONG ) ;
BOOL FAR PASCAL _export AboutDlgProc ( HWND, UINT, UINT, LONG ) ;
```

```
/*------
  #define
  ------*/
#define IDM_QUIT       1   /* The Quit    option in the menu. */
#define IDM_ABOUT      2   /* The About   option in the menu. */
#define IDM_PLAY       3   /* The Play    option in the menu. */


/*---------------
  Global variables
  ---------------*/
char        gszAppName[] = "WhoAmI" ; /* Our application name. */
HINSTANCE   ghInst;                   /* current instance.      */
```

Listing 10.2. WhoAmI.c.

```
/*===========================================================
  PROGRAM: WhoAmI.c
  -------
  (C) Copyright 1992, 1993 Gurewich. (R) All rights reserved.

  How to compile and link this program, and create a stand-alone
  program:
  =====================================================================

    1. If you are using the Microsoft C compiler, make sure that
       this file uses __argv (not _argv)
          [] Make sure that your PC is in protected mode.
          [] Log into the directory c:\spSDK\Samp4Win\
          [] At the DOS prompt type:
                 NMAKE  WhoAmI.mak [Enter}
    2. If you are using the Borland C compiler, make sure that
       this file uses _argv (not __argv)
          [] Log into the directory c:\spSDK\Samp4Win\
          [] At the DOS prompt type:
              MAKE  -f WhoAmI.bmk [Enter}
    3. At the DOS prompt type:
       c:\spSDK\Util\Tslink WhoAmI.exe c:\spSDK\TSfiles\Hello.ts
       Who.exe {Enter}
You now have a file: Who.exe which is a stand-alone file.
  =========================================================*/
```

continues

Listing 10.2. continued

```c
/*--------
 #include
 --------*/
/*-----------------------------------
 Required for all Windows applications.
 ---------------------------------*/
#include <windows.h>

/*--------------------------------------------------------------------
 Required so that "sp_" functions, "SP_" macros and #definitions
 from the TS C Sound library may be used in this applications.
 -----------------------------------------------------------------*/
#include "c:\spSDK\TegoWlib\sp4Win.h"

/*------------------------------------------------------
 Definitions & prototypes specific to this application.
 ----------------------------------------------------*/
#include "c:\spSDK\Samp4WIN\WhoAmI.h"

/*--------------------------------------------------
 For standard C functions used in this application.
 ------------------------------------------------*/
#include <ctype.h>
#include <stdlib.h>
#include <stdio.h>

/*=========== For the Microsoft C compiler ===================*/
extern char ** __argv;

/*=========== For the Borland C compiler ===================*/
/*** extern char ** _argv; ***/


/*==================
 FUNCTION: WinMain()
 ==================*/
int PASCAL WinMain ( HANDLE hInstance,
                     HANDLE hPrevInstance,
                     LPSTR  lpszCmdLine,
                     int    nCmdShow )
{
/*------------------------
 Local and static variables.
 ------------------------*/
HWND      hWnd;   /* Handler to the window of our application.   */
MSG       msg;    /* Message to be processed by our application. */
WNDCLASS  wc;     /* Window class of our application.            */
```

```
/*-----------------------------------------------
  Make the hInstance variable a global variable.
  -------------------------------------------*/
  ghInst = hInstance;

/*-----------------------------------------------
  Update the window class structure and register
  the window class.
  -------------------------------------------*/
  if ( !hPrevInstance )
     {
     /*--------------------------------------------
     The "if" is satisfied, this is the very 1st
     run of this application.
     ------------------------------------------*/
     wc.style          = CS_HREDRAW | CS_VREDRAW ;
     wc.lpfnWndProc    = WndProc ;
     wc.cbClsExtra     = 0 ;
     wc.cbWndExtra     = 0 ;
     wc.hInstance      = ghInst ;
     wc.hIcon          = LoadIcon  ( ghInst, "IconOfTape" ) ;
     wc.hCursor        = LoadCursor ( NULL, IDC_ARROW      ) ;
     wc.hbrBackground  = GetStockObject ( WHITE_BRUSH );
     wc.lpszMenuName   = gszAppName ;
     wc.lpszClassName  = gszAppName ;

     /*-----------------
     Register the window.
     ----------------*/
     RegisterClass ( &wc );

     }/* end of if(!hPrevInstance) */


/*------------------------------------
  Create the window of our application.
  ----------------------------------*/
  hWnd = CreateWindow ( gszAppName,
                        gszAppName,
                        WS_OVERLAPPEDWINDOW,
                        CW_USEDEFAULT,
                        CW_USEDEFAULT,
                        CW_USEDEFAULT,
                        CW_USEDEFAULT,
                        NULL,
                        NULL,
                        ghInst,
                        NULL );
```

continues

Listing 10.2. continued

```
/*--------------------------------------------
 Show and update the window of our application.
 -----------------------------------------*/
ShowWindow   ( hWnd, nCmdShow );
UpdateWindow ( hWnd );

/*----------------
 The message loop.
 ---------------*/
while ( GetMessage ( &msg, NULL, 0, 0 ) )
      {
      TranslateMessage ( &msg );
      DispatchMessage  ( &msg );
      }

return msg.wParam ;

} /* end of function. */
/*========================= end of WinMain() ===================*/

/*==================
 FUNCTION: WndProc()
 =================*/
/*------------------------------
 DESCRIPTION: Processes messages.
 ---------------------------*/
long FAR PASCAL _export WndProc ( HWND hWnd,
                                  UINT message,
                                  UINT wParam,
                                  LONG lParam )
{
/*-------------------------
 Local and static variables.
 ---------------------*/
static FARPROC lpfnAboutDlgProc;  /* For the "About" dialog box.  */

static int     iOpenResult;

switch ( message )
      {
      case WM_CREATE:
            /*----------------------
            Open the sound session.
            --------------------*/
            iOpenResult = sp_OpenSession (
                        __argv[0],
                        SP_STAND_ALONE,
```

```
                    0L,
                    SP_TS_TYPE);

        /*--------------------------
        Quit if can't open the file.
        --------------------------*/
        if ( iOpenResult != SP_NO_ERRORS )
            {
            MessageBox ( NULL,
                    "Failed to open the sound session!",
                    "Message from WhoAmI.c",
                     MB_ICONINFORMATION );

            /*--------------------
            Quit the application.
            -------------------*/
            SendMessage ( hWnd,
                    WM_DESTROY,
                    0,
                    0 );
            }

        /*---------------------------------------
        Obtain the lpfnAboutDlgProc of the "About"
        the dialog box.
        ---------------------------------------*/
        lpfnAboutDlgProc =
        MakeProcInstance (( FARPROC) AboutDlgProc, ghInst);
        return 0;

    case WM_COMMAND:
        /*------------------
        Process menu items.
        -----------------*/
        switch (wParam)
            {
            case IDM_QUIT:
                /*------------------------
                User clicked on Quit option.
                ------------------------*/
                DestroyWindow (hWnd);
                return 0L;

            case IDM_ABOUT :
                /*----------------------------
                User clicked on "About" option.
                ---------------------------*/
```

continues

Listing 10.2. continued

```
                                DialogBox ( ghInst,
                                            "AboutBox",
                                            hWnd,
                                            lpfnAboutDlgProc );
                                return 0L;

                        case IDM_PLAY :
                                /*-----------------------------------
                                User clicked on "Play" option.
                                -----------------------------------*/
                                MessageBox ( NULL,
                                             __argv[0],
                                             "The value of argv[0] is:",
                                             MB_ICONINFORMATION );

                                sp_PlayF ( SP_START_OF_FILE,
                                           SP_END_OF_FILE ) ;

                                return 0L;

                        }/* end of switch (wParam) */


        case WM_DESTROY:
                PostQuitMessage (0);
                return 0;
        }/* end of switch (message) */

/*------------------------
 Message was not processed.
 ----------------------*/
return DefWindowProc ( hWnd, message, wParam, lParam ) ;

}/* end of WndProc() */
/*================== end of WndProc() ====================*/

/*=======================
 FUNCTION: AboutDlgProc()
 =======================*/
/*-------------------------------------------
 DESCRIPTION:
 This is the "About" dialog box procedure.
 -------------------------------------------*/
BOOL FAR PASCAL _export AboutDlgProc ( HWND hDlg,
                                       UINT message,
                                       UINT wParam,
                                       LONG lParam )
```

```
{
switch ( message )
      {
      case WM_INITDIALOG :
             return TRUE;

      case WM_COMMAND :
            switch ( wParam )
                 {
                 case IDOK :
                 case IDCANCEL :
                     EndDialog ( hDlg, 0 );
                     return TRUE;
                 }
      }/* end of switch(message) */
return FALSE ;
}/* End of function. */
/*=============== end of AboutDlgProc() ==============*/
```

Listing 10.3. WhoAmI.rc.

```
/*===================================================
FILE NAME: WhoAmI.rc
.........

FILE DESCRIPTION:
................
The resource file.

(C) Copyright Gurewich 1992, 1993

=================================================*/

/*........
#include
.......*/
#include <windows.h>
#include "WhoAmI.h"

/*....
Menu
....*/
WhoAmI   MENU
```

continues

Listing 10.3. continued

```
BEGIN
   POPUP   "&Menu"
      BEGIN
         MENUITEM "&Quit",          IDM_QUIT
         MENUITEM "&About",         IDM_ABOUT
         MENUITEM "&Play",          IDM_PLAY
      END
END

/*-----------------------------------------
 Definition of the Cassette tape icon.
 Filename: Tape.ico
 Icon name: IconOfTape
 -----------------------------------------*/
IconOfTape ICON Tape.ico


/*--------------------
 The About dialog box.
 --------------------*/
AboutBox DIALOG 81, 43, 160, 100
STYLE DS_MODALFRAME ¦ WS_POPUP ¦ WS_VISIBLE ¦ WS_CAPTION ¦ WS_SYSMENU
CAPTION "About the WhoAmI program"
FONT 8, "MS Sans Serif"
BEGIN
    PUSHBUTTON       "OK", IDOK, 64, 75, 40, 14
    CTEXT            "(C) Copyright Gurewich 1992, 1993",
                     -1, 13, 47, 137, 18
    ICON             "IconOfTape", -1, 14, 12, 18, 20
END
```

Listing 10.4. WhoAmI.def.

```
;=======================================
; module-definition file for WhoAmI.c
;=======================================

NAME           WhoAmI

DESCRIPTION    'The WhoAmI program. (C) Copyright Gurewich 1992, 1993'

EXETYPE        WINDOWS

STUB           'WINSTUB.EXE'
```

```
CODE   PRELOAD MOVEABLE DISCARDABLE

DATA   PRELOAD MOVEABLE MULTIPLE

HEAPSIZE       1024
STACKSIZE      8192
```

Listing 10.5. WhoAmI.mak.

```
#==============
# WhoAmI.mak
#==============

WhoAmI.exe : WhoAmI.obj WhoAmI.h WhoAmI.def WhoAmI.res
    link /nod WhoAmI.obj, WhoAmI.exe, NUL, \
        slibcew.lib oldnames.lib libw.lib commdlg \
        c:\spSDK\TegoWlib\TegoWin.lib, \
        WhoAmI.def
    rc -t WhoAmI.res

WhoAmI.obj : WhoAmI.c WhoAmI.h
    cl -c -G2sw -Ow -W3 -Zp  WhoAmI.c

WhoAmI.res : WhoAmI.rc WhoAmI.h Tape.ico
    rc -r WhoAmI.rc
```

Compiling and Linking the WhoAmI Program

To compile and link the WhoAmI program with the Microsoft C compiler:

- Make sure the WhoAmI.c file uses __argv, not _argv.

- Make sure your PC is in a DOS-protected mode.

- Log into c:\spSDK\Samp4Win\.

- At the DOS prompt type

    NMAKE WhoAmI.mak   {Enter}

To compile and link the WhoAmI program with the Borland C compiler:

- Make sure the WhoAmI.c file uses _argv, not __argv.

- Log into c:\spSDK\Samp4Win\.

- At the DOS prompt type

    ```
    MAKE -f WhoAmI.bmk   {Enter}
    ```

Linking the WhoAmI Program with a Sound File

The sp_OpenSession() statement of the WhoAmI program uses a TS-Type file:

```
iOpenResult = sp_OpenSession (
                  __argv[0],
                  SP_STAND_ALONE,
                  0L,
                  SP_TS_TYPE);
```

The first parameter of sp_OpenSession() specifies that the sound file to be opened is the program itself. The second parameter of sp_OpenSession() specifies that the program is a stand-alone program. The third parameter of sp_OpenSession() has no meaning in the short version of the SP library, so we supplied the value 0L. The fourth parameter of sp_OpenSession() specifies that the program should be linked with a TS-Type sound file.

To link the TS-Type sound file Hello.ts to WhoAmI.exe, at the DOS prompt type

```
c:\spSDK\Util\TSlink WhoAmI.exe c:\spSDK\TSfiles\Hello.ts Who.exe {Enter}
```

The resultant file Who.exe is a stand-alone sound program.

The *lpszCmdLine* Variable

Remember that the third parameter of the WinMain() function is lpszCmdLine:

```
int PASCAL WinMain ( HANDLE hInstance,
                     HANDLE hPrevInstance,
                     LPSTR  lpszCmdLine,
                     int    nCmdShow )
```

```
{
 . . . . . . . . . . . . . .
 . . . . . . . . . . . . . .
 . . . . . . . . . . . . . .
}
```

The `lpszCmdLine` variable contains the parameters that were typed to execute the Windows application. That is, suppose you write a Windows application called PlayAny.exe. To execute the PlayAny program from the DOS prompt, the user must type

WIN PlayAny <Sound file name>   {Enter}

If the user executes the PlayAny program from within Windows by selecting Run from the File menu, the user must type

PlayAny <Sound file name>

The name of the sound file to be played can be extracted from the third parameter of the `WinMain()` function.

In stand-alone programs, the sound file to be played is the program itself. Unfortunately, the `lpszCmdLine` variable does not include the program name. This is the reason for using `argv[0]`.

Using a Sound Card from Within a Windows Application

Some users have sound cards installed in their PCs. Naturally, these users enjoy a better sound quality than users who use the internal built-in speaker. When you write a Windows application, you can write the code so that it accommodates both types of PC systems: PCs *with* and *without* an installed sound card. The program code may detect the presence or absence of a sound card in the system, and accordingly direct the sound to either the internal built-in speaker or to the sound card.

There are two major differences between playing through the internal built-in speaker and playing through a sound card. To begin with, the sound card produces better sound quality. Secondly, the sound card does not use the CPU resources for playing. This means that once the CPU issues a command to the sound card to play a sound section, the sound card is on its own, playing the sound section without any help from the PC's CPU. The PC is free to perform other tasks while the playback is going on. For example, move graphic objects such as multimedia.

The Windows Operating System and Sound Cards

One of the main advantages of using the Windows operating system is that as a Windows programmer, you may assume that your users have a large amount of code already installed in their PCs.

For example, when displaying text or graphics on the monitor, your code does not have to worry about the type of monitor your user owns. It is the responsibility of the Windows operating system to display the text and graphics on the user's monitor. As a programmer, you may safely assume that your user already installed the proper monitor driver in his or her system, and that the Windows operating system accepted that particular driver. If the monitor's driver is incompatible with the Windows operating system, then the user would experience problems operating Windows. Your program assumes that the PC is already configured and accepted by Windows.

The same, of course, applies to the printer. If your program has to print something, it does not assume any particular printer brand. The only assumption your program makes is that the printer works well with the Windows operating system. This concept is known as the *device independency* feature of Windows.

The same device independency applies to sound cards. Therefore, as long as the installed sound card is Windows compatible, all the programs presented in this chapter and in subsequent chapters will work well with this sound card.

Installing the Sound Card

Installing the sound card into your PC involves two separate steps:

1. Hardware and software installation of the sound card.

2. The Windows drivers installation.

Hardware and Software Installation of the Sound Card

To install a sound card into the PC, follow the installation manual that came with the sound card package. The manual explains how to install the sound card into one of the slots of the PC, and how to install the software that came with the sound card package.

The sound card that was installed by the authors of this book is the *Sound Blaster Pro* by Creative Labs. When we completed the installation of this sound card, we ran a test utility called *TEST-SBP.EXE* that came with this sound card. The TEST-SBP.EXE utility (residing in C:\SBPRO\) tests the installation and displays the various settings of the sound card. These settings are the I/O address, the interrupt number, and the DMA channel number.

If the sound card that you use is also the Sound Blaster Pro, then you'll need to know these settings for the Windows driver installation, so make sure to write down the I/O address, the interrupt number, and the DMA channel as reported by the TEST-SBP.EXE utility.

If you have a different sound card, you'll have to extract the hardware settings of the card by using an equivalent software utility that came with that sound card.

Windows Drivers for the Sound Card

To use the sound card from within Windows applications, you need to install the sound card drivers (if you haven't installed them yet).

Examining and Verifying Your Current Installed Drivers

To examine the current installed drivers on your system, follow these steps:

- From the Main group of icons, click the Control Panel icon (see Figure 11.1). The Control Panel window appears, as shown in Figure 11.2.

- Select the Drivers icon from the Control Panel group of icons. The Drivers window appears, as shown in Figure 11.3. As shown, the Drivers window contains a list of Installed Drivers (that is, drivers that are already installed).

Figure 11.1. The Control Panel icon.

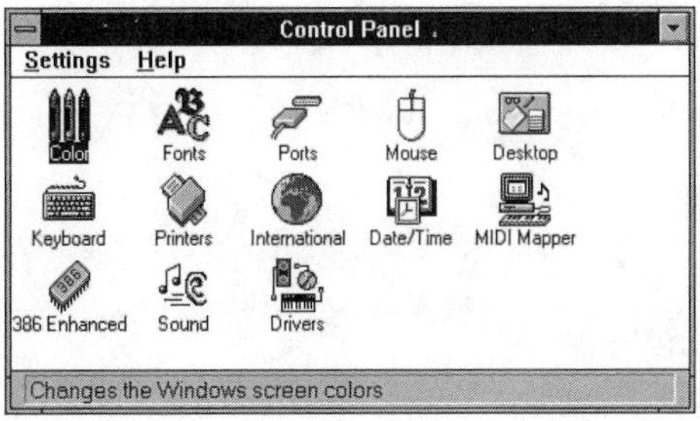

Figure 11.2. The Control Panel window.

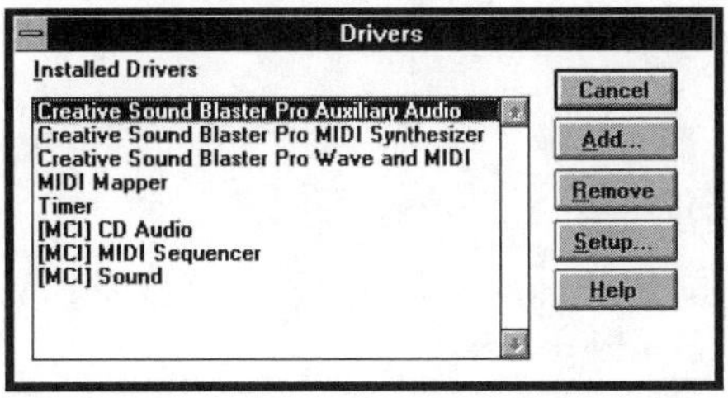

Figure 11.3. The Drivers window.

As you can see, the drivers we want to install (the Creative Sound Blaster Pro drivers) are in the list of the already installed drivers. We will use the other drivers that appear in the Driver window for the programs that we will write in this chapter (and in subsequent chapters).

The Drivers

The first three drivers shown in Figure 11.3 are

- Creative Sound Blaster Pro Auxiliary Audio
- Creative Sound Blaster Pro MIDI Synthesizer
- Creative Sound Blaster Pro Waves and MIDI

These drivers are needed for the Sound Blaster Pro card. If you have a different Creative Labs sound card (or a sound card from a different manufacturer), then you have to install the drivers that came with your card.

The other installed drivers shown in the list of Figure 11.3 are

- MIDI Mapper
- Timer
- [MCI] CD Audio
- [MCI] MIDI Sequencer
- [MCI] Sound

These drivers came with your Windows package. They are needed for various multimedia operations.

Installing the Drivers

In case any of the drivers shown in Figure 11.3 are not installed in your system, here is how you add them:

- Select the Add push button from the Drivers window.

  The Add window appears, as shown in Figure 11.4. This window contains a list of drivers that you can add.

  For example, to add the [MCI] Sound driver, highlight it, and then push the OK push button.

If the driver you want to install does not appear in the Add list, highlight the Unlisted or Updated Driver item. Then push the OK push button, and follow the prompts. Windows will ask you to specify the drive and directory of the driver you want to install.

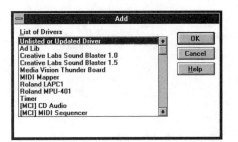

Figure 11.4. The Add window.

NOTE   After you complete the installation of a driver, Windows asks whether you wish to restart the system. A driver becomes effective only after restarting the system.

The Hello2 Program

We will now write our first sound card Windows application, the Hello2 program.

Recording the .WAV File for the Hello2 Program

The Hello2 program plays a .WAV file called c:\spSDK\WAV\Hello2.wav. Here is how you create this .WAV file:

- Select the Sound Recorder icon from the Accessories group of icons (see Figure 11.5).

- The Sound Recorder window appears, as shown in Figure 11.6.

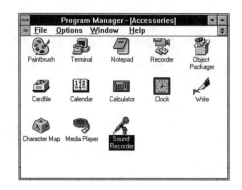

Figure 11.5. The Sound Recorder icon.

Figure 11.6. The Sound Recorder window.

The Sound Recorder program came with your Windows package. This program lets you record .WAV files and play them back using a sound card. Later in this book you will learn how to write programs like the Sound Recorder program by yourself. For now, however, continue recording the sound file needed by the Hello2 program.

- Make sure your microphone is properly connected to your sound card, and prepare to record something.

  Select the Microphone push button (the button that has a picture of a microphone on it—the rightmost push button).

  As soon as you press the microphone push button, speak into the microphone and say

  Hello. This is my first sound Windows program!

- To stop the recording, select the Stop push button (the button located to the left of the Microphone push button).

To listen to what you just recorded:

- Push the Play push button (the button located to the left of the Stop push button).

If you are satisfied with the recording, save the sound file by selecting the Save As option from the File menu. Save your recording as c:\spSDK\ WAV\Hello2.wav. If you are not satisfied with your recording, select the New option from the File menu and repeat this entire process until you are happy with your recording.

Compiling, Linking, and Executing the Hello2 Program

To gain a better understanding of what the program code can do, we recommend that you compile, link, and execute the Hello2 program before going over its code.

To compile and link the Hello2 program with the Microsoft compiler:

- Make sure your PC is in a DOS-protected mode.

- Log into c:\spSDK\Samp4Win\.

- At the DOS prompt type

  `NMAKE Hello2.mak` {Enter}

To compile and link the Hello2 program with the Borland compiler:

- Log into c:\spSDK\Samp4Win\.

- At the DOS prompt type

  `NMAKE -f Hello2.bmk` {Enter}

Before executing the Hello2 program make sure that a Windows-compatible sound card is installed in your PC, that all the appropriate drivers are installed, and that the file Hello2.wav resides in c:\spSDK\WAV\.

To execute the Hello2 program

- Select Run from the File menu of the File Manager of Windows.

- Click Browse and select the file

  `c:\spSDK\Samp4Win\Hello2.exe`

The main window of Hello2 appears, as shown in Figure 11.7.

Figure 11.7. The main window of Hello2.

The Hello2 program menu contains two options: Quit and About (see Figure 11.8).

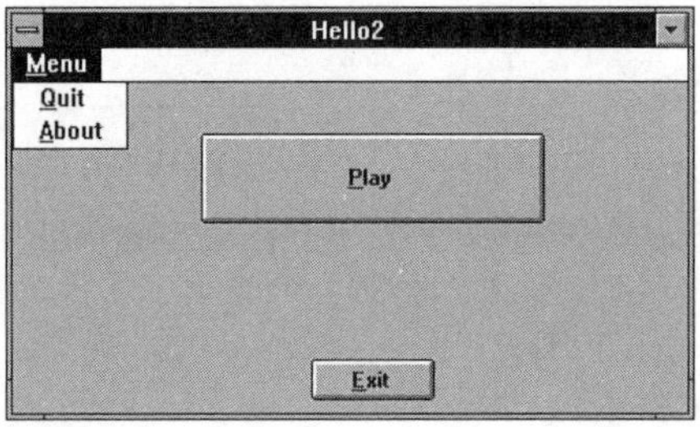

Figure 11.8. The Hello2 program menu.

When the user selects the Quit option, the program terminates. When the user selects the About option, the About dialog box appears, as shown in Figure 11.9.

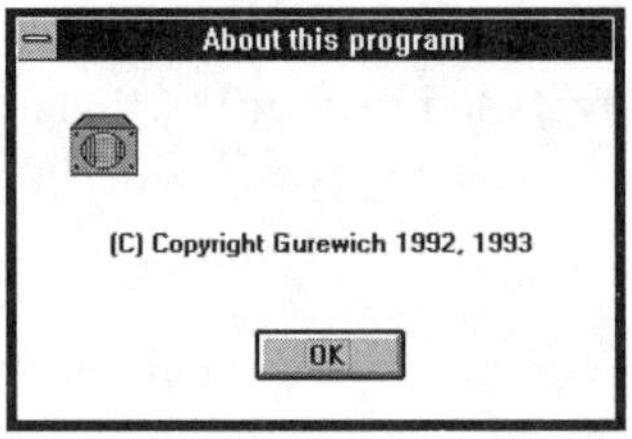

Figure 11.9. The About dialog box of the Hello2 program.

When the user selects the Play button, the WAV sound file c:\spSDK\WAV\Hello2.wav is played through the sound card hardware. During playback, the mouse is available and the user may switch to other Windows applications.

The Files of the Hello2 Program

The Hello2 program consists of the following files:

Hello2.h	The #include file of the program.
Hello2.c	The C code of the program.
Hello2.rc	The resource file of the program.
Hello2.def	The module definition file of the program.
Hello2.mak	The make file of the program.
ExtSpkr.ico	The icon of the program.

These files are provided for you in c:\spSDK\Samp4Win\.

The complete listing of Hello2 is shown in Listings 11.1 through 11.5.

Listing 11.1. Hello2.h.

```
/*=====================================================
 FILE NAME: Hello2.h

 (c)Copyright Gurewich 1992, 1993
 ====================================================*/

/*--------
 prototypes
 --------*/
long FAR PASCAL _export WndProc       ( HWND, UINT, UINT, LONG );
BOOL FAR PASCAL _export AboutDlgProc ( HWND, UINT, UINT, LONG ) ;

/*------
 #define
 ------*/
#define IDM_QUIT  1  /* The Quit  option in the menu */
#define IDM_ABOUT 2  /* The About option in the menu */

#define PLAY_PB  100  /* The Play  push button. */
#define EXIT_PB  101  /* The Exit  push button. */
```

continues

Listing 11.1. continued

```
/*--------------
 Global variables
 -------------*/
char      gszAppName[] = "Hello2" ; /* Our application name. */
HINSTANCE ghInst;                   /* current instance.     */
```

Listing 11.2. Hello2.c.

```
/*============================================================
  PROGRAM: Hello2.c
  ------
  (c)Copyright 1992, 1993 Gurewich. (R) All rights reserved.

  PROGRAM DESCRIPTION:
  -----------------
  This is a Generic1 based program.

  The program plays a WAV file through a sound card.
  ============================================================*/

/*---------
 #include
 --------*/
/*-----------------------------------
 Required for all Windows applications.
 ----------------------------------*/
#include <windows.h>

/*-----------------------------------------------------------
 Required so that ts_ functions, TS_ macros, and #definitions
 from the TS C multimedia sound library may be used in this
 application.
 -----------------------------------------------------------*/
#include "c:\spSDK\TegoWlib\ts4Win.h"

/*----------------------------------------------------------
 Definitions & prototypes specific to this application.
 ---------------------------------------------------------*/
#include "c:\spSDK\Samp4WIN\Hello2.h"

/*----------------------------------------------------------
 For C functions that require the standard C #include files.
 ---------------------------------------------------------*/
```

```c
#include <stdlib.h>
#include <stdio.h>


/*==================
 FUNCTION: WinMain()
 ==================*/
int PASCAL WinMain ( HANDLE hInstance,
                     HANDLE hPrevInstance,
                     LPSTR  lpszCmdLine,
                     int    nCmdShow )
{
/*-------------------------
 Local and static variables.
 -------------------------*/
HWND     hWnd;   /* Handler to the window of our application.   */
MSG      msg;    /* Message to be processed by our application. */
WNDCLASS wc;     /* Window class of our application.            */

HBITMAP  hBitmapOfBkGnd; /* Handle to the bit map of the background. */
HBRUSH   hBrushOfBkGnd;  /* Handle to the brush   of the background. */

/*---------------------------------------------
 Make the hInstance variable a global variable.
 ---------------------------------------------*/
ghInst = hInstance;

/*----------------------------------------------------------------
 Load the background bit map, and create a brush.
 "BackGround" is defined in the .RC file, and it is based on the
 file: BACK2.bmp.
 ----------------------------------------------------------------*/
hBitmapOfBkGnd = LoadBitmap ( ghInst, "BackGround" );
hBrushOfBkGnd = CreatePatternBrush ( hBitmapOfBkGnd );

/*----------------------------------------------
 Update the window class structure and register
 the window class.
 ----------------------------------------------*/
if ( !hPrevInstance )
   {
   /*----------------------------------------
   The "if" is satisfied, this is the very 1st
   run of this application.
   ----------------------------------------*/
   wc.style         = CS_HREDRAW ¦ CS_VREDRAW ;
   wc.lpfnWndProc   = WndProc ;
   wc.cbClsExtra    = 0 ;
```

continues

Listing 11.2. continued

```
    wc.cbWndExtra    = DLGWINDOWEXTRA ;  /* Dialog box as the */
                                         /* main window.      */

    wc.hInstance     = ghInst ;
    wc.hIcon         = LoadIcon  ( ghInst, "IconOfExtSpkr" ) ;
    wc.hCursor       = LoadCursor ( NULL, IDC_ARROW         ) ;

    wc.hbrBackground = hBrushOfBkGnd;  /* The brush that we created */
                                       /* with the bit map.         */

    wc.lpszMenuName  = gszAppName ;
    wc.lpszClassName = "Hello2Class" ; /* As appears in the CLASS */
                                       /* in the .RC file.        */

    /*-----------------
    Register the window.
    ----------------*/
    RegisterClass ( &wc );

    }/* end of if(!hPrevInstance) */

/*------------------------------------------------------------
NOTE: In this application the main window is a dialog box.
      "Hello2Box" is the name of the dialog box as defined
      in the .RC file (before the DIALOG keyword).
      ------------------------------------------------------*/
hWnd = CreateDialog ( ghInst, "Hello2Box", 0, NULL );

/*---------------------------------------------
Show and update the window of our application.
-----------------------------------------*/
ShowWindow   ( hWnd, nCmdShow );
UpdateWindow ( hWnd );


/*---------------
The message loop.
--------------*/
while ( GetMessage ( &msg, NULL, 0, 0 ) )
      {
      TranslateMessage ( &msg );
      DispatchMessage  ( &msg );
      }

/*------------------------------------------------------------
Delete the memory and brush objects used for the background.
----------------------------------------------------------*/
```

```
DeleteObject ( hBitmapOfBkGnd );
DeleteObject ( hBrushOfBkGnd );


return msg.wParam ;

} /* end of function. */
/*========================= end of WinMain() ====================*/

/*==================
 FUNCTION: WndProc()
 =================*/
/*------------------------------
 DESCRIPTION: Processes messages.
 ------------------------------*/
long FAR PASCAL _export WndProc ( HWND hWnd,
                                  UINT message,
                                  UINT wParam,
                                  LONG lParam )
{
/*--------------------------
 Local and static variables.
 -------------------------*/
int    iOpenResult;  /* Result of opening the session. */
int    iPlayResult;  /* Result of playing the session. */

char   sWAVFileName[125]; /* Name of the WAV file to play. */
char   sMessage[125];

/*-------------------------------
 Needed for the About dialog box.
 -------------------------------*/
static FARPROC lpfnAboutDlgProc ;


switch ( message )
        {
        case WM_CREATE:
             /*--------------------------------------------------
             Obtain the lpfnAboutDlgProc of the About dialog box.
             --------------------------------------------------*/
             lpfnAboutDlgProc =
             MakeProcInstance (( FARPROC) AboutDlgProc, ghInst);

             /*-----------------------------------------
             Is there a sound card in the system that is
             able to play Wave files?
             -----------------------------------------*/
```

continues

Listing 11.2. continued

```c
if ( ts_WaveDeviceCanPlay() == 0 )
   {
   MessageBox ( NULL,
                "No sound card was found!",
                "Message",
                MB_ICONSTOP );

      /*-----------------
      Quit the application.
      ------------------*/
      SendMessage ( hWnd,
                    WM_DESTROY,
                    0,
                    0 );
      return 0;
      }

/*--------------------
Open the sound session.
--------------------*/
lstrcpy( sWAVFileName, "c:\\spSDK\\WAV\\Hello2.wav");
iOpenResult =
ts_OpenWaveSession ( sWAVFileName );

if ( iOpenResult != 1 )
   {
   lstrcpy ( sMessage, "Failed to open a session for: ");
   lstrcat ( sMessage, sWAVFileName );
   MessageBox ( NULL,
                 sMessage,
                 "Message",
                 MB_ICONINFORMATION );

      /*-----------------
      Quit the application.
      ------------------*/
      SendMessage ( hWnd,
                    WM_DESTROY,
                    0,
                    0 );
      return 0;
      }

   return 0;
```

```
case WM_CHAR:
    /*---------------------
    Process the pressed key.
    --------------------*/
    wParam = toupper ( wParam );
    switch (wParam)
            {
            case 'P':
                    SendMessage ( hWnd,
                                  WM_COMMAND,
                                  PLAY_PB,
                                  0);
                    break;

            case 'E':
                    SendMessage ( hWnd,
                                  WM_COMMAND,
                                  EXIT_PB,
                                  0);
                    break;
            }

    return 0L;

case WM_COMMAND:
    /*---------------
    Process menu items.
    -----------------*/
    switch (wParam)
            {
            case PLAY_PB:
                    /*--------------------------
                    Play a sound section.
                    Range to play:
                    From: Beginning of sound file.
                      To: End of file.
                    --------------------------*/
                    iPlayResult =
                    ts_PlayWave ( hWnd,
                                  TS_START_OF_FILE,
                                  TS_END_OF_FILE,
                                  TS_IN_MILLISECONDS );

                    if ( iPlayResult != 1 )
                        {
                        MessageBox ( NULL,
                                     "Failed to play the session.",
                                     "Message",
```

continues

Listing 11.2. continued

```
                                    MB_ICONINFORMATION );
                        }

                    return 0L;

            case EXIT_PB:
            case IDM_QUIT:
                /*---------------------------
                User clicked on Quit option.
                --------------------------*/
                DestroyWindow (hWnd);
                return 0L;

            case IDM_ABOUT :
                /*---------------------------
                User clicked on About option.
                --------------------------*/
                DialogBox ( ghInst,
                            "AboutBox",
                            hWnd,
                            lpfnAboutDlgProc );
                return 0;
            }/* end of switch (wParam) */

    case MM_MCINOTIFY:
        switch ( wParam )
            {
            case MCI_NOTIFY_SUCCESSFUL:
                break;
            case MCI_NOTIFY_ABORTED:
                break;
            case MCI_NOTIFY_SUPERSEDED:
                break;
            case MCI_NOTIFY_FAILURE:
                MessageBox ( NULL,
                            "Failure!",
                            "Message",
                             MB_ICONINFORMATION );
                break;
            }/* end of switch() */

        return 0L;
```

```
        case WM_DESTROY:
                /*--------------------
                Close the Wave session.
                ---------------------*/
                ts_CloseWaveSession();
                PostQuitMessage (0);
                return 0;
        }/* end of switch (message) */

/*-----------------------
 Message was not processed.
 -----------------------*/
return DefWindowProc ( hWnd, message, wParam, lParam ) ;

}/* end of WndProc() */
/*================== end of WndProc() ====================*/


/*=======================
 FUNCTION: AboutDlgProc()
 ======================*/
/*---------------------------------------
 DESCRIPTION:
 This is the About dialog box procedure.
 ---------------------------------------*/
BOOL FAR PASCAL _export AboutDlgProc ( HWND hDlg,
                                       UINT message,
                                       UINT wParam,
                                       LONG lParam )
{
switch ( message )
        {
        case WM_INITDIALOG :
                return TRUE;

        case WM_COMMAND :
                switch ( wParam )
                        {
                        case IDOK :
                        case IDCANCEL :
                            EndDialog ( hDlg, 0 );
                            return TRUE;
                        }
        }
return FALSE ;
}/* End of function. */
/*=============== end of AboutDlgProc() ==============*/
```

Listing 11.3. Hello2.rc.

```
/*=====================================================
 FILE NAME: Hello2.rc
 --------

 FILE DESCRIPTION:
 ----------------
 The resource file.

 (c)Copyright Gurewich 1992, 1993

 =====================================================*/

/*------
 #include
 ------*/
#include <windows.h>
#include "Hello2.h"

/*--
 Menu
 --*/
Hello2  MENU
BEGIN
   POPUP  "&Menu"
      BEGIN
         MENUITEM "&Quit",            IDM_QUIT
         MENUITEM "&About",           IDM_ABOUT
      END
END

/*-----------------------------------------
 Definition of the external speaker icon.
 File name: ExtSpkr.ico
 Icon name: IconOfExtSpkr
 -----------------------------------------*/
IconOfExtSpkr ICON ExtSpkr.ico

/*--------
 Bit maps.
 --------*/
BackGround    BITMAP Back2.bmp

/*-------------------
 The About dialog box.
 -------------------*/
AboutBox DIALOG 81, 43, 160, 100
STYLE DS_MODALFRAME ¦ WS_POPUP ¦ WS_VISIBLE ¦ WS_CAPTION ¦ WS_SYSMENU
CAPTION "About this program"
```

```
FONT 8, "MS Sans Serif"
BEGIN
    PUSHBUTTON      "OK", IDOK, 64, 75, 40, 14
    CTEXT           "(c)Copyright Gurewich 1992, 1993", -1,
                    13, 47, 137, 18
    ICON            "IconOfExtSpkr", -1, 14, 12, 18, 20
END


/*----------------------------------------------------
The the main dialog box.
This dialog box appears upon starting the application.
--------------------------------------------------*/
Hello2Box DIALOG PRELOAD 59, 59, 221, 124

STYLE WS_MINIMIZEBOX ¦ WS_POPUP   ¦ WS_VISIBLE ¦
                     WS_CAPTION ¦ WS_SYSMENU ¦
                     WS_THICKFRAME
CAPTION "Hello2"
FONT 8, "MS Sans Serif"
CLASS "Hello2Class"
BEGIN
    PUSHBUTTON      "&Play", PLAY_PB, 62, 17, 112, 31
    PUSHBUTTON      "&Exit", EXIT_PB, 98, 94, 40, 14
END
```

Listing 11.4. Hello2.def.

```
;=====================================
; module-definition file for Hello2.c
;=====================================

NAME        Hello2

DESCRIPTION 'The Hello2 program. (c)Copyright Gurewich 1992, 1993'

EXETYPE     WINDOWS

STUB        'WINSTUB.EXE'

CODE  PRELOAD MOVEABLE DISCARDABLE

DATA  PRELOAD MOVEABLE MULTIPLE

HEAPSIZE    1024
STACKSIZE   8192
```

Listing 11.5. Hello2.mak.

```
#=============
# Hello2.mak
#=============

Hello2.exe : Hello2.obj Hello2.h Hello2.def Hello2.res
    link /nod Hello2, Hello2, NUL, \
        slibcew oldnames libw commdlg \
        c:\spSDK\TegoWlib\TSWlib, \
        Hello2.def
    rc -t Hello2.res

Hello2.obj : Hello2.c Hello2.h
    cl -c -G2sw -Ow -W3 -Zp Hello2.c

Hello2.res : Hello2.rc Hello2.h ExtSpkr.ico
    rc -r Hello2.rc
```

The #*includes* of Hello2

The Hello2 program includes the following #include statement:

```
#include "c:\spSDK\TegoWlib\ts4Win.h"
```

This statement #included the file ts4Win.h that resides in c:\spSDK\TegoWlib\. Remember that in previous chapters we #included the file c:\spSDK\TegoWlib\TegoWlib.h.

For programs that use sp_ functions and #definitions, your program must #include the c:\spSDK\TegoWlib\TegoWlib.h file. For programs that use ts_ functions and #definitions, your program must #include the c:\spSDK\TegoWlib\TSWLib.h file.

All the names of the functions from the TSWlib.lib library start with the characters ts_. These ts_ functions handle sound cards, MIDI operations, CD hardware, and other multimedia and animation functions. The TSWlib.lib library supplied with the diskette of this book is the short version of the library, and it contains only a limited amount of ts_ functions. However, it contains enough functions to enable you to compile and link all the program examples presented in this book.

NOTE   FOR MICROSOFT COMPILER USERS:

The c:\spSDK\TegoWlib\TegoWin.lib file is a library that contains sp_ functions. These functions enable programs to produce sound through the internal built-in speaker of the PC.

To use sp_ functions from the TegoWlib.lib library, your program must #include the statement:

```
#include "c:\spSDK\TegoWlib\SP4Win.h"
```

The c:\spSDK\TegoWlib\TSWlib.lib file is a library that contains ts_ functions. These functions enable programs to produce sound and other multimedia tasks through multimedia hardware such as sound cards, MIDI, CDs, joysticks, and other multimedia hardware.

To use ts_ functions from the TSWlib.lib library, your program must #include the statement:

```
#include "c:\spSDK\TegoWlib\TS4Win.h"
```

If your program uses both sp_ functions and ts_ functions, then it must #include the SP4Win.h file and the TS4Win.h file.

The book's diskette contains the short versions of the TegoWlib.lib and TSWlib.lib libraries.

NOTE   FOR BORLAND COMPILER USERS:

The c:\spSDK\TegoWlib\TegoWBL.lib file is a library that contains sp_ functions. These functions enable programs to produce sound through the internal built-in speaker of the PC.

To use sp_ functions from the TegoWBL.lib library, your program must #include the statement:

```
#include "c:\spSDK\TegoWlib\SP4Win.h"
```

If your program uses both sp_ functions and ts_ functions, then it must #include the SP4Win.h file and the TS4Win.h file.

The book's diskette contains the short versions of the TegoWBL.lib and TS4BL.lib libraries.

The Make File of the Hello2 Program

Because the Hello2 program uses functions from the TSWlib.lib library, we must include this library in the list of libraries to be linked. Indeed, the link statement in the Hello2.mak file contains this library:

```
link /nod Hello2, Hello2, NUL, \
    slibcew oldnames libw commdlg \
    c:\spSDK\TegoWlib\TSWlib, \
```

The file Hello2.bmk is the make file of Hello2 that is used with the Borland Compiler.

Because the Hello2 program uses functions from the TS4BL.lib library, we must include this library in the list of libraries to be linked. Indeed, the link statement in the Hello2.bmk file contains this library:

```
tlink /c /n  Tw /L\borlandc\lib c0ws Hello2, Hello2, NUL, \import
mathws cws c:\spSDK\TegoWlib\TS4BL.lib, \
```

The *WinMain()* of Hello2

The WinMain() function of Hello2 has the Generic1-type message loop:

```
while ( GetMessage ( &msg, NULL, 0, 0 ) )
    {
    TranslateMessage ( &msg );
    DispatchMessage  ( &msg );
    }
```

The advantage of using a sound card (besides the improved sound quality), is that once the program issues a command to the sound card to play a sound section, the sound card is on its own, playing without any help from the PC. Thus, during playback the CPU is free to perform other tasks, without the need to control the sound card.

A Dialog Box as the Main Window

Hello2 uses a dialog box as its main window. This is accomplished by updating the wc.cbWndExtra element with DLGWINDOWEXTRA:

```
wc.cbWndExtra     = DLGWINDOWEXTRA ;  /* Dialog box as the */
                                      /* main window.      */
```

and by updating the `wc.lpszClassName` element with `Hello2Class`:

```
wc.lpszClassName = "Hello2Class" ; /* As appears in the CLASS */
                                   /* in the .RC file.       */
Hello2.rc defines a dialog box Hello2Box as a "Hello2Class" CLASS:
    Hello2Box DIALOG PRELOAD 59, 59, 221, 124
    ......................................
    ......................................
    CLASS "Hello2Class"
    BEGIN
       ........................
       ........................
    END
```

This dialog box serves as the main window of the program.

To create a yellow background to this dialog box (which is the main window of the program), we load the `BackGround` bit map and create a brush using this bit map:

```
hBitmapOfBkGnd = LoadBitmap ( ghInst, "BackGround" );
hBrushOfBkGnd = CreatePatternBrush ( hBitmapOfBkGnd );
```

The element `wc.hbrBackground` is updated with this brush:

```
wc.hbrBackground = hBrushOfBkGnd;   /* The brush that we created */
                                    /* with the bit map.         */
```

The Icon of Hello2

The icon of the Hello2 program is defined as `IconOfExtSpkr` by updating `wc.hIcon`:

```
wc.hIcon  = LoadIcon ( ghInst, "IconOfExtSpkr" ) ;
```

`IconOfExtSpkr` is defined in Hello2.rc as the `ExtSpkr.ico` icon:

```
IconOfExtSpkr ICON ExtSpkr.ico
```

This icon displays a picture of an external speaker. (This icon is appropriate because the program requires an external speaker.) This icon was prepared by using the Image Editor that came with the SDK for Windows (see Figure 11.10).

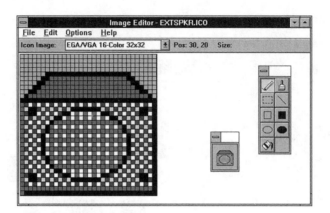

Figure 11.10. The ExtSpkr.ico icon.

The *WndProc()* of Hello2

The WndProc() function of Hello2 processes the various events that correspond to events that take place during the program execution.

The *WM_CREATE* Case of Hello2

Under the WM_CREATE case we obtain the lpfnAboutDlgProc of the About dialog box, and then determine whether a Windows-compatible sound card is installed in the system.

Determining Whether a Sound Card Is Installed in the System

The ts_ function ts_WaveDeviceCanPlay() is used to determine whether the system contains a Windows-compatible sound card that can play .WAV files. If the ts_WaveDeviceCanPlay() function returns 0, then a message box is displayed, telling the user that the PC is not equipped with a compatible sound card:

```
/*-----------------------------------------
Is there a sound card in the system that is
able to play Wave files?
-----------------------------------------*/
```

```
if ( ts_WaveDeviceCanPlay() == 0 )
   {
   MessageBox ( NULL,
                "No sound card was found!",
                "Message",
                MB_ICONSTOP );

   /*------------------
   Quit the application.
   ------------------*/
   SendMessage ( hWnd,
                 WM_DESTROY,
                 0,
                 0 );
   return 0;
   }
```

NOTE

Function Name: `ts_WaveDeviceCanPlay()`

Description: This function determines whether the PC is equipped with a Windows-compatible sound card that can play .WAV files.

Prototype: `int ts_WaveDeviceCanPlay ( void );`

Parameters: None.

Return: Int. A returned value of 1 means that the system is equipped with a Windows-compatible sound card that can play .WAV files. A returned value of 0 means that the system does not have such a sound card installed.

The `ts_WaveDeviceCanPlay()` returns 0 whenever it finds an incompatible sound card, or if one of the drivers is missing.

The *ts_* Functions

Throughout this chapter and in subsequent chapters you will encounter and use multimedia-related functions from the TSWlib.lib library or the TSWBL.lib library. As you'll see, these `ts_` functions start with the characters `ts_` and include the word *Wave*. For example, `ts_WaveDeviceCanPlay()`, `ts_OpenWaveSession()`. The *Wave* word means that these functions handle .WAV sound files. The TSWlib.lib library (or the TSWBL.lib library) enclosed with the diskette of this book is the short version of the library. The full version of the TSWlib.lib library includes more `ts_Wave` functions, as well as other `ts_` functions that control other multimedia hardware. For example, the `ts_CD` functions control CD equipment, the `ts_MIDI` functions control MIDI equipment, and so on.

Directing Sound to Either the Sound Card or the Internal Built-In Speaker

We terminate the Hello2 program when we discover that the system is not equipped with a Windows-compatible sound card. However, your program should update a static (or a global) variable that indicates whether sound should be directed to the sound card or to the internal built-in speaker. If the `ts_WaveDeviceCanPlay()` reports that there is no sound card in the system, then you should update the flag accordingly. Throughout the program, your code may examine the value of the flag, and based on its value, will either direct the sound to the internal built-in speaker or to a sound card. This way, your program will consist of a single .EXE file that accommodates both the PC users that *have* a sound card in their system, as well as the PC users that *do not have* a sound card in their system. In addition, your program will not have to ask the user during program setup whether or not a sound card is installed. And finally, the description of your program may include a statement such as:

SOUND SUPPORTED!

This program plays sound through a sound card if one is installed in your PC. (If no sound card is installed, sound is played through the internal built-in speaker of the PC WITHOUT any additional hardware or software.)

Depending on your program, you may choose not to make any statements regarding its sound capabilities. This way, your users will be surprised and fascinated by your program's sound capability.

If you do not inform your users that your program or demo speaks real human voice, they will be amazed and surprised to actually *hear* your program when they run it. A user without a sound card will be even more surprised to hear human voice played through the PC speaker. (Most PC users are not aware of the fact that the PC speaker can produce more than just primitive beeps.)

Opening a Wave Session

Once the program determines that a Windows-compatible sound card is installed in the system, the .WAV sound file opens by using the ts_OpenWaveSession() function:

```
/*--------------------
Open the sound session.
--------------------*/
lstrcpy( sWAVFileName, "c:\\spSDK\\WAV\\Hello2.wav");
iOpenResult =
ts_OpenWaveSession ( sWAVFileName );

if ( iOpenResult != 1 )
    {
    lstrcpy ( sMessage, "Failed to open a session for: ");
    lstrcat ( sMessage, sWAVFileName );
    MessageBox ( NULL,
                 sMessage,
                 "Message",
                 MB_ICONINFORMATION );

    /*-----------------
    Quit the application.
    -----------------*/
    SendMessage ( hWnd,
                  WM_DESTROY,
                  0,
                  0 );
    return 0;
    }
```

NOTE

Function Name: ts_OpenWaveSession ()

Description: This function opens a Wave session.

Prototype: int ts_OpenWaveSession (LPSTR lpstrFileName);

> *Parameters:* A NULL terminated string. The name of the .WAV file to be opened.
>
> *Returns:* Int. A returned value of 1 means that the Wave session opened successfully. Any other returned value indicates an error.

The `ts_OpenWaveSession()` function may fail to open a Wave file if the specified Wave file does not exist, if the Wave file is corrupted, if a certain driver is missing, or because of other similar mishaps.

Stand-Alone Programs

Just like the programs discussed in previous chapters, Windows applications that support sound cards may be built as stand-alone sound programs or as non-stand-alone sound programs. To convert a non-stand-alone sound program to a stand-alone sound program, use a utility that links the .WAV sound file to your program. This utility is part of the TS Sound Editor. Because we assume that you do not have a copy of the TS Sound Editor, all the programs discussed in this chapter and in subsequent chapters are built as non-stand-alone programs.

The *WM_CHAR* Case of Hello2

Under the `WM_CHAR` case the key pressed by the user is converted to uppercase and examined. If the pressed key is the **P** key, then the `WM_COMMAND` message is sent with `wParam` equal to `PLAY_PB` by using the `SendMessage()` function. This yields the same effect as pushing the Play push button.

Similarly, upon discovering that the **E** key was pressed, the `SendMessage()` function is issued, causing the same effect as pushing the Exit push button:

```
case WM_CHAR:
     /*---------------------
     Process the pressed key.
     --------------------*/
     wParam = toupper ( wParam );
     switch (wParam)
```

```
        {
    case 'P':
            SendMessage ( hWnd,
                           WM_COMMAND,
                           PLAY_PB,
                           0);
            break;

    case 'E':
            SendMessage ( hWnd,
                           WM_COMMAND,
                           EXIT_PB,
                           0);
            break;
        }

    return 0L;
```

The WM_COMMAND Case of Hello2

Under the WM_COMMAND case the PLAY_PB message is processed. This message was generated as a response to the user pushing the Play push button:

```
case PLAY_PB:
    /*--------------------------
    Play a sound section.
    Range to play:
    From: Beginning of sound file.
      To: End of file.
    ---------------------------*/
    iPlayResult =
    ts_PlayWave ( hWnd,
                  TS_START_OF_FILE,
                  TS_END_OF_FILE,
                  TS_IN_MILLISECONDS );

    if ( iPlayResult != 1 )
        {
        MessageBox ( NULL,
                     "Failed to play the session.",
                     "Message",
                      MB_ICONINFORMATION );
        }

    return 0L;
```

The *ts_PlayWave()* Function

To play the Wave file, the function `ts_PlayWave()` is used. The parameters of this function contain the beginning coordinate, the ending coordinate, and the units of the coordinates. For example, to play a section of the Wave sound file from coordinate 3 milliseconds to coordinate 432 milliseconds, the following statement should be issued:

```
ts_PlayWave ( hWnd, 3, 432, TS_IN_MILLISECONDS );
```

The fourth parameter, `TS_IN_MILLISECONDS`, indicates that the coordinates (the second and third parameters) are supplied in units of milliseconds.

NOTE

Function Name: `ts_PlayWave()`

Description: This function plays a section of the Wave file through a Windows-compatible sound card.

Prototype: `int ts_PlayWave ( HWND hWnd,`
`                    long lStartingCoordinates,`
`                    long lEndingCoordinates,`
`                    int  iUnits);`

Returns: The returned integer is 1 if the sound section may be played. A returned value other than 1 means that the sound section cannot be played.

Parameters: `HWND hWnd`: During the playback process messages related to the playback process are sent to the `hWnd` window.

`long lStartingCoordinates`: The starting coordinate of the section to be played.

`long lEndingCoordinates`: The ending coordinate of the section to be played.

`int  iUnits`: The coordinate units. If the second and third parameters are supplied in units of milliseconds, then `iUnits` should be equal to `TS_IN_MILLISECONDS`.

The *MM_MCINOTIFY* Message

As previously discussed, once our program issues the ts_PlayWave() function, the sound card is on its own, playing the Wave file without any additional help from our program.

For our program to know when the playback of the Wave file is over, we need to pass to the ts_PlayWave() function the hWnd of our program, so that when the playback of the sound section is over or when the playback fails for some reason, our program will be notified with the MM_MCINOTIFY message.

Here is how the MM_MCINOTIFY message is processed in WndProc():

```
case MM_MCINOTIFY:
switch ( wParam )
     {
     case MCI_NOTIFY_SUCCESSFUL:
          break;
     case MCI_NOTIFY_ABORTED:
          break;
     case MCI_NOTIFY_SUPERSEDED:
          break;
     case MCI_NOTIFY_FAILURE:
          MessageBox ( NULL,
                      "Failure!",
                      "Message",
                       MB_ICONINFORMATION );
          break;
     }/* end of switch() */

          return 0L;
```

This code illustrates all the possible values of the wParam that may accompany the MM_MCINOTIFY message. As the name suggests, the value of wParam is equal to MCI_NOTIFY_SUCCESSFUL whenever the playback was successfully completed. The other wParam values indicate that the playback was aborted, superseded, or failed.

In the Hello2 program, the code under the MCI_NOTIFY_ cases does not do anything. Generally speaking, these messages arrive due to stopping the playback in the middle by using the ts_StopWave() function, or by issuing a new ts_PlayWave() function before the current playback is completed. (The ts_StopWave() function is discussed later in the chapter.)

If the MCI_NOTIFY_SUPERSEDED is received, it means that the playback was interrupted by the issuing of another command to the sound card. Because there may be several reasons that caused the superseding, your program may include the code that prevents the user from issuing unreasonable commands to the sound card. Our next program example includes the Play, Stop, and Record push buttons. To prevent a MCI_NOTIFY_SUPERSEDED message, we disable the Record push button while a playback is in progress, and we disable the Play push button while a recording is in progress.

A Single Session for Each Sound Card

Most sound cards cannot play and record at the same time. If your program needs to perform both recording and playing simultaneously, then you'll have to install two sound cards in the PC. For example, in a multimedia call conference program, there is a need to send and receive audio simultaneously.

The *WM_DESTROY* Case of Hello2

Before terminating the program, we close the Wave sound file. This is accomplished by using the ts_CloseWaveSession() function:

```
case WM_DESTROY:
    /*-------------------
    Close the Wave session.
    -------------------*/
    ts_CloseWaveSession();
    PostQuitMessage (0);
    return 0;
```

NOTE

Function Name: ts_CloseWaveSession()

Description: This function closes the Wave sound session.

Prototype: int ts_CloseWaveSession (void);

Return value: The return value is always 1.

Parameters: None.

The Record Program

The Record program uses `ts_` functions to record and play .WAV sound files.

We recommend that you compile, link, and execute the Record program before studying its code. This way you will gain a better understanding of what the program can do.

Compiling, Linking, and Executing the Record Program

To compile and link the Record program with the Microsoft compiler:

- Make sure your PC is in a DOS-protected mode.

- Log into c:\spSDK\Samp4Win\.

- At the DOS prompt type

  `NMAKE Record.mak`   {Enter}

To compile and link the Record program with the Borland compiler:

- Log into c:\spSDK\Samp4Win\.

- At the DOS prompt type

  `NMAKE -f Record.bmk`   {Enter}

Before executing the Record program make sure that a Windows-compatible sound card is installed in your PC, and that all the appropriate drivers are installed.

To execute the Record program:

- Select Run from the File menu of the Program Manager of Windows.

- Click Browse and select the file

  `c:\spSDK\Samp4Win\Record.exe`

The main window of Record appears, as shown in Figure 11.11.

Figure 11.11. The main window of Record.

The Record program menu contain two options: Quit and About (see Figure 11.12). When the user selects Quit, the program terminates. When the user selects the About option, the About dialog box appears, as shown in Figure 11.13.

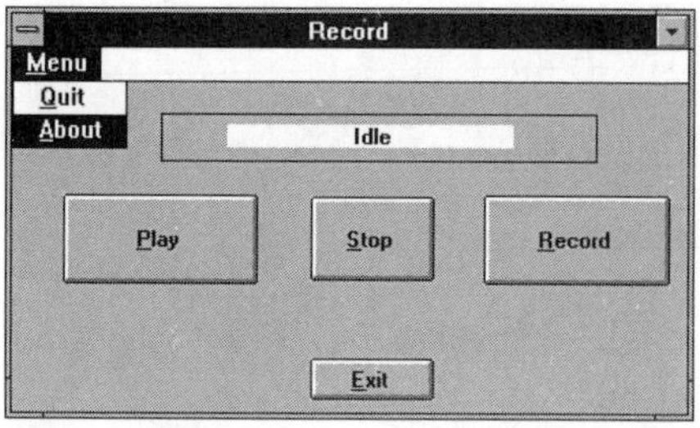

Figure 11.12. The Record program menu.

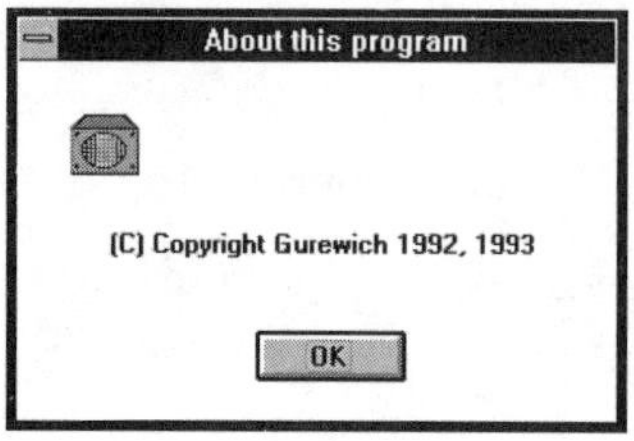

Figure 11.13. The About dialog box of the Record program.

The main window of Record contains four push buttons: Play, Stop, Record, and Exit. To record a .WAV file, press the Record push button, and speak into the microphone. To stop the recording, press the Stop push button. To play the file that you recorded, press the Play push button. To exit the main window, press the Exit push button.

During playback, the mouse is available and the user may switch to other Windows applications.

The Record program does not let the user save the recorded Wave file. (A later program in this chapter covers the topic of saving a recording.)

The Files of the Record Program

The Record program consists of the following files:

Record.h	The #include file of the program.
Record.c	The C code of the program.
Record.rc	The resource file of the program.
Record.def	The module definition file of the program.
Record.mak	The make file of the program.
ExtSpkr.ico	The icon of the program.

These files are provided for you in c:\spSDK\Samp4Win\.

The *WM_CREATE* Case of Record

Under the WM_CREATE case, we determine the capabilities of the sound card. The function ts_WaveDeviceCanPlay() determines whether a sound card that is capable of playing Wave files (.WAV files) is installed in the PC.

Similarly, the function ts_WaveDeviceCanRecord() determines whether a sound card that is capable of recording Wave files is installed in the PC.

> **NOTE**
>
> *Function Name:* `ts_WaveDeviceCanRecord()`
>
> *Description:* This function determines whether the PC is equipped with a Windows-compatible sound card that is able to record .WAV files.
>
> *Prototype:* `int ts_WaveDeviceCanPlay ( void );`
>
> *Parameters:* None.
>
> *Return:* Int. A returned value of 1 means that the system is equipped with a Windows-compatible sound card that is capable of recording .WAV files. A returned value of 0 means that the system does not have such a sound card installed in it.

If a sound card that is capable of recording and playing .WAV files is installed in the system, a sound session opens with the `ts_OpenWaveSession()` function. Because the open sound session is for a sound file that does not exist yet, we supply a null string as the name of the .WAV file:

```
/*-------------------------
Open the Multimedia session.
-------------------------*/
lstrcpy( sWAVFileName, "" );
iOpenResult =
ts_OpenWaveSession ( sWAVFileName );

if ( iOpenResult != 1 )
   {
   lstrcpy ( sMessage,
           "Failed to open a session." );
   MessageBox ( NULL,
               sMessage,
               "Message",
               MB_ICONINFORMATION );

   /*-----------------
   Quit the application.
   ------------------*/
   SendMessage ( hWnd,
               WM_DESTROY,
               0,
               0 );

   return 0;
   }
```

Handling the Play Request Under the *WM_COMMAND* Case

When the user presses the Play push button, the PLAY_PB case under the WM_COMMAND case is executed. Because we want the Play and Record push buttons to be disabled during playback, the DisablePlayAndRecord() function is executed. Then the DisplayStatus() function is executed, displaying the text: Playback is in progress..., and finally the ts_PlayWave() function is executed.

If for some reason the sound card cannot accept the play command, the returned value of ts_PlayWave() is not 1. In that case, we enable the Play and Record push buttons so that the user will be able to play (or record) again.

Here is the PLAY_PB case:

```
case PLAY_PB:
        /*-----------------------------
        User pressed the Play push button.
        ------------------------------*/
        /*------------------------------------
        Disable the Play and Record push buttons.
        ------------------------------------*/
        DisablePlayAndRecord ( hWnd );

        /*---------------------------
        Display the status title.
        (Playback in progress)
        ---------------------------*/
        DisplayStatus( hWnd, 'P' );

        /*---------------------------
        Play a sound section.
        Range to play:
        From: Beginning of sound file.
          To: End of file.
        ---------------------------*/
        iPlayResult =
        ts_PlayWave ( hWnd,
                     TS_START_OF_FILE,
                     TS_END_OF_FILE,
                     TS_IN_MILLISECONDS );

        if ( iPlayResult != 1 )
           {
           /*-------------------------------------------
           The sound card is unable to accept the play
           command.
           -------------------------------------------*/
```

```
/*----------------------------------------
Enable the Play and Record push buttons.
---------------------------------------*/
EnablePlayAndRecord ( hWnd );

/*----------------------------
Display the status title.
(Idle)
---------------------------*/
DisplayStatus ( hWnd, 'I' );
}
return 0L;
```

Once the `ts_PlayWave()` function is executed, the sound card is on its own, and the PC is free to perform other tasks while the playback is in progress.

If the user did not press the Stop push button during playback, the playback will automatically terminate when the playback range specified in the `ts_PlayWave()` function is completed. Our program will be notified that the playback range is completed by receiving the MM_MCINOTIFY message.

Handling the Record Request Under the WM_COMMAND Case

Similarly, we process the Record push button message. The code under the RECORD_PB case makes sure that during the recording the only enabled push buttons are the Stop push button and the Exit push button.

Before starting the recording, the function `ts_DeleteWave()` is executed, deleting the current Wave file (if any). Once the `ts_DeleteWave()` is executed, the `ts_RecordWave()` function is executed. Here is the RECORD_PB case:

```
case RECORD_PB:
    /*----------------------------
    User pressed the Record push button.
    ----------------------------*/
    /*---------------------------------------
    Disable the Play and Record push buttons.
    ---------------------------------------*/
    DisablePlayAndRecord ( hWnd );
```

```
/*----------------------------
Display the status title.
(Recording in progress)
----------------------------*/
DisplayStatus( hWnd, 'R' );

/*-----------------------------------
Delete the previous recording (if any).
-------------------------------------*/
ts_DeleteWave( TS_START_OF_FILE,
               TS_END_OF_FILE,
               TS_IN_MILLISECONDS );

/*-------------------------------------------
Record a sound section.
Range to record:
From: Beginning of sound file.
  To: 30 seconds.
--------------------------------------------*/
iRecordResult =
ts_RecordWave ( hWnd,
               TS_START_OF_FILE,
               30000L,
               TS_IN_MILLISECONDS );

if ( iRecordResult != 1 )
    {
    /*-----------------------------------------
    The sound card is unable to accept the record
    command.
    ------------------------------------------*/
    /*-----------------------------------------
    Enable the Play and Record push buttons.
    ------------------------------------------*/
    EnablePlayAndRecord ( hWnd );
    }

return 0L;
```

The *ts_RecordWave()* Function

The ts_RecordWave() function is used to cause the sound card to start recording a Wave file. The recording range is specified in the function parameters.

NOTE

Function Name: `ts_RecordWave()`

Description: This function records a .WAV file.

Prototype: `int ts_RecordWave ( HWND hWnd,`
`                                 long lStartingPoint,`
`                                 long lEndingPoint,`
`                                 int  iUnits );`

`HWND hWnd:` The window's handle that will receive the `MM_MCINOTIFY` message.

`long lStartingPoint:` The starting point from which recording starts.

`long lEndingPoint:` The ending point of the recording range.

`int iUnits:` The units of `lStartingPoint` and `lEndingPoint`.

Returned Value: Int. A returned value of 1 means that the recording command was issued successfully. A returned value other than 1 means that the sound card can't accept the recording command.

Just like the `ts_PlayWave()` function, once the `ts_RecordWave()` function is executed, the sound card is on its own, and the PC is free to perform other tasks while the recording is in progress.

If the user did not push the Stop push button during the recording, the recording will automatically terminate when the recording range specified in the `ts_RecordWave()` function is completed. Our program will be notified that the recording range is completed by receiving the `MM_MCINOTIFY` message.

The *ts_DeleteWave()* Function

Under the `RECORD_PB` case, the `ts_DeleteWave()` function is executed prior to the execution of the `ts_RecordWave()` function. The `ts_DeleteWave()` function deletes the previous recording if one exists. (If you do not execute the `ts_DeleteWave()` function prior to executing the `ts_RecordWave()` function, the new recording will automatically be inserted into the existing recording.)

NOTE

Function Name: `ts_DeleteWave()`

Description: This function deletes a section of a .WAV file.

Prototype: `int ts_DeleteWave ( long lStartingPoint,`
`                                 long lEndingPoint,`
`                                 int  iUnits);`

`long lStartingPoint:` The starting point of the sound section to be deleted.

`long lEndingPoint:` The ending point of the sound section to be deleted.

`int iUnits:` The units of `lStartingPoint` and `lEndingPoint`. *Returned Value:* Int. A returned value of 1 means that the deletion was performed successfully. A returned value other than 1 means that the deletion was not performed.

Under the `RECORD_PB` case we deleted the entire .WAV file:

```
/*------------------------------------
Delete the previous recording (if any).
------------------------------------*/
ts_DeleteWave( TS_START_OF_FILE,
               TS_END_OF_FILE,
               TS_IN_MILLISECONDS );
```

Limiting the Recording Length

Under the `RECORD_PB` case, the `ts_RecordWave()` function limits the recording length to a maximum of 30 seconds (30 seconds = 30,000 milliseconds):

```
iRecordResult =
ts_RecordWave ( hWnd,
                TS_START_OF_FILE,
                30000L,
                TS_IN_MILLISECONDS );
```

There is a very good reason for limiting the recording length. Suppose the

There is a very good reason for limiting the recording length. Suppose the user starts recording, and then leaves the room without stopping the recording. Upon returning, the user may find that the recording filled the entire hard drive! This is because the recording is temporarily saved as a temporary file on the hard drive. Thus, it is always a good idea to limit the recording length.

When the recording is performed, it is up to the ts_RecordWave() function to handle the various memory chores. If there is no place in RAM for the recording, it is the responsibility of the ts_RecordWave() function to swap the recording to the hard drive.

Inserting a New Recording into an Existing .WAV File

In the Record program we deleted the previous recording. Then we started a new recording from the 0 seconds position up to a maximum of 30 seconds (or until the user presses the Stop push button).

Although the Record program did not use the insert capabilities of the recording process, you can experiment with the insert capability yourself. Here is how the insert capability works:

Suppose that you recorded a .WAV file that is 30 seconds long, from 0 seconds position to 30 seconds position. If you then issue the ts_RecordWave() function and specify the recording range to be from 10 seconds to 20 seconds without first executing the ts_DeleteWave() function, then the final result is a .WAV file that is 40 seconds long. The new recording from 10 seconds to 20 seconds is inserted in the original recording. You may keep inserting a section to any desired location in the recording. Naturally, the range of recording must make sense. For example, if the current recording is from 0 seconds to 40 seconds, you cannot specify a recording range of 50 seconds to 60 seconds.

Stopping the Recording and the Playback

When the user pushes the Stop push button, the ts_StopWave() function is executed. This function stops either the playback or the recording, whichever is in progress:

```
case STOP_PB:
    /*-----------------------------
    User pressed the Stop push button.
    ------------------------------*/
    /*------------------------------------
    Enable the Play and Record push buttons.
    -------------------------------------*/
    EnablePlayAndRecord ( hWnd );

    /*---------------------------
    Display the status title.
    (Idle)
    ---------------------------*/
    DisplayStatus( hWnd, 'I' );

    ts_StopWave();

return 0L;
```

NOTE

Function Name: ts_StopWave()

Description: This function stops the recording or the playback (which-ever is currently in progress).

Prototype: int ts_StopWave (void);

Parameters: None.

Returned Value: Int. A returned value of 1 means that the sound card accepted the stop command. A returned value other than 1 means that the sound card can't accept the command.

The *MM_MCINOTIFY* Case

The MM_MCINOTIFY message is received whenever there is a message from the sound card. For example, when the sound card completes the recording or the playback, the WndProc() function of the Record program receives the MM_MCINOTIFY message.

In the Record program, we wrote the code so that the user is unable to cause the sending of unreasonable commands to the sound card. We do that by disabling the Play and Record push buttons during the play (and during the record) so that the user will not be able to push the Play push button or the Record push button while the playback or recording is already in progress.

The reason for writing our program this way is to avoid the need of writing code that handles the various MCI_NOTIFY_ messages. In fact, in the Record program, the MM_MCINOTIFY message is received only when the playback or recording process is terminated. When the MM_MCINOTIFY message is received, we enable the Play and Record push buttons:

```
case MM_MCINOTIFY:
     /*-----------------------------------
     Enable the Play and Record push buttons.
     ----------------------------------*/
     EnablePlayAndRecord ( hWnd );

     /*----------------------------
     Display the status title.
     (Idle)
     ---------------------------*/
     DisplayStatus ( hWnd, 'I' );

     switch ( wParam )
            {
            case MCI_NOTIFY_SUCCESSFUL:
                  break;
            case MCI_NOTIFY_ABORTED:
                  break;
            case MCI_NOTIFY_SUPERSEDED:
                  break;
            case MCI_NOTIFY_FAILURE:
                  MessageBox ( NULL,
                              "Failure!",
                              "Message",
                               MB_ICONINFORMATION );
                  break;
            }/* end of switch() */

     return 0L;
```

The code under each of the MCI_NOTIFY_ cases is a simple break statement. The only reason for including these cases in the Record program is to illustrate that these messages are available. These messages are especially useful during development time, where a MessageBox() statement may be used for debugging purposes.

The *WM_DESTROY* Case of Record

Under the WM_DESTROY case, the ts_CloseWaveSession() is executed, closing the sound session:

```
case WM_DESTROY:
     /*-------------------
     Close the Wave session.
     --------------------*/
     ts_CloseWaveSession();
     PostQuitMessage (0);
     return 0;
```

The Sampling Rate of the Recording and Additional *ts_* Functions

As you may have noticed, the Record program does not specify the sampling rate of the recording. Hence, the recording performs at a default sampling rate (11,025 Hertz).

The full version of the TS library includes additional ts_ functions that enable you to perform the recording at any desired sampling rate.

The full version of the TS library includes other powerful ts_ functions that enable you to control other aspects of the recording and the playback.

The Record2 Program

We will now upgrade the Record program to let the user save the recording into a .WAV file, as well as load .WAV files and play them. The new upgraded program is called Record2.

Compiling, Linking, and Executing the Record2 Program

To compile and link the Record2 program with the Microsoft compiler:

- Make sure your PC is in a DOS-protected mode.

- Log into c:\spSDK\Samp4Win\.

- At the DOS prompt type

  NMAKE Record2.mak   {Enter}

To compile and link the Record2 program with the Borland compiler:

- Log into c:\spSDK\Samp4Win\.

- At the DOS prompt type

  NMAKE -f Record2.bmk   {Enter}

Before executing the Record2 program make sure that a Windows-compatible sound card is installed in your PC, and that all the appropriate drivers are installed.

To execute the Record2 program:

- Select Run from the File menu of the Program Manager of Windows.

- Click Browse and select the file

  c:\spSDK\Samp4Win\Record2.exe

The main window appears, as shown in Figure 11.14. It contains two menu options: File and Exit (see Figures 11.15 and 11.16).

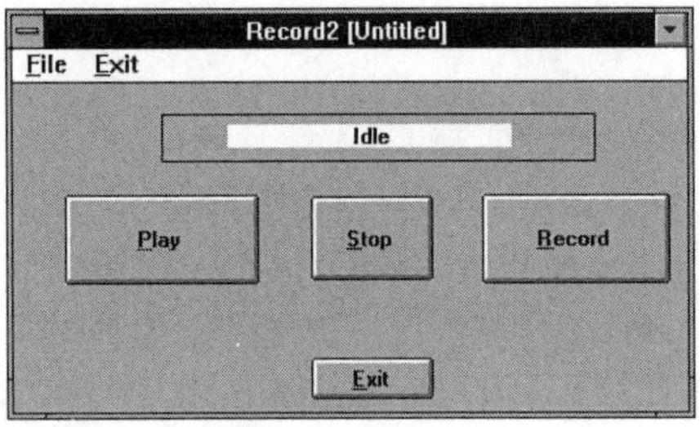

Figure 11.14. The main window of Record2.

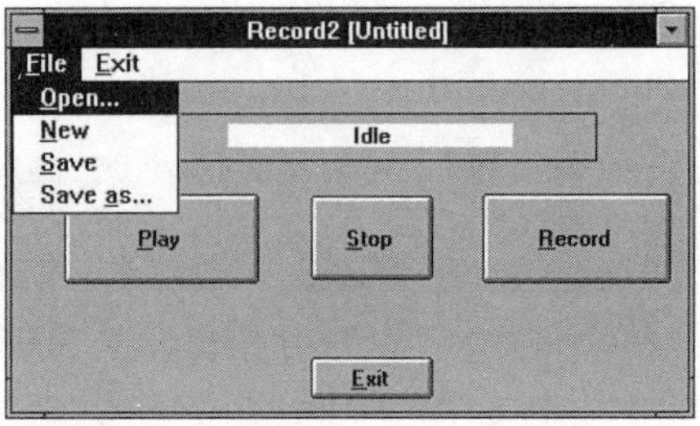

Figure 11.15. The File menu of Record2.

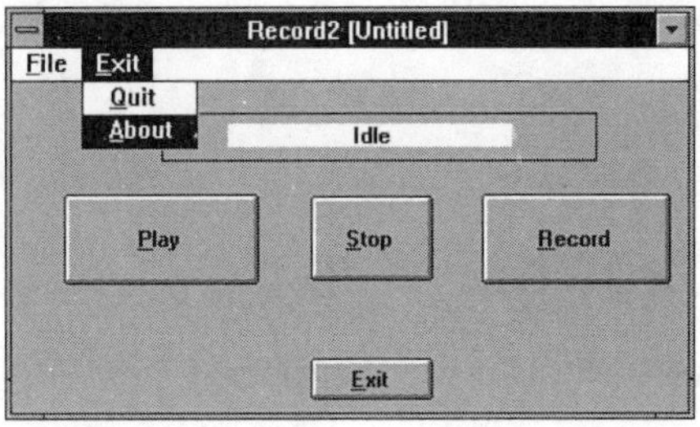

Figure 11.16. The Exit menu of Record2.

The Exit menu contains two options: Quit and About. When the user selects Quit, the program terminates. When the user selects About, the About dialog box appears, as shown in Figure 11.17.

Figure 11.17. The About dialog box of the Record2 program.

The File menu has four items in it: Open, New, Save, and Save As. These items are the standard file-opening and file-saving options.

The main window of Record2 contains four push buttons: Play, Stop, Record, and Exit. To record a .WAV file, press the Record push button, and speak into the microphone. To stop the recording, push the Stop push button. To play the file that you recorded, push the Play push button. To exit the main window, press the Exit push button.

During playback, the mouse is available and you may switch to other Windows applications.

The Record2 program lets you save the recorded Wave file by selecting the Save or Save As menu options. A Wave file may also be loaded by using the Open menu option.

The Files of the Record2 Program

The Record2 program consists of the following files:

Record2.h	The #include file of the program.
Record2.c	The C code of the program.
Record2.rc	The resource file of the program.
Record2.def	The module definition file of the program.
Record2.mak	The make file of the program.
ExtSpkr.ico	The icon of the program.

These files are provided for you in c:\spSDK\Samp4Win\.

The *WM_COMMAND* Case of Record2

The Record2 program is very similar to the Record program. The only difference is that Record2 can load and save .WAV files.

The New Option of the File Menu

When the user selects the New option from the File menu, the WM_COMMAND message is received with wParam equal to IDM_NEW. Under the IDM_NEW case, the ts_OpenWaveSession() is executed with

```
file name equals to the null string:
          lstrcpy( gsWaveFileName, "" );
          iOpenResult =
          ts_OpenWaveSession ( gsWaveFileName );
```

The Open Option of the File Menu

When the user selects the Open option from the File menu, the WM_COMMAND message is received with wParam equal to IDM_OPEN. Under the IDM_OPEN case, we let the user select a .WAV file by using the standard Open dialog box of Windows, as shown in Figure 11.18. We do that by executing the ts_SelectWaveDIalog() function. This function returns a nonzero integer if the user did not select a file. If the user selected a file, the second parameter of the ts_SelectWaveDialog() function is updated with the name and path of the selected file, and the third parameter of the ts_SelectWaveDialog() function is updated with the name of the selected file (without its path).

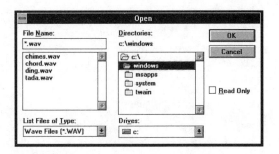

Figure 11.18. The standard Open dialog box of Windows.

NOTE

Function Name: `ts_SelectWaveDialog()`

Description: This function lets the user select a .WAV file via a standard Windows Open File dialog box.

Prototype: `int ts_SelectWaveDialog ( HWND hWnd,`
`                                LPSTR lpstrFileName,`
`                                LPSTR lpstrTitle );`

Parameters: `HWND hWnd`: The handler of the window in which the Open dialog box appears.

`LPSTR lpstrFileName`: The string that will be updated with the name and path of the file selected by the user.

`LPSTR lpstrTitle`: The string that will be updated with the name (without the path) of the file selected by the user.

Returned Value: Int. A returned value of zero means that the user did not select a file. For example, the user pushed the Cancel push button of the Open dialog box.

After the user selects a file, a sound session opens with the selected file:

```
/*----------------------------------
Open the Multimedia session with the
selected Wave file.
----------------------------------*/
iOpenResult =
ts_OpenWaveSession ( sSelectedPathAndFile );
```

If the sound session opening with the selected file fails, we reopen the session with the current Wave file:

```
if ( iOpenResult != 1 )
   {
   lstrcpy ( sMessage,
           "Failed to open a session with " );
   lstrcat ( sMessage, sSelectedPathAndFile );
   MessageBox ( NULL,
                sMessage,
                "Message",
                MB_ICONINFORMATION |
                MB_SYSTEMMODAL);
```

```
/*-------------------------------------
Since we failed to open a session with
the selected file, open the session with
the previous file.
-------------------------------------*/
iOpenResult =
ts_OpenWaveSession ( gsWaveFileName );
DisplayWindowTitle ( hWnd );
return 0;
}
```

If the sound opening is successful, the variable gsWaveFileName is updated with the selected Wave file name. The variable gsWaveFileName is maintained throughout the program to hold the name of the currently opened Wave file. The function DisplayWindowTitle() is used throughout the program to display the name of the currently opened Wave file in the title of the Record2 window:

```
lstrcpy( gsWaveFileName,
         sSelectedPathAndFile );

DisplayWindowTitle ( hWnd );
```

The Save Option of the File Menu

When the user selects the Save option from the File menu, the WM_COMMAND message is received with wParam equal to IDM_SAVE. Under the IDM_SAVE case we first check to see if the current Wave file name is the null string. If the current Wave file name is the null string, it means that the user did not yet save the Wave file. Thus, we treat this case as a Save As case by sending the IDM_SAVE_AS message with the SendMessage() function. This has the same effect as the user selecting the Save As menu option.

If however, gsWaveFileName is not null, then the Wave session is saved as a .WAV file by using the ts_SaveWave() function:

```
case IDM_SAVE:
    if ( gsWaveFileName[0] == '\0' )
       {
       SendMessage ( hWnd,
                     WM_COMMAND,
                     IDM_SAVE_AS,
                     0);
       return 0L;
       }
```

```
ts_SaveWave ( gsWaveFileName );

return 0L;
```

The Save As Option of the File Menu

When the user selects the Save As option from the File menu, the WM_COMMAND message is received with wParam equal to IDM_SAVE_AS.

Under the IDM_SAVE_AS case we provide the user with a Save As dialog box that lets the user select the name and the directory of the .WAV file to be saved. This is accomplished with the ts_SaveAsWaveDialog() function. If the user cancelled the Save As dialog box, the if(!SaveAsResult) is satisfied, and the case is terminated with a return 0L statement. If the user selected a file from the Save As dialog box, then the ts_SaveWave() function is executed, saving the Wave session as a .WAV file:

```
case IDM_SAVE_AS:
    lstrcpy ( sSelectedPathAndFile, "");
    lstrcpy ( sSelectedFile, "");

    iSaveAsResult =
    ts_SaveAsWaveDialog ( hWnd,
                          sSelectedPathAndFile,
                          sSelectedFile);
```

```
if ( !iSaveAsResult )
    {
    /*--------------------------------
    User did not select a file from the
    Save As dialog box.
    -------------------------------*/
    return 0L;
    }

lstrcpy( gsWaveFileName,
         sSelectedPathAndFile );
DisplayWindowTitle ( hWnd );
ts_SaveWave ( gsWaveFileName );
return 0L;
```

NOTE

Function name: `ts_SaveAsDialog()`

Description: This function lets the user select a .WAV file via a standard Windows Save As dialog box.

Prototype: `int ts_SaveAsDialog ( HWND hWnd, LPSTR lpstrFileName,LPSTR lpstrTitle );`

Parameters: `HWND hWnd`: The handler of the window in which the Save As dialog box will appear.

`LPSTR lpstrFileName`: The string that will be updated with the name and path of the file selected by the user.

`LPSTR lpstrTitle`: The string that will be updated with the name (without the path) of the file selected by the user.

Returned Value: Int. A returned value of zero means that the user did not select a file. For example, the user pushed the Cancel push button of the Save As dialog box.

The Dog2 Program

In a previous chapter we presented the Dog program—a program that displays a dog and its bone. When the user tries to steal the bone (by clicking the bone or by pressing the **B** key), the dog starts barking. In the Dog program the barking plays through the PC internal speaker. We will now rewrite the Dog program so that the barking plays through the sound card. The new program is called Dog2.

The Dog2 program introduces several new `ts_` functions. These functions are useful for writing animation programs.

Compiling, Linking, and Executing the Dog2 Program

To compile and link the Dog2 program with the Microsoft compiler:

- Make sure your PC is in a DOS-protected mode.

- Log into c:\spSDK\Samp4Win\.

- At the DOS prompt type

    NMAKE Dog2.mak   {Enter}

To compile and link the Dog2 program with the Borland compiler:

- Log into c:\spSDK\Samp4Win\.

- At the DOS prompt type

    NMAKE -f Dog2.bmk   {Enter}

Before executing the Dog2 program make sure that a Windows-compatible sound card is installed in your PC, and that all the appropriate drivers are installed.

To execute the Dog2 program:

- Select Run from the File menu of the Program Manager of Windows.

- Click Browse and select the file

    c:\spSDK\Samp4Win\Dog2.exe

The main window appears, as shown in Figure 11.19. The Dog2 program menu contains three options: Quit, About, and Instructions (see Figure 11.20).

The About dialog box of the Dog2 program is shown in Figure 11.21, and the Instructions dialog box is shown in Figure 11.22.

Figure 11.19. The main window of Dog2.

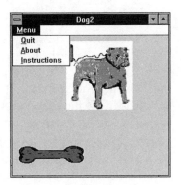

Figure 11.20. The Dog2 program menu.

Figure 11.21. The About dialog box of the Dog2 program.

Figure 11.22. The Instructions dialog box of the Dog2 program.

When the user clicks the bone (or presses the **B** key), the dog starts jumping and barking. The barking plays through the sound card.

The Files of the Dog2 Program

The Dog2 program consists of the following files:

Dog2.h	The #include file of the program.
Dog2.c	The C code of the program.
Dog2.rc	The resource file of the program.
Dog2.def	The module definition file of the program.
Dog2.mak	The make file of the program.
ExtSpkr.ico	The icon of the program.

These files are provided for you in c:\spSDK\Samp4Win\.

The Animation of the Dog2 Program

There are two types of animation: *asynchronous animation* and *synchronous animation.*

In asynchronous animation, the played sound is not synchronized with the moving pictures. The Dog2 program is an example of asynchronous animation.

In synchronous animation, the played sound is synchronized with the moving pictures; each picture is associated with its own sound section. Later in this chapter a program that uses synchronous animation is discussed.

The Process of Creating an Asynchronous Show

This section explains the process of creating an asynchronous show, which includes the setting of the timer.

Preparing a Timer

Before starting an asynchronous show, a timer needs to be set. In the Dog2 program, the timer is prepared in WinMain() as follows:

```
/*--------------
Prepare a timer.
-------------*/
if ( !SetTimer ( hWnd,
     1,
     175,  /* Every 175 msec. */
     NULL ))
   {
   MessageBox ( NULL,
               "No more timers available!",
               "Timer problems!",
               MB_ICONINFORMATION );
   /*------------------
   Quit the application.
   -------------------*/
   SendMessage ( hWnd,
               WM_DESTROY,
               0,
               0 );
   }/* end of if() */
```

This SetTimer() statement causes the Windows operating system to generate a WM_TIMER message every 175 milliseconds. The value of the timer setting (175 milliseconds) determines the frequency at which frames change during the show. Although we used the value of 175 milliseconds, you may experiment with other values.

Preparing the Frames of the Show

The show is composed of several frames (.BMP pictures). The ts_EditFrame() function is used to prepare frames for the show.

Under the WM_PAINT case the PrepareShow1() function is executed. The PrepareShow1() function prepares show number 1, a show that is composed of two pictures: the bone, and the dog with its mouth closed. Here is how the PrepareShow1() function prepares the bone bit-map picture:

```
ts_EditFrame (0,        /* Frame number.                     */
           ghInst,      /* The instance of the application.  */
           ghBone,      /* The bitmap handler.               */
           10,          /* Upper left X-coordinate in pixels. */
           200,         /* Upper left Y-coordinate in pixels. */
           125,         /* Width in pixels.                  */
           32,          /* Height in pixels.                 */
           -1L,         /* Starting Sound coordinate: None   */
           -1L );       /* Ending Sound coordinate: None     */
```

Similarly, the ts_PrepareShow1() function prepares the Dog bit-map picture:

```
ts_EditFrame (1,        /* Frame number.                     */
           ghInst,      /* The instance of the application.  */
    ghDogWithOpenMouth,  /* The bitmap handler.               */
           100,         /* Upper left X-coordinate in pixels. */
           10,          /* Upper left Y-coordinate in pixels. */
           125,         /* Width in pixels.                  */
           125,         /* Height in pixels.                 */
           -1L,         /* Starting Sound coordinate: None   */
           -1L );       /* Ending Sound coordinate: None     */
```

The last thing that the PrepareShow1() function does is mark frame #1 as the last frame of the show. This is accomplished by using the ts_MarkLastFrame() function:

```
/*----------------------------
Mark Frame #1 as the last frame.
----------------------------*/
ts_MarkLastFrame (1);
```

NOTE

Function Name: `ts_EditFrame()`

Description: This function edits a bit-map frame for the show.

Prototype:
```
int ts_EditFrame (int          iFrameNumber,
                  HINSTANCE    hInstance,
                  HBITMAP      hBitMap,
                  int          iX,
                  int          iY,
                  int          iWidth,
                  int          iHeight,
                  long         lStartSND,
                  long         lEndSND);
```

Parameters:

`int iFrameNumber`: The frame number to be edited.

`HINSTANCE hInstance`: The instance of the program.

`HBITMAP hBitMap`: The bit-map handler of the frame.

`int iX`: The X-coordinate in pixels of the frame.

`int iY`: The Y-coordinate in pixels of the frame.

`int iWidth`: The width in pixels of the frame.

`int iHeight`: The height in pixels of the frame.

`long lStartSND`: Not applicable for asynchronous animation.

`long lEndSND`: Not applicable for asynchronous animation.

Returned Value: This function always returns 1.

NOTE

Function Name: ts_MarkLastFrame()

Description: This function marks a frame as the last frame of the show.

Prototype: int ts_MarkLastFrame (int iFrameNumber);

Parameter: int iFrameNumber, the frame number to be marked as the last frame of the show.

Returned Value: This function always returns 1.

Once the show is prepared, the ts_DisplayFrozenFrame() function may be used to display individual frames of the show. Under the WM_PAINT case, we display the bone picture and the dog picture:

```
/*-----------
Paint the bone.
--------------*/
ts_DisplayFrozenFrame ( hWnd, 0 );

/*--------------------------------
Paint the Dog with its mouth closed.
--------------------------------*/
ts_DisplayFrozenFrame ( hWnd, 1 );
```

Note that show number 1 is merely the displaying of the bone and the dog. This show does not involve any sound playing, and does not involve any animation.

NOTE

Function Name: ts_DisplayFrozenFrame ()

Description: This function displays one frame.

Prototype: int ts_DisplayFrozenFrame (HWND hWnd,
                                          int iFrameNumber);

Parameters: HWND hWnd: The handler of the window in which the frame will be displayed.

int iFrameNumber: The frame number to be displayed.

Returned Value: This function always returns 1.

Now that show number 1 is completed; we are now ready to prepare show number 2. This is accomplished with the PrepareShow2() function.

The *PrepareShow2()* Function

Show number 2 involves two frames: the dog with its mouth open, and the dog with its mouth closed. Thus, the prepareShow2() function executes the ts_EditFrame() twice. Because show number 2 is composed of two frames, the PrepareShow2() function marks the second frame as the last frame of the show with the ts_MarkLastFrame() function:

```
void PrepareShow2 ( void )
{
/*-----------------------------------------------
Build Frame #0: The dog with its mouth closed
-------------------------------------------*/
ts_EditFrame (0,           /* Frame number.                        */
            ghInst,       /* The instance of the application.     */
   ghDogWithCloseMouth, /* The bitmap handler.                  */
            100,          /* Upper left X-coordinate in pixels.   */
            10,           /* Upper left Y-coordinate in pixels.   */
            125,          /* Width in pixels.                     */
            125,          /* Height in pixels.                    */
            -1L,          /* Starting Sound coordinate: None      */
            -1L );        /* Ending Sound coordinate: None        */


/*-----------------------------------------------
  Build Frame #1: The dog with its mouth open
-------------------------------------------*/
ts_EditFrame (1,           /* Frame number.                        */
            ghInst,       /* The instance of the application.     */
   ghDogWithOpenMouth,   /* The bitmap handler.                  */
            100,          /* Upper left X-coordinate in pixels.   */
            10,           /* Upper left Y-coordinate in pixels.   */
            125,          /* Width in pixels.                     */
            125,          /* Height in pixels.                    */
            -1L,          /* Starting Sound coordinate: None      */
            -1L );        /* Ending Sound coordinate: None        */
```

```
/*------------------------------
 Mark Frame #1 as the last frame.
----------------------------*/
ts_MarkLastFrame (1);

}/* end of function. */
```

Starting the Sound Playback of the Show

Show number 2 includes in it playback of sound through the sound card. The playback is initiated when the user presses the **B** key, or when the user clicks the bone.

When the user presses the **B** key, the playback of the sound starts, and the global variable giTheShowMustGoOn is set to 1.

```
case 'B':
     /*---------------------
     Prepare the barking show.
     --------------------*/
     PrepareShow2();

     /*-------------
     Make the dog bark.
     ---------------*/
     if ( ts_PlayWave ( hWnd,
                        TS_START_OF_FILE,
                        TS_END_OF_FILE,
                        TS_IN_MILLISECONDS ) == 1)
        {
        giTheShowMustGoOn = 1;
        }
     return 0;
```

The Animation

Remember that the timer is set to 175 milliseconds. This means that the WndProc() function receives a WM_TIMER message every 175 milliseconds. Under the WM_TIMER case, the giTheShowMustGoOn is checked. If the value of the flag is 1, the ts_ShowAsync() function is executed:

```
case WM_TIMER:
     if ( giTheShowMustGoOn == 1 )
        {
```

```
      ts_ShowAsync ( hWnd );
      }
   return 0L;
```

> **NOTE**
>
> *Function Name:* `ts_ShowAsync();`
>
> *Description:* This function displays the next sequential frame of the show. Once the last frame (the frame that was marked as the last frame) is displayed, the next frame to be displayed is the first frame of the show.
>
> *Prototype:* `int ts_ShowAsync ( HWND hWnd );`
>
> *Parameter:* `HWND hWnd`: The handler of the window in which the frame will be displayed.
>
> *Returned Value:* This function always returns 1.

Ending the Show

We terminate the show upon receiving the `MM_MCINOTIFY` message. Remember that the `MM_MCINOTIFY` message with `wParam` equal to `MCI_NOTIFY_SUCCESSFUL` is received when the sound card completes the playback. Under the `MCI_NOTIFY_SUCCESSFUL` case, the show is terminated by resetting the `giTheShowMustGoOn` flag to 0. Then the dog (with its mouth closed) and its bone are displayed by preparing and showing the frames of show number 1:

```
case MM_MCINOTIFY:

   switch ( wParam )
      {
      case MCI_NOTIFY_SUCCESSFUL:
         giTheShowMustGoOn = 0 ;
         /*-----------------------------------------
         The show is over, so leave the dog with its
         mouth closed.
         -----------------------------------------*/
         PrepareShow1();
         ts_DisplayFrozenFrame ( hWnd, 0 );
         ts_DisplayFrozenFrame ( hWnd, 1 );
         break;
```

```
             case MCI_NOTIFY_ABORTED:
                  ts_StopWave();
                  giTheShowMustGoOn = 0;
                  break;
             case MCI_NOTIFY_SUPERSEDED:
                  ts_StopWave();
                  giTheShowMustGoOn = 0;
                  break;
             case MCI_NOTIFY_FAILURE:
                  ts_StopWave();
                  giTheShowMustGoOn = 0;
                  break;
             }/* end of switch() */

        return 0L;
```

The PressAny Program

We will now write the PressAny program. This program illustrates synchronous animation. The animation show synchronizes the text Press any key to continue... with the audio phrase *Press any key to continue....* The audio phrase plays through the sound card.

Compiling, Linking, and Executing the PressAny Program

To compile and link the PressAny program with the Microsoft compiler:

- Make sure your PC is in a DOS-protected mode.
- Log into c:\spSDK\Samp4Win\.
- At the DOS prompt type

  NMAKE PressAny.mak   {Enter}

To compile and link the PressAny program with the Borland compiler:

- Log into c:\spSDK\Samp4Win\.
- At the DOS prompt type

  NMAKE -f PressAny.bmk   {Enter}

Before executing the PressAny program make sure that a Windows-compatible sound card is installed in your PC, and that all the appropriate drivers are installed.

To execute the PressAny program:

- Select Run from the File menu of the Program Manager of Windows.

- Click Browse and select the file

    `c:\spSDK\Samp4Win\PressAny.exe`

The main window appears, as shown in Figure 11.23.

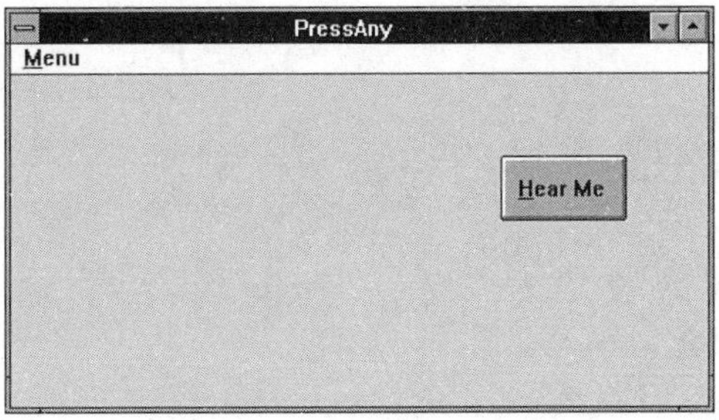

Figure 11.23. The main window of PressAny.

The PressAny program menu contains three options: Quit, About, and Instructions (see Figure 11.24). The About dialog box of the PressAny program is shown in Figure 11.25, and the Instructions dialog box is shown in Figure 11.26.

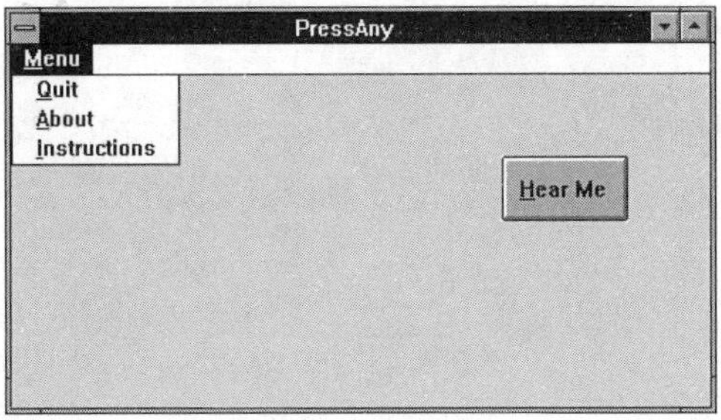

Figure 11.24. The PressAny program menu.

Figure 11.25. The About dialog box of the PressAny program.

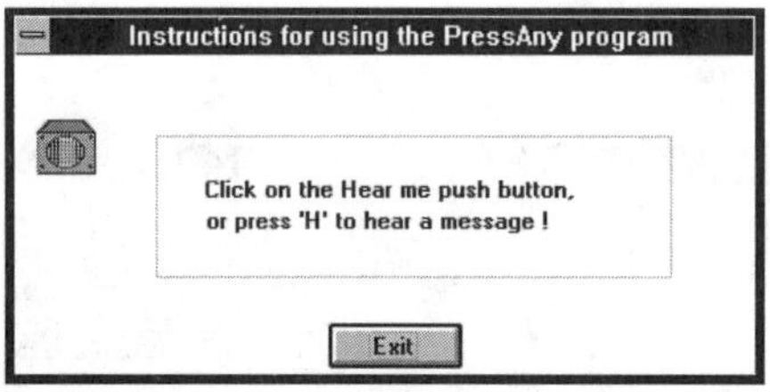

Figure 11.26. The Instructions dialog box of the PressAny program.

When the user clicks the Hear Me push button (or presses the H key), the phrase `Press any key to continue...` is displayed simultaneously and in synchronization with the audio prompt *Press any key to continue...* (see Figure 11.27).

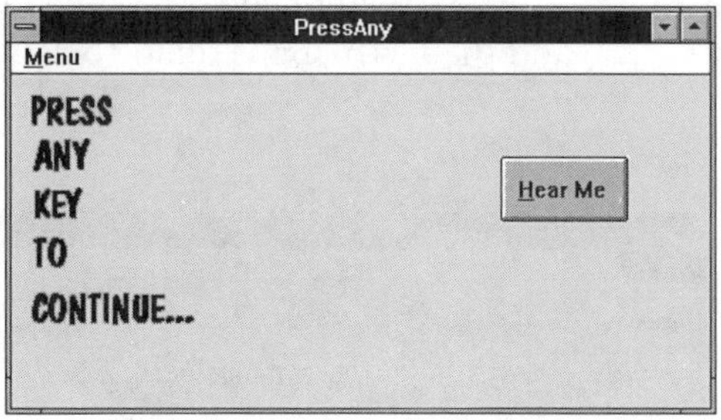

Figure 11.27. The phrase `Press any key to continue...` is displayed.

The Files of the PressAny Program

The PressAny program consists of the following files:

PressAny.h	The #include file of the program.
PressAny.c	The C code of the program.
PressAny.rc	The resource file of the program.
PressAny.def	The module definition file of the program.
PressAny.mak	The make file of the program.
ExtSpkr.ico	The icon of the program.

These files are provided for you in c:\spSDK\Samp4Win\.

The bit-map files used in the PressAny program are Wait6.bmp, Wait7.bmp, Wait8.bmp, Wait9.bmp, and Wait10.bmp. These bit-map files are shown in Figure 11.28, and they are provided for you in c:\spSDK\Samp4Win\.

(a) Wait6.bmp   **PRESS**

(b) Wait7.bmp   **ANY**

(c) Wait8.bmp   **KEY**

(d) Wait9.bmp   **TO**

(e) Wait10.bmp   **CONTINUE...**

Figure 11.28. The bit-map files used in the PressAny program.

The Show of the PressAny Program

The PressAny program is very similar to the Dog2 program. The only difference is that the show of PressAny is a synchronized show—the animation is synchronized with the sound sections of the sound file.

Preparing the Timer

The timer is set in `WinMain()` to generate a `WM_TIMER` message every 75 milliseconds:

```
/*--------------
Prepare a timer.
--------------*/
if ( !SetTimer ( hWnd,
                 1,
                 75,    /* Every 75 msec. */
                 NULL ))
   {
   MessageBox ( NULL,
                "No more timers available!",
                "Timer problems!",
                MB_ICONINFORMATION );

   /*-------------------
   Quit the application.
   -------------------*/
   SendMessage ( hWnd,
                 WM_DESTROY,
                 0,
                 0 );

   }/* end of if() */
```

Preparing the Show

The show is prepared in the `PrepareShow()` function. This function executes the `ts_EditFrame()` function five times (for five frames) and then marks the fifth frame as the last frame by using the `ts_MarkLastFrame()` function.

Because the show is synchronized, the last two parameters of the `ts_EditFrame()` represent the *sound hook* range. The frame should appear whenever the sound file reaches this range.

Here is the `ts_EditFrame()` statement that corresponds to frame number 0:

```
/*--------------------------
 Build Frame #0: "PRESS"
--------------------------*/
ts_EditFrame (0,           /* Frame number.                     */
              ghInst,      /* The instance of the application.  */
              ghPress,     /* The bit-map handler.              */
              10,          /* Upper left X-coordinate in pixels. */
```

```
10,        /* Upper left Y-coordinate in pixels.  */
60,        /* Width in pixels.                     */
25,        /* Height in pixels.                    */
0L,        /* Starting Sound coordinate.           */
800L );    /* Ending Sound coordinate.             */
```

The preceding ts_EditFrame() function specifies the range 0 to 800 milli-seconds (the last two parameters of the function). This means that the bit map that corresponds to the ghPress handler should appear whenever the played sound is within this range.

Similarly, the ts_EditFrame() function sets the sound hooks for the other frames. Here are the sound hooks of the five frames:

Frame Number	Bit-Map Handler	Sound Range (in milliseconds)	Audio Content
0	ghPress	0 - 800	*Press*
1	ghAny	800 - 1,100	*any*
2	ghKey	1,100 - 1,600	*key*
3	ghTo	1,600 - 2,080	*to*
4	ghContinue	2,080 - 2,780	*continue*

Starting the Show

When the user selects the Hear Me push button, the WM_COMMAND message is received with wParam equal to HEARME_PB. Under the HEARME_PB case the show is prepared by executing the PrepareShow() function. The show is then started by starting the playback of the sound file with the ts_PlayWave() function. If the returned value of ts_PlayWave() is 1, it means that the sound card accepted the play command, in which case the giTheShowMustGoOn flag is set to 1:

```
case HEARME_PB:
    /*--------------
    Prepare the show.
    ---------------*/
    PrepareShow();

    /*-------------
    Perform the show.
    ---------------*/
    if ( ts_PlayWave ( hWnd,
                    TS_START_OF_FILE,
                    TS_END_OF_FILE,
```

```
                        TS_IN_MILLISECONDS ) == 1)
        {
        giTheShowMustGoOn = 1;
        }
    return 0L;
```

The giTheShowMustGoOn variable is used as a flag to enable or disable the show under the WM_TIMER case.

The *WM_TIMER* Message

As we just discussed, the SetTimer() function was set to generate a WM_TIMER message every 75 milliseconds. The synchronized show is performed under the WM_TIMER case:

```
case WM_TIMER:
    if ( giTheShowMustGoOn == 1 )
        {
        ts_ShowSync ( hWnd );
        }
    return 0L;
```

The ts_ShowSync() function displays the frame that corresponds to the currently played sound section. Remember that the ts_EditFrame() function assigned a sound range to the frames. Thus, the ts_ShowSync() function examines the currently played byte, and based on the value, displays the corresponding frame.

NOTE

Function Name: ts_ShowSync()

Description: This function displays the frame that corresponds to the currently played sound section.

Prototype: int ts_ShowSync (HWND hWnd);

Parameter: HWND hWnd: The handler of the window in which the frame will be displayed.

Returned Value: The returned value is always 1.

In order not to miss the displaying of any of the frames, the timer has to be set to a value that is small enough. In our timer setting, we set the timer to 75 milliseconds. This value is small enough to catch all the frames of the show.

Ending the Show

We terminate the show upon receiving the MM_MCINOTIFY message. Remember that the MM_MCINOTIFY message with wParam equal to MCI_NOTIFY_SUCCESSFUL is received when the sound card completes the playback. Under the MCI_NOTIFY_SUCCESSFUL case, the show is terminated by resetting the giTheShowMustGoOn flag to 0. The InvalidateRect() and UpdateWindow() functions are used to cause the generation of a WM_PAINT message so that the window will clear:

```
case MM_MCINOTIFY:

    switch ( wParam )
            {
            case MCI_NOTIFY_SUCCESSFUL:
                InvalidateRect ( hWnd, NULL, TRUE );
                UpdateWindow ( hWnd );
                giTheShowMustGoOn = 0;
                break;
            case MCI_NOTIFY_ABORTED:
                InvalidateRect ( hWnd, NULL, TRUE );
                UpdateWindow ( hWnd );
                giTheShowMustGoOn = 0;
                ts_StopWave();
                break;
            case MCI_NOTIFY_SUPERSEDED:
                InvalidateRect ( hWnd, NULL, TRUE );
                UpdateWindow ( hWnd );
                giTheShowMustGoOn = 0;
                ts_StopWave();
                break;
            case MCI_NOTIFY_FAILURE:
                InvalidateRect ( hWnd, NULL, TRUE );
                UpdateWindow ( hWnd );
                giTheShowMustGoOn = 0;
                ts_StopWave();
                break;
            }/* end of switch() */

    return 0L;
```

The *ts_* Animation Functions

The ts_ animation functions introduced in this program were designed to make life easier for the programmer. By using these high-level functions, you can concentrate on the artistic aspects of the show, experimenting with the show without the need to write lengthy repetitive code. For example, to add more frames to the show, simply add more frames in PrepareShow() by using the ts_EditFrame() function.

The short version of the TS library contains only a limited amount of ts_ animation functions.

Playing MIDI Files

MIDI files (Musical Instruments Digital Interface files) are useful in music programs. The MIDI files are short, and may be used as background music in your programs.

We'll now write the PlayMIDI program, which plays MIDI files.

The Files of the PlayMIDI Program

The PlayMIDI program consists of the following files:

PlayMIDI.h	The #include file of the program.
PlayMIDI.c	The C code of the program.
PlayMIDI.rc	The resource file of the program.
PlayMIDI.def	The module definition file of the program.
PlayMIDI.mak	The make file of the program.
MIDI.ico	The icon of the program.

These files are provided for you in c:\spSDK\Samp4Win\.

Compiling, Linking, and Executing the PlayMIDI Program

To compile and link the PlayMIDI program with the Microsoft compiler:

- Make sure your PC is in a DOS-protected mode.

- Log into c:\spSDK\Samp4Win\.

- At the DOS prompt type

```
NMAKE PlayMIDI.mak   {Enter}
```

To compile and link the PlayMIDI program with the Borland compiler:

- Log into c:\spSDK\Samp4Win\.

- At the DOS prompt type

```
NMAKE -f PlayMIDI.bmk   {Enter}
```

Before executing the PlayMIDI program make sure that a Windows-compatible sound card that is able to play MIDI files is installed in your PC (for example, the Sound Blaster). You must also make sure that all the appropriate drivers are installed.

To execute the PlayMIDI program:

- Select Run from the File menu of the Program Manager of Windows.

- Click Browse and select the file

```
c:\spSDK\Samp4Win\PlayMIDI.exe
```

Select the Open option from the menu, and open a MIDI file. MIDI files usually have a .MID file extension. The Windows directory has a sample MIDI file called c:\Windows\Canyon.mid.

You may now play the selected MIDI file by pushing the Play push button.

The Code of the PlayMIDI Program

The PlayMIDI program is very similar to the Record2 program. The only difference is that the PlayMIDI program does not have the Record push button, and that all the ts_Wave_ functions were replaced with ts_MIDI_ functions:

ts_WaveDeviceCanPlay() was replaced with ts_MIDIDeviceCanPlay().

ts_SelectWaveDialog() was replaced with ts_SelectMIDIDialog().

ts_OpenWaveSession() was replaced with ts_OpenMIDISession().

ts_PlayWave() was replaced with ts_PlayMIDI().

ts_StopWave() was replaced with ts_StopMIDI();

ts_CloseWaveSession() was replaced with ts_CloseMIDISession().

Other *ts_* MIDI Functions

The TS library supplied with the book's diskette is a short-version library; it contains a limited number of ts_MIDI_ functions. However, the full-version library contains additional ts_MIDI functions that enable you to increase and decrease the MIDI volume, record MIDI files, extract the current position of the played file (for sound hooks), and perform other useful tasks.

Mixing .WAV Files and MIDI Files

Many programs play MIDI files simultaneously with .WAV files. To see it in action, you may execute the PlayMIDI program, start playing a MIDI file, and while the .MID file plays, switch to the Dog2 program and play the barking. You'll hear the MIDI music played simultaneously with the barking. You may, of course, play .WAV files and MIDI files from within the same program. This feature is useful for adding background music (the MIDI file) to vocal music (the .WAV file).

CHAPTER

TWELVE

Sound C Programming for DOS

Previous chapters discussed sound C programming for the Windows operating system. This chapter teaches how to write C sound programs for DOS.

In this chapter, you will learn about playing sound through the internal PC speaker. You will learn about playing sound through the Sound Blaster sound card in the next chapter.

Writing C Programs for DOS That Play Through the Internal Speaker of the PC

If you are a "hooked on Windows" programmer, you are probably asking yourself why you should bother learning how to write C programs for DOS when this powerful Windows operating system is available. We'll avoid answering this question, and get right to business, writing C sound programs for DOS.

When writing C programs for DOS, your program should be easily distributed—that is, your program should not require the use of any special driver or any other preinstalled software. To accomplish this objective, your programs must be linked with the TegoMS.lib library. The book's diskette includes a short version of this library. This short version includes enough functions to enable you to compile and link all the programs that are presented in this book.

The MAKEexe.bat File

The directory c:\spSDK\SampMS\ includes the file MAKEexe.bat. This batch file contains the compile/link (cl) command line for compiling and linking with the Microsoft C compiler. Here is the listing of MAKEexe.bat:

```
echo off
cls
Echo ******************************************************************
Echo *                                                                *
Echo *     Compiling and linking with the Microsoft C compiler        *
Echo *   and the TegoSoft C for DOS sound library (short version).    *
Echo *                                                                *
Echo ******************************************************************
cl -AH  %1   C:\spSDK\Lib\TegoMS.lib C:\c700\lib\Graphics.lib
```

The cl parameters include two libraries:

1. c:\spSDK\Lib\TegoMS.lib

2. c:\c700\lib\Graphics.lib

The first library is the short version of the library TegoMS.lib. This library is for use with the Microsoft C compiler.

The second library is the Graphics.lib library that came with your Microsoft C compiler. If your programs do not include any C functions from the Graphics library, then you may delete this library from the MAKEexe.bat file.

Similarly, the directory c:\spSDK\SampBL\ includes the file MAKEexe.bat. This batch file contains the compile/link (bcc) command line for compiling and linking with the Borland C compiler. Here is the listing of c:\spSDK\SampBL\MAKE.exe.bat:

```
echo off
cls
Echo
Echo
Echo       Compiling and linking with the Borland C Compiler
Echo      and the TegoSoft C for DOS sound library (short version).
Echo
Echo
bcc -mh %1   C:\spSDK\Lib\TegoBL.lib
```

The bcc parameter includes the library c:\spSDK\Lib\TegoBL.lib. This library is the short version of the TegoBL.lib. This library is for use with the Borland C compiler.

The PlayTS.c Program

The PlayTS program enables the user to play any TS sound file from the DOS command line. Playing other types of sound files (for example, .WAV files, .VOC files) is discussed later.

Generating TS Sound Files

A TS-type sound file may be generated from a .WAV file by using the WAV2TS.exe utility.

> **Example   Converting a .WAV Sound File To a .TS Sound File**
>
> The WAV2TS.exe utility converts any .WAV file to a TS-type sound file.
>
> For example, to convert the Hello.wav sound file to a TS sound file, you have to use the WAV2TS.exe utility as follows:
>
> At the DOS prompt type `WAV2TS Hello.wav Hello.ts`   {Enter}
>
> The resultant file is the sound file Hello.ts.

Note that the WAV2TS.exe utility is not included in the book's diskette. This utility is an integral part of the TS Sound Editor. Because we assume that you do not have a copy of the TS Sound Editor, we recorded the file Hello.wav, and then used the WAV2TS.exe utility to create the file Hello.ts. The Hello.ts file resides in c:\spSDK\TSfiles\.

We recommend that you compile, link, and execute the PlayTS program prior to going over its code. This way you'll gain a better understanding of what the code can accomplish.

Compiling and Linking the PlayTS Program

To compile and link the PlayTS program with the Microsoft compiler:

- Make sure your PC is in protected mode.

- Log into c:\spSDK\SampMS\.

- At the DOS prompt type

    `MAKEexe PlayTS.c` {Enter}

Alternatively, you may use the Programmer Work Bench (PWB) program that comes with the Microsoft C compiler to compile and link the PlayTS.c file. When opening a project with the PWB, don't forget to include the c:\spSDK\Lib\TegoMS.lib and c:\c700\lib\Graphics.lib libraries.

To compile and link the PlayTS program with the Borland compiler:

- Log into c:\spSDK\SampBL\.

- At the DOS prompt type

    `MAKEexe PlayTS.c` {Enter}

Executing the PlayTS.exe Program

The PlayTS program enables you to play any TS-type sound file through the internal PC speaker.

To play the file c:\spSDK\TSfiles\Hello.ts:

- Make sure your PC is at the DOS prompt (that is, if you are in a DOS shell of Windows, exit from the Windows session, and return to the DOS prompt).

- Log into c:\spSDK\SampMS\.

- At the DOS prompt type

    `PlayTS c:\spSDK\TSfiles\Hello.ts` {Enter}

The sound file Hello.ts is played in an endless loop.

You can stop the playback by pressing any key.

Similarly, you may play the other TS files that reside in c:\spSDK\TSfiles\.

Note: If you compiled and linked the program with the Borland compiler, then this is how to execute the program:

- Log into c:\spSDK\SampBL\.

- At the DOS prompt type

```
PlayTS c:\spSDK\TSfiles\Hello.ts  {Enter}
```

Naming the Sound Files

The TS files supplied in the book's diskette all have a .ts file extension. However, the extension of the sound files may have any legal DOS extension. This enables you to name your sound files in any colorful name that is applicable to your program. For example, you may name your sound file as Play.Me, Hear.Me, Fun2Hear, and so on.

The C Code of the PlayTS Program

The C code of the PlayTS program is in the file c:\spSDK\SampMS\PlayTS.c.

The PlayTS file is listed in Listing 12.1.

Listing 12.1. PlayTS.c.

```
/*=================================================================
PROGRAM NAME: PlayTS.c

(C) Copyright Gurewich 1992, 1993 (R) All Rights Reserved.

PROGRAM DESCRIPTION:
--------------------
This program plays a .TS sound file from beginning to end in an
endless loop.

User may stop the playback by pressing any key during the playback.

=================================================================*/

/*=========
  #include
  =========*/
```

```
/*-----------------------
  Standard C header files.
  -----------------------*/
#include <conio.h>
#include <graph.h>
#include <signal.h>
#include <stdio.h>
#include <string.h>

/*-----------------------------------------------------
   Standard TegoSoft Sound+ header files (short version).
   ----------------------------------------------------*/
#include "c:\spSDK\h\sp1.h"
#include "c:\spSDK\h\sp2.h"
#include "c:\spSDK\h\sp3.h"

/*=========
  prototypes
  =========*/
void display_status_line ( char * message_s );

/*================
  FUNCTION: main()
  ================*/
void main ( int argc, char *argv[ ] )
{
/*---  Name of the Sound file to be played. ---*/
char    file_name_to_play_s[125];
/*--- Results of opening the sound session. ---*/
int     open_result_i;

/*------------------
  The last byte played.
  ----------------*/
long    current_byte_l;

/*---------------
  Clear the screen.
  ---------------*/
_clearscreen ( _GCLEARSCREEN );

/*-----------------------------------------------------
  Pick up the Sound file name from the DOS command line.
  ----------------------------------------------------*/
strcpy ( file_name_to_play_s, argv[1] );

/*---------------------------------
  Tell the TSEngine to open a session.
  --------------------------------*/
```

continues

Listing 12.1. continued

```
display_status_line ("Opening a session. Please wait...");
open_result_i =
sp_open_tsengine_session ( file_name_to_play_s, SP_TS_FILE );
if ( open_result_i != 1 )
   {
   printf ( "\n Can't open a session for sound file:%s",argv[1]);
   exit(0);
   }

/*-------------------------------------------------------
  Wait until user presses a key to start the playback.
  ------------------------------------------------*/
display_status_line ("Press any key to start playing...");
SP_CLEAR_TYPEAHEAD;
getch();

display_status_line ("Now playing, press any key to stop playback..." );
current_byte_l = 0L;

_disable();

while ( 1 )
     {
     current_byte_l =
     sp_play_byte_range ( current_byte_l, current_byte_l + 15000L );

     /*-----------------------------------
      Start playback from the beginning if
      the sound file was fully played.
      ----------------------------------*/
     if (current_byte_l == -1L )
        {
        current_byte_l = 0L;
        }
     /*-----------------------------------
     Terminate playback if user presses any key.
     -----------------------------------*/
     if ( kbhit() )
        break;
     } /* end of while(1) */
_enable();

display_status_line ( "Good bye" );
_settextposition ( 24, 1 );

}/* end of main() */
/*=== end of main() ===*/
```

```
/*==========
  FUNCTION
  ========*/
/*---------------------------------------------
DESCRIPTION:
 This function erases row number 22, and then
 displays a message at the center of this row.
 This function is used to display status and
 instruction messages.
 ---------------------------------------------*/
void display_status_line ( char * message_s )
{
int message_length_i;   /* Length of the message to be displayed. */
int i;                  /* Used as a counter.                     */

/*---------------------------------------------
 Find the message length (for centering purpose).
 ---------------------------------------------*/
message_length_i = strlen ( message_s );

/*------------------
 Clear the status line.
 ------------------*/
_settextposition ( 22, 1 );
for (i=0;i<79;i++)
    printf(" ");

/*---------------------------------------------
 Display the message at the center of the row.
 ---------------------------------------------*/
_settextposition ( 22, 40-message_length_i/2 );
printf("%s", message_s);

}
/*=== end of function. ===*/
```

The #include Files

There are two groups of #include files, the standard C header files (for example, conio.h, graph.h), and the standard TegoSoft Sound+ header files. These #include files are called sp1.h, sp2.h, and sp3.h; they reside in c:\spSDK\h\.

> **NOTE** To incorporate sound into your C for DOS programs, your
> program must #include the files: sp1.h, sp2.h, and sp3.h. These
> #include files contain the macro and the prototypes of the C sound
> functions.

Picking Up the Name of the Sound File from the DOS Command Line

The main() function uses argc and *argv[] as its parameters:

```
void main ( int argc, char *argv[ ] )
{
.............
.............
.............
}
```

The path and name of the sound file is then copied to the string variable file_name_to_play_s:

```
strcpy ( file_name_to_play_s, argv[1] );
```

Note our name convention for the C variables: each variable name is terminated with a letter that indicates the type of the variable. Thus, the string variable file_name_to_play_s is terminated with the characters _s, the long variable current_byte_l is terminated with the characters _l, and so on. This is our variable name convention; you, of course, may use any naming technique that suits you best.

Opening a Sound Session

Before a sound file may be played, a sound session must be opened by using the sp_open_tsengine_session() function:

```
open_result_i =
sp_open_tsengine_session ( file_name_to_play_s, SP_TS_FILE );
if ( open_result_i != 1 )
   {
```

```
printf ( "\n Can't open a session for sound file:%s",argv[1]);
exit(0);
}
```

You may recognize the fact that sp_open_tsengine_session() is a function from the short version of the c:\spSDK\Lib\TegoMS.lib library, because the function name starts with the characters sp_.

NOTE   All functions from the c:\spSDK\Lib\TegoMS.lib (or c:\spSDK\TegoBL.lib) library start with the characters sp_. All macros and #definitions start with characters SP_.

Function name: sp_open_tsengine_session()

Description: This function opens a sound session. The prototype of *sp_open_tsengine_session()* is declared in c:\spSDK\h\sp1.h as:

```
int sp_open_tsengine_session ( char * file_name_to_play_s,
                               int file_type_i );
```

Parameters: char * file_name_to_play_s: a null terminated string that holds the path and name of the sound file to be opened.

int file_type_i: The type of the sound file to be opened.

Examples of valid values for the file type:

SP_S_FILE	S-type sound files.
SP_TS_FILE	TS-type sound files.

The full version of the library enables you to open a sound session with file-type SP_WAV_FILE (for .WAV files), SP_VOC_FILE (for .VOC files), and SP_SND_FILE (for .SND files).

These identifiers enable you to play .WAV files, .VOC files, and other popular sound files without the need to use the conversion utilities— that is, when supplying the SP_WAV_TYPE as the second parameter of sp_open_tsengine_session, the sound file to be opened is a .WAV file, so there is no need to use the WAV2TS.exe utility.

Returned value: The returned value from the sp_open_tsengine_session is an integer that indicates whether the TSEngine was successful in opening the sound session. A returned value other than 1 means that the TSEngine failed to open the sound session.

Clearing the Keyboard Buffer

Once the program opens the sound file, the program prompts the user to press any key to start the playback. It is always a good idea to clear the keyboard buffer prior to waiting for the user key pressing. This way we make sure that the playback starts because the user pressed a key, not because of a character that was previously stored in the keyboard buffer. Because clearing the keyboard buffer is so common in the C programs that include sound, the SP_CLEAR_TYPEHEAD macro is #defined in sp1.h as

```
#define SP_CLEAR_TYPEAHEAD  while(kbhit()) \
                                  getch()
```

Playing the Sound File

The sound file is played by using the sp_play_byte_range() function.

NOTE

Function Name: sp_play_byte_range()

Description: This function plays a sound file (or a section of a sound file).

Prototype: long sp_play_byte_range (long req_start_l, long req_end_l   );

Parameters: long req_start_l: The first byte in the sound section to be played.

long req_end_l: The last byte in the sound section to be played.

Returned Value: The returned value is a long integer that represents the last byte played. A negative returned value means that the sound section cannot be played.

The Play Loop

The playback is accomplished in a `while(1)` loop as follows:

```
while ( 1 )
    {
    current_byte_l =
    sp_play_byte_range ( current_byte_l,
                         current_byte_l + 15000L );

    /*----------------------------------------
    Start playback from the beginning if
    the sound file was fully played.
    ----------------------------------------*/
    if (current_byte_l == -1L )
        {
        current_byte_l = 0L;
        }

    /*----------------------------------------
    Terminate playback if user presses any key.
    ----------------------------------------*/
    if ( kbhit() )
        break;
    } /* end of while(1) */
```

The sound file is played in groups of 15,000 bytes each. Once a 15,000 bytes group is played, the variable `current_byte_l` is examined. During the very first loop iteration, the sound section played is from `current_byte_l=0L` to byte location 15,000. Upon completing playing this group, the returned value from the `sp_play_byte_range` is equal to 15000L. On the next loop iteration, the played section is from `current_byte_played_l=15000L` to byte location 30,000. This playing-in-groups process continues until the second parameter of the `sp_play_byte_range` exceeds the size of the sound file.

For example, if the size of the sound file is 35,000 bytes (in the first iteration the played sound section is 0 to 15,000), the second playback is from 15,000 to 30,000, and in the third iteration the played section is from 30,000 to 35,000. In the third iteration the TSEngine was instructed to play the section from byte location 30,000 to 45,000. However, because the total size of the sound file in this example is only 30,000 bytes, the TSEngine responds by playing the range from byte location 30,000 up to byte location 35,000, and the returned value from the `sp_play_byte_range` is -1L, an indication that the playback reached the end of the sound file.

Within the while(1) loop, the value of the returned value from the sp_play_byte_range() function is examined to see whether it is equal to -1. If so, it means that the whole sound file was played, in which case the variable current_byte_1 is initialized to 0L. (You may modify the program so that upon discovering that the returned value is -1, the program breaks from the while(1) loop. This changes the program so that the sound file is played only once instead of in an endless loop.)

Breaking from the *while(1)* Loop

To allow the user to break from the while(1) loop by pressing any key, the if(kbhit()) statement is executed, examining whether the user pressed a key on the keyboard. If so, the if(kbhit()) is satisfied, and the while(1) loop is broken with the break statement:

```
if ( kbhit() )
   break;
```

The _*disable()* and _*enable()* Standard C Functions

The _disable() and _enable() functions are standard C functions that disable and enable interrupts. The sound quality is better if the _disable() function is executed prior to executing the sp_play_byte_range() function. The _enable() function is executed at the end of the playback to enable the interrupts.

Although there is no mandatory requirement to disable the interrupts during the playback, it makes sense to assume that the quality of sound is improved if the interrupts are disabled. You should be aware, however, that if your program uses the mouse device, the mouse can be disabled if the _disable() function is executed. The mouse will again be active after the execution of the _enable() function.

Note that using the mouse during the playback may have degrading effects on the sound quality. Thus, you may consider disabling the mouse during the playback by using the _disable() function.

Other *sp_play_* Functions

The `sp_play_byte_range()` function belongs to a family of `sp_play_` functions. As implied by its name, the range of the sound section to be played by the `sp_play_byte_range()` function is supplied in units of byte coordinates. Other functions in the `sp_play_` family of functions include `sp_play_fsec_range()` and `sp_play_label_range()`.

The `sp_play_fsec_range()` function is similar to the `sp_play_byte_range()` function. The only difference is that the range of the sound section to be played by `sp_play_fsec_range()` is specified in units of seconds. For example, to play the sound section from 1.32 seconds to 4.32 seconds, the following statement must be issued:

```
sp_play_fsec_range ( 1.32, 4.32 );
```

The `sp_play_label_range()` function enables you to specify the sound range to be played in terms of sound labels. To take advantage of this powerful function, you need to insert sound labels in the sound file. Sound labels are inserted by using the TS Sound Editor.

Here is how sound labels are used in a typical program:

As you develop your program, you build a single sound file composed of several sound files. Thus, the sound file may include the audio phrases *Good-Bye*, *Welcome*, *Press any key to continue...*, *Having fun?*, and other audio phrases (or music) applicable to your program. The Sound Editor program enables you to add these sound files to a single sound file. The Sound Editor program also enables you to insert sound labels. Thus, you may insert the label `Press starts here` at the beginning of the audio section `Press any key to continue...`, and you may insert the label `Press ends here` at the end of this sound section. Similarly, you may insert other sound labels at the beginning and end of the other sound sections.

To play a particular sound section, your program may issue the `sp_play_label_range()` function. For example, to play *Press any key to continue...*, the following statement is executed:

```
sp_play_label_range ( "Press starts here",
                      "Press ends here");
```

Because the Sound Editor is not included in the book's diskette, we assume you do not have a copy of the Sound Editor program. Therefore, all the program examples of this book use the `sp_play_byte_range()` function.

Memory Management and Virtual Memory

One of the best features of the c:\spSDK\Lib\TegoMS.lib library is that it manages all the disk access, disk swapping, and memory allocation chores for you. All you have to do is to simply specify the range of the sound file to be played. For example, suppose you have a sound file that is 10 megabytes long. Regardless of the amount of RAM the PC has, you may safely use the sp_play_byte_range() function to play any desired range in the sound file. If the PC does not have enough RAM in it to hold 10 megabytes of sound, sp_play_byte_range() will automatically do all the necessary swapping, unloading, loading, and whatever it takes to play the specified range.

The PlayS Program

The PlayS program is similar to the PlayTS program. The only difference is that PlayS enables the user to play .S files from the DOS prompt.

Compiling, Linking, and Executing the PlayS Program

To compile and link the file c:\spSDK\SampMS\PlayS.c with the Microsoft compiler:

- Make sure your PC is in a DOS-protected mode.

- Log into c:\spSDK\SampMS\.

- At the DOS prompt type

    MAKEexe PlayS.c {Enter}

To compile and link the file c:\spSDK\SampMS\PlayS.c with the Borland compiler:

- Log into c:\spSDK\SampMS\.

- At the DOS prompt type

    MAKEexe PlayS.c {Enter}

To execute the PlayS program:

- If you compiled with the Microsoft compiler, log into
  c:\spSDK\SampMS\.

  If you compiled with the Borland compiler, log into
  c:\spSDK\SampBL\.

- At the DOS prompt type

  PlayS c:\spSDK\Sfiles\Press.s {Enter}

You may use the PlayS program to play any of the .S files that reside in
c:\spSDK\Sfiles\.

The Code of PlayS.c

The PlayS.c file is almost identical to the PlayTS.c file. The only difference is
that the second parameter of the `sp_open_tsengine_session()` function is
`SP_S_FILE`:

```
sp_open_tsengine_session ( file_name_to_play_s, SP_S_FILE );
```

Using .S Files

As you may have noticed by examining c:\spSDK\TSfiles\ and
c:\spSDK\Sfiles\, .S files are much shorter than .TS files.

A type S sound file may be generated from a .WAV file by using the
WAV2S.exe utility.

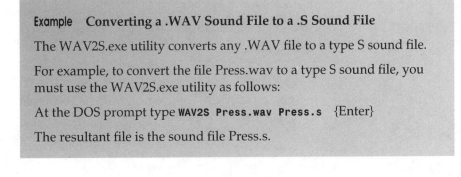

Example   Converting a .WAV Sound File to a .S Sound File

The WAV2S.exe utility converts any .WAV file to a type S sound file.

For example, to convert the file Press.wav to a type S sound file, you
must use the WAV2S.exe utility as follows:

At the DOS prompt type **WAV2S Press.wav Press.s** {Enter}

The resultant file is the sound file Press.s.

Note that the WAV2S.exe utility is not included in the book's diskette. This utility is an integral part of the TS Sound Editor. Because we assume you do not have a copy of the TS Sound Editor, we recorded the file Press.wav, and then used the WAV2S.exe utility to create the file Press.s. The Press.s file resides in c:\spSDK\Sfiles\.

The Size of the Playback Group

The while(1) loop of PlayS.c plays the .S file in groups of 15,000 bytes each. By using the conversion formula for .S files

$$[\text{ Length in seconds }] = \frac{[\text{ Length in bytes }] \times 8}{[\text{Sampling rate in Hertz}]}$$

we see that each 15,000 bytes of the Press.s sound file (recorded at a sampling rate of 40,000 Hertz) represents a playback of 3 seconds:

$$[\text{ Length in seconds }] = \frac{15,000 \times 8}{40,000} = 3 \text{ Seconds.}$$

The size of the playback group determines how fast the program responds to a key pressed by the user. In the PlayS program, a user might have to wait 3 seconds after pressing a key before the playback is interrupted. To expedite the response time, you can change the size of the playback section to a smaller size.

In the PlayTS program, the played file is a .TS file. The formula that converts bytes to seconds for a TS-type sound file is

$$[\text{ Length in seconds }] = \frac{[\text{ Length in bytes }]}{[\text{Sampling rate in Hertz}]}$$

Thus, 15,000 TS bytes of a TS file recorded at 8,000 Hertz represent

$$[\text{ Length in seconds }] = \frac{15,000}{8,000} = 1.875 \text{ Seconds.}$$

Thus, in the PlayTS program, a user might have to wait 1.875 seconds after pressing a key before the playback is interrupted.

Stand-Alone Programs

So far, all the C programs we developed for DOS have been non-stand-alone sound programs. This means that the distribution disk (the disk that contains all the files of the complete program) of each of these programs must contain the .EXE program, as well as the sound file(s) that are used in the program. For example, suppose you want to send someone a sound file that contains the audio message *Hello. Have a nice day. Good-Bye.* Your distribution disk should include two files: PlayTS.exe and Hello.ts

The fact that your distribution disk contains more than one file is inconvenient. In addition, there is always a possibility that your user will separate or lose one of the files.

To overcome this inconvenience, you can convert a non-stand-alone program to a stand-alone Program. For example, suppose you want to send somebody a stand-alone HearMe.exe file. Upon receiving the HearMe.exe file, the user simply types **HearMe** at the DOS prompt. The user can now hear whatever you want him to hear.

Your distribution disk contains a single file, the HearMe.exe file. The sound file is an integral part of the HearMe.exe file.

Converting the PlayTS Program to a Stand-Alone Sound Program

As an exercise, we will now convert the non-stand-alone PlayTS program that was discussed earlier to a stand-alone program.

To convert PlayTS.c to a stand-alone Program, perform the following steps:

STEP 1:

Copy the PlayTS.c file to TSalone.c:

```
COPY playTS.c TSalone.c   {Enter}
```

We will now make a change to the code of TSalone.c.

STEP 2:

Replace the `sp_open_tsengine_session()` with the following statement:

`sp_open_tsengine_session_sa ( argv[0], 0L, SP_TS_FILE );`

In this statement we replaced the `sp_open_tsengine()` function with the `sp_open_tsengine_sa()` function. The sa in the function name stands for *Stand-Alone*.

> **NOTE**
>
> *Function Name:* `sp_open_tsengine_session_sa()`
>
> *Description:* This function is used to open a sound session in a stand-alone sound program. The prototype of `sp_open_tsengine_session_sa()` is declared in c:\spSDK\h\sp1.h as:
>
> `int sp_open_tsengine_session_sa( char * file_name_to_play_s,`
> `long not_applicable_l, int file_type_i );`
>
> *Parameters:* `char * file_name_to_play_s`: A null terminated string that holds the path and name of the sound file to be opened. For stand-alone programs this parameter should be equal to `argv[0]` (that is, the path and name of the stand-alone .EXE file).
>
> `long not_applicable_l`: This parameter is not applicable for the short version library. You may supply the value 0L for this parameter.
>
> `int file_type_i`: This parameter indicates the type of sound file to be opened.
>
> Examples of valid values for the file type
>
>   `SP_S_FILE`   S-type sound files
>
>   `SP_TS_FILE`   TS-type sound files
>
> The full version of the library enables you to open a sound session with `SP_WAV_FILE` (for .WAV files), `SP_VOC_FILE` (for .VOC files), and `SP_SND_FILE` (for .SND files).
>
> These identifiers enable you to play .WAV files, .VOC files, and other popular sound files without the need to use the conversion utilities—that is, when supplying the `SP_WAV_TYPE` as the third parameter of

sp_open_tsengine_session, the sound file to be opened is a .WAV file, so there is no need to use the WAV2S.exe utility.

Returned Value: The returned value from the sp_open_tsengine_session_sa is an integer that indicates whether the TSEngine was successful in opening the sound session. A returned value other than 1 means that the TSEngine failed to open the sound session.

Replacing the sp_open_tsengine_session() function with sp_open_tsengine_session_sa() is the only change needed to be made in the C source code in order to convert a non-stand-alone sound program into a stand-alone program.

STEP 3:

In this step we compile and link the stand-alone TSalone.c program:

- Make sure your PC is in a DOS-protected mode.

- Log into c:\spSDK\SampMS\ (for the Microsoft compiler)

  or,

  log into c:\spSDK\SampBL\ (for the Borland compiler).

- At the DOS prompt type

  ```
  MAKEexe TSalone.c   {Enter}
  ```

STEP 4:

The last step is to link the file TSalone.exe (generated in step 3) with the sound file c:\spSDK\TSFiles\Hello.ts.

The TSlink Utility

The TSlink utility resides in c:\spSDK\Util\. This utility enables you to link an .EXE file with a single sound file. The sound file may be a type S sound file or a type TS sound file.

The TSlink utility included with the book's disk is a short-version utility. The full-version TSlink utility is an integral part of the TS Sound Editor program, and it enables you to link other types of sound files, such as .WAV sound files and .VOC sound files.

To use the TSlink utility

- Log into c:\spSDK\SampMS\ (for the Microsoft compiler)

  or,

  log into c:\spSDK\SampBL\ (for the Borland compiler).

- At the DOS prompt type

```
c:\spSDK\Util\TSlink TSalone.exe c:\spSDK\TSFiles\Hello.ts
NiceDay.exe
```

The first parameter of the TSlink utility is the name of the .EXE file to be linked; the second parameter is the name of the sound file to be linked to the .EXE file; and the third parameter is the name of the resultant stand-alone .EXE file. You must provide the file extension—that is, the first parameter must be TSalone.exe, not TSalone; the second parameter must be Hello.ts, not Hello; and the third parameter must be NiceDay.exe, not NiceDay.

NOTE   The TSlink.exe utility links a .EXE file with a sound file.

Syntax: TSlink <1st parameter> <2nd parameter> <3rd parameter>

First parameter: The name of the .EXE file to be linked.

Second parameter: The name of the sound file to be linked.

Third parameter: The name of the resultant .EXE file.

Executing the Stand-Alone NiceDay Program

You may now execute the stand-alone program from the DOS prompt:

- Log into c:\spSDK\SampMS\ (for the Microsoft compiler)

  or,

  log into c:\spSDK\SampBL\ (for the Borland compiler).

- At the DOS prompt type

```
NiceDay   {Enter}
```

The stand-alone program consists of a single file, NiceDay.exe. This file may reside in any drive and any directory.

The TSlink utility linked the sound file Hello.ts with the TSalone.exe file, and created a new file called NiceDay.exe. The size of NiceDay.exe is approximately the sum of the sizes of the files TSalone.exe and Hello.ts. The distribution disk will consist of a single file, the NiceDay.exe file. There is no need to distribute the sound file Hello.ts.

Converting Other Programs

You may now convert all the other non-stand-alone sound programs presented in this chapter to stand-alone sound programs in the same manner just described.

Additional sp_ Functions from the TegoSoft Sound Library

In addition to the sp_open_ family of functions and the sp_play_ family of functions, the TegoMS.lib library includes other sp_ functions that enable you to manipulate sound files in a variety of ways and extract information from the sound files. The following program illustrates how information can be extracted from sound files.

The Info4TS Program

The file Info4TS.c resides in c:\spSDK\SampMS\. This program uses various functions from the sp_get_ family of functions.

Compiling, Linking, and Executing the Info4TS Program

To compile and link the Info4TS program:

- Make sure your PC is in a DOS-protected mode.

- Log into c:\spSDK\SampMS\ (for the Microsoft compiler)

  or,

  log into c:\spSDK\SampBL\ (for the Borland compiler).

- At the DOS prompt type

  `MAKEexe Info4TS.c` {Enter}

To execute the Info4TS program:

- Log into c:\spSDK\SampMS\ (for the Microsoft compiler)

  or,

  log into c:\spSDK\SampBL\ (for the Borland compiler).

- At the DOS prompt type

  `Info4TS <Path and Name of a .TS file>` {Enter}

  For example, to execute the Info4TS program with the c:\spSDK\TSfiles\Music.ts, at the DOS prompt type

  `Info4TS c:\spSDK\TSfiles\Music.ts` {Enter}

Similarly, you may execute the Info4TS program with any of the other .TS files that appear in c:\spSDK\TSfiles\.

Upon executing the Info4TS program, various information is extracted from the sound file and displayed on-screen. The user is then prompted to press any key to start the playback. During the playback, the current position of the played sound file is displayed. The user may interrupt the playback by pressing any key during the playback.

The Code of the Info4TS.c Program

The code of the Info4TS program resides in c:\spSDK\SampMS\Info4TS.c.

As always, the #include section of the file contains the various .h files of the TegoMS.lib library:

```
/*--- Standard TegoSoft Sound+ header files. ---*/
#include "c:\spsdk\h\sp1.h"
#include "c:\spsdk\h\sp2.h"
#include "c:\spsdk\h\sp3.h"
```

Disabling Ctrl-C

It is a good idea to disable the Ctrl-C key in order to prevent the user from terminating the program by pressing Ctrl-C. The Ctrl-C key is disabled at the beginning of the program by using the signal() function:

```
/*------------------------------------------------------------
 Disable the Ctrl_C plus other signals so that the user is
 unable to terminate the program by pressing Ctrl-C.
 ----------------------------------------------------------*/
signal(SIGINT,SIG_IGN);
```

Extracting Information from the .TS File

Once the .TS session opens with the sp_open_tsenngine_session() function, the program can extract various data and information from the sound file.

The size (in bytes) of the sound file is extracted by using the sp_get_size_of_file_in_lbytes() function:

```
/*-- Extract the size of the TS file in bytes. --*/
size_of_file_in_bytes_l = sp_get_size_of_file_in_lbytes();
```

The lbytes is a reminder that the returned value of the function is a long integer that represents the size of the sound file in bytes.

The size (in seconds) of the sound file is extracted by using the sp_get_size_of_file_in_lsec() function:

```
/*-- Extract the size of the TS file in lsec. --*/
size_of_file_in_lsec_l = sp_get_size_of_file_in_lsec();
```

The lsec is a reminder that the returned value of the function is a long integer that represents the size of the sound file in seconds.

The size (in seconds) of the sound file is extracted by using the sp_get_size_of_file_in_fsec() function:

```
/*-- Extract the size of the TS file in fsec. --*/
size_of_file_in_fsec_f = sp_get_size_of_file_in_fsec();
```

The fsec is a reminder that the returned value of the function is a float number that represents the size of the sound file in seconds.

The sampling rate is extracted by using the sp_get_sampling_rate() function:

```
 /*-- Sampling rate. --*/
sampling_rate_l = sp_get_sampling_rate();
```

The current playback speed is extracted by using the sp_get_playback_speed() function:

```
/*-- playback speed. --*/
playback_speed_f = sp_get_playback_speed();
```

Displaying the Current Position During Playback

The playback is accomplished by executing a while(1) loop. The sound file is played in groups of 8,000 bytes each. Between the playback of the groups, the sp_get_position_in_fsec() function is used to extract the current position:

```
_disable();
/*-- Play the file. --*/
display_message("Now playing...");
current_byte_l = 0L;
while ( 1 )
     {
     current_byte_l =
     sp_play_byte_range ( current_byte_l,
                          current_byte_l + 8000L );

     /*-- break if TS file was fully played.--*/
     if (current_byte_l == -1L )
        break;

     /*-- Terminate playback if key was pressed. --*/
     if ( kbhit() )
        break;
```

```
/*-- Position in fsec. --*/
position_in_fsec_f = sp_get_position_in_fsec();
_settextposition ( row_number_i, 10 );
printf ("Current position of TS file is %.2f fsec.",
         position_in_fsec_f);

    }
_enable();
```

The Info4S Program

The Info4S program is almost identical to the Info4TS program. The only difference is that the Info4S program works with .S files.

Compiling, Linking, and Executing the Info4S Program

To compile and link the Info4S program:

- Make sure your PC is in a DOS-protected mode.
- Log into c:\spSDK\SampMS\ (for the Microsoft compiler)

  or,

  log into c:\spSDK\SampBL\ (for the Borland compiler).
- At the DOS prompt type

  MAKEexe Info4S.c {Enter}

To execute the Info4S program:

- Log into c:\spSDK\SampMS\ (for the Microsoft compiler)

  or,

  log into c:\spSDK\SampBL\ (for the Borland compiler).
- At the DOS prompt type

  Info4S <Path and Name of a .S file> {Enter}

  For example, to execute the Info4S program with the c:\spSDK\Sfiles\Press.s, at the DOS prompt type

  Info4S c:\spSDK\TSfiles\Press.s {Enter}

Similarly, you may execute the Info4S program with any of the other .S files that appear in c:\spSDK\Sfiles\.

Using the *sp_get_* Family of Functions for Other Types of Sound Files (.WAV, .VOC, .SND)

As you may see, the only difference between Info4TS and Info4S is the second parameter of the `sp_open_tsengine_session()` function. Once the sound session opens, all the `sp_` functions may be used regardless of the type of sound file. Thus, the `sp_get_` family of functions (as well as all the other `sp_` functions) may be applied to .S files, .TS files, .WAV files, .VOC files and other types of sound files. (Note that the library supplied with the book's diskette is a short-version library that supports only .S and .TS sound files.)

Changing the Playback Speed

In some programs you may want to either decrease or increase the playback speed. For example, suppose you create a HearMe program that plays a sound file that is 25 minutes long. Naturally, you don't expect the user to sit down and listen to you continuously for 25 minutes! Even if what you have to say is interesting, the user may be forced to stop listening because of something like a telephone interruption. Thus, it is best to equip your HearMe program with a Pause feature, as well as Rewind and Fast Forward features. This way users will be able to pause and do all the other manipulations that are available on a regular tape-recorder. It is recommended that you also provide a variable playback speed capability in your HearMe program. This way users will be able to scan the recording faster, until they reach the desired location.

To set the playback speed to any desired value, use the `sp_set_playback_speed()` function. The prototype of this function is declared in c:\spSDK\h\sp2.h as

```
void  sp_set_playback_speed ( float );
```

For example, to set the playback to twice the natural speed, use the statement

```
sp_set_playback_speed ( 2.0 );
```

To set the playback speed to half the natural speed, use the statement

```
sp_set_playback_speed ( 0.5 );
```

To set the playback speed to its natural speed, use the statement

```
sp_set_playback_speed ( 1.0 );
```

The full version of the TegoMS.lib library includes many other `sp_` functions that enable you to manipulate sound files in almost any conceivable way, enabling you to create many fascinating and exciting sound programs.

Synchronizing Moving Text with Sound

The SayPress program is an example of a program that synchronizes text with speech.

Compiling, Linking, and Executing the SayPress Program

To compile and link the SayPress program:

- Make sure your PC is in a DOS-protected mode.
- Log into c:\spSDK\SampMS\ (for the Microsoft compiler)

  or,

  log into c:\spSDK\SampBL\ (for the Borland compiler).
- At the DOS prompt type

  MAKEexe SayPress.c {Enter}

To execute the SayPress program:

- Log into c:\spSDK\SampMS\ (for the Microsoft compiler)

  or,

  log into c:\spSDK\SampBL\ (for the Borland compiler).

- At the DOS prompt type

`SayPress` {Enter}

The phrase `Press any key to continue...` is displayed in synchronization with the playback of the phrase.

The Code of the SayPress Program

The code of the SayPress program is in the file c:\spSDK\SampMS\SayPress.c (or c:\spSDK\SampBL\SayPress.c). The program plays the sound file in sections. Each section corresponds to a different word in the phrase *Press any key to continue....* To extract the word\sound partitions of the sound file, you can use the TS Sound Editor program. Because we assume you do not have a copy of the TS Sound Editor program, here is the breakdown of the c:\spSDK\Sfiles\Press.s file:

Byte Coordinates	*Audio Phrase*
0 - 3,896	*Press*
3,896 - 6,224	*any*
6,224 - 10,137	*key*
10,137 - 11,228	*to*
11,228 - SP_END_OF_FILE	*continue*

Text to Speech

Once you master the art of playing sound from within your programs, you'll be able to construct very interesting programs. For example, you may develop a program that converts text to speech. To write such a program you'll need to record all the possible phonemes that exist in the English language. Depending on the particular algorithm that you use, the number of phonemes may vary (typically 36 phonemes are enough to construct any English word). For example, the word *Bravo* may be constructed from the following phonemes:

`Bravo = B- R - ah - V - o`

The .TS file (or .WAV file) used by your program should consist of the 36 phonemes. To play a certain word, your program has to dissect the word to its phonemes, and then play the appropriate sound sections that correspond to each of these phonemes.

Animation, Graphics, and Playback

The c:\spSDK\Util\ directory includes two sample programs, GR1.exe and GR2.exe. These sample programs illustrate how sound may be played simultaneously with the displaying and moving of graphic objects.

To execute the GR1.exe program:

- Log into c:\spSDK\Util\.

- At the DOS prompt type

    `GR1 <Path and name of .S file>` {Enter}

    For example, to execute the GR1.exe sample program with the sound file Day.s:

- At the DOS prompt type

    `GR1 c:\spSDK\Sfiles\Day.s` {Enter}

The GR2.exe is a similar sample program. For example, to execute the GR2.exe sample program with the sound file Day.s:

- At the DOS prompt type

    `GR2 c:\spSDK\Sfiles\Day.s` {Enter}

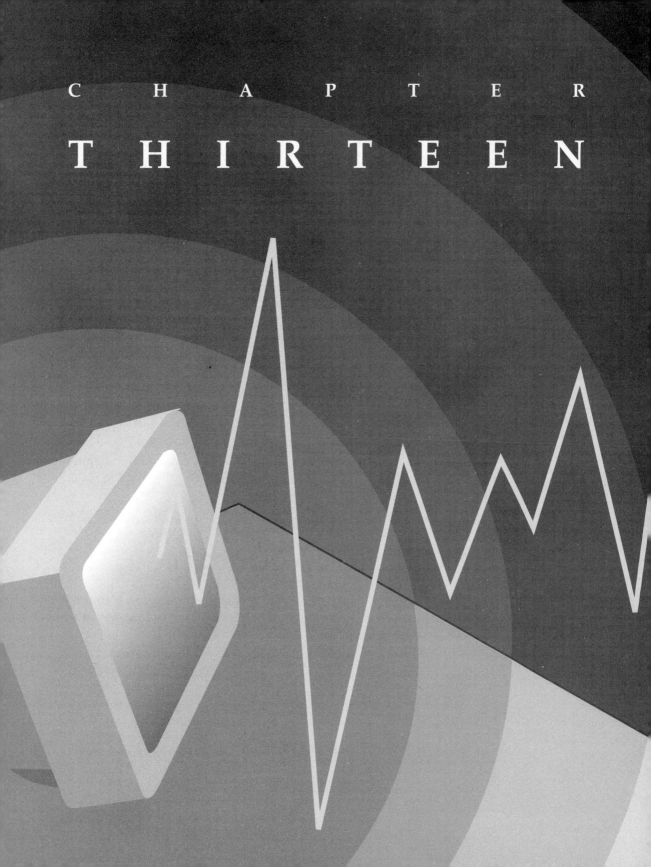

The Sound Blaster Card Under DOS

Previous chapters presented several Windows applications that utilize the Sound Blaster sound card. In fact, these programs can use any Windows-compatible sound card. Indeed, this is the advantage of using the Windows operating system.

As a programmer, you do not care who the vendor of the PC peripherals is. As long as the sound card is a Windows-compatible device, the programs will be able to use it. Unfortunately, this is not the case when programming for DOS. Thus, when programming for DOS, the sound functions are specific for the particular sound card vendor. In this chapter we write a DOS application called PlayVOC.c. This program plays .VOC files through the Sound Blaster sound card.

Executing the PlayVOC Program

The PlayVOC program uses the Sound Blaster driver CT-VOICE.DRV, and it assumes that this driver resides in c:\SBpro\DRV\. Before executing PlayVOC, you must make sure that the driver CT-VOICE.DRV resides in c:\SBpro\DRV\.

To execute PlayVOC:

- Log into c:\spSDK\Samp4SB\.

- From the DOS prompt type

```
PlayVOC  < Path & Name of .VOC file >   {Enter}
```

For example, to play the .VOC file c:\sbpro\vedit2\conga.voc, at the DOS prompt type

```
PlayVOC c:\sbpro\vedit2\conga.voc   {Enter}
```

Compiling and Linking PlayVOC with the Borland C Compiler

To compile and link PlayVOC.C with the Borland C compiler:

- Log into c:\spSDK\Samp4SB\.

- At the DOS prompt type

```
MKBLEXE PlayVOC.c   {Enter}
```

Compiling and Linking PlayVOC with the Microsoft C Compiler

To compile and link PlayVOC.C with the Microsoft C compiler:

- Make sure your PC is in a DOS-protected mode.

- Log into c:\spSDK\Samp4SB\.

- At the DOS prompt type

```
MKMSEXE PlayVOC.c   {Enter}
```

The Code of PlayVOC

For your convenience, the PlayVOC.c file resides in c:\spSDK\Samp4SB\. This file is compatible with both the Microsoft and the Borland compilers.

Loading and Initializing the Sound Blaster Driver Program

To use the Sound Blaster card from within the program, a Sound Blaster driver program must be loaded. The PlayVOC program uses the Sound Blaster driver CT-VOICE.DRV. PlayVOC assumes that this driver resides in c:\SBpro\DRV\.

The CT-VOICE.DRV driver is loaded into memory and initialized by using the load_driver() function.

The load_driver() function is responsible for loading the driver. The driver c:\SBpro\DRV\CT-VOICE.DRV is opened with the _dos_open() function:

```
if ( _dos_open ("C:\\SBpro\\DRV\\CT-VOICE.DRV",
                O_RDONLY,
                &handler_to_driver_i) != 0 )
   {
   printf("\n Can't open the CT-VOICE driver!");
   exit (0);
   }
else
   {
   printf("\n Driver was opened successfully!");
   }
```

If the CT-VOICE.DRV driver opens successfully, the load_driver() function proceeds to allocate memory for the driver:

```
filesize_ul  = filelength ( handler_to_driver_i );
blocksize_ui = (filesize_ul + 15L) / 16;
result_uc = _dos_allocmem ( blocksize_ui, &segment_ui );
if ( result_uc !=0 )
   {
   printf ("\n Can't allocate memory for the driver!");
   return -1;
   }
```

If the memory allocation is accomplished successfully, the load_driver() function proceeds and loads the driver into memory:

```
/*-----------------------------
Loading the driver into memory.
-----------------------------*/
FP_SEG (pointer_to_driver) = segment_ui;
FP_OFF (pointer_to_driver) = 0;
driver_buffer = (char huge*) pointer_to_driver;
```

```
_dos_read ( handler_to_driver_i,
            driver_buffer,
            32000,
            &bytes_read_ui );
_dos_close ( handler_to_driver_i );
```

Note that the _dos_read() statement reads a maximum of 32,000 bytes. If your driver is greater than 32,000 bytes, the _dos_read() function has to be called in a loop until the complete driver is loaded. (However, most drivers are less than 32,000 bytes.)

Once the driver is successfully loaded into memory, the load_driver() function checks that bytes 3 through 10 contain the characters: CT-VOICE:

```
/*---------------------------------------------------------
Check if the loaded driver has the characters "CT-VOICE"
starting at the 4th character.
---------------------------------------------------*/
temp_s[0] = driver_buffer[3];
temp_s[1] = driver_buffer[4];
temp_s[2] = driver_buffer[5];
temp_s[3] = driver_buffer[6];
temp_s[4] = driver_buffer[7];
temp_s[5] = driver_buffer[8];
temp_s[6] = driver_buffer[9];
temp_s[7] = driver_buffer[10];
temp_s[8] = '\0';
if ( strcmp(temp_s, "CT-VOICE") != 0 )
    {
    printf("\n Can't find CT-VOICE Not a valid driver!");
    return -1;
    }
```

This check makes sure that the loaded driver is indeed the CT-VOICE driver. Of course, this check is not a full-proof check because it checks only eight bytes of the driver.

Now that the CT-VOICE.DRV driver is loaded into memory, the program may start calling various functions from this driver by using in-line assembly code. To call a specific function of the driver, the bx register must be filled with the function number to be called.

To initialize the sound card, function number 3 is called:

```
/*--------------------
Initialize the driver.
--------------------*/
__asm {
```

```
mov        bx,3
call       pointer_to_driver
mov        out_result,ax
}
```

The result of the initialization is checked by examining the value of the out_result variable:

```
/*------------------------------------------------
Checking the results of the initialization
-----------------------------------------*/
switch ( (int)out_result )
      {
      case 1: printf ("\n No sound card was found!");
              return -1;
      case 2: printf ("\n Incorrect port address!");
              return -1;
      case 3: printf ("\n Incorrect interrupt number!");
              return -1;
      }
```

The last thing to be done in the load_driver() function is set up a variable for communications with the Sound Blaster card. The status_word_i variable is an integer that serves as a mailbox between the program and the sound card. The sound card reports various status conditions by updating this variable. This means that PlayVOC needs to tell the sound card what the address of this variable is.

First, the physical address of the status_word_i variable is calculated:

```
/*------------------------------------------------
Calculate the address of the status word.
-----------------------------------------*/
p_status_word_i = &status_word_i;
seg_address = FP_SEG(p_status_word_i);
ofs_address = FP_OFF(p_status_word_i);
```

Then the Sound Blaster card is notified about this address by using function number 5 of the CT-VOICE.DRV driver:

```
/*------------------------------------------------
Inform the driver the address of the
status word.
-----------------------------------------*/
__asm {
    mov        bx,5
    mov        es,seg_address
    mov        di,ofs_address
    call       pointer_to_driver
    }
```

Loading the .VOC File into Memory

The .VOC file is loaded into memory by using the load_voc() function.

The load_voc() function uses the _dos_read() function to read the .VOC file into the buffer address_of_voc_buffer[].

After the buffer is filled, load_voc() checks to see if the loaded file is a .VOC file by checking the first two bytes of the buffer. All valid .VOC files should start with the characters Creative Voice File. If the loaded file is a valid .VOC file, then the first two characters of the buffer should be Cr:

```
if ( ( address_of_voc_buffer[0] != 'C') ¦¦
     ( address_of_voc_buffer[1] != 'r'))
   {
   printf("\n .VOC should contain Cr as its first characters");
   exit(0);
   }
```

This check, of course, is not a full-proof check because you check only two characters.

Playing the Sound File

The .VOC file is played by using the play_it() function.

The play_it() function first enables the sound card output by calling function number 4 of the CT-VOICE.DRV driver with al=1:

```
/*------------------------
Enable sound card output.
--------------------*/
_ _asm {
    mov  bx,4              /* Function number 4.          */
    mov  al,1              /* al=1 means enable output. */
    call pointer_to_driver /* Execute the function.       */
    }
```

After enabling the sound card output, the segment and offset addresses of the .VOC file buffer are calculated:

```
seg_address = FP_SEG ( address_of_voc_buffer );
ofs_address = FP_OFF ( address_of_voc_buffer )
             + length_of_voc_header_uc;
```

Finally, the sound card is told to start playing the .VOC file buffer by calling function number 6 of the CT-VOICE.DRV driver:

```
__asm {
    mov   bx, 6              /* Function number 6                */
    mov   es, seg_address    /* The segment address of the buffer */
    mov   di, ofs_address    /* The offset address of the buffer  */
    call pointer_to_driver   /* Execute the function.            */
    }
```

Stopping the Playback

After the playback is started by the play_it() function, the sound card is on its own. The sound card keeps playing the .VOC file buffer without any help from the PlayVOC program.

The main() function of PlayVOC stops the playback when the user presses any key, or when the sound card completes playing the sound file.

Remember that in load_driver() the variable status_word_i was set as the mailbox for communications between the sound card and the program. The sound card updates this variable with 0 when the playback is completed.

The status of the sound card is examined within a while(1) loop in main(), by checking the value of status_word_i. If the value is 0, it means that the sound card completed playing the .VOC file, in which case the while(1) loop terminates.

The playback also terminates when the user presses any key on the keyboard. If the user presses any key, the while(1) loop breaks, and the playback stops by calling function number 8 of the CT-VOICE.DRV:

```
__asm {
    mov bx,8                /* Function number 8.    */
    call pointer_to_driver  /* Execute the function. */
    }
```

Freeing the .VOC Buffer and Releasing the Sound Card

Before exiting the program, the memory allocated for the .VOC file is freed by using the _dos_freemem() function, and the sound card is released by using the release_card() function:

```
_dos_freemem(FP_SEG(address_of_voc_buffer));
release_card();
```

The *release_card()* Function

The `release_card()` function releases the sound card by calling function number 9 of the CT-VOICE.DRV driver:

```
_ _asm {
  mov  bx,9                /* Function number 9.    */
  call pointer_to_driver   /* Execute the function. */
  }
```

Other Sound Blaster Functions

As demonstrated in the code of the PlayVOC program, knowing how to use the Sound Blaster amounts to knowing how to load the Sound Blaster driver, how to load the .VOC file, how to analyze the status word, and how to use in-line assembly for sending commands to the Sound Blaster.

Here are the various CT-VOICE.DRV functions that are available to you:

Function Number 0: Determining the Driver Version

> **Inputs:**   BX=0 (The function number)
>
> **Outputs:**   AH (The main version number)
>   AL (The sub version number)

After executing this function, the AH and AL registers are updated with the main version number and the sub version number of the driver.

Function Number 1: Setting the Port Address

> **Inputs:**   BX = 1 (The function number)
>   AX   (The port address)
>
> **Outputs:**   None

This function sets the port address of the Sound Blaster card. For this function to be effective, it must be called before function 3.

Function Number 2: Setting the Interrupt Number

Inputs: BX = 2 (The function number)
            AX (The interrupt number)

Outputs: None

This function sets the interrupt number of the Sound Blaster card. For this function to be effective, it must be called before function 3.

Function Number 3: Initializing the Driver

Inputs: BX = 3 (The function number)

Outputs: AX = 0: Initialization was successful.
            AX = 1: The Sound Blaster card was not found.
            AX = 2: There is a problem with the I/O address
                    setting of the card.
            AX = 3: There is a problem with the interrupt
                    setting of the card.

Function Number 4: Setting the Speaker On and Off

Inputs: BX = 4 (The function number)
            AL = 0 (Set the speaker off)
            AL = 1 (Set the speaker on)

Outputs: None

Function Number 5: Setting the Status Word Address

Inputs: BX = 5 (The function number)
            ES:DI (Status address)

Outputs: None

Function Number 6: Starting the Playback

Inputs: BX = 6 (The function number)
ES:DI (The address of the .VOC buffer)

Outputs: None

Function Number 7: Starting the Recording

Inputs: BX = 7 (The function number)
AX   (The sampling rate)
DX:CX (Maximum length of recording)
ES:DI (The address of the .VOC buffer)

Outputs: None

Function Number 8: Stopping the Playback or the Recording

Inputs: BX = 8 (The function number)

Outputs: None

After executing this function, the status word will be 0.

Function Number 9: De-installing the Driver

Inputs: BX = 9 (The function number)

Outputs: None

Function Number 10: Pausing the Playback

Inputs: BX = 10 (The function number)

Outputs: AX = 0 (The pausing was successful)
AX = 1 (The pausing failed)

Upon executing this function, the current playback is paused.

Function Number 11: Resuming the Playback

Inputs: BX = 11 (The function number)

Outputs: AX = 0 (The resuming was successful)
              AX = 1 (The resuming failed)

Upon executing this function, the playback that was previously paused with function number 10 is resumed.

Creating Multimedia Programs for DOS with the Sound Blaster Sound Card

To create multimedia programs for DOS with the Sound Blaster you may use the same techniques that were introduced in the Windows applications. That is, you have to design a table that outlines the sound range that should be played with each of the frames. During the playback, the frame that corresponds to the currently played sound range is displayed.

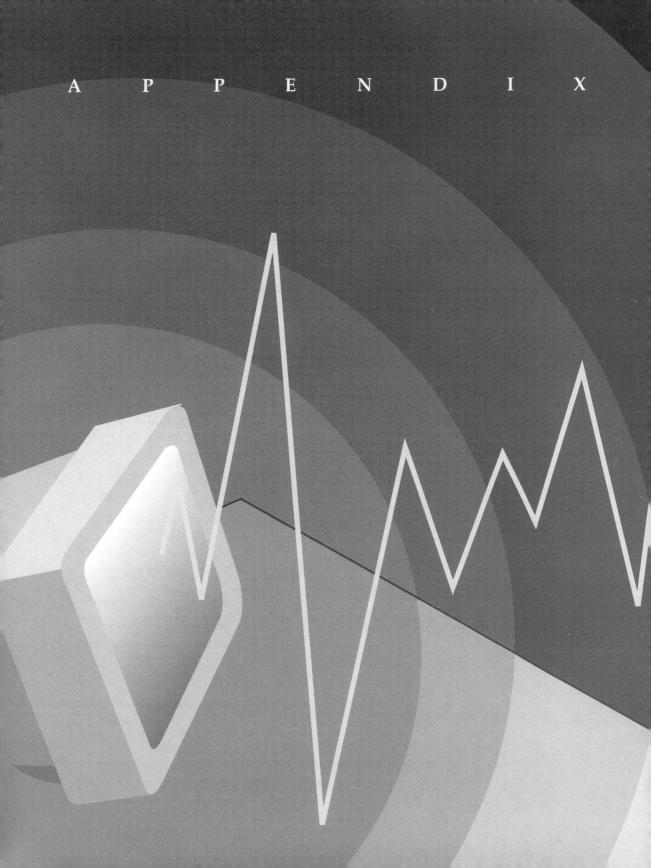

Sound DLL

This book discusses Windows applications that utilize the static libraries that are supplied in c:\spSDK\TegoWlib\. An alternative method is to write Windows applications that utilize DLL libraries.

There are advantages, as well as disadvantages, in writing programs that utilize DLL functions.

Advantages of Using DLL Sound Functions

Suppose your application is composed of several programs, and each program calls sp_ functions. In such a case, it is probably better to utilize the DLL.

The DLL file resides on the hard drive and is shared by all the programs that use it. Because the DLL is not part of the executable programs, your program's size decreases.

Using the DLL Sound Library for Visual Basic and Other Windows Programming Languages

Another advantage of using a DLL is that it can be used from other Windows programming languages, such as Visual Basic for Windows. It can also be used from any other Windows programming language that can utilize DLL.

Disadvantage of Using DLL Sound Library

The disadvantage of using a DLL is that your application assumes that the end user has the DLL installed on the hard drive. Because most users do not have the DLL sound library, your distribution disk must include the DLL, and your Install program must copy the DLL into the user's hard drive.

Using the Sound DLL

In this appendix we will rewrite the HearMe application so that it uses a DLL library instead of a static library.

The DLL that HearMe uses is called TegoSND.DLL. This DLL is not included on the book's disk. However, you can order it directly from TegoSoft Inc. (See last page of the book for order information.)

Using the DLL4Snd.DLL Dynamic Link Library (DLL)

Converting an application that was linked with the static library TegoWin.lib to an application that uses the DLL library TegoSND.DLL is easy.

Follow these steps to convert the HearMe application:

Step 1

To use the DLL, you must #include the TegoSND.h file. Thus, in the HearMe.c file, replace the statement

```
#include "c:\spSDK\TegoWlib\sp4Win.h"
```

with the statement

```
#include "c:\spSDK\DLL\TegoSND.h"
```

(Note: The file TegoSND.h is not included in the book's disk.)

The TegoSND.h file contains the prototype declarations of the sp_ functions that are part of the DLL.

Step 2

The application uses sp_ functions from the DLL. Therefore, the .DEF file must contain the appropriate IMPORTS statement. This IMPORTS statement contains all the sp_ functions that the application imports from the DLL.

Because the HearMe.c uses only two sp_ functions, here is the IMPORTS state-ment that must be included in the file HearMe.def:

```
IMPORTS
        TegoSND.sp_OpenSession
        TegoSND.sp_PlayF
```

Step 3

The link statement in the HearMe.mak file needs to be modified because now the static library c:\spSDK\TegoWlib\TegoWin.lib is not used anymore.

Here is the modified HearMe.mak file:

```
#==============
# Hearme.mak
#==============

Hearme.exe : Hearme.obj Hearme.h Hearme.def Hearme.res
    link /nod Hearme.obj, Hearme.exe, NUL, \
        slibcew.lib oldnames.lib libw.lib commdlg, \
        Hearme.def
    rc -t Hearme.res

Hearme.obj : Hearme.c Hearme.h
    cl -c -G2sw -Ow -W3 -Zp  Hearme.c

Hearme.res : Hearme.rc Hearme.h Tape.ico
    rc -r Hearme.rc
```

These are all the changes you need to make the HearMe application work with the DLL.

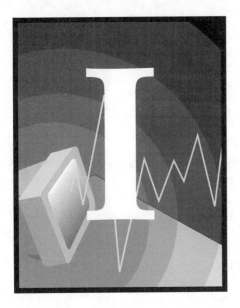

Index

A

H

I

What's on the Disk

The disk contains original programs that enable you to include sound in your DOS or Windows programs. You can use the programs and code examples with the Borland or Microsoft C compilers. The disk includes the following:

- Source code examples from the book

- Source code and executables for complete sound programs

- Libraries of C functions for including sound in your DOS or Windows applications

- Software utilities

Installing the Floppy Disk

The software included with this book is stored in a compressed form. You cannot use the software without first installing it on your hard drive.

1. From a DOS prompt, set your default drive to the drive that contains the installation disk. For example, if the disk is in drive A:, type A: and press Enter.

2. Type INSTALL and press Enter.

This will create a new directory called C:\SPSDK and install all the files in that directory on your hard drive. Read the file README.TXT for more information on the files.

 NOTE   To install the files, you'll need at least 4.6M of free space on your hard drive.